# The Art & Science of Project Management

John

We know you have contributed to the art and science of PM in more than one way. Best wishes.

Miles
Roger

# The Art and Science of Project Management

*Attitude*

*Books, and*

*Conversations*

*by*
Roger D. H. Warburton
Vijay Kanabar

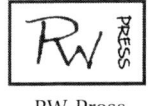

RW-Press

Copyright © Roger Warburton and Vijay Kanabar, 2012.

All rights reserved. No part of this book may be reproduced or transmitted in any form or by any means without the written permission of the authors.

Published int the United States of America by *RW-Press*, Newport, RI.

*First Printing, April 2012.*

    *Version 1.31*

ISBN: 978-0-9831788-0-4

*RW-Press*
150 Eustis Avenue,
Newport, RI 02840
U.S.A.

www.RW-Press.com

Cover photograph: A digital print of "The Canyon" by Maxfield Parrish.
Print used with permission from Robert Dennis, Director of the Lewis Wayne Gallery, Dallas, TX.

*To Eileen and Dina
—still and again.*

# CONTENTS

| | |
|---|---|
| **The Art & Science of Project Management** | iii |
| **Contents** | viii |
| **List of Figures** | xviii |
| **List of Tables** | xxii |
| **Preface** | xxvii |
|     Why Project Management? | xxviii |
|         Project Management and Business | xxix |
|         Project Management and Education | xxx |
|     Why Now? | xxxi |
|     Acknowledgments | xxxi |
| **Introduction** | xxxiii |
|     Structure of the Book | xxxiv |
|     Advice to the Beginner | xxxvi |
|     Conventions | xxxvii |
|     The Cases | xxxviii |
|         The PMA Case | xxxviii |
|         The New Kitchen | xxxix |
|     Challenge Everything! | xxxix |
| **I  Projects And Their Environment** | **1** |
| **1  Projects** | **3** |

|       |       |                                          |     |
|-------|-------|------------------------------------------|-----|
| 1.1   |       | The Project Management Institute         | 4   |
| 1.2   |       | What is a Project?                       | 5   |
|       | 1.2.1 | Project Time Scales                      | 8   |
| 1.3   |       | Project Management                       | 8   |
| 1.4   |       | The Project Manager                      | 10  |
|       | 1.4.1 | Interactions                             | 12  |
| 1.5   |       | Benefits of Project Management           | 12  |
|       | 1.5.1 | Project Success                          | 13  |
| 1.6   |       | The Project Management Office            | 14  |

## 2 The Project Environment    17

|       |        |                                          |     |
|-------|--------|------------------------------------------|-----|
| 2.1   |        | The Environment                          | 17  |
| 2.2   |        | The Internal Environment                 | 17  |
| 2.3   |        | The External Environment                 | 18  |
| 2.4   |        | The Project's Rationale                  | 19  |
| 2.5   |        | Programs                                 | 19  |
| 2.6   |        | Portfolios                               | 20  |
| 2.7   |        | Mission, Goals, Objectives, and Strategy | 20  |
|       | 2.7.1  | Mission                                  | 21  |
|       | 2.7.2  | Goals                                    | 21  |
|       | 2.7.3  | Objectives                               | 22  |
|       | 2.7.4  | Strategy                                 | 22  |
| 2.8   |        | Portfolio Management                     | 22  |
|       | 2.8.1  | Critical Success Factors                 | 24  |
| 2.9   |        | The Scoring Matrix                       | 24  |
|       | 2.9.1  | PMA Project Selection                    | 26  |
|       | 2.9.2  | Calibration                              | 29  |
|       | 2.9.3  | Project Selection                        | 30  |
| 2.10  |        | Financial Evaluation Criteria            | 31  |
|       | 2.10.1 | Payback                                  | 32  |
|       | 2.10.2 | Net Present Value                        | 32  |
|       | 2.10.3 | I work at a Non-Profit!                  | 34  |

## 3 Deliverables and Milestones    35

|       |       |                           |     |
|-------|-------|---------------------------|-----|
| 3.1   |       | Deliverables              | 35  |
|       | 3.1.1 | Measuring Deliverables    | 36  |
|       | 3.1.2 | Small Deliverables        | 37  |
|       | 3.1.3 | Progressive Elaboration   | 38  |
| 3.2   |       | Milestones                | 39  |

## 4 Projects and Companies — 41
- 4.1 Projects Goals vs. Company Goals — 42
- 4.2 Cultures — 43
  - 4.2.1 The Abilene Paradox — 46
  - 4.2.2 A Cultural Clash — 47
  - 4.2.3 Rewards — 47
- 4.3 Project Structures — 48
  - 4.3.1 Functional Organizations — 50
  - 4.3.2 Matrix Organizations — 50
  - 4.3.3 Projectized Organizations — 51

## 5 Project Life Cycles — 53
- 5.1 Products and Services Life Cycles — 54
- 5.2 The Project Life Cycle — 55
- 5.3 Industry Life Cycle Examples — 57
  - 5.3.1 The Software Development Life Cycle — 57
  - 5.3.2 The Pharmaceutical Industry Life Cycle — 58
  - 5.3.3 The Construction Industry Life Cycle — 59
- 5.4 Agile Project Management — 59
  - 5.4.1 The Old Way: The Waterfall — 59
  - 5.4.2 Evolutionary — 60
  - 5.4.3 Agile — 61
- 5.5 Choosing a Development Model — 63

# II The Process Groups — 65

## 6 The Process Groups — 67
- 6.1 Project Phases — 68
- 6.2 The Process Groups — 69
- 6.3 Processes — 72
  - 6.3.1 The Knowledge Areas — 74

## 7 Initiating Process Group — 77
- 7.1 Develop Charter — 79
  - 7.1.1 Develop Charter Inputs — 80
  - 7.1.2 Develop Charter Tools and Techniques — 81
  - 7.1.3 Develop Charter Outputs — 81
  - 7.1.4 Charter Example — 81
- 7.2 Identify Stakeholders — 82

|  |  |  |  |  |
|---|---|---|---|---|
|  |  | 7.2.1 | How Stakeholders Influence the Project | 85 |
|  |  | 7.2.2 | Identify Stakeholders Inputs | 85 |
|  |  | 7.2.3 | Identify Stakeholders Tools and Techniques | 85 |
|  |  | 7.2.4 | Identify Stakeholder Outputs | 87 |
|  |  | 7.2.5 | Summary | 87 |

## 8 Planning Process Group — 89

- 8.1 Develop Project Management Plan — 92
- 8.2 Scope Planning — 92
  - 8.2.1 Collect Requirements — 92
  - 8.2.2 Define Scope — 95
  - 8.2.3 Create WBS — 96
- 8.3 Time Planning — 98
  - 8.3.1 Estimate Activity Resources — 101
  - 8.3.2 Estimate Activity Durations — 103
  - 8.3.3 Develop Schedule — 103
- 8.4 Cost Planning — 107
  - 8.4.1 Estimate Costs — 108
  - 8.4.2 Determine Budget — 109
- 8.5 Risk Planning — 112
  - 8.5.1 Plan Risk Management — 112
  - 8.5.2 Identify Risks — 115
  - 8.5.3 Perform Qualitative Risk Analysis — 117
  - 8.5.4 Perform Quantitative Risk Analysis — 117
  - 8.5.5 Plan Risk Responses — 118
- 8.6 The Sub-Plans — 118
  - 8.6.1 Plan Quality — 118
  - 8.6.2 Develop Human Resources (HR) Plan — 121
  - 8.6.3 Plan Communications — 122
  - 8.6.4 Plan Procurements — 125

## 9 Executing Process Group — 127

- 9.1 Direct and Manage Project Execution — 128
- 9.2 Perform Quality Assurance — 129
- 9.3 Acquire Project Team — 130
- 9.4 Develop Project Team — 131
- 9.5 Manage Project Team — 133
- 9.6 Distribute Information — 134
- 9.7 Manage Stakeholder Expectations — 135
- 9.8 Conduct Procurements — 136

## 10 Monitoring and Controlling — 139
- 10.1 Monitor and Control Project Work — 141
- 10.2 Perform Integrated Change Control — 142
- 10.3 Verify Scope — 144
- 10.4 Control Scope — 145
- 10.5 Control Schedule — 146
- 10.6 Control Costs — 147
- 10.7 Perform Quality Control — 148
- 10.8 Report Performance — 149
- 10.9 Monitor and Control Risks — 151
- 10.10 Administer Procurements — 152

## 11 Closing Process Group — 155
- 11.1 Close Project or Phase — 157
- 11.2 Close Procurement — 160

# III The Knowledge Areas — 163

## 12 Integration — 165
- 12.1 The Charter — 167
  - 12.1.1 Enterprise Environmental Factors — 169
  - 12.1.2 Organizational Process Assets — 170
- 12.2 The Business Case — 170
- 12.3 The Project Management Plan — 171
- 12.4 Direct and Manage Project Execution — 172
- 12.5 Monitor and Control Project Work — 173
- 12.6 Perform Integrated Change Control — 174
- 12.7 Close Project or Phase — 174

## 13 Scope — 175
- 13.1 Scope Definition — 175
  - 13.1.1 What? How? When? Who? — 176
  - 13.1.2 The Theme — 177
  - 13.1.3 Complete and Precise — 177
- 13.2 The Specification — 178
- 13.3 Scope Contents — 179
  - 13.3.1 The Project's Justification — 179
  - 13.3.2 Deliverables and Milestones — 180
  - 13.3.3 Budget — 180

|  |  | 13.3.4 | Acceptance Criteria | 180 |
|---|---|---|---|---|
|  |  | 13.3.5 | Risks | 181 |
|  |  | 13.3.6 | Constraints | 181 |
|  |  | 13.3.7 | Limits and Exclusions | 182 |
|  |  | 13.3.8 | Assumptions | 182 |
|  |  | 13.3.9 | Technical Requirements | 183 |
|  | 13.4 | Statement of Work (SOW) | | 184 |
|  | 13.5 | The Triple Constraints | | 185 |
|  | 13.6 | The Priority Matrix | | 186 |
|  |  | 13.6.1 | Scope Creep | 188 |
|  | 13.7 | Writing the Scope | | 189 |

## 14 The WBS  191
| | 14.1 | The Work Breakdown Structure (WBS) | | 191 |
|---|---|---|---|---|
| | 14.2 | Some Bad WBS Practices | | 195 |
| | 14.3 | Graphical vs. Outline WBS | | 196 |
| | | 14.3.1 | Graphical WBS | 196 |
| | | 14.3.2 | Outline WBS | 198 |
| | 14.4 | WBS Design | | 200 |
| | | 14.4.1 | Work Packages | 201 |
| | | 14.4.2 | Work Package Size | 202 |
| | | 14.4.3 | Control Accounts | 202 |
| | | 14.4.4 | WBS Dictionary | 203 |
| | | 14.4.5 | WBS and the Cost Estimate | 203 |

## 15 Time  205
| | 15.1 | From WBS to Activities | | 206 |
|---|---|---|---|---|

## 16 The Network Diagram  209
| | 16.1 | A Simple Example | | 209 |
|---|---|---|---|---|
| | | 16.1.1 | Nodes | 211 |
| | | 16.1.2 | Arrows and Predecessors | 211 |
| | | 16.1.3 | The Activity Properties Box | 212 |
| | 16.2 | The Forward Pass | | 213 |
| | 16.3 | The Backward Pass | | 215 |
| | | 16.3.1 | Slack | 217 |
| | 16.4 | The Critical Path | | 218 |
| | | 16.4.1 | Please Finish Earlier! | 220 |
| | | 16.4.2 | Milestones | 221 |
| | | 16.4.3 | Managing the Critical Path | 221 |

CONTENTS

   16.4.4 Analyzing the Critical Path .................... 222
 16.5 Activity Sequencing Relationships .................... 223
 16.6 Leads and Lags ........................................ 224
   16.6.1 Loops and Conditional Branches ............... 226
   16.6.2 AOA and AON ................................. 227

## 17 Cost   229
 17.1 Cost Politics ........................................ 229
   17.1.1 It's an Estimate! ........................... 229
   17.1.2 It's about the Future ....................... 230
   17.1.3 The Dream Factor ............................ 230
   17.1.4 The Optimism Factor ......................... 231
   17.1.5 Cost Estimation Errors ...................... 231
   17.1.6 Marketing vs. Technical Estimates ........... 232
   17.1.7 Will it get canceled? ....................... 232
   17.1.8 Protect the Valuables! ...................... 232
 17.2 Cost Estimation ..................................... 232
   17.2.1 Parametric Techniques ....................... 237
   17.2.2 The Delphi Technique ........................ 241
   17.2.3 Bottom-Up Estimation ........................ 242
   17.2.4 Cost Drivers ................................ 243
   17.2.5 The Budget .................................. 244
   17.2.6 Cost Estimation Summary ..................... 244
 17.3 PERT ................................................ 244
 17.4 Overhead Costs ...................................... 249
   17.4.1 What Does $1 Cost? .......................... 250
   17.4.2 Cost vs. Price .............................. 254
 17.5 PMI and Estimating .................................. 255

## 18 Earned Value Management   257
 18.1 How ya doin'? ....................................... 257
   18.1.1 EV and Efficiency ........................... 260
 18.2 Formal Definitions .................................. 261
   18.2.1 Planned Value, $PV$ ......................... 261
   18.2.2 Earned Value, $EV$ .......................... 261
   18.2.3 Actual Cost, $AC$ ........................... 261
   18.2.4 Cost Variance ............................... 262
   18.2.5 Schedule Variance ........................... 262
   18.2.6 Cost Performance Index (CPI) ................ 263
   18.2.7 Schedule Performance Index (SPI) ............ 264

|  |  |  |  |
|---|---|---|---|
| 18.3 | The Estimate at Completion, *EAC* | | 266 |
| | 18.3.1 | The Average *CPI* Method | 266 |
| | 18.3.2 | The *EAC* Formula | 266 |
| | 18.3.3 | Measuring Progress | 267 |
| 18.4 | EV Example: The Re-Paving Project | | 269 |
| | 18.4.1 | Month Three | 269 |
| | 18.4.2 | Plot Everything | 271 |
| 18.5 | Using Earned Value | | 274 |
| | 18.5.1 | Using Hours | 274 |
| | 18.5.2 | No Progress! | 275 |
| | 18.5.3 | Throw Money At It! | 276 |
| | 18.5.4 | Rotten Quality! | 277 |
| | 18.5.5 | At Major Milestones | 277 |
| 18.6 | TCPI | | 277 |
| | 18.6.1 | *TCPI* Example | 278 |
| | 18.6.2 | Hints of Trouble Ahead: The TCPI Calculation | 278 |
| | 18.6.3 | 2 Months Later | 279 |
| | 18.6.4 | The TCPI does not lie | 280 |
| | 18.6.5 | PMBOK to the Rescue! | 281 |
| | 18.6.6 | $TCPI = CPI$? | 283 |
| | 18.6.7 | Oh-Oh. The customer knows | 283 |
| 18.7 | Further Reading: | | 284 |

## 19 Quality   285

| | | |
|---|---|---|
| 19.1 | Key Concepts | 286 |
| 19.2 | Tools and Techniques for Quality Planning | 287 |
| 19.3 | Tools and Techniques for Quality Assurance | 291 |
| 19.4 | Tools and Techniques for Quality Control | 291 |

## 20 Human Resources   295

| | | | |
|---|---|---|---|
| 20.1 | Develop Human Resource (HR) Plan | | 296 |
| 20.2 | Acquire Project Team | | 297 |
| 20.3 | Develop Project Team | | 298 |
| | 20.3.1 | Recognition and Rewards | 299 |
| 20.4 | Manage Project Team | | 301 |
| | 20.4.1 | The Technical Director | 303 |

## 21 Communications   305

| | | |
|---|---|---|
| 21.1 | Identify Stakeholders | 306 |
| 21.2 | Communications Planning | 308 |

## Contents

- 21.3 Identify Communication Requirements Techniques ... 309
- 21.4 Distribute Information Tools & Techniques ... 311
- 21.5 Manage Stakeholder Expectations Tools and Techniques ... 311
  - 21.5.1 Report Performance Tools & Techniques ... 311

### 22 Risk Management — 313
- 22.1 Risks ... 314
  - 22.1.1 Good Risks and Bad Risks ... 315
  - 22.1.2 Known Unknowns and Unknown Unknowns ... 316
- 22.2 Risk Strategies ... 316
  - 22.2.1 Strategies for negative risks ... 317
  - 22.2.2 Strategies for positive risks ... 318
- 22.3 Tools for Plan Risk Management ... 318
- 22.4 Tools for Identify Risks ... 319
- 22.5 Tools for Risk Assessment ... 320
- 22.6 Techniques for Qualitative Risk Assessment ... 321
- 22.7 Tools for Quantitative Risk Analysis ... 324
  - 22.7.1 Expected Monetary Value (EMV) ... 324
  - 22.7.2 Decision Tree Analysis ... 325
- 22.8 Risk Monitoring and Control ... 329
  - 22.8.1 Tools for Risk Response ... 329
- 22.9 Tools to Monitor and Control Project Risk ... 330
- 22.10 Risk Occurrence Over Time ... 330

### 23 Procurement Management — 333
- 23.1 Contract Types ... 335
- 23.2 Selecting a Contract ... 337
  - 23.2.1 Fixed Price Contracts ... 337
  - 23.2.2 Cost-Plus Contracts ... 337
- 23.3 Incentive Fee Contract Example ... 339
- 23.4 The Scope and Contract Types ... 341
- 23.5 Statement of Work ... 343
- 23.6 DoD Contracts and Costs ... 344

### 24 Ethics — 347
- 24.1 An Example of an Ethical Issue ... 348
- 24.2 More Ethical Examples ... 351
- 24.3 TD vs. PM Revisited ... 352
- 24.4 PMI Sample Ethical Problem ... 353
- 24.5 Ethical Situations Test ... 354

24.5.1 Sleeping at Night . . . . . . . . . . . . . . . . . . . . . . . . 354

# IV The "New Kitchen" Project   357

## 25 A New kitchen   359
   25.1 Conceptual Development . . . . . . . . . . . . . . . . . . . . . . 359
   25.2 The Requirements Analysis Phase . . . . . . . . . . . . . . . . . . 361
   25.3 The Bidding Cycle . . . . . . . . . . . . . . . . . . . . . . . . . 363
   25.4 The Charter . . . . . . . . . . . . . . . . . . . . . . . . . . . . 363
   25.5 The Scope . . . . . . . . . . . . . . . . . . . . . . . . . . . . . 364
       25.5.1 Deliverables . . . . . . . . . . . . . . . . . . . . . . . . 364
       25.5.2 Milestones . . . . . . . . . . . . . . . . . . . . . . . . . 365
   25.6 WBS . . . . . . . . . . . . . . . . . . . . . . . . . . . . . . . . 366
   25.7 Cost Estimate . . . . . . . . . . . . . . . . . . . . . . . . . . . 367
   25.8 The Network Diagram . . . . . . . . . . . . . . . . . . . . . . . 368
       25.8.1 Designing the Schedule . . . . . . . . . . . . . . . . . . 368
   25.9 Risks . . . . . . . . . . . . . . . . . . . . . . . . . . . . . . . . 373
       25.9.1 Known Unknowns . . . . . . . . . . . . . . . . . . . . 373
       25.9.2 Unknown Unknowns . . . . . . . . . . . . . . . . . . . 374
       25.9.3 Enhance Risks . . . . . . . . . . . . . . . . . . . . . . . 375
   25.10 Acceptance . . . . . . . . . . . . . . . . . . . . . . . . . . . . . 375

## 26 Acknowledgments and Copyrights   377

## Notes   387

## Bibliography   393

## Index   397

# List of Figures

| | | |
|---|---|---|
| 5.1 | The product life cycle | 55 |
| 6.1 | The process groups | 72 |
| 6.2 | The inputs and outputs for the *Identify Risks* process. | 73 |
| 7.1 | The *processes* contained in the *initiating* process group. | 78 |
| 7.2 | A summary of the *Develop Charter* process. | 79 |
| 7.3 | The inputs to the *Develop Charter* process. | 80 |
| 7.4 | The inputs to the *Identify Stakeholder* process. | 86 |
| 7.5 | The tool to create the stakeholder management *strategy*. | 86 |
| 8.1 | Overview of the *planning* process group, and the processes within it. | 90 |
| 8.2 | The graphical *WBS* for the PMA case. | 98 |
| 8.3 | A portion of the high level network diagram for the PMA case. | 102 |
| 8.4 | *Resource Breakdown Structure* for the PMA case. | 103 |
| 8.5 | A portion of the network diagram for the PMA case. | 105 |
| 8.6 | A portion of the GANTT chart for the PMA case. | 105 |
| 8.7 | A portion of the Timeline diagram for the PMA case. | 106 |
| 8.8 | A summary of the status after completing *Scope* and *Time* planning. | 106 |
| 8.9 | The time-phased budget for the PMA project | 111 |
| 8.10 | The cumulative net cash position for the PMA project | 111 |
| 8.11 | *Risk Management Plan* for the PMA case. | 114 |
| 8.12 | PMA Quality Management Plan. | 120 |
| 8.13 | The organizational chart for the PMA project. | 122 |
| 8.14 | HR Plan for the PMA case. | 123 |
| 9.1 | The *Executing Process Group* and its associated *Processes*. | 128 |
| 10.1 | The *Monitoring and Control* process groups and the associated *Processes*. | 140 |

## List of Figures

10.2 Monitoring and controlling project work is about tracking, reviewing, and regulating project progress. . . . . . . . . . . . . . . . . . . . . . . . 141
10.3 The Change Control System (CCS). . . . . . . . . . . . . . . . . . . . . 142
10.4 The *Change Management Plan* for the PMA web site . . . . . . . . . . 144
10.5 A *Performance Report* showing the status of the PMA project, which uses Earned Value to determine that the project is over budget. . . . . 150
10.6 A *Forecast Report* showing the revised forecast for the estimate at completion (EAC). . . . . . . . . . . . . . . . . . . . . . . . . . . . . . . . . . 151

11.1 The *Closing* process group and its associated *Processes*. . . . . . . . . . 156
11.2 Project Closeout Report and Lessons Learned . . . . . . . . . . . . . . 159

12.1 Vicky's Party Charter! . . . . . . . . . . . . . . . . . . . . . . . . . . . . 167

13.1 The Jello® Triangle: The triple constraints of scope, cost and schedule. 185

14.1 A portion of the WBS for a *Make Party Invitations* project. . . . . . . . 192
14.2 Some WBS No-nos. . . . . . . . . . . . . . . . . . . . . . . . . . . . . . 195
14.3 Preliminary WBS for a kitchen re-modeling project. . . . . . . . . . . . 197
14.4 Outline WBS Format for the kitchen re-modeling. . . . . . . . . . . . . 198
14.5 Outline WBS numbered starting with 1.0. . . . . . . . . . . . . . . . . . 199
14.6 Outline WBS using letters for major subsystems. . . . . . . . . . . . . . 200

15.1 From WBS to ordered activities. . . . . . . . . . . . . . . . . . . . . . . 206

16.1 Rough Network Diagram. . . . . . . . . . . . . . . . . . . . . . . . . . . 211
16.2 The completed *Forward Pass*. . . . . . . . . . . . . . . . . . . . . . . . . 215
16.3 The completed backward pass. . . . . . . . . . . . . . . . . . . . . . . . 217
16.4 The slack and the *Critical Path*. . . . . . . . . . . . . . . . . . . . . . . . 218
16.5 The completed backward with an earlier finish date. . . . . . . . . . . . 220
16.6 A classic Lag: Purchasing takes 1 day, but waiting for the part takes 10 days. . . . . . . . . . . . . . . . . . . . . . . . . . . . . . . . . . . . . . . 225
16.7 An illegal loop in a network diagram. . . . . . . . . . . . . . . . . . . . 226
16.8 An *activity on arrow* (AOA) diagram, equivalent to Figure 16.1. . . . . 227

17.1 The scope dreams often crash on the reality rocks of cost and schedule. 231
17.2 The Accuracy of cost estimation during the project life cycle. . . . . . . 236
17.3 A portion of the micro (or, bottom-up) estimate for the PMA project derived using Microsoft Project. . . . . . . . . . . . . . . . . . . . . . . 243

## List of Figures

17.4 A comparison of the $\beta$ and normal distributions for projects with the same total cost. $\beta$ is asymmetric, with less likelihood of being early, and more likely to take longer. . . . . . . . . . . . . . . . . . . . . . . . . . 245

18.1 *SPI* for the 4 page project. The $SPI \to 1$ at the end of the project, which here, is on Day #8. . . . . . . . . . . . . . . . . . . . . . . . . . . . . . . 265
18.2 *CPI* and *SPI* in month 2 for the repaving project. . . . . . . . . . . . 271
18.3 Miles (planned and completed) for the repaving project. . . . . . . . 272
18.4 CPI and SPI for the repaving project. . . . . . . . . . . . . . . . . . . . . 273
18.5 EAC for the repaving project. . . . . . . . . . . . . . . . . . . . . . . . . . 273
18.6 CPI and SPI when there is not much progress. . . . . . . . . . . . . . . 275
18.7 CPI and SPI when the project manager throws money at it to get back on schedule. . . . . . . . . . . . . . . . . . . . . . . . . . . . . . . . . . . . . 276
18.8 The *TCPI* is the efficiency required to complete the rest of the project on budget. It rises dramatically, clearly demonstrating the project is in trouble. $TCPI \to \infty$ in month 8! . . . . . . . . . . . . . . . . . . . . . . . 281

19.1 A simple control chart with one data point outside the control limits. This point should be investigated. . . . . . . . . . . . . . . . . . . . . . . 289
19.2 A control chart showing an out of control process: There are more than seven data points on the same side of the mean–the rule of seven. . . 290
19.3 A simple flow chart. . . . . . . . . . . . . . . . . . . . . . . . . . . . . . . . 290
19.4 An *Ishikawa Diagram* analyzing the causes of late pizza delivery on weekends. . . . . . . . . . . . . . . . . . . . . . . . . . . . . . . . . . . . . . 292

20.1 A simple organization chart. . . . . . . . . . . . . . . . . . . . . . . . . . 296
20.2 An RACI Matrix. . . . . . . . . . . . . . . . . . . . . . . . . . . . . . . . . 297
20.3 Maslow's hierarchy of needs. . . . . . . . . . . . . . . . . . . . . . . . . . 300

21.1 A portion of the *Communications Plan* for the PMA web site . . . . . 309
21.2 Maslow's hierarchy of needs. . . . . . . . . . . . . . . . . . . . . . . . . . 310

22.1 The *Risk Assessment Matrix* tool for *Qualitative* assessment. . . . . . 322
22.2 A *Decision Tree* analyzing the investment in new web site tools. . . . 326

23.1 Buyer risk versus contract type. . . . . . . . . . . . . . . . . . . . . . . . 342
23.2 Seller risk versus contract type. . . . . . . . . . . . . . . . . . . . . . . . 342
23.3 Statement of Work for the PMA contract. . . . . . . . . . . . . . . . . . 343
23.4 Norman Augustine's data on combat aircraft price. . . . . . . . . . . . 344
23.5 A linear plot of Norman Augustine's data on combat aircraft prices. . . 345
23.6 Norman Augustine's Law: The DoD budget vs. combat aircraft prices. 345

# List of Figures

23.7 The same graph as Fig. 23.6, which is just not as impressive in this log form. . . . . . . . . . . . . . . . . . . . . . . . . . . . . . . . . 346

25.1 Conceptual plan. The dotted lines show the proposed new position of the kitchen and closet walls. The arrow indicates the goal of creating a sight line from the front door through to the garden. . . . . . . . . . . . 360

25.2 The preliminary design for the new kitchen, which was used for the bidding cycle. The lav in the middle of the kitchen had to go! . . . . . . 362

25.3 *Charter* for the new kitchen project. . . . . . . . . . . . . . . . . . . 364

25.4 The detailed specification: The detailed design, showing the new entry closet, pantry and kitchen island. . . . . . . . . . . . . . . . . . . . . 365

25.5 The graphical form of the WBS. . . . . . . . . . . . . . . . . . . . . 366

25.6 Outline WBS Format for the new kitchen. . . . . . . . . . . . . . . . 367

25.7 The Microsoft Project look in GANTT chart format. . . . . . . . . . . 370

25.8 The GANTT chart for the end of the project. . . . . . . . . . . . . . 371

25.9 The network diagram for the start of the project. . . . . . . . . . . . 371

25.10 The portion of the network diagram that follows on from Figure 25.9. . 372

25.11 The WBS output from *Microsoft Project*. . . . . . . . . . . . . . . . 373

# LIST OF TABLES

| | | |
|---|---|---|
| 1 | McDonald's six forces, which are redefining the future of management, and their relation to *current* project management concepts. | xxx |
| 1.1 | Project time scales by industry. | 8 |
| 1.2 | The technical and sociocultural skills of project management. | 10 |
| 1.3 | The CHAOS data on project failure. | 14 |
| 2.1 | A comparison of portfolios, programs, and projects. | 20 |
| 2.2 | SMARTO objectives. | 22 |
| 2.3 | A sample scoring model. | 25 |
| 2.4 | Scoring values defined for the Research CSF. | 27 |
| 2.5 | The scoring matrix for the PMA project. | 27 |
| 2.6 | PMA Winners and Losers. | 28 |
| 2.7 | NPV Example #2. | 33 |
| 4.1 | Project Goals vs. Company Goals. | 42 |
| 4.2 | Cultural Characteristics and Project vs. Company Goals. | 45 |
| 4.3 | Cultural Characteristics and their Extremes. | 46 |
| 4.4 | Advantages and disadvantages of projects in *Functional* organizations. | 51 |
| 4.5 | Advantages and Disadvantages of Projects in Matrix Organizations. | 51 |
| 4.6 | Advantages and Disadvantages of Projectized Organizations. | 52 |
| 5.1 | Example of Activities, Deliverables, and Decision Gates. | 57 |
| 5.2 | Considerations for selecting either waterfall, evolutionary, or agile development. | 63 |
| 6.1 | The PMA membership project phases and their major deliverables | 68 |
| 6.2 | Percent of effort spent in each of the project's process groups. | 71 |
| 6.3 | Project Management *Process Groups* mapped to *Knowledge Areas*. Page 1 of 2 | 75 |

## List of Tables

| | | |
|---|---|---|
| 6.4 | Project Management *Process Groups* mapped to *Knowledge Areas*. Page 2 of 2 | 76 |
| 7.1 | The charter for the PMA web site. | 82 |
| 7.2 | Stakeholders for the repaving project outside the classroom. | 84 |
| 7.3 | Stakeholder Register & Management Strategy: A tool for identifying the expectations and creating a strategy to manage stakeholders. | 87 |
| 8.1 | The *Develop Project Management Plan* process inputs and outputs | 92 |
| 8.2 | The *Collect Requirements* process inputs and outputs | 93 |
| 8.3 | *Requirements document* for the PMA case study. | 94 |
| 8.4 | *Requirements Traceability Matrix* for the PMA case study | 95 |
| 8.5 | The *Define Scope* process Inputs and Outputs | 96 |
| 8.6 | The *Create WBS* process inputs and outputs | 97 |
| 8.7 | The *Time Planning* processes with their associated inputs and outputs. Important outputs are in bold. | 99 |
| 8.8 | *Activity List* for the PMA Case | 100 |
| 8.9 | *Milestone List* for the PMA case. | 101 |
| 8.10 | Some examples of *Estimate Activity Resources* for the PMA case. | 102 |
| 8.11 | *Activity Durations* for the PMA case | 104 |
| 8.12 | *Cost Planning* processes, inputs, and outputs. | 107 |
| 8.13 | *Time Phased Costs by Resource* for the PMA project. Output from Microsoft Project | 110 |
| 8.14 | The Risk Management Processes, Inputs and Outputs. | 113 |
| 8.15 | *Risk Identification* for the PMA case. | 115 |
| 8.16 | *Risk Identification Updates* for the PMA case. | 115 |
| 8.17 | Definition of of *impact* of risks for the PMA case. | 117 |
| 8.18 | Risk response categories. | 118 |
| 8.19 | The *Plan Quality* inputs and outputs. | 119 |
| 8.20 | The *Develop HR Plan* inputs and outputs | 122 |
| 8.21 | The *Plan Communication* inputs and outputs. | 124 |
| 8.22 | The PMA *Communication Management Plan*. | 124 |
| 8.23 | *Plan Procurements* Inputs and Outputs | 126 |
| 9.1 | The *Direct and Manage Project Execution* process inputs and outputs. | 129 |
| 9.2 | The *Perform Quality Assurance* process inputs and outputs. | 130 |
| 9.3 | PMA Quality Assurance Audit Results | 130 |
| 9.4 | PMA Staffing Assignments | 131 |
| 9.5 | The *Develop Project Team* process inputs and outputs. | 132 |
| 9.6 | PMA Team Directory | 132 |

## List of Tables

| | | |
|---|---|---|
| 9.7 | PMA Team Operating Agreement | 133 |
| 9.8 | PMA Team Performance Assessment | 133 |
| 9.9 | The *Manage Project Team* process inputs and outputs. | 134 |
| 9.10 | The *Distribute Information* process inputs and outputs. | 134 |
| 9.11 | The *Manage Stakeholder Expectations* process inputs and outputs. | 135 |
| 9.12 | The PMA *Stakeholders' Issues Log*. | 136 |
| 9.13 | *Conduct Procurements* Inputs and Outputs. | 137 |
| 10.1 | The *Monitor and Control Project Work* inputs and outputs | 141 |
| 10.2 | The *Perform Integrated Change Control* inputs and outputs. | 144 |
| 10.3 | The *Verify Scope* process inputs and outputs. | 144 |
| 10.4 | PMA Scope Verification | 145 |
| 10.5 | The *Control Scope* process inputs and outputs. | 146 |
| 10.6 | The *Control Schedule* process inputs and outputs | 146 |
| 10.7 | Variance Analysis and Work Performance Results | 147 |
| 10.8 | The *Control Costs* process inputs and outputs. | 148 |
| 10.9 | The *Perform Quality Control* process inputs and outputs. | 148 |
| 10.10 | PMA Quality Control Measurements. | 149 |
| 10.11 | The *Report Performance* process inputs and outputs. | 149 |
| 10.12 | The *Monitor and Control Risks* process inputs and outputs. | 152 |
| 10.13 | Updated Risk Register | 152 |
| 10.14 | PMA *Risk Audit* tool. | 152 |
| 10.15 | The *Administer Procurements* process inputs and outputs. | 153 |
| 11.1 | The *Close Project or Phase* inputs and outputs. | 157 |
| 11.2 | The *Close Procurement* inputs and outputs. | 160 |
| 12.1 | The *Integration* knowledge area processes and their associated *process groups*. | 166 |
| 12.2 | The deliverables (outputs) from the processes in the *Integration* knowledge area. | 166 |
| 12.3 | The charter for the PMA web site. | 169 |
| 12.4 | The *Business Case* for the PMA web site. | 171 |
| 13.1 | *Deliverables and Milestones* for a party. | 180 |
| 13.2 | The *Priority Matrix* for a fighter jet. | 186 |
| 13.3 | The *Priority Matrix* for my Dad's birthday party. | 187 |
| 14.1 | *WBS Dictionary Element* for PMA Case | 203 |
| 16.1 | Table of activities, durations, and predecessors. | 210 |

# List of Tables

| | | |
|---|---|---|
| 16.2 | The activity properties box. | 212 |
| 16.3 | Table of *earliest* properties for A. | 213 |
| 16.4 | Table of *earliest* properties for B. | 214 |
| 16.5 | Table of *earliest* properties for C. | 214 |
| 16.6 | Table of *latest* properties for D. | 216 |
| 17.1 | When to use Top-Down vs. Bottom-up Cost Estimates. | 236 |
| 17.2 | Sample job mix cost rates. | 240 |
| 17.3 | Driving to the interview: The PERT optimistic, pessimistic, and most likely estimates. | 247 |
| 17.4 | PERT interview chances of being on time. | 247 |
| 17.5 | PMA Function Point Analysis. | 248 |
| 17.6 | The overhead calculation for the Small Beer Company. | 252 |
| 17.7 | The overhead summary for the Small Beer Company. | 254 |
| 17.8 | The bid for the special party from the Small Beer Company. | 254 |
| 18.1 | The SPI for the 4 page project. | 265 |
| 18.2 | The status of the repaving project after month 3. | 269 |
| 18.3 | The repaving project after month 3 with cumulative costs. | 270 |
| 18.4 | $CPI$, $SPI$, and $EAC$ for the repaving project after month 2. | 270 |
| 18.5 | The status of the book project after month 3. | 279 |
| 18.6 | The status of the book project after month 5. | 280 |
| 21.1 | Stakeholder identification for the PMA web site. | 307 |
| 21.2 | Issues tracking for the PMA web site. | 312 |
| 22.1 | Sources of risk on the Kitchen project. | 315 |
| 22.2 | Definition of risk *Likelihood* values. | 321 |
| 22.3 | Definition of risk *Impact* values. | 321 |
| 22.4 | The *Risk Assessment* for the PMA web site. | 323 |
| 22.5 | Calculation of the contingency budget. | 325 |
| 22.6 | Calculation of the contingency budget using multiple outcomes. | 325 |
| 22.7 | Risk events and some potential responses. | 330 |
| 23.1 | The positive and negative aspects of a fixed price contract. | 338 |
| 23.2 | The positive and negative aspects of a cost plus contract. | 339 |
| 24.1 | An *Ethical Analysis* of the TD vs. APM positions. | 353 |
| 24.2 | Ethical Issues Test. | 355 |
| 25.1 | The cost estimate for the new kitchen | 368 |

## LIST OF TABLES

25.2 The time estimates for the activities in the new kitchen . . . . . . . . . 369

# PREFACE

> **I like prefaces. I read them. Sometimes I do not read any further.**
>
> *Malcolm Lowry*

Is project management an art or a science? *Both!*

While studying project management, we hope you will learn to appreciate the beauty of analysis and the elegance of precision.

There is a tendency for project management to be presented as *Plan, Do*, as if one can perfectly plan a project, and then with your shiny plan in hand, just go out and do it. Unfortunately, the real world doesn't work that way.

We believe that to be successful in project management requires an extra ingredient: *Challenge Everything!* Look at a paragraph, a chart, or a number and ask yourself if it makes sense. Examine it and formulate an opinion. Does your experience tell you something? It is a theme we will return to.

We also believe that as a project manager, there are no excuses. It is your problem.

A magician makes the trick look easy, but it takes thousands of hours of practice to make it look effortless. Success in project management is not magic either. It takes hard work, training, practice and continuous education.

PREFACE

| | |
|---|---|
| My customer is | unreasonable |
| | too demanding |
| | crazy |
| | keeps changing his mind |
| My boss is | relentless |
| | unreasonable |
| | meddling |
| My staff is | untrained |
| | inexperienced |
| The project is | impossible. |

You are the project manager, just get on with it.

## Why Project Management?

At this point, many books about project management claim that using the book will allow you to: *Deliver your projects on time! Deliver on budget!*

Unfortunately, most projects fail to meet their objectives in either cost, schedule, or more importantly, customer satisfaction. It seems self-serving, perhaps even arrogant, therefore, to guarantee that reading a book can cure this endemic problem.

We prefer to say that there are excellent reasons for studying project management, and rather than make some outrageous claim about delivering on time, we prefer to tell you the truth, as in "Earned value will tell you precisely how much over budget your project is."

In our opinion, the excellent reasons for studying project management include:

- You are not alone, others have left breadcrumbs along the path for you to follow.

- There are powerful tools, and proven techniques that are pretty easy to use. In fact, there's no excuse not to use them.

- There are jobs for project managers.[1]

- The stress of project management can be reduced by working smart. The critical path might only involve 25% of the project's activities, so worry about those, and then enjoy the weekend.

[1] OK, we admit this is pandering to the reader!

The number of projects in the world is increasing. This is due to selection factors, changing industries, and a superb job of marketing by the Project Management Institute. Many companies are only recently realizing that they are project-oriented. The legal profession used to be all about billable hours, for example, but more and more clients are requesting (quite reasonably, we believe) a fixed price, up-front bid for services.

Small, non-profit organizations, such as theaters, charities, and arts groups host fund raising events—all projects. We claim that the skills and techniques of project management are applicable to these small organizations. Project management need not be large and bureaucratic.

**Project Management and Business**

Project Management is revolutionizing the world of business.

The study of traditional management is at a cross-roads.[2] There has been much speculation about the future of work, and the forces that are re-defining and shaping organizations.

Paul McDonald suggests that *Management 1.0* was founded on the industrial manufacturing paradigm, which has reached the limits of its relevance. It is time to consider a new *Management 2.0*, based on the global, information age paradigm in which modern businesses compete. [1]

McDonald argues that six forces will redefine the future of management, forces that are already making themselves felt, and that will require a new kind of management thinking. McDonald's forces are: The virtualization of work, open source practices, the decline of organizational hierarchy, the rise of Generation-Y values, the tumult of global markets, and the imperative of business sustainability.

The transition to *Management 2.0* is is typified by companies such as Apple and Google, who now overshadow one-time giants such as General Motors. This is often described as a transition from an industry-driven economy to a knowledge-based economy.

While some people view McDonald's theory as extreme and futuristic, we believe that the concepts underlying his six forces are woven throughout *current project management thinking*. We illustrate the similarity between McDonald's forces and established project management thinking in Table 1.

It is not hard to conclude that project management is at the forefront of modern management.

[2] General Management, as distinct from Project Management.

Table 1: McDonald's six forces, which are redefining the future of management, and their relation to *current* project management concepts.

| Management 2.0 | Current Project Management Concepts |
| --- | --- |
| **Virtualization of Work** <br> Employee trust and teamwork. | **Virtual Teams and Virtual Projects** <br> Structures to manage and drive project success based on positive team behaviors. |
| **Open Source Work Practices** <br><br> Interpersonal relationships in fluid, flexible communities | **Shift from tools and techniques toward managing behaviors** <br> Motivation of project team members and the building of commitment and trust. |
| **Decline of organizational hierarchy** <br> Cultivators and brokers within network structures | **Re-definition of the project manager's role** <br> Project champions broker PM expertise to drive measurable project success. |
| **Rise of Gen-Y Values** <br> A focus on fun, gratification and creativity with work-life balance | **Focus on evolving stakeholder relationships** <br> Creating an environment that balances all stakeholder interests. |
| **The Tumult of Global Markets** <br> Workplace diversity and multi-culturalism | **Global Projects** <br> Embracing team diversity. Managing multiple subject matter experts. |
| **The Imperative of Business Sustainability** <br> Integration of sustainability and Corporate Social Responsibility into management education | **The imperative of sustainability in projects** <br> Integration of ethics and governance, sustainability and CSR into project management education. |

## Project Management and Education

Project Management is revolutionizing the world of education.

Many of the new, most innovative, and interesting ideas are emerging from business, rather than academics. Traditionally, the teaching of project management has been buried in a course on Operations. The explosive growth in project management in the past two decades has left an academic vacuum, which has been filled by non-traditional academic units. The teaching of project management is dominated by online courses and professional, non-credit training.

Many people seeking project management education are graduate professionals, and the way to meet their need is through online education, and project management is at the forefront of the emerging trend: online education in non-traditional academic units.[3]

---

[3]We should explain, in the interest of honesty, that the authors both teach online courses in Boston University's Metropolitan College, a college whose mission has been redefined the past two decades to provide *Graduate Professional Education.*

# Why Now?

Writing this book has been a satisfying project. The first time we do a project, we are excited and we can't wait to get into it. As we proceed, we learn and wish we'd done things differently. By the end of the project, we *really* know how to do it. The second time around, we get to *do it right!*

This is the second time for us, and we leave it to the reader to decide if we indeed did it right.

# Acknowledgments

First, we thank all the students who have put up with our methods. "It's is hard," they cry. We do not apologize for that, we relentlessly challenge our students. We prefer to think that by challenging students, we are preparing them for real world projects.

We are fortunate to work for a brilliant and dedicated department chair, Dr. Kip Becker. Kip constantly challenges us to improve, to innovate, and to grow. Without him, we'd still be teaching 10 students at a blackboard. How far Kip has dragged us.

Our lives are made so much easier by the endless hard work of the superb Administrative Sciences department staff: Susan Sunde, Lucille Dicker, and Fiona Niven. Thanks!

Our department's student services staff handle dozens of daily details in the non-academic lives of our students. Without them, there would be no students left to teach. Thank you Frank Cassidy and Marlene Suarez.

We would like to acknowledge the leadership of Dean Jay Halfond who whole-heartedly supported the introduction of the project management curriculum, and continues to push us to excel. Our warm thanks also go out to our Associate Dean for Academic Affairs, Tanya Zlateva for her consistent dedication to, and nurturing of, the program. Without her technical and emotional support, we would be much poorer.

We have benefited enormously from the efforts of the first-class Boston University Distance Education department. Under the leadership of Nancy Coleman, the group has flourished, diversified, and technologically advanced. To everyone there, a huge, grateful *Thank You!*

## PREFACE

To Nancy Coleman (who invariably says 'Yes' to our radical experiments and crazy ideas); to videographers Charles Southworth and Rob Haley ("sure, we can shoot on location"); to Eric Friedman, Daisy Cerritos, Jenn Sullivan, and Thomas Adams Martin at students services ("only 10 student crises this week"); and to our dedicated instructional designers, Steve Hufsmith and Brad Kay-Goodman ("Sure, we can probably implement that for you today!"). To all of them at Distance Ed, we owe a huge debt of thanks.

Jan Morris tracked down the details of the quotations, and double checked their authorship. Her dedication, not to say zeal, for the task relieved us immensely.

Eileen Warburton copy-edited the entire book. Without her superb talents, there would be random commas, spellings, and peculiar wordings throughout.

Any mistakes remain our responsibility.

# Introduction

> **The important thing is not to stop questioning.
> Curiosity has its own reason for existence.**
>
> *Albert Einstein*

Project management and Boston made us who we are. Despite our diverse backgrounds, Boston is where our project management grew to maturity. We love the Big Dig, baked beans, and the Red Sox. We really are Bostonians.

The subtitle of the book is an ABC:

- Attitude . . . because we believe project management is about clear and strong communication, with an attitude. Challenge everything!

- Books . . . because books and research are the foundation of what we are.

- Conversations . . . because the book challenges the reader, and invites comment. Our reader is not a passive subject.

Besides, ABC is a good metaphor for an introductory textbook, what's new, and Boston is "The New World."

This book introduces the student to the world of project management. We assume nothing, we start from zero.

Almost all of the students taking our project management classes know nothing about formal project management. Therefore, we spend a good deal of effort defining concepts, and establishing first principles. This also aided us in our goal of producing a useful reference. When it comes to definitions and principles, we firmly believe that precision is important. Therefore, we have added lots of index entries, notes and references.

# Introduction

Many of our students have been project managers for years, but have never studied formal project management. We call such a person an *Accidental Project Manager*. Typically, you get called into your boss's office and are told, "Congratulations, you are now the project manager for the company's new project!"

Visions of pay raises and glory stream through your mind. Then you wake up early the next morning realize you know nothing about project management!

For the accidental project manager, our job is to define the concepts clearly and precisely, and without too much surrounding clutter. We hope that combining your valuable practical experience with the established, powerful theoretical concepts, all expressed in the correct vocabulary, will take your project skills to new heights.

The content of the book is based on introductory and advanced courses, both undergraduate and graduate, that we have taught for many years. Our students range from those who are new to project management to experienced professionals seeking a formal grounding for their accumulated knowledge. At Boston University's Metropolitan College, our students are non-traditional, and whether they are undergraduate or graduate students, are usually older with families and careers, they are committed to their education, and motivated. Therefore, we have the luxury of assuming an intelligent and dedicated reader.

As a result, you will not find in this book sections entitled *What you will learn in this chapter*. Rarely will you find *Overviews*.[4] We believe all that just clutters up a book and adds useless pages.[5]

Our mission is to provide a readable, easy to understand book that carefully defines the tools and techniques of project management, is up to date in accepted wisdom (i.e., research), and can serve long-term as a reference for the working professional. To accomplish our mission we established the goals of covering all project management concepts, supporting the concepts with examples, explaining the technical tools and techniques and providing practical worked examples, pointing the reader towards relevant research if they want more depth, and eliminating junk.

## Structure of the Book

A project manager needs two types of skills:

1. *Sociocultural Skills:* A project manager interacts with diverse stakeholders, many of whom have different goals. The project manager also reports to

---

[4] When our students ask if we will provide a study guide for the exam, we reply "No. If it was important, it's in the book. If we thought it was unimportant, we left it out."

[5] We wrote the book, and then deleted almost 20%. We do try to practice what we preach. According to Stephen King: Rewrite formula: 2nd Draft = 1st Draft - 10%. This is the 2nd draft.

upper management and customers. Communication skills are therefore a critical aspect of project management.[6] A project manager must acquire the team, and since a project has not been done before, develop their skills.

These are often referred to as soft skills, but we prefer to think of them as the *art* of project management.

2. *Technical Skills:* A project manager must to be able to perform a variety of technical analyses, such as determining the financial value of a project, performing a cost estimate, constructing a work breakdown structure, building a network diagram, and calculating the earned value. These are essential skills, as each one performs a vital role. If you cannot convincingly demonstrate the value of your project, it may be canceled. Every customer wants to know the cost estimate and the schedule, which emerges from the network diagram. During the project, earned value management shows whether the project is on schedule and/or on budget.

These analyses often referred to as the *science* of project management.

In reality, there is science in the artistic aspect. You can't expect to be good at communication without understanding technical issues such as Maslow's hierarchy. There are also artistic aspects to the analyses. Personally, we find the earned value formulas particularly elegant. The dichotomy between art and science is a false one, in project management and the world. We hope you will enjoy both aspects of the book, simultaneously and throughout.

The book is divided into four parts:

- *Part I Projects:* We define a project, and explore the domain to which project management applies. We also cover the different functions of projects in organizations, and in particular, their roles in accomplishing the mission of the company.

- *Part II Process Groups:* The *process groups* are the activities that the project manager follows during the planning and execution of the project: Initiating, Planning, Executing, Monitoring and Controlling, and Closing. We discuss the *processes* that make up each *process group*,[7] as well as the inputs and outputs for each.

  In Part II, we generally follow the order established in the PMBOK, which defines the terminology but does not provide technical details or examples. For example, Chapter 1 of the PMBOK defines projects, programs, and portfolios, but does not explain how to select projects to make up a portfolio. We

[6] Vijay is often heard to say that "Communication is 90% of project management."

[7] All 42 of them!

provide the underlying technical rationale for portfolio management and show how to use the established tools and techniques with practical examples. Our goal with this book is to get the reader to a place where he or she should be able, after some practice, to implement a portfolio management system.

On a first reading the student may wish to cruise lightly through Part II to get an overview of the PMI processes and knowledge areas. The beginner can use Part II as a checklist for what should happen and look up the processes, their inputs and outputs, as needed.

- *Part III Knowledge Areas:* There are nine *Knowledge Areas* that a project manager must master to be effective, and in Part III, we develop these technical skills. After becoming familiar with Part I, the beginning student should work carefully through the chapters in Part III.

The chapters in Part III again follow the order in the PMBOK and they also follow the stages of a project as it develops. Therefore, it makes sense to follow them in the order presented here. In class, we follow these chapters in order, covering more or less one chapter per week in a one semester course.

- *Part IV The Kitchen Project:* This illustrates the entire project management process and its deliverables with a real-world, practical example: The New Kitchen.

## Advice to the Beginner

Projects surround us, but only recently have people begun to define carefully the characteristics of a project. Many people throw around the term "project" without understanding that it is a very precisely defined concept. Also, projects are often confused with programs, which are totally different. As a result, there is a lot of confusion surrounding the word *project*.

In the first week of classes, we cover the formal definition of a project. In the second week, many students come to class having heard the word *project* bandied about in meetings, and often incorrectly.[8]

This illustrates one of the problems of project management. Many of the terms are thrown around by people who do not understand their meaning.[9] In that situation, we always give the same advice: Keep your mouth shut, no one likes a smarty pants.

[8] We love it when that happens! Actual learning is going on.

[9] It's even worse when they think they understand them!

# Conventions

One of the challenges students face is to learn to master the large, intimidating terminology. Therefore, throughout the book, formal project management terms are italicized. This includes project management processes, e.g., *Define Scope*; key documents, e.g. *Risk Register*; and important terms, e.g., *critical path*. This should help the student become familiar with the terminology.

There are two types of notes, page notes and chapter notes. Page notes are numbered sequentially throughout each chapter.[10] Page notes appear on the same page as the number, and so are easy to find. They contain immediate information, mostly personal observations and comments.

Chapter notes are informal references; they provide explanatory and bibliographic information, and are collected at the end of the book in the *Notes* Chapter. Chapter notes explain where the reader can find more information on a topic, what the research says, and where to find more information. Chapter notes are also numbered sequentially throughout a chapter.

While the appearance of two sets of numbers may at first appear confusing, they have completely different jobs to do.[1] For the sharp-eyed, the two types of note numbers have microscopically different type fonts.[11]

More practically, if you don't see a note at the bottom of the page corresponding to that number, it is a chapter note and you can find it at the back of the book. If you find two notes with the same number on a page, one is a page note, and its content is below. The other is a chapter note at the end of the book.

Formal references to other works are given by citations, and collected at the end in the *Bibliography* section at the end of the book. Citations are provided as numbers in brackets. For example, our previous book on project management said that "this is a great time to study project management." [2]

Definitions appear as follows:

> *This is not a definition, but it sure looks like one.*

We decided that the use of "we" in this book was perfectly appropriate. When we express an opinion, we want it to be clear that it is *our opinion*. We do not do this lightly. We have strong views that are backed by years of experience with both projects and teaching. Hopefully, we have backed our opinions with research supported by references. But if you want to challenge our opinions, feel free to do so. Challenge everything.

---

[10]This is a page note. It falls towards the bottom of the page.

[11]This is another page note. The superscript '1' at the end of the previous sentence is a chapter note, and you can find it in the *Notes* section at the end of the book. The fact that there is no '1' at the bottom of this page, also indicates that it is a chapter note.

INTRODUCTION

There is only one index, because we think that looking up authors separately is confusing. For example, should you look up *Maslow's Hierarchy* under *Maslow* in an author index, or in the subject index? In this book, everything and everyone is in a single index.

Neither is there a separate glossary, as that duplicates information. Terms are defined in their context, and indexed.

## The Cases

Throughout the book, we use two cases to illustrate project management concepts. We also provide sample documents, which students can use a model for their own projects. We use two practical case studies: The Project Management Association (PMA) case, and the New Kitchen case.

### The PMA Case

Throughout the book, we use the *PMA Case* to illustrate project management concepts, and to provide real examples of documents, tools and techniques. The Project Management Association (PMA) is a small organization that is Boston-based. PMA is dedicated to educating its members in project management, to providing networking opportunities, and to making available useful summaries of the latest research. PMA would like to improve the services it offers to its members, and so is considering implementing a new web site with the following features:

- Pages of useful research materials for members.
- A Conference Management System (CMS) with:
    - Online conference participant registration, online submission, review, and acceptance of papers.
    - Download of papers by members.
- Administration of memberships, payments and receipts.
- Social networking for members.
- Marketing emails to members.

We will provide more details about the case in the appropriate sections throughout the book.

**The New Kitchen**

We follow the design and implementation of a new kitchen project through all its phases, and give examples of the process, the issues involved, and give examples of tools and techniques.[12]

# Challenge Everything!

We tell our students to challenge everything. When reading a paragraph, ask yourself: Does this make sense to me? Do I have experience that either reinforces or contradicts the premise of what I am reading?

To challenge everything is not to be a cynic. A cynical person is someone who denies the sincerity of people's motives, and is often sarcastic or sneering. This is not a useful attitude. Even worse than a cynic is a misanthrope, who has a deep seated hatred or distrust of people in general.[3]

But challenges must be backed up. We want you to challenge from an intellectual perspective, which means that you are expected to back up your challenge with facts, data and, preferably, references.[13] When it comes to citing references, the gold standard is to quote from an academic journal. We are nor being pedantic here, but setting the standard. Over time, academic journals embody the accepted state of the art, the accepted wisdom. Random quotations found in a quick Google search carry no weight.

In our previous book, Vijay wrote "A talented PM can work magic with a doomed project." This caused a lot of discussion among students. As his friend and colleague, I defend his use of the poetic word *magic* as an aspirational goal. You can challenge it, but you'd better come armed.

---

[12] Vijay was overheard to say that if he had to listen to Roger's obsessing over the kitchen, at least he was going to make him put it to practical use as a case in the book.

[13] Otherwise, you are plagiarizing!

# Part I

# Projects And Their Environment

# CHAPTER 1

# PROJECTS

> **Don't undertake a project unless it is manifestly important and nearly impossible.**
>
> *Edwin Land*

Projects are everywhere.

Examples of projects include building a house or skyscraper, organizing and holding a birthday or anniversary party, developing a new drug, designing a new air plane or ship, filming a movie or producing a play, or developing a new web site.

The chief distinguishing characteristic of projects is that they are new endeavors, they have never been attempted before. This is in contrast to routine activities, which are performed repetitively. Examples of routine activities include cutting your grass, cooking daily meals, manufacturing drugs, maintaining an airplane or ship, showing a movie or performing a play, and maintaining a web site.

The concept of a project is very old. The Pyramids of Ancient Egypt and the Roman Colosseum were magnificent, sophisticated and complicated projects. However, it is only recently that the precise definition of a project has emerged.

Projects are not necessarily large endeavors. Small, non-profit organizations also engage in projects, for example, when they conduct fund-raisers, or introduce new performances, such as plays and dances. They resort to routine activities when they take tickets and their performances go into a regular run.

The techniques of modern project management are applicable to both large and small projects. There is a tendency for students to look at the jargon, the vast quantity of information, and the diverse collection of tools and assume that project management only applies to large projects. Not so! The tools and techniques of project management can be easily adapted to small projects.

For example, a key lesson is that the scope document, which precisely describes the project, is a project's most important document. Therefore, taking time to carefully define the scope is worthwhile. Even for a small project, it is still worth the effort to produce a clear and concise scope document. The scope need not be a long, bureaucratic tome.

Also, modern network diagram tools operate on small computers and are relatively easy to learn. The application of such tools to manage cost and schedules is very cost effective, even for small projects.

As you go about your daily life, you often hear people talking about their "projects," but not all of these activities will satisfy the precise definition, and as a result, there is considerable confusion as to what constitutes a project. This confusion is exacerbated by the fact that all organizations have their own terminology and procedures. Once the word "project" is embedded in a company, it is likely to stick, even if the outside world does not regard what they are doing as projects.

For example, almost all of the activities in a manufacturing plant are routine, non-projects: parts are ordered, delivered into inventory, and then assembled into products. These operations are much the same from week to week. However, people who work in manufacturing often describe their activities as projects. They may refer to the week's manufacturing target as their project for the week.

It is easy to develop standardized procedures for routine activities. Since projects typically have not been done before, it is much harder to develop a standardized approach, and this presents one of the challenges of project management.

## 1.1 The Project Management Institute

> I think it's wrong that only one company makes the game Monopoly.
>
> *Stephen Wright*

The Project Management Institute (PMI) is the professional organization devoted the the furthering of project management. PMI is growing rapidly, which is one indicator of the growing importance of project management.[1]

PMI has done an excellent job of defining the characteristics of projects through global standards. These standards are widely accepted and, as claimed by PMI, "when consistently applied, they help you, your global peers and your organization achieve professional excellence."

The most important standard published by PMI is known as the *PMBOK*.[2] The official title of the *PMBOK* is *A guide to the Project Management Body of Knowledge* [4]. PMI defines the *PMBOK* as the standard formal document that describes established norms, methods, processes, and practices.

> *The PMBOK® Guide is the standard for managing projects most[3] of the time across many types of industries. This standard describes the project management processes, tools, and techniques used to manage a project towards a successful outcome.*

The *PMBOK* mostly addresses project management, but it also contains information about the project environment, such as program and portfolio management. It also contains information from other disciplines, such as communications theory, risk management, and quality control.

While the *PMBOK* is the definitive standard, we do not feel obligated to slavishly follow every word. Project management is a complex endeavor and applicable to a wide range of industries. We are quite comfortable challenging the *PMBOK* when we have experience, data or research to suggest a better approach. In fact, we encourage our students to examine critically all their readings, not just the *PMBOK*.[4]

## 1.2 What is a Project?

We begin with the formal PMBOK definition of a project:

> *A project is a temporary endeavor undertaken to create a unique product, service, or result.*

A project is considered to be a unique endeavor, in that it has never been done before. Projects must be carefully distinguished from routine activities, which are repetitive in nature.

[1] The PMI website *pmi.org* has a massive collection useful information on all aspects of project management.

[2] *PMBOK* is usually pronounced as pim-bock.

[3] Most?! Some standard!

[4] Challenge Everything!

## 1. Projects

This is a somewhat cryptic definition that obscures a lot of important information. For example, the word "temporary" is expanded to mean that a project has definite beginning and end dates.[5] The word "temporary" is also a little unusual because it implies a short duration activity while projects often continue for long periods. A skyscraper may take many years to build. Even so, the project to create the skyscraper is referred to as a temporary effort.

The word "unique" is also a loaded term. Here, the word means that the project has not been done before. There are of course, repetitive aspects of a project, even if the overall result is unique. In our skyscraper example, the building may be highly original in design, and therefore unique. Within the construction, however, many activities are quite routine, e.g., installing the light fixtures in each floor.

The uniqueness of projects requires further clarification. Suppose one is building several houses in a development, and all of the houses have the same design. One might argue that the first house is a project, since it is unique. Building the remaining houses might be considered routine, and not really projects. It is likely, though, that one would continue to treat the other houses as projects, and manage their construction in a disciplined way.

A definition should stand alone, and precisely define a concept. We believe the above definition does not work very well in this regard, e.g., it needed several paragraphs just to clarify the idea of "temporary." Therefore, we provide another definition that we believe is more helpful:

> *A project is unique, non-routine effort, limited by time and budget, defined by a performance specification, and designed to meet stakeholder needs.*

Rather than defining a project as temporary, we used the phrase "unique, non-routine." This clarifies the idea that a project is different from anything that went before. Also by avoiding the word "temporary," we eliminate the confusion about projects that take many years, or even decades to complete. The definition also clarifies the important distinction between routine activities and projects.

The limitations on cost and schedule are also important additions. Often, some of the first questions asked about a project are: How much will it cost? When will it be completed? Since every project is limited by cost and schedule, it is appropriate to include these ideas in the definition.

Including the performance specification explains how the project is defined. The performance specification is the most important document in the project, and highlighting it in the definition elevates its importance.

---

[5] An activity without an end date is technically, not a project. This is a favorite trick question on exams.

Finally, the project must meet stakeholder needs. We note the use of the word, "stakeholder," who is anyone with a stake in the project. Sometimes, the word, "customer," is used in the definition, but the customer is only one of many stakeholders.

It is not unusual to have stakeholders who would be happy to see the project fail, and managing such naysayers is a challenging activity. For example, in the construction of a new side walk, the owners of the stores lining the route may be negatively affected during construction, and might prefer that the project not be done at all.

Projects are characterized as follows:

- *Projects have an established objective.*

  In the early stages of a project's conceptual development, the project is defined by its charter, which is a short overview of the goals and objectives, and perhaps a desired schedule and rough budget. The first activity of the project is typically the development of the scope, which precisely defines the project.

- *Projects have a well-defined life span.*

  Projects have a beginning date and an end date. If activities continue indefinitely into the future, then technically it is not a project. In general, it is a good idea to break up long projects into several shorter projects, each with a well defined objective, budget, and completion date.

- *Projects require staff participation from across the organization.*

  Projects are inherently multi-disciplinary. For example, when building a house, the project manager must interact with the architect and the contractor, as well as assorted subcontractors such as roofers, plumbers, electricians, and carpenters. There are also technical requirements such as the permitting process, gas company installation and approval procedures, and voluminous fire codes, electrical codes, and environmental regulations.

  Project managers must also interact with professionals such as accountants, lawyers, engineers, and human resources personnel. Project managers will quickly find themselves immersed in many disciplines.[6]

- *Projects have defined schedules and budgets.*

  No project has the luxury of an infinite cost or schedule. Customers always have an assigned budget and a preferred delivery schedule.

[6]There is a fascinating debate about whether a project manager can be successful if he or she does not possess technical expertise in the project's discipline. Does a project manager need to be a subject matter expert, or are project management skills universally applicable?

- *Projects have limited resources.*

  Resources include staff and equipment, which must be managed. Other factors may limit the performance of the project, such as competition with other projects for staff and the availability of funds.

- *Projects have multiple, often competing, stakeholders.*

  The project manager and the team are obvious stakeholders, but there are many more, including the sponsor (who pays the bill), customers, users, and trainers. Upper management also has a stake in the project's success, but if things are not going well, it may be in their best interest to cancel the project!

### 1.2.1 Project Time Scales

Projects have widely different time scales. Table 1.1 shows typical time scales for projects in different industries.

Table 1.1: Project time scales by industry.

| Industry | Typical Project Time Scale |
| --- | --- |
| Military Jet | 15-20 years |
| Mega Project Construction | 10-15 years |
| Skyscraper Construction | 3-5 years |
| House Construction | 3-6 months |
| Software System | 1-2 years |
| Web Site Construction | 3-6 months |
| Insurance Product | 1 month |
| Proposal | 30 days |

## 1.3 Project Management

> You want to study project management?
> Read more, sleep less!
>
> *John Cable*

## 1.3. Project Management

Project management is the term applied to the process of managing projects.

Because projects are unique, it is difficult to develop a completely standardized approach. There is seldom a "right" way to proceed, one is always dealing with uncertainty. On the other hand, standardized methods have evolved which reduce the risks associated with dealing with the unknown.

The Project Management Institute (PMI) defines project management as:

> *Project Management is the application of knowledge, skills, tools, and techniques to project activities to meet the project requirements.*

As with professions such as law, medicine, and accounting, the body of knowledge rests with the practitioners and academics who apply and advance it. The PMBOK includes proven traditional practices that are widely applied, as well as innovative practices that are emerging. As a result, the PMBOK is constantly evolving.[7]

> *The PMBOK Guide® provides guidelines for managing individual projects. It defines project management and related concepts and describes the project management life cycle and the related processes.*

How should the PMBOK be used? The project team should consult the PMBOK to identify the processes that are relevant to their own individual project objectives.

For example from the planning process group, a process called *Identify Risks* may be selected to be integrated into their specific project life cycle. When considering a process for inclusion in a project, it is useful to identify the relevant inputs and outputs, any forms or company templates that already exist, and any related documents. Company and environmental factors may also constrain project options, and therefore affect the selection of relevant processes.

The entire life cycle should be tailored to meet the project's and sponsor's requirements in the most efficient manner. The work load of including a process must be balanced against the elimination of the associated deliverables. Every project needs a well-constructed *scope*, and so eliminating the *Define Scope* process is a bad idea. On the other hand, if there are no subcontractors, then one can safely eliminate *Procurement Management Planning*.[8]

As an illustration of tailoring the PMBOK, for small projects we frequently combine the following four PMBOK risk management processes: *Identify Risks*; *Perform Qualitative Risk Analysis*; *Perform Quantitative Risk Analysis*; and *Plan Risk*

---

[7] That the standard is evolving is often neglected. However, as a student of project management, your job is to question the standard, and to improve it, wherever possible.

[8] We do not recommend eliminating this entirely from the Management Plan. It is better to briefly state "No subcontractors are planned." That way, if you later decide you need subs, you have a place to put the information in the plan.

*Responses.* We define a customized process that we call *Create Risk Management Plan.*[9]

Since every project is unique, no two life cycles will be the same. Also, the rigor with which each process is executed varies from one project to another. If the project is mission critical, or if the project team is not experienced, one should use more rigor in implementing and executing each process. An example of 'more rigor' is to enforce better process and deliverable documentation in order to reduce the risks of mis-communication.

Table 1.2: The technical and sociocultural skills of project management.

| Technical Skills | Sociocultural Skills |
| --- | --- |
| Scope Production | Stakeholder Management |
| Work Breakdown Structure | General Management |
| Cost & Schedule Management | Staff Management |
| Resource Contention | Leadership |
| Critical Path Management | Negotiation Skills |
| Earned Value Management | Politics |

Project management involves two types of skills:

- *Sociocultural Skills.* These are the "soft" skills, including general management skills, interpersonal communications, and staff development.

- *Technical Skills.* These include the ability to produce and manage work breakdown structures, network diagrams, critical paths, and track cost and schedule performance.

Table 1.2 lists project management skills and classifies them. Fortunately, coming to the aid of the modern project manager is a discipline and methodology that provides support and professionalism in both arenas.

## 1.4 The Project Manager

**Managing is essentially a loser's job, and managers are about the most expendable pieces of furniture on the earth.**

*Ted Williams, The Splendid Splinter.*

---

[9] Note that we actually use the PMBOK as a checklist to ensure that we include all the necessary pieces. It would do no good if we forgot to plan the risk responses!

## 1.4. The Project Manager

Let's begin with the definition:

*The project manager is the person assigned to to achieve the project's objectives.*

In this book, we are always going to assume that you, dear reader, are the project manager. Whenever we ask a question, or expect you to analyze a problem, we always assume that you should answer it from the project manager's point of view.

The project manager must possess three characteristics: Knowledge about project management; the ability to perform as a project manager; and personal effectiveness, which encompasses both skills and personality traits.

The project manager often has responsibility without authority. Rarely does the project manager have the luxury of being able to order people around. The interdisciplinary nature of projects, and the diverse skills required, means that few, if any, of the staff work directly for the project manager. One of the key skills, therefore, of project management is being able to induce the right people to do the right thing at the right time. This includes their staff, stakeholders, customers, and even upper management. This leads to one of our most cherished beliefs:

*Project managers induce people to perform.*

The role of the PM is to:

1. Plan and organize the project from start to finish.
2. Manage relations with stakeholders, and in particular, customers.
3. Manage relations with the parent company.
4. Develop and manage the project team.
5. Monitor and control project progress, particularly the costs and schedule.
6. Deal with uncertainty and changes.
7. Deliver the product or service, and get the customer's acceptance.

Project managers must exercise control and provide leadership to their team. At the same time, they cannot do everything and so must learn to delegate, follow up, and provide training and encouragement as needed.

Since projects have not been done before, project managers must deal with uncertainty. Almost everything in project management is a compromise, there are rarely correct answers. Projects are inherently messy, and change is a fact of life. Project managers must be able to deal with complexity, and prioritize.

Project managers live in a permanent competition for resources. They compete for staff and with other projects for resources. They referee stakeholders, all of whom have differing objectives and priorities.

### 1.4.1 Interactions

The project manager interacts with many different constituencies:

- *Stakeholders.* This is the most important group. Failure to carefully manage stakeholders will jeopardize the project. Stakeholders are usually a diverse group with competing priorities.

- *Upper Management.* The project manager must understand the role of the project in the company's strategy, and be able to defend its budget.[10]

- *Sponsor.* The person who pays for the project will want regular cost and schedule updates.

- *Customers.* The people who set the expectations for the final product or service.

- *Project Team.* It is the project manger's job to induce the team to perform to the best of their ability.

- *Functional Areas.* These are typically the company departments that provide the staff to the project, and may include:
    - System designers and architects.
    - Subject matter experts.
    - Business analysts, lawyers, and accountants.
    - Contractors and subcontractors.
    - Testers and quality control staff.

## 1.5 Benefits of Project Management

There are two main benefits to a disciplined approach to project management:[11]

---

[10] We regard this a nothing less defending one's job security!

[11] As explained in the introduction, we are resisting the urge to say that you will deliver your project on schedule and on budget.

- *You are not alone.* There is a mountain of information available: Literature, templates, and advice. You can access it, and learn from others. Someone has probably done something similar.

- *Powerful Tools.* The critical path tells you which activity is the most important one to work on now. Earned value tells you how much your project is over budget and behind schedule. You may not like the answers, but at least you'll know the truth.

### 1.5.1 Project Success

A significant challenge of project management is that every project must aim to be successful. In a routine manufacturing environment, the failure of a few products (out of a million) might not be regarded as catastrophic. However, the failure of a project critical to the mission of a company might lead to a crash of the entire company. Finally, projects are almost always produced to a tight deadline with constrained funds. This all adds pressure to the project manager to succeed.

When discussing "success," however, it is important to distinguish between:[5]

1. *Project management success.* This is typically measured by the traditional factors of following a quality process, and delivering on schedule and within budget.

2. *Project success.* This is usually defined in terms of product quality, and measured by whether the project met its overall objectives, e.g., its critical success factors.[12]

One should also distinguish between size and importance because the importance of a project is not necessarily related to its size. Small, mission-critical projects are much more important than their larger non-critical cousins. Neither is technical complexity related to size. Small, mission-critical, technically challenging projects will require the best from a project manager.

The subject of project failure garners a lot of attention. First, we point out that *failure* is a complex concept: Is a project a failure if it successfully meets stakeholder needs but comes in late and over budget? Is a project successful that is on time and on budget, but leaves some stakeholders unhappy?

One of the most quoted sources of project failure is the *CHAOS Report* by the Standish Group who studied 365 companies with a total of 8,380 Information Sys-

[12]Another way of understanding this distinction is with the oft-heard saying that "the operation was a success, but the patient died."

tem applications. [6] The report divided projects into three distinct outcomes, as shown in Table 1.3.

Table 1.3: The CHAOS data on project failure.

| Project Outcome | 1994 | 2009 | Definition |
|---|---|---|---|
| *Successful* | 16% | 32% | Completed on time and budget, with all features as specified. |
| *Challenged* | 53% | 44% | Completed, but were over cost, over time, and/or lacking features |
| *Impaired/Failed* | 31% | 24% | Abandoned or canceled **Total losses!** |

The first percentage is for the original data from 1994, and the second is for 2009. While these are IT projects, similar data exists for other types of projects in other countries and industries. The point is that while things have improved somewhat in 15 years, the CHAOS data suggest that most projects fail!

There are major criticisms, however, of the Standish interpretation of "failure." [7] For example, a project 25% over budget that meets stakeholder needs and is on-time is a failure according to the Standish criteria. Also, the data is biased in that it ignores projects that under-run in cost and time.

Another interesting factor is the forecast bias. That is, most people underestimate their forecast,[13] and without taking these biases into account, the Standish data are highly suspect.

This is an excellent example of the technique that we wish to inculcate into our reader: Challenge Everything![14]

## 1.6 The Project Management Office

[13]Whether by design or ignorance is another fascinating question

[14]Just because you read it in a fancy report, you don't have to take it for granted. Ask questions. Examine assumptions. Find your own data.

A Project Management Office (PMO) is a responsible for the coordinated management of projects. The job is to:

- Develop and manage the company standards, policies and procedures that apply to projects.

- Invest in project management technology, best practices, tools and techniques and implement them across projects.

- Manage the information technology system

- Supervise functions that are managed centrally, such as the portfolio selection system, and risk pools.

- Collect and manage lessons learned.

# CHAPTER 2

# THE PROJECT ENVIRONMENT

## 2.1 The Environment

> **There are two ways of being creative. One can sing and dance.**
> **Or one can create an environment in which singers and dancers flourish.**
>
> *Warren G. Bennis*

A project manager must be aware of the environment surrounding the project, as well as creating a positive internal environment for the team.

## 2.2 The Internal Environment

The internal project environment influences team members' attitudes and their desire to perform. For a project to succeed, team members must be committed to the project's goals and care about producing a quality product or service.[1] A positive internal environment includes:

1. A corporate culture that acknowledges and appreciates the efforts of team members.

[1] Again, we see the idea that you cannot 'order' someone to succeed, you can only create an environment which helps them to succeed.

2. Good working relationships among team members.

3. Clear and open communications.

4. An environment of trust.

5. A willingness to take risks.

6. Recognition of efforts and achievements.

Apart from the first item, which depends on the corporate climate, these qualities are the responsibility of the project manager. They are important because they relate directly to the characteristics of a project. Since projects are unique, the project manager must ensure that everyone understands both the objectives and their own roles. A willingness on the part of the team to take risks is required because they are venturing into uncharted territory.

## 2.3 The External Environment

The external environmental influences include:

1. The parent company, including upper management.

2. Organizational assets, including policies and procedures, lessons from previous projects, etc.

3. The company culture, existing staff, and company investment in tools and technologies.

4. The political environment, including government policies, tax incentives, etc.

5. The business climate, including company strength, business strategies, and access to funds.

6. The geographical setting, including environmental issues.

7. Social commitments, including benefits and working conditions.

## 2.4 The Project's Rationale

An important and critical aspect of the external environment is the business need of the project—its rationale for existence. This need is documented in the business case, and must be aligned with company objectives. (This is covered in the section on portfolio management 2.6.)

If the need for the project disappears, the project will also disappear. A threat to all projects is the evolution of the business that eliminates the need for the project. Project managers must be on the lookout for this.[2]

## 2.5 Programs

Programs are collections of projects that have a natural association, and are managed together for mutual benefit. The definition of a program is:

*A program is a group of related projects managed in a coordinated way to obtain benefits and control not available from managing them individually.*

Suppose a company's marketing department creates a program to launch a new product. That program might include the following projects:

- Launch the product at a national trade show.
- Plan and implement a marketing campaign.
- Create the supply chain for the product.
- Create new marketing channels for the product.

Sometimes a program has routine activities as part of its mission. In the above example, routine activities might include updating the marketing materials and brochures and publication of a weekly sales brochure to selected clients.

An organization that uses the term "program" in the way we have defined it is NASA. For example, NASA's Mars exploration program consisted of many projects, including Spirit and Opportunity Launches, 2001 Mars Odyssey, Mars Express, and the Mars Reconnaissance Orbiter.

Program management is often accomplished in a Program Management Office (PMO).

[2] No project, no job!

## 2.6 Portfolios

A portfolio is usually managed as a business unit. That is, a portfolio consists of all the activities necessary to make a product (or line) successful. Portfolios, therefore, include projects, programs, as well as routine activities.

Developing a new product is a project, but the activities to make the product successful include many routine activities such as marketing, product maintenance, inventory control, and customer service. A new product cannot be successful without all of these non-project activities, so it makes sense for a company to manage it all as a coherent whole.

*A portfolio is a collection of programs, projects, products, and routine activities managed together for mutual benefit.*

A comparison of portfolios, programs and projects is shown in Table 2.1, which is based on a similar table in the PMBOK.

Table 2.1: A comparison of portfolios, programs, and projects.

|  | **Projects** | **Programs** | **Portfolios** |
| --- | --- | --- | --- |
| Scope | Clearly defined objective | Wider scope with corporate objectives | Business objectives aligned with corporate strategy |
| Planning | Progressive elaboration of project objectives | Program plan | Business Plan |
| Management | The project | The program | The portfolio |
| Success | Meets stakeholder objectives, within cost & schedule | Meets business objectives | Meets corporate objectives |

## 2.7 Mission, Goals, Objectives, and Strategy

A project manager must be able to link their project to the company's mission, goals, and objectives. Projects compete for both client and company funds and resources, and projects without a clear link to the mission are at risk of cancellation. It is simply job security for the project manager to be able to defend his or her project.

Every project manager should have an "elevator speech" about why the company cannot possibly survive without their project.[3]

It is important to understand the precise difference between mission, goals, objectives, and strategy, as well as their relation to portfolios, programs, and projects.

### 2.7.1 Mission

The mission is the company's reason for existing. The mission statement is often aspirational, providing the vision and values for the company. It defines who you are, what you do, and why. Every project must have a clear link to the mission and strategy. Otherwise, why do it?

For example, Google's mission is to "organize the world's information and make it universally accessible and useful." Notice that this does not say anything about search engines. If I had asked you what Google is known for, you'd probably say something about web searching.

Google's is an excellent example of mission statement. It is concise and clear, and sets out their goals for everyone to see. An excellent example of how that mission statement helped to guide Google is to think about what happened when digital mapping became available. If the Google mission had been to create a great search engine, then digital mapping might have been viewed as outside the realm of their mission. But since their mission is to 'organize information,' and maps are an organizational tool, digital mapping was clearly within their domain.

Many companies had the capabilities to include mapping in their portfolios, but failed to see the link to the organization of information. Google understood that mapping was a clearly linked to their mission and became one of the leading mapping companies.

### 2.7.2 Goals

The goals are what you wish to accomplish. For example, a company goal might be to: *Diversify our products to get into new markets.*

---

[3]The notion of an elevator speech is that if you find yourself in the elevator with the President of the corporation, you have about 60 seconds to justify your existence. Practice it.

### 2.7.3 Objectives

Objectives are detailed, specific statements about what the company wishes to achieve. When listing objectives, the acronym SMARTO is often used—see Table 2.2[4]

An example of a specific objective related to the above goal of diversifying into new markets is *Increase market share by 15% in 3 years*. This objective satisfies all of the SMARTO criteria.

Table 2.2: SMARTO objectives.

| S | Specific | in the target objective |
|---|---|---|
| M | Measurable | indicators of progress |
| A | Assignable | to a specific person |
| R | Realistic | in what can be done |
| T | Timed | with schedules and deliverables |
| O | Open | for everyone to see |

### 2.7.4 Strategy

The strategy defines precisely how the company will accomplish the objectives. For example, the strategy to accomplish the above objective of increasing market share by 15% in 3 years might be:

- Invest $50,000 in new product development.
- Set up a new portfolio evaluation method.
- Develop 3 new innovative products and dramatically enhance the existing lines.
- Diversify the portfolio into 2 totally new product areas.

## 2.8 Portfolio Management

Which projects should a company select? If the literature is to be believed, most companies are very poor at this. Also, there is a huge difference in effectiveness

---

[4] Actually, most textbooks use the acronym SMART (without the 'O' at the end). We believe that a vital part of successful project selection and evaluation is openness. Everyone in the company should see what is being funded and what rejected.

between the best and worst companies in selecting projects. In this section, we briefly describe the key aspects of the scoring matrix, which is the most appropriate tool to use for portfolio management.

A portfolio consists of many different projects, all with different goals, stakeholders, and priorities. Projects must align with corporate objectives, and choosing between projects is a vital skill.

Projects may spring up in unexpected areas. For example, when tax and environmental regulations change, systems and processes must be upgraded. These so-called "compliance projects" are not glamorous, they cost money, and do not improve the bottom line. However, the project selection mechanism must also permit the selection of these types of projects.

But what makes for a successful project? Research has established that there are a few critical success factors (CSF).[1]

A good portfolio is characterized by:

- *The right number of projects.* Many companies take on too many projects. The result is that their projects do not have enough resources, either money or staff, and it should therefore come as no surprise that their portfolio performs poorly. Therefore, one of the essential aspects of good portfolio management is *killing projects.*

- *Good balance.* Portfolios need to have a mix of highly innovative projects, moderate extensions to existing lines, and compliance projects. One of the excellent attributes of the scoring matrix is that it achieves a balanced portfolio.

- *Clearly tied to the business mission and strategy.* Projects need a clear and coherent link to the business objectives. Spending and investment must be linked to corporate goals.

There are many ways of prioritizing and selecting projects. Financial methods are popular and until recently dominated the selection process. However, selecting a project based on its return on investment is generally considered to be the *worst* way to select projects. Early in the life of a project quantities such as cash flow, profitability, and return on investment are very difficult to estimate.

### 2.8.1 Critical Success Factors

> **I don't know the key to success, but the key to failure is trying to please everybody.**
>
> *Bill Cosby*

Many studies have been conducted on what makes a successful product.[2] Successful products have a few *Critical Success Factors* in common. The most important CSFs are:

1. *A unique, differentiated product that provides significant benefits and superior value to the customer.* This is the most important CSF and is much more important than any other factor in the eventual success of a product.

2. *A strong market-driven, customer focused orientation aimed at an "attractive market."* An attractive market is one in which there is lots of money[5] and, preferably, no competitors. Also an attractive market is defined from the customer's perspective and so it is vital to build in the voice of the customer. That is, solicit opinions from potential customers: The project's value is determined by customers, not the project manager. Also, one should carefully assess the competition and their potential responses.

3. *Solid up-front project definition.* The project's most important document is the scope, so investment of time up front is critical. Don't rush in. Clearly define the project.

4. *Don't stray from core competencies.* What are you good at? You can branch out into new areas, but if you do, be sure you know that it is risky.

5. *Execute a disciplined process.* Practice good project management and garner upper management support. Implement a portfolio management system with tough Go/Kill decisions. Continually check costs, margins, and revenues.

## 2.9 The Scoring Matrix

> **If it doesn't matter who wins or loses, then why do they keep score?**
>
> *Vince Lombardi*

---

[5] If there is not lots of money, why bother?

## 2.9. The Scoring Matrix

A sample scoring matrix is shown in Table 2.3. The top row lists the evaluation criteria, which are the factors against which projects will be scored. The CSFs established above are the foundation of the evaluation criteria in the scoring matrix. For example, knowing that a unique, differentiated project is the #1 CSF, we need a way to evaluate projects against this criterion. Other company goals may be added as criteria.

Each evaluation criterion is assigned a weight, which is shown in the second row of Table 2.3. These weights represent how important the criterion is to the company. Weights are typically scored from 1 – 5, where 5 represents a criterion vital to the company. For example, a company with an aging portfolio may add "Innovativeness" as a criterion and give it a weight of 4. Projects that score high in the Innovativeness will then rise to the top of the list.

The projects to be evaluated are listed down the left hand side. Each projects is given a score out of 10 for each of the criteria. For example, Project #1 is assigned a score of 9/10 for the Unique criterion, and a 4 in Return on Investment (ROI).

The total project score is obtained by multiplying the weights by the scores. For example, the Project #1 score is:

$$9 \times 5 + 8 \times 4 + 4 \times 2 = 45 + 32 + 8 = 85. \tag{2.1}$$

Once all projects have been scored, they can be ranked and dollars assigned.

Table 2.3: A sample scoring model.

| Criteria | Unique | Innovative | ROI | |
|---|---|---|---|---|
| **Weight** | 5 | 4 | 2 | **Score** |
| Project #1 | 9 | 8 | 4 | 84 |
| Project #2 | 6 | 2 | 3 | 44 |
| Project #3 | 9 | 9 | 9 | 99 |
| Project #4 | 6 | 4 | 5 | 56 |

Scoring models are efficient: They fit management's style in that they are simple to understand, do not take a lot of time, and do not require a tedious bureaucracy. While that is useful, it is more important that scoring models:

## 2. THE PROJECT ENVIRONMENT

- yield portfolios with high value projects,
- support go/kill decisions,
- assign investment that reflects strategic priorities, and
- result in well-balanced portfolios.

### 2.9.1 PMA Project Selection

As an example, suppose the Project Management Association (PMA) is considering implementing several new projects. Proposed new projects usually emerge from strategy sessions, internal solicitations throughout the company, and the marketing department. Each project has a project manager[6] and a *Charter*, which briefly describes the project, its budget, and the primary objectives. PMA's list of proposed projects is as follows:

1. A new web site to communicate with members.
2. A fundraiser solicitation by email to members.
3. A course in project management for members.
4. A membership drive to increase the membership.

**The CSFs**

The mission and goals of PMA were established in the Introduction: PMA is dedicated to project management research and to the education of its members. We might establish, therefore, the following criteria to evaluate the proposed projects:

- **Research.** Projects will be scored high if they increase the research knowledge of members and, since this is the primary mission, this will carry a weight of 5.

- **Education.** Projects will be scored high if they increase the education of members. This is important, but not quite as important as the research goal, and so it is assigned a weight of 4.

- **Growth.** Projects will be scored high if they grow the membership of the organization. This is not so important as research and education, and so it is assigned a weight of 2.

---

[6]At this stage, the project manager is the person who will champion the project.

Each CSF should be carefully defined, and the definition is elaborated during discussions. For example, the **Research** CSF might be scored as in Table 2.4:

Table 2.4: Scoring values defined for the Research CSF.

| Score | Definitions for Scoring the Criteria |
|---|---|
| 9-10 | Valuable research information for most members. |
| 7-8 | Valuable research information for many members, or useful research capabilities for majority of members. |
| 4-7 | Research information useable by a few members. |
| 0-3 | No useful research information. |

**The Scoring Matrix**

Once the CSF scoring criteria are defined, each project is given a score for each CSF–see Table 2.5. The projects are then ordered by their score (high scores at the top) to rank the projects. This is shown in Table 2.6.

Table 2.5: The scoring matrix for the PMA project.

| Criteria | Research | Education | Growth | |
|---|---|---|---|---|
| Weight | 5 | 4 | 2 | Score |
| #1. Web Site | 9 | 8 | 4 | 85 |
| #2. Fundraiser | 2 | 2 | 9 | 44 |
| #3. PM Course | 0 | 10 | 7 | 99 |
| #4. Membership | 0 | 0 | 8 | 56 |

**The Budgets**

When the projects were initially proposed, a rough budget was included. So far, we have not considered the budgets, we have evaluated them solely on their match to

## 2. THE PROJECT ENVIRONMENT

Table 2.6: PMA Winners and Losers.

| Criteria | Research | Education | Growth | Score | Budget | Allocated |
|---|---|---|---|---|---|---|
| **Weights** | 5 | 4 | 2 | | | |
| **Funded Projects** | | | | | | |
| #3. PM Course | 0 | 10 | 7 | 99 | 5,000 | 5,000 |
| #1. Web Site | 9 | 8 | 4 | 85 | 5,000 | 10,000 |
| **Losers** | | | | | | |
| #4. Membership | 0 | 0 | 8 | 56 | 1,000 | 11,000 |
| #2. Fundraiser | 2 | 2 | 9 | 46 | 1,000 | 12,000 |

the CSFs. The next step involves the costs of the projects, which are entered in the fourth column in Table 2.6.

The next piece of data we need is the total funds allocated to be spent on projects by the organization. Suppose for PMA, this amount is $10,000. In the fifth column in Table 2.6, we calculate the running total of the funded amount. The top project gets funded, so at this point we have spent $5,000. Then the next highest score is funded, and the total allocated at this point is $10,000.

**The Winners**

Projects are funded until we reach the allocated amount, which here is $10,000. Project #3 does not get funded.

**The Strategy**

The final step in the process is to decide if the funded projects make sense from a strategic perspective *as a group*. To do that, we look at the overall match to the company mission, and also such things as synergy between projects. At this stage, the committee evaluating the projects often makes changes, such as:

- *Cut the budgets.* Budgets are not sacred. Project managers may have padded their bids, assuming they would get cut. Very expensive projects need to be looked at carefully, even if they score high. Consider the web site (project #1), we could do *all* the other projects if we chose not to do the web site!

- *Combine similar projects.* The fund-raiser and the membership drive look very similar. We could ask the project managers to rebid with synergy.

- *Beware of "false precision."* That is, projects with similar scores should be considered to be equally valuable, after all there is a lot of guesswork in the scoring process. Also, a high score in one highly weighted category can dramatically affect the ranking of a project.

- *Conduct a sensitivity analysis.* After the projects are ranked, you should examine the scores to see if small changes affect the order. If so, think about the score to make sure that it is reasonable.

### 2.9.2 Calibration

Projects are funded based on their ranking in the scoring matrix, and the major factor that affects the ranking is the weight (the second row in Table 2.6). While the weights are somewhat subjective, they are defined in a way that is meaningful to the company.

However, the weights are somewhat arbitrary. We assigned them based on what we thought was important. For a company starting out on the project selection process, this is about the best that can be done. Over time, however, the weights can be calibrated, making the selection process more reliable.[7]

Calibration is accomplished by having the organization go through the scoring process using historical projects. Typically, several small teams are assigned to score a dozen or so projects, including several successes, several failures, and other projects of interest that will help calibrate the matrix. The teams first suggest values for the weights, and then come together to negotiate their differences.

Next, the teams use the agreed upon weights to score selected historical projects. This must be done by returning to what the opinion of the projects was when they were first proposed.[8] The teams then rank the projects so that the highest score projects are at the top.

If the weights are correct, the company's most successful projects will be at the top of the list. Or, as is often the case, the projects that people thought were going to be successful, but that failed for surprising reasons.

[7] Remember, we are predicting the future, so nothing is guaranteed!

[8] Otherwise, hindsight on successes and failures will corrupt the process.

In practice, the process usually works surprisingly well in that successful projects do tend to float to the top, and the failures to the bottom. The weights, the project scores, and the relative rankings should all be analyzed and discussed, and if appropriate, some of the weights might be adjusted.

### 2.9.3 Project Selection

Project selection can be done in two ways:

- *Calibration of the weights is performed first.* A dozen projects that the company performed in the past are selected. These historical projects should provide a representative sample of company projects, including spectacular successes and failures, as well as a wide range of ordinary projects. The scoring matrix process is followed through using the historical projects.

  The objective is to determine a set of weights that allow the best projects to float to the top, while the poor projects congregate at the bottom. Once everyone agrees that the results are reasonable, the weights are fixed and cannot be changed. The matrix is then ready for use in the selection of future projects.

  This is the preferred approach, as the calibration process is an effective way to train people in the scoring matrix process. Once training is complete, and the weights established, the process can be put in place for the evaluation and selection of proposed (i.e., future) projects.

- *New projects are evaluated first with estimated weights.* Projects are evaluated first, and then calibration is performed over time as data become available. This is usually only done if the company does not have historical data on project success.

Project selection should be done by an independent committee.[9] The project selection process typically begins with a widely distributed solicitation for new project ideas.

All ongoing projects should be included in the selection process, and compete for funds with the new projects. Existing projects are included to assess their progress, and to ensure that they still match the company mission and objectives. That is, funding is allocated on a year-to-year basis, and ongoing projects are not automatically funded.

---

[9] Research data suggest that the president's pet project fails more often than most.

## 2.10. Financial Evaluation Criteria

Project managers should be called in to defend their projects in front of the committee, which then assigns the project scores.

In practice, once the matrix with winners and losers is produced, a great deal of negotiation takes place. Good projects naturally rise to the top, while poor ones sink to the bottom. Most of the discussion takes place in the middle, with several projects with similar scores competing for funds. At this point, a number of factors can be considered:

- The scoring model is based on opinions and future projections, so it is not an exact science. The scores must not be taken too literally. Projects whose scores do not differ by much should be considered as equal.

- Budgets are not sacred. The committee will often take funds from projects and reallocate the money to projects considered worthwhile.

- Sometimes, there is synergy between projects that the individual projects managers are not aware of. The committee can combine projects and reassign budgets to get two for the price of one.[10]

The rankings are not absolute; the important idea is the overall strategy. After the scores have been analyzed, the budgets massaged, and the synergies exploited, there should be a coherence to the list of projects to be funded. When asked, you should have a simple, coherent answer the following question: *What was funded this year?*

A decent answer might be: *We funded growth projects this year, as membership has declined.* [11]

## 2.10 Financial Evaluation Criteria

Project managers must be able to calculate, evaluate, and most importantly, defend the financial implications of their projects. This is generally referred to as return on investment, (ROI). The following methods are typically used:

- Payback

- Net Present Value (NPV)

[10]Dear PM:
We have good news and bad news. The bad news is that your project was not funded. The good news is that if you talk to the project manager for the fund-raiser project and combine your efforts, we believe that together you have an excellent chance of being funded.

[11]Note the explicit link to the strategy. A poor answer is: Umm ... Joe's and Betsy's projects.

### 2.10.1 Payback

Payback is a simple calculation of the time it will take to recover the investment. We propose a project that will cost $30,000. As a result of completing the project, we estimate that there will be an improvement in cash flow of $10,000 per year. The payback is:

$$Payback = \frac{Investment}{Cash\ Flow\ Improvement} = \frac{\$30,000}{\$10,000} = 3\ years. \quad (2.2)$$

Shorter paybacks are obviously more desirable. Payback emphasizes cash flow, and ignores interest rates. It also does not consider whether the project will have an impact on profitability.

Like all financial evaluation criteria, payback depends on an estimate of future cash flows, which are uncertain. Payback is usually used to see if the project is viable. If so, then more sophisticated analyses may be conducted.

### 2.10.2 Net Present Value

Would you rather have $1 now, or wait a year for it?

If I give you $1 now, you can invest it and a year from now you will have more. Therefore, the value of cash is a function of time. Cash now is more valuable than cash received in the future. Therefore, when evaluating a project, income received sooner is better. To allow for this, we use the net present value formula, which is usually referred to as just NPV:

$$NPV = -I + \sum_{n=0}^{n=N} \frac{CF_n}{(1+i)^n}, \quad (2.3)$$

where $I$ is the amount invested in the project; $N$ is the total number of years for which we will carry out the calculation; $n$ is a quantity that indexes the years; $CF_n$ is the net cash flow in year $n$; and $i$ is the discount rate.

If the NPV is positive, then the project meets the minimum desired rate of return, and the project is eligible for consideration–at least from a financial perspective. A project with a negative NPV is rejected.

The following examples might help. First, we do an example that shows how to perform the mechanics of the calculation.

*NPV Example #1*

## 2.10. Financial Evaluation Criteria

We invest $2 in a project. As a result, we expect that at the end of year 1, we will receive an **additional** $1. In years 2 and 3, we will receive an additional $2 and $3 respectively. We will use a discount rate of 10%.

$$\begin{aligned} NPV &= -2 + \frac{1}{(1+0.1)} + \frac{2}{(1+0.1)^2} + \frac{3}{(1+0.1)^3} \\ &= -2 + 0.909 + 1.653 + 2.254 \\ &= 2.81 \end{aligned} \quad (2.4)$$

The project is financially viable, since the NPV is positive. Note that if we just added the cash flows we would have: $-2+1+2+3 = 4$. The fact that the NPV is less than 4 is because the future value of cash is considered less valuable.

*NPV Example #2*

A company is planning to purchase a machine which will improve productivity. The machine costs $30,000, and has a potential life of 3 years. The machine is expected to improve productivity by 10%, resulting in a cost savings of $15,000 per year. The company considers that any investment should pay off significantly better than a stock market return, and so insists on a discount rate of 20%. Should the company buy the machine?

Table 2.7: NPV Example #2.

| Year | Cash Flow | Rate | NPV | Net NPV |
|---|---|---|---|---|
| 0 | -30,000 | 1.0 | -30,000 | -30,000 |
| 1 | 15,000 | $\frac{1}{1+0.2}$ | $\frac{15,000}{1.2} = 12,500$ | -17,500 |
| 2 | 15,000 | $\frac{1}{(1+0.2)^2}$ | $\frac{15,000}{1.44} = 10,417$ | -7,084 |
| 3 | 15,000 | $\frac{1}{(1+0.2)^3}$ | $\frac{15,000}{1.728} = 8,681$ | **1,598** |

The project has a positive NPV, and so is financially viable (but only just!).

In any NPV calculation, one should examine the validity of all parameters: Are the cash flows realistic and sustainable? Is the discount rate reasonable? Has the calculation been carried out for an unreasonably long term?

In the above example, we should ask a number of questions. Is a 3 year life a reasonable assumption? The machine may last for 3 years, but we have not considered maintenance costs, which would negatively affect the cash flow.

We also note that any extra costs will significantly reduce the attractiveness of the investment. For example, if the cash flow is reduced to $14,000 per year, the NPV is negative ($NPV = -509$). So the calculation is very sensitive to the error in the cash flow, and since we are attempting to predict the future, this does not look like a very good investment.

### 2.10.3 I work at a Non-Profit!

When we teach ROI, a few students often comment that they work for a non-profit agency, and that their mission has little to do with cash flows and profits. However, NPV can still be applied, once just has to be creative about the quantity to measure instead of cash.

One student who took our course worked for an agency whose mission was to help the homeless. She established the specific objective of helping more people (see SMARTO, section 2.7.3).

After the class on NPV, she realized that helping people sooner was better than helping people later. Just as the traditional NPV formula is based on the idea that it is preferable to have a dollar now rather than later, she realized that it was also better to help someone now rather than to help them later. Instead of applying the NPV formula to cash flow in dollars, she applied it to the *number of people helped*.

In deciding which projects the organization should pursue, and what design alternatives to implement within projects, her form of NPV gave priority to projects that helped more people sooner. It was a brilliant adaptation of NPV.[12]

---

[12] We like this example, because it breaks the obsession of measuring everything in dollars. Often, there are more natural units to work in. Look at your projects, and ask yourself what units the deliverables are really measured in? Then think about using those to report the true measure of progress.

# CHAPTER 3

# DELIVERABLES AND MILESTONES

**Life isn't a matter of milestones but of moments.**

*Rose Fitzgerald Kennedy*

## 3.1 Deliverables

Deliverables and milestones are so important, they deserve their own chapter.

Projects begin with an end deliverable. That is, you'll know your project when you see it.[1] But how do you tell? More importantly, how will other people know it when they see it? The answer is *Deliverables*.

When a project is complete, it is because the end result is delivered. No deliverable, no project. So a project is assessed and measured by its final deliverable. It naturally follows that the ongoing status and progress of the project is also measured by intermediate deliverables. Deliverables are the key to everything when it comes to assessing the project.[2]

The focus of most processes and tools is the development, completion, and assessment of the deliverables. e.g., the *Work Breakdown Structure* is a "deliverable-

---
[1] Just like love.

[2] If you think about this for a moment, you will realize that it is hard to measure anything else.

oriented hierarchy." Further, the entire theory of earned value depends on measuring the status of the project through the assessment of deliverables.

But what, exactly, are deliverables?

*Deliverables are the tangible outputs of the project.*

Deliverables are *tangible*, meaning you you can see them and touch them.[3] It is important to recognize that deliverables are *outputs* of the project.

A project begins with an end-deliverable, which is the project itself. There are also intermediate deliverables, such as the design and deliveries of components. The project management process results in deliverables such as documentation and managerial reports. Examples of intermediary deliverables include:

- *The Scope.* This might actually consist of several, separate deliverables as the project proceeds: Preliminary Requirements, Conceptual Design, and Detailed Design.

- *Cost and Schedule Estimates.* These are required at major milestones to report on the status of the project.

- *Intermediate project components.* These might include early prototypes and partial project deliveries.

- *Project Management Reports.* These include monthly reports, containing cost and schedule data, project status, risk updates, stakeholder issues, etc.

Sometimes, items are delivered *to* the project, but these are not considered to be deliverables. For example, in a construction project, the delivery of 2x4s, paint, and cabinets are not examples of deliverables; they are *deliveries*.

### 3.1.1 Measuring Deliverables

A project manager spends a lot of time and effort assessing deliverables. Every deliverable must be checked for compliance with the scope, whether it is on-time or not, and if it is within its budget. All of these questions hinge on some kind of assessment or measurement of the quality and acceptability of the deliverable. Therefore, when the deliverables are proposed, the project manager must consider how they are to be measured.

---

[3]Even if they are electronic documents, we are still going to use the word *tangible*. We prefer the idea of a tangible deliverable, even if it electronic.

Some deliverables are actually quite easy to measure. Examples of easily measured deliverables are:

- Miles of roadway completed.[4]

- Linear meters of steel girders erected.

- Square meters of wall painted.

- Pages of documentation written.

Let's examine the last item a little more closely. When you propose a document as a deliverable, someone knowledgeable about the project should be able to provide an outline, a decent estimate of the number of chapters, and maybe even a rough page count. This is essential because it provides a foundation for cost and schedule estimation, as most organizations have a good idea of how many pages per week a typical employee can produce.

When the activity of writing the document is assigned, you can communicate what is expected. After two weeks, you can reasonably measure the progress against expectations. If you expect 10 pages and you receive 5, you immediately know you have a problem and should investigate.

### 3.1.2 Small Deliverables

Suppose you assign Tom to write a 100-page technical document. From experience with similar documents, the company estimates the typical production rate at about 5 pages per day. Therefore, the document should take Tom (whom we assume is about average) about 20 days (4 weeks) to produce. After 4 weeks, Tom delivers only 50 pages, half of what you expected, with several major sections missing. You ask, "Tom! What happened?" Tom replies,

*"The document was much more difficult than I anticipated!"*

This is not Tom's fault. This is bad project management.

Deliverables should be divided into small, discrete, manageable pieces. The above document should have been divided into chapters (or sections) of 10-15 pages each. Then after the first week, you should ask Tom, *"How ya doin'?"*

If the document is more difficult than anticipated, you know immediately, not after four weeks. You still have the problem of a difficult-to-write document, but you know about it much earlier. You now have options: You can assign more people.

[4] Drive by any road construction project, and you can measure for yourself the miles completed.

You can assign different people. You can revise the table of contents. You can even ask the customer if any sections can be deleted.

They key is to divide all deliverables into small, discrete, manageable pieces. In fact, a good rule for the size of deliverables is:

> *A deliverable should be able to be produced by one-to-two people in one-to-two weeks.*

Break all the deliverables into pieces with the above rule. That way, you can manage them. If someone gets into trouble, you will know immediately.

When dividing up a deliverable, there are three things to consider:

- *Small.* The earlier you can tell if the deliverable is in trouble, the more options you have to fix it. Small deliverables make this possible.

- *Discrete.* The more separable the deliverable is into independent units, the less interaction there is among both the content and the staff. When building a house, one naturally divides deliverables between the plumber, electrician, carpenter, etc. The pieces are more manageable when divided into discrete technical sections that have little interaction.

- *Manageable.* Dividing the document into pieces also makes them manageable. It is easier to determine their cost and schedule, and to track them during production.

Also, many smaller deliverables can often be assembled in different ways. When it comes to the network diagram later, many small deliverables will give the project manager more options to work on the activities in parallel, which shortens the schedule.

### 3.1.3 Progressive Elaboration

Since a project has not been done before, you learn as you go. The project manager must take special care to manage changes. The gradual evolution of a project is a process called progressive elaboration.

## 3.2 Milestones

> **It's a funny kind of month, October. For the really keen cricket fan it's when you discover that your wife left you in May.**
>
> *Denis Norden*

Milestones allow you to track the status of the project. For example, the completion of the scope is a major milestone for all projects. Every milestone should have a date associated with it. During project planning the date is the planned milestone, and after successful execution, it becomes the actual completion date.

*A milestone is a significant point or event in the project.*

For example, the completion of project planning is a major milestone for a project. The milestone is marked by the completion of the *Project Management Plan*, and its acceptance by the customer. It is appropriate, therefore, to create a milestone called *Planning Complete* when the plan is accepted by the customer.

A milestone is also considered to be:[1]

*A milestone is a an activity with zero duration.*

For example, in the PMA project, we scheduled an activity called *Database Design Complete*, and gave it a zero duration (which makes it a milestone). We then linked it to the *Design Database* activity. That way, if the design is delayed, the completion milestone will automatically be delayed as well.

The following are examples of milestones from the New Kitchen project, as of June 1st:

- *Demolition Complete.* Planned: March 31st. Actually completed March 31st.
- *Gas line installed.* Planned: April 15th. Delayed by the gas company; completed May 15th.
- *Cabinet Delivery.* Planned: June 22nd. Not complete, on schedule.

Notice how the milestones accurately communicated the status of the project. In fact, project status meetings are usually all about milestones: Were they delivered on time?

## 3. Deliverables and Milestones

Major milestones are associated with major deliverables. Since the *scope* is an important document, it is vital to track its status, and this would be reported through a major milestone called *Scope Complete*.

Consider the PMA web site project, the major milestones are: Scope delivery; completion of prototype user interface; completion of database design; installation of web server; delivery of the major functional modules (there are several of these); documentation delivery; integration; testing; user training; and customer acceptance.

The status of the project at any point in time is clearly indicated by the completed milestones. Therefore, a project manager is expected to regularly report on the status of all deliverables during the execution of the project. If a milestone is late, the customer will immediately ask, "How late?" We leave the task of precisely determining the exact status of the cost and schedule of the deliverables to Chapter 18–Earned Value.

More milestones, mean better project management. Customers and stakeholders will be better able to see what is going on. But the milestones must make sense: They must be distributed appropriately throughout the project, and matched to major deliverables.

# CHAPTER 4

# PROJECTS AND COMPANIES

**There's no crying in baseball!**

*Tom Hanks, A League of Their Own*

The project manager is *responsible* for the project. This means that project managers must do whatever it takes to get the job done and satisfy stakeholders. What happens, when these ideas conflict with the goals or culture of the company?

This is an important issue for all project managers, because in most respects, companies and project have completely different goals.

Both companies and projects must be successful: companies must flourish while project goals are achieved. The trick is to balance the needs of a project with the needs of the company.

The competition between projects and companies is inherent in their structures, and the stress created on project managers is a fundamental part of the job. If you wonder why organizations structure themselves in the complex ways discussed below, they are trying the balance the goals of the company and the goals of their projects.

But remember, as a project manager, you are responsible. No excuses.[1].

[1] Paraphrasing Tom Hanks, *There's no crying in project management!*

# 4. Projects and Companies

## 4.1 Projects Goals vs. Company Goals

Projects violate most of ideas that companies consider as good management.[2] To be specific, projects and companies have completely different and competing goals. Project goals are almost always in direct conflict with those of the company that sponsors it.

The goal of a company is to manage efficiently, which implies repetitive actions that can be continuously improved. The Japanese have a word for it: *kaizen*. A simple example is travel expenses: Every company has a standard for processing travel expense claims. It doesn't make any sense to allow each department to have their own travel forms and procedures. Companies therefore, insist on a standardized travel reimbursement process.

On the other hand, by definition, projects are unique. How can you improve something if you only do it once?

Many of the key characteristics of projects are listed in Table 4.1, along with the opposite characteristic, which companies desire. We argue that for almost all project characteristics, the goals of the project (on the left) are completely opposite to the goals of the company (on the right).

Table 4.1: Project Goals vs. Company Goals.

| Projects | Companies |
| --- | --- |
| Unique | Manage efficiently |
| Creative, individualistic | Routine, repetitive |
| Inter-Disciplinary | Departments with expertise |
| Integration skills | Technical expertise development |
| Project expertise | Creation of subject matter experts |
| Specific, narrow needs | Wide, general capabilities |
| PM in charge | Department managers in charge |
| Staff rewarded for project performance | Staff rewarded for company performance |

Projects are inherently interdisciplinary, while companies are organized into departments, usually with a single expertise. Departments are good for companies because they acquire and develop their expertise by investing in the skills of their

---

[2] This is a strong statement, but we firmly believe it to be true in most instances.

employees, which generally enhances the capabilities of the company. Company departments stay current by investing in technology, staff training, etc.

On the other hand, projects are typically short-sighted because a project's technology may be static. Once the project team has learned enough about the technology to implement the current project, there is no incentive on the part of the project to invest in staff growth. In fact, projects are defined by their scope document, to which changes are actively discouraged. Therefore, it is not unusual for the skills of people working on long-term projects to become obsolete.

Departments are silos of expertise, and they have little or no incentive to become interdisciplinary. In fact, this is often discouraged as it dilutes their capabilities. An accounting department needs expertise in accounting, and doesn't really care about environmental regulations or web design. On the other hand, projects are inherently interdisciplinary, and a project manager may have to worry about accounting, environmental regulations, and web design.

## 4.2 Cultures

**A nation's culture resides in the hearts and in the soul of its people.**

*Mahatma Gandhi*

You need to make sure your project does not infringe on cultural norms, which are the values, beliefs, and expectations that permeate the company. The project team can either adopt or reject the organization's values, beliefs, and expectations, and their attitude will directly affect the project environment. It can be empowering or destructive.

The aspect of culture that we will be considering here is 'organizational culture,' and in particular, those aspects that apply to projects and the project teams. Cultures are defined by 'cultural norms.' [8]

*Norms* include the common knowledge regarding how to get the work done, what is acceptable, and who is influential. All organizations have norms, and these typically include:

1. Shared visions and beliefs: What makes your company good?

2. Unspoken company expectations: Is quality work expected? Can you slip a deadline to get it right?

## 4. Projects and Companies

3. Explicit policies and procedures: Every company has a P&P manual.

4. Views of authority and power: Can you approach the President of the company?

5. Work hours: Are you expected to work extra hours to get the job done?

6. Ethics. What is considered right?

Often, there is a whole collection of unwritten rules that one has to learn when you join a new organization. For example, is the CEO a gregarious person who chats with everyone, or is the CEO a tyrant that nobody dares speak to?

Think about the culture of your own organization. What are the myths and stories that get passed down between employees? What are the first things you tell a new employee, especially the off-the-record stuff? When you changed jobs, what was the first thing you noticed about your new organization?

A project manager needs to understand the culture of the organization because it is very difficult to go against the culture. For example, if the company allows and encourages flexibility in its working hours, then a project manager cannot arbitrarily impose a regime of time-clock punching. In a flexible working situation, the project manager must insist on deliverables, and let the team figure out how to best accomplish them. You can measure the progress of deliverables without asking what time they showed up for work.

One of my favorite examples of the culture clash between organizations occurred when I was much younger and assigned to write a piece of a proposal teamed with another company. I had to work at their site and the assignment lasted several weeks. Near the end, we all had to work over a weekend. I was told that dress was informal for weekends and I could wear anything I wanted. (This was a long time ago, and we all wore ties back then!)

I showed up in jeans and a Red Sox T-shirt.[3] They all showed up identically dressed in khakis and polo shirts. I was not dressed correctly! Their khakis and polos were just another uniform, and I was definitely not regulation. This is a good example of an organizational norm: It was unwritten but very specific. Everyone eventually learns to comply with these unwritten expectations.

Research suggests that there are 10 characteristics which capture the essence of an organization's culture and these are described in Table 4.2.

Each of the characteristics in Table 4.2 has two extremes, which are defined in Table 4.3. Often, the desires of projects and companies favor opposite extremes.

---

[3] This was deliberate, because I was in Orioles country.

## 4.2. Cultures

Table 4.2: Cultural Characteristics and Project vs. Company Goals.

| Cultural Characteristic | Project vs. Company Goal |
|---|---|
| Member identity | Do you identify with the project or the company? In projectized organizations, the team tends to identify with the project, while in functional organizations they identify more with their department and company. |
| Group emphasis | Do you prefer to work in a group, or as an individual? Projects favor group work, although a project needs good technical skills to solve problems. |
| People focus | Do management decisions incorporate the views of the employees, or do they tend to strictly focus on projects, or even the bottom line? |
| Unit integration | Are departments structured to work independently, or are they encouraged to work together? |
| Control | Do rules, policies and procedures tend to dominate employee behavior? Does the company encourage independent thinking? Can PMs bend the rules? |
| Risk tolerance | Are employees encouraged to take risks, and even allowed to fail occasionally? Projects require innovation, which means voyaging into uncharted territory. |
| Reward criteria | Are salary increases and promotions awarded according to project or department performance, or other secret criteria? |
| Conflict tolerance | Are employees encouraged to speak out, and air their views openly? How does the company handle dissent? |
| Means-ends orientation | Does management focus on the outcomes and results or the processes to achieve them? Projects need to have discipline and procedures (means) but must deliver (ends). |
| Open focus | Does the organization encourage open discussion? Who is allowed to talk to customers? |

For example, a project would probably prefer the team member to identify with the task at hand (i.e., the project), while the company might prefer identification with the organization.

The interesting question is: How do the above characteristics affect projects? Gen-

## 4. Projects and Companies

erally, projects tend to prefer the right hand extreme in Table 4.3.

Table 4.3: Cultural Characteristics and their Extremes.

| Project Dominance | Cultural Characteristic | Company Dominance |
|---|---|---|
| Task | 1. Member Identity | Organization |
| Individual | 2. Group Emphasis | Group |
| Task | 3. People Focus | People |
| Independent | 4. Unit Integration | Interdependent |
| Loose | 5. Control | Tight |
| Low | 6. Risk Tolerance | High |
| Project Performance | 7. Reward Criteria | Department Performance |
| Low | 8. Conflict Tolerance | High |
| End | 9. Means-Ends Orientation | Means |
| Internal | 10. Open Communications | External |

### 4.2.1 The Abilene Paradox

It was a hot day in Coleman Texas, but Jerry Harvey was cool and enjoying lemonade on his back porch, playing dominoes with his wife and in-laws. Harvey's father-in-law was concerned that the others were bored, so he suggested that they all drive to Abilene for lunch. No one wanted to go, but nobody spoke up.

So they all drove 106 miles, ate really bad food, and then drove back.

Nobody wanted to leave the back porch, the fan, the lemonade, or the dominoes. But no one spoke up, and they all went to Abilene. Nobody wanted to go to Abilene, but they all went anyway.

Harvey describes this as an inability to manage agreement. [9] But it also includes aspects of speaking up. Does your organization encourage speaking up? If a project manager does not encourage people to speak up, then everyone will drive to Abilene!

Upper management's power to hire and fire can squelch speaking up. Does the company discourage a frank and outspoken discussion when safety is being compromised for profit? The Abilene paradox is profound because it explains the inability of the participants to speak the truth when faced with policies they do not support. Discouraging dissent confuses telling the truth with disloyalty, and even betrayal.

A person experiencing this conflict may be left with ethical and emotional challenges related to self-betrayal, shame, guilt, and even moral failure for not having acted upon his or her appraisal of the situation.

### 4.2.2 A Cultural Clash

My son experienced two really good examples of the clash of norms on the same project. He is an animator, and when the movie he was working on was close to its scheduled release date, everyone was forced to work 60 hours per week. Ok, so far. But every morning, the producer sent around junior assistant producers to see what time the animators arrived at their desks.

Animators are bunch of independent arty types, who love what they do, but usually don't respond well to authority. One Friday morning in LA, there was a huge pile-up on the freeway, and everyone arrived late. Most of them had worked late the night before, so didn't think much of it. You can imagine how the 'creatives' (as they refer to themselves) reacted to a junior assistant producer (the 'suits') yelling that they should be at their desks by 9 am.

### 4.2.3 Rewards

A second example from the same project illustrates the problem of attempting to reward productivity. In order to encourage the completion of shots, the producer decided to reward the team that completed the most shots. (A reasonable goal.) The producer chose as the reward a free Sunday lunch at the animators' favorite watering hole.

My son's team connived to come in second every week. That way, they were seen as productive team players. But they were already working 6 days and 60 hours, and the last thing they wanted to do was to give up their Sunday—their only day off!

This shows how problematical the use of rewards can be. People will manipulate the system in creative ways to achieve goals you would never have thought of.

If you insist on checking every detail of the team's work, then you cannot expect the team to take any risks. You cannot have it both ways. If you curtail freedom, you cannot expect people to experiment. If you yell at people when they fail, they will never try anything new without checking with you first. There will be no independent thought.

When the project manager does not understand the culture, the team tends to find ways around the system and things get very unproductive. We've seen many project failures when project managers tried to impose unreasonable discipline on creative types. The key is the "deliverable." If they deliver, who cares how they do it?[4]

## 4.3 Project Structures

> **Peace is a daily, a weekly, a monthly process, gradually changing opinions, slowly eroding old barriers, quietly building new structures.**
>
> *John F. Kennedy*

Companies set up three types of structures in which to execute projects:

1. Functional.

    A functional organization is dominated by departments that have a specific mission. When a project arises, a team is assembled from the departments. Once the project is over, the team members return to their home departments. The managers of the departments are referred to as *functional managers*.

    An example of a functional organization is a university, which is organized into academic departments. Occasionally, a project arises that needs an interdisciplinary team. Examples include: hiring senior administrators, developing a marketing strategy, and rewriting the web site. Each of these requires expertise from many departments, and so a committee is formed to accomplish the project. The team members meet and work to accomplish the project, but do not leave their departments.

    Suppose the Dean calls me up and asks me to chair a committee to hire a new Director for the student admissions department. I say OK[5] But I do not work directly for the Dean., I work for my department chair who signs my pay raises, so you can bet that I will want to keep him happy. In this example, the academic department manager is a *functional manager*.

[4] Of course, we could just be explaining our personal philosophy here.

[5] Because she is the Dean, and I have no real choice!

## 4.3. Project Structures

But I still need to do a good job on the search committee. This is an example of a functionally organized project. I can expect to get subject area help from the student admissions department, because they have the expertise. As the chair, I have been assigned as the project manager, so I am responsible for schedule (the Dean wants the person to start at the beginning of next semester), the budget (can I take the candidates out to lunch at expensive restaurants?), and the resources (the committee assignments). But I am a classic project manager in that I cannot order them around. I have to *induce* them to perform.

The project is important to the University, but it is not my major priority. In a choice between answering emails from students and my committee assignment, which will I chose? Student emails. Nothing makes a professor's life more miserable than a bunch of angry students. In this example, we see all of the the issues associated with performing projects in functionally structured organizations.

2. Matrix.

    In a matrix organization, two parallel structures exist simultaneously: A departmental structure which contains the technical staff, and a project structure that houses the project managers. Matrix organizations are classified as strong, balanced, or weak, where the adjective applies to the power of the project manager.

    A strong matrix behaves like a projectized organization (see below), while a weak matrix looks somewhat like a functional organization. The balanced matrix is the traditional form, where the project manager is responsible for the project and the functional managers have responsibility for its technical performance. Most large Defense Contractors are organized in a matrix structure.

    The matrix structure is the most important one to understand, and for two reasons:

    a) It is a powerful way of accomplishing complex projects, while simultaneously balancing the needs of the organization and the needs of the project.

    b) All of the managerial, staffing, and technical issues that occur in the matrix structure also occur in the other structures. The issues are much clearer in the matrix structure and easier to understand, so it is useful to study it in detail. If you understand the problems in matrix orga-

# 4. Projects and Companies

nizations, you will understand the issues wherever or whenever they occur.

3. Projectized.

    In a projectized organization, most of the work of the company is dedicated to projects.

    An example of a projectized organization is a construction company. Each new building is a project, and teams are assembled as needed. When the project is complete, the team members all move on to other projects. That is a polite way of saying that either there is another project for the team to work on or they are unemployed. They also hire subcontractors as needed: steel workers, plumbers, carpenters, etc. Everyone is dedicated to the project.

    Another example of a projectized organizations is the movie business. The team for a movie is assembled from independent contractors: the director, scriptwriters, actors, lighting techs, grips, etc. When the project is over, they all move on, to the the next movie or unemployment.

Each of these organizational structures has different characteristics, strengths and weaknesses. Rarely does the project manager get to choose the organizational structure, it is inherited from the company, so it is important to understand the role of projects in the organization, and the challenges that will arise.

## 4.3.1 Functional Organizations

In a functional organization, the interests of the departments dominate. The functional approach is common in small organizations, which do not want to create an expensive project structure. Management is handled through normal departmental channels. Table 4.4 describes the advantages and disadvantages of doing projects in functional organizations.

## 4.3.2 Matrix Organizations

The matrix structure is a hybrid in which the project team is assembled from the departmental assets. There are two chains of command: A project chain and a department (or functional) chain. As a result, project team members report to two managers: The project manager on project matters, and their functional manager on technical matters. This is a source of pressure for the team members, who must keep two bosses happy.

Table 4.4: Advantages and disadvantages of projects in *Functional* organizations.

| Advantages | Disadvantages |
| --- | --- |
| No organizational changes required | Unclear motivation for a project |
| Easy to create teams | Hard to prioritize projects |
| Departments build expertise | Staff are loyal to their department |
| Staff have expertise | Hard to coordinate interdisciplinary activities |
| Team returns to department when project is complete | Lack of ownership for the project |

While complex, the matrix organization gives companies the best of both worlds. Projects get the advantage of a dedicated project manager, and a Project Management Office that invests in projects. The company realizes the long-term benefits and efficiencies of departmental structures, which are better at nurturing technical expertise and moving staff between projects.

Table 4.5: Advantages and Disadvantages of Projects in Matrix Organizations.

| Advantages | Disadvantages |
| --- | --- |
| Clear project management Investment by PMO | Conflict between PM and TD |
| Easy to create teams | Team members have two bosses |
| Departments build expertise | Staff are loyal to their department |
| Departments provide resources to projects | Stressful |
| Team returns to department when project is complete | Department goals compete with project goals |
| Flexible assignment of staff to small and large projects | Can be slow and bureaucratic |
| Standard corporate policies and procedures for all projects | Corporate goals may conflict with project goals |

### 4.3.3 Projectized Organizations

In a projectized organization, each project has its own team that operates under the leadership of its project manager, who is usually dedicated to the project.

## 4. Projects and Companies

Table 4.6: Advantages and Disadvantages of Projectized Organizations.

| Advantages | Disadvantages |
|---|---|
| Teams are easily assembled | No standard policies |
| Clear authority–the PM | Resources may be duplicated |
| Responsive | Rivalries between project teams |
| Cohesive and committed | Limited technical expertise |
| Efficient communication | No place for staff when project is complete |
| Explicit staff expertise | No long-term growth plan for staff |

# CHAPTER 5

# PROJECT LIFE CYCLES

**Life is what happens to you while you're busy making other plans.**

*John Lennon*

All projects go through natural life cycle patterns or phases. The details differ from one industry to another, but all projects have an orderly sequence of phases and activities. We describe a few project life cycles from various industries to illustrate the diversity of patterns.

Before we do so, we want to reinforce the difference between a product life cycle and a project life cycle. A simple, informal way to remember the project life cycle is by what we call the C-D-E-F stages:

1. **Conceive** the project: The project is chartered.

2. **Define** the project: The project plan is developed.

3. **Execute** the project: The project is designed and developed.

4. **Finish** the project: The project is tested, accepted, and closed.

## 5. Project Life Cycles

Projects may have sub-projects, which also follow the same life cycle. A well-balanced life cycle seamlessly integrates project management functions and processes into the technical aspects of the project. Life cycle activities include:

- *Organizing:* Determining the quality and quantity of resources needed and using communication skills to obtain and manage them.

- *Motivating:* Creating an environment that provides satisfaction to the team members and encourages them to do their best.

- *Directing:* Providing management and leadership to stakeholders, and influencing them to achieve project goals

### 5.1 Products and Services Life Cycles

We first carefully distinguish between the *product* and *project* life cycles. The Product Life Cycle begins when a product is conceived and put into development. It is then introduced to the market, followed by a growth in sales, a sales peak, and a gradual decline. See Figure 5.1.

Profits follow a different curve. There is an investment early on when the product is in development, and profits do not accrue until the product has been in the marketplace for a while. Eventually, if the product is successful, there is a period of profitability, called the mature stage, followed by a decline, and the product's withdrawal from the market.

The reality is complicated by many issues. Successful products rarely exist in isolation. They evolve through product lines, which enhances their life. Successful products engender competition and technological innovations may make products obsolete. Also, sales are not necessarily a good measure of the health of the product, since they are influenced by the state of the economy, the behavior of competitors, and customer whims.

The development of a new service may also be a project. The services life cycle generally follows that of Figure 5.1, although many services are not designed to be profitable, e.g., renewal of a driver's license and computer telephone support. Other services are designed to be profitable, such as legal and accounting, restaurants, and bars. Many services are large non-profit organizations, such as universities and theaters.[1]

For new products and services, the development stage is typically a project. Once the product or service is introduced to the market, it is no longer a project, as the

---

[1] While most universities are 'non-profits,' they operate with all the same constraints on sales, staff utilization, and overhead as profit-making entities.

54

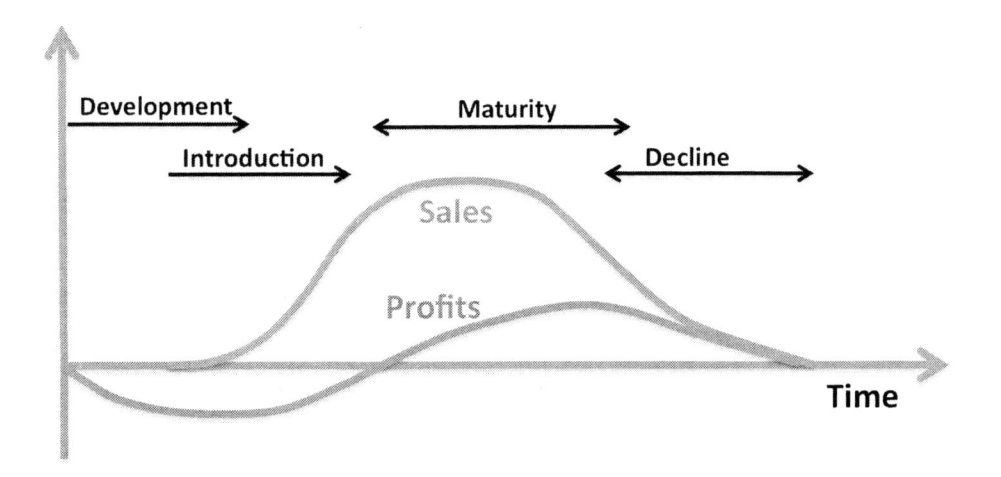

Figure 5.1: The product life cycle

activities become routine: manufacturing, sales, distribution, etc. There may be occasional projects along the way, such as an improvement in the product or service, a new advertising campaign, or the implementation of a new supply chain.

## 5.2 The Project Life Cycle

Projects have their own life cycles (often within the product life-cycle) that have orderly sequences of integrated activities[2] There are three stages in the project life cycle:

1. *Pre-Project Phase*

   Activities in the pre-project include such things as recognizing a business opportunity and creating a business case for the project, as well as obtaining seed funding.

   The primary job of the pre-project phase is to ensure that there is a viable project, before one invests money in it. This is sometimes referred to as requirements definition, although ensuring viability requires some design work. To ensure viability at this stage requires work on the cost estimate, the schedule, and the major technical issues.

[2] Project life cycles are different from the project management *process groups*.

Building a prototype is often an efficient way to determine feasibility, estimate the cost and schedule, and analyze major risks. Of course, this can be a separate project.

2. *Implementation Phase*

During the project implementation phase, a project goes through a structured development life cycle, where the product or service is defined, designed, built, tested, and accepted by the sponsor.

The activities in this phase are described in the PMBOK. The products of this phase are the project deliverables, including the product or service itself, as well as intermediate deliverables such as the design. Outputs from this phase also include the project management process outputs, e.g., *The Charter* is an output of the *Create Charter* PMBOK Process; and the *Budget Forecast* is an output of *Control Costs*.

Each phase should have a clearly specified a *Decision Gate*, which is a critical decision point, where the deliverables are carefully reviewed, along with the cost and schedule. At a decision gate, the team, customer, and stakeholders review the products and select among three possible outcomes: move to next phase; fix the products by revisiting activities; or kill the project.

3. *Post-Project Phase*

The post-project phase begins as soon as the product or service is commissioned and operational.

The activities in this phase are typically not part of the project, consisting of such things as manufacturing (for products), routine provision of services, and maintenance activities (painting bridges when they rust).

In some industries, the post-project phase is very expensive. For example, the decommissioning and retirement of a nuclear plant is extensive and rigorous. Obtaining funding approval from various environmental and regulatory organizations can take several years. The building of the nuclear plant is the project phase, while the post-project phase would be both the operation and taking the plant out of operation and moth-balling it.

They key idea is that each phase consists of activities with deliverables, and is concluded with a decision gate. Table 5.1 gives examples of activities, deliverables, and decision gates.

Table 5.1: Example of Activities, Deliverables, and Decision Gates.

| Activities | Deliverables | Decision Gate Questions |
|---|---|---|
| Feasibility Study | Business Case<br>Preliminary Plan<br>Stakeholder Register | Customer support exists?<br>Customers perceive value?<br>Delivery dates acceptable?<br>Cost & Schedule acceptable? |
| Requirements Analysis | Specification<br>Scope<br>Risk Register | Is the project feasible?<br>Performance metrics acceptable?<br>Risks acceptable?<br>Contingency funds available? |

## 5.3 Industry Life Cycle Examples

### 5.3.1 The Software Development Life Cycle

The software development life cycles consists of:

1. *Definition Phase:* During this phase the customer's problems are defined and the requirements elicited. The team conducts systems analyses and develops the project plan. The deliverable is the specification document, which contains the user requirements, and a test plan to measure compliance.

2. *Design phase:* The software and business analysts design an acceptable solution for the customer. The deliverable is the design document. Also, the project manager finalizes the baseline cost and schedule.

3. *Construction phase:* The software is coded, and unit testing may occur here.

4. *Testing phase:* The product or service is tested against the specification.

5. *Acceptance phase:* The customer analyzes the acceptance test results and if satisfactory, signs the acceptance agreement. Customer training may also occur during this phase. The operation phase begins upon completion of the acceptance phase.

The software development cycle is made up of four phases, but depending on the size of the project, you may want to create additional phases and sub phases. What's important is that each phase and sub phase must have a clear objective, well-defined milestones and deliverables.

## 5. Project Life Cycles

For example, the design phase usually has two parts: First, the high level system architecture is proposed and validated. This is followed by a detailed design that refines the implementation and defines the lower level components.

**Major Documents and Milestones**

For the definition phase the major deliverables are the project plan, the specification, and the acceptance criteria.[3]

For the design phase, the design itself is the major deliverable and an important milestone for the project.[4]

For the construction phase the key activity is coding and testing, and the major milestone is the successful validation and verification of these activities.

For the acceptance phase, the deliverable is the project itself, and the milestones are the completion of all project documentation and the formal acceptance agreement.

### 5.3.2 The Pharmaceutical Industry Life Cycle

To contrast with the software development life cycle, we present a brief overview of a typical pharmaceutical life cycle, which consists of:[1]

- *Research and Development*: New potential drugs are identified.

- *Discovery and Screening*: Drugs are refined and tested.

- *Preclinical Development*: The effects on trial populations are determined.

- *Clinical Trial Phase*: The drug goes from laboratory sample to pilot production, and finally to commercial production.

- *Registration Phase*: Government forms and compliance documentation are completed and, hopefully, approved.

- *Post Registration Phase*: Packaging and marketing occurs.

---

[3] The Definition Phase focuses on "What, not How"

[4] Here you focus on the "How". For software, the completion of the detailed design represents about the 40% completion point.

### 5.3.3 The Construction Industry Life Cycle

The key stages in the construction life cycle are:[2]

- *Apply for Permits.*

- *Site Work*: Clear ground, install temporary power and utilities. Inspection.

- *Foundation*: Excavate, concrete, basement walls, waterproof and insulate. Inspection.

- *Framing*: Install joists, frame walls. Inspection.

- *Dry In*: Sheathing, roof decking, shingles, doors and windows. Inspection.

- *Utilities*: Plumbing, electrical, HVAC, phone, cable, computers, alarms. Inspection.

- *Interior Finishing*: Insulating, dry wall, paint and wallpaper, cabinets, tile and appliances. Inspection.

- *Landscaping and Groundwork*: Driveway, sod, plantings. Inspection.

- *Final Acceptance*: Walk-through, inspection and complete punch list. Conduct final acceptance for Certificate of Occupancy.

Notice how in the construction life cycle, each phase explicitly ends with an inspection. This is a useful lesson for other industries.

## 5.4 Agile Project Management

The focus of this discussion is software projects, however, the basic principles hold true for all other industries as well. Agile software development processes are the most mature, and so represent the best state of the art.

### 5.4.1 The Old Way: The Waterfall

Historically, the *Waterfall* development cycle was the most widely used method for software development and is regarded as the classical approach. The waterfall approach is characterized by sequential steps. Once a process has been completed,

## 5. Project Life Cycles

it is not visited again. In this respect it is rather like a waterfall in that the water trickles down, and it only goes one way.

A second aspect of the waterfall method is that the requirements are developed up-front and frozen. Then the software is designed and tested. The drawback is that the final software may arrive long after the requirements were discussed with the users. Often the user requirements have evolved and the resulting system is not useful.

It is widely acknowledged that the key strength of the waterfall is its strong managerial control over the process and, in particular, the schedule and costs.[5]

### 5.4.2 Evolutionary

To address the limitations of the waterfall model, researchers and practitioners introduced alternate paradigms for software development, which we classify as *evolutionary*. One such model is rapid prototyping or rapid application development (RAD).[3] Widespread agreement on what this approach actually entails is difficult to achieve, however, rapid prototyping typically involves the following characteristics:

- *Throwaway prototypes.* These are developed to clarify the user requirements and to test design approaches. The prototype is discarded and one subsequently moves to a more structured approach (perhaps even waterfall).

- *Built-upon development.* Development is iterative, designed to clarify user requirements and analyze the system design. The entire development process is continually repeated to incrementally deliver capabilities and gradually refine the final product.

- *Gathering requirements.* Focus groups are used to define requirements.

- *Reusing software components.* This enhances productivity, and reduces errors by using previously tested components.

- *Iterating the software design.* This ensures the system continues to meet performance requirements, even as the system loads and user base increase.

- *Deferring major improvements and enhancements to the next version.* Builders resist the urge to implement changes, preferring to successfully implement the current version.

---

[5] Since the requirements are nailed down, scope creep is minimized, and the cost should be relatively stable. Unless, of course, the problem is poorly defined, in which case, all bets are off.

- *Less formality throughout the software development life cycle.* The focus is on the products and whether they satisfy the customer, rather than writing everything down.[6]

- *Continuously evaluating the outcome with users.* To keep them happy.

### 5.4.3 Agile

An important and growing trend is that of *agile* project management. In fact, agile is rapidly becoming the rage!

Agile development models are evolutionary in nature, the requirements evolve as the product is developed. There is flexibility in the development of components, as well as their cost and schedule. The model is particularly appropriate when the system requirements are unclear or when the feasibility of the project itself is in doubt.

There are several variations of the agile development approach but they all share the following characteristics:

- The development process, the product, the cost, and the schedule all evolve.

- Proactive development of test cases and user scenarios ahead of time to analyze and test both the current and future iterations of the product.

- Periodic delivery and installation of product versions in the operational environment to ensure timely and increasingly effective functionality.

- Continuous evolution based on user input.

The agile approach has its roots in *The Agile Manifesto* and consists of 12 philosophical aspirations:[4]

1. Customer satisfaction by rapid delivery and integration of useful software.
2. Welcoming changing requirements from users even if it is late in development.
3. Working software is delivered in weeks rather than months.
4. Working software is the principal measure of progress.
5. Sustainable development–maintaining a constant pace.

[6]This appears to imply that formality is burdensome but necessary. We prefer to emphasize that the focus is on satisfying the customers by providing real products, rather than on attempting to define every detail in a document.

6. Frequently daily co-operation between business people, users and developers.

7. Face-to-face conversation is strongly preferred.

8. Projects are built around motivated individuals, who should be trusted.

9. Continuous attention to technical excellence and good design.

10. Simplicity is the key in everything.

11. Self-organizing teams.

12. Regular adaptation to changing circumstances.

The Scrum model is another popular framework based on agile principles. [5] *Scrum* consists of the following attributes:

- The customer is the Product Owner.

- The Project Manager is the Scrum Master.

- The Software developers are the Team.

- Development iterations are called *sprints* which are typically 30 days in duration.

- The product features to be implemented in a sprint are determined during a sprint planning meeting.

- Brief 15 minute stand-up meetings are held each day during a sprint to review work accomplished the previous day and to plan the work for the current day.

- Daily meetings allow the Scrum Master to determine the productivity rate (and refine estimates and schedules) and to manage risks.

- A sprint ends with a *sprint retrospective* to review the work process and plan for a future sprint.

## 5.5 Choosing a Development Model

We wrap up our discussion by presenting some considerations for selecting either the waterfall, evolutionary, or agile process. Your selection should be based on the characteristics of the project's requirements, the project team, and the commitment and availability of the user community. Table 5.2 is a guide.[6]

Table 5.2: Considerations for selecting either waterfall, evolutionary, or agile development.

| Considerations Based On | Project Attribute | Preferred Model |
|---|---|---|
| Stakeholders | Flexibility in approach needed | Agile |
| | Evolution of User Requirements | Evolutionary or Agile |
| | Extensive User involvement | Evolutionary or Agile |
| | Strict PM Control Required | Waterfall |
| | Flexibility in Development | Evolutionary or Agile |
| | Completion on schedule | Waterfall |
| Requirements | Well known, easily defined | Waterfall or Agile |
| | Defined during development | Waterfall |
| | Likely to change often | Evolutionary or Agile |
| | Demonstrations needed to develop the requirements | Evolutionary or Agile |
| | Proof of concept needed to determine Feasibility | Evolutionary |
| Team | New to the problem domain | Evolutionary |
| | New to the technology domain | Evolutionary |
| | Might be reassigned | Waterfall & Evolutionary |
| Users | Limited availability | Waterfall or Evolutionary |
| | New to requirements definition | Evolutionary |
| | Want to be involved | Evolutionary and Agile |
| Risk | New area for organization | Evolutionary |
| | Involves system integration | Waterfall |
| | Involves Enhancements | Any |
| | Funding Is Unstable | Evolutionary or Agile |
| | Schedule Is Constrained | Waterfall or Agile |

# Part II

# The Process Groups

# CHAPTER 6

# THE PROCESS GROUPS

*When one has finished building one's house, one suddenly realizes that in the process one has learned something that one really needed to know in the worst way —before one began!*

*Friedrich Nietzsche*

The PMBOK defines four major components of project management:

- Project Phases

- Process Groups

- Processes

- Knowledge Areas

In this chapter, we briefly describe the above components, and the interactions between them.

# 6. The Process Groups

## 6.1 Project Phases

Projects are divided into phases, which are logical divisions that allow for efficient development. Each project phase follows the process groups.[1]

The number of phases depends on the size and complexity of the project, and they may occur in series or in parallel. Some phases may even be iterated or repeated. In the usual case, the phases are sequential, and the outputs from one phase are evaluated and the decision to proceed allows the next phase to begin.

Some phases can genuinely proceed in parallel. An example might be a system with software and hardware components. Once the formal specification is complete, and the interfaces defined, then the hardware and software development phases can proceed in parallel. Conducting the phases in parallel incurs risks, since mistakes can result in re-work of both hardware and software components. Therefore, when deciding whether to proceed with parallel phases, the project manager must spend time to precisely define the inputs to the phases.

Iteration is often imposed when changes are required. For example, a change to the scope, will require the team to execute the same processes as when the scope was developed. The processes may be conducted in less detail than when the scope was first developed, but the steps are the same.[2] The cost and schedule impact of the proposed change must be estimated, and the risks assessed. Finally, a go/kill decision is made on whether to implement the proposed change.

For example, the management at PMA may decide that they want to increase their membership. This is not yet a project. They decide to study the problem and evaluate methods for increasing the membership (e.g., email blast, advertising, networking at conferences, etc.), and evaluate the costs vs. potential growth. Once they have collected the data, then they can decide whether to proceed, and if so, with which method. This project, therefore, has two phases, as described in Table 6.1.

Table 6.1: The PMA membership project phases and their major deliverables

| Phase | Name | Major Deliverable |
|---|---|---|
| #1 | Growth Strategy Selection | Cost/Benefit Analysis |
| #2 | Implement Growth Strategy | Increased Membership |

Phases always share the same characteristics:

- *A phase is formally initiated and closed.* Phases typically produce specific

---

[1] Note that project *phases* are not the same as *process groups*.

[2] We believe that this is not really an iteration, but a kind of a mini walk-through of the steps. We have yet to find a situation where there is a genuine, complete iteration of a phase.

deliverables, which are the basis for the decision of whether to continue to the next phase. For example, in the PMA growth strategy project, the end point of the first phase is a cost benefit analysis, which is the basis for the decision of whether to proceed with a membership growth phase or not, and if so, with which strategy. Note that one explicit outcome of a phase is whether to continue with the project or to kill it.

- *A phase is coherent and distinct.* The work of a phase should be as independent as possible from other phases or projects. This means that a phase uses specific skills (and organizational assets).[3]

- *A phase's major deliverables are carefully controlled.* The output is a go/kill decision, and so careful attention must be paid to the deliverables.

- *A phase follows the process groups.* See section 6.2

## 6.2 The Process Groups

**If you want to build a ship, don't drum up people together to collect wood, but rather teach them to long for the endless immensity of the sea.**

*Antoine de Saint-Exupery*

The PMBOK does not define the process group, it merely says that the 42 processes are combined into 5 process groups. For our purposes, a process group is a logical grouping of the project management processes.

The process groups are inter-dependent, and must be performed in the same sequence on each project. Many of these dependencies are intuitive; for example you cannot rank risks in order of importance unless you identify them first. And of course, you cannot create a risk response plan unless you have both identified risks and ranked them.

There are still some fuzzy areas, however. The PMBOK specifies that resources (people and materials) are identified before the durations of the activities are estimated. While desirable, we frequently have to estimate project costs without having a list of resources available. In fact, companies often bid jobs with "standardized" labor mixes, and actual resources are identified only when the project is underway.

Finally, it is worth noting that project management process groups are not project phases. The term project phase is used in the product life-cycle.

[3] If a phase is closely inter-related with another phase, the phase is badly specified—the phases probably should have been combined.

## 6. THE PROCESS GROUPS

There are five process groups:

1. *Initiating Process Group*

    The purpose of this process group is to charter the project and to identify the stakeholders. The *initiating* processes authorize a new project, the start of a phase of a multi-phase project, or the re-start of a halted project. This is also where a project is divided into phases and large projects into sub-projects.

    It is important to note that a significant portion of *initiating* is often accomplished outside the project. For example, a project may be created and authorized by the company or the program office, often as part of the portfolio management process.

    There are only two processes in this group: *Develop Project Charter* and *Identify Stakeholders.*

2. *Planning Process Group*

    The *planning* process group is the largest group with twenty processes. It is the heart and soul of project planning: creating a successful road map for the project.

    This process group defines action plan for the entire project, from start to finish. The processes in this group include defining and refining the scope, developing the project management plan, and identifying and scheduling all project activities.

    Many planning processes interact and depend on each other and many of them can be worked on concurrently. For example, *quality planning, risk management planning*, and *human resource planning* can all be done concurrently.

    Changes to a project are inevitable and the planning processes allow for revisiting and re-planning one or more processes. In fact, planning is an iterative process and the incremental and progressive detailing of the project plan is referred to as *rolling wave planning.*

3. *Executing Process Group*

    The *executing* process group dominates the work load and, therefore, the expenditure of funds. This is where the work on the project actually occurs. There are eight processes in this group and the key project management activities include acquiring and developing the project team, generally coordinating people and resources, and getting the work completed on schedule and within budget.

As work proceeds and the project is refined, other aspects of the project manager's job include distributing information, managing stakeholder expectations, and assuring quality.[4]

4. *Monitoring and Controlling Process Group*

    In this group the project manager tracks, reviews, and regulates the performance. There are ten processes in this group. The project manager identifies required changes, monitors and controls the cost, schedule, and risks, and manages any variances to the plan.

5. *Closing Process Group*

    The *closing* processes are those performed to formally terminate all activities of a project.[5] There are two processes in this group and the most important activity is to obtain acceptance of the project by customers, sponsors, or stakeholders. These processes may also be used to close a canceled project.

We wrap up our discussion of process groups by presenting research data on the average amount of effort spent by teams in the various process groups. [10] Data gathered from 860 project managers is presented in Table 6.2. The results are intuitive and suggest that the executing processes, where the work is completed, consume most of the budget and effort on a project.

Table 6.2: Percent of effort spent in each of the project's process groups.

| Process Group | Effort in Group |
|---|---|
| Initiating Process: | 1% to 2% |
| Planning Process: | 11% to 21% |
| Executing: | 69% to 82% |
| Monitoring and Control: | 4% to 5% |
| Closing: | 2% to 3% |

The relations between the process groups is shown in Figure 6.1.

Each of the process groups is divided into *processes*. For example, the first process in the *Initiating* group is *Develop Project Charter*.

[4] Note that we are concerned here with managing the project, not doing the project. The project manager does not actually do the work!

[5] Or phase of a multi-phase project.

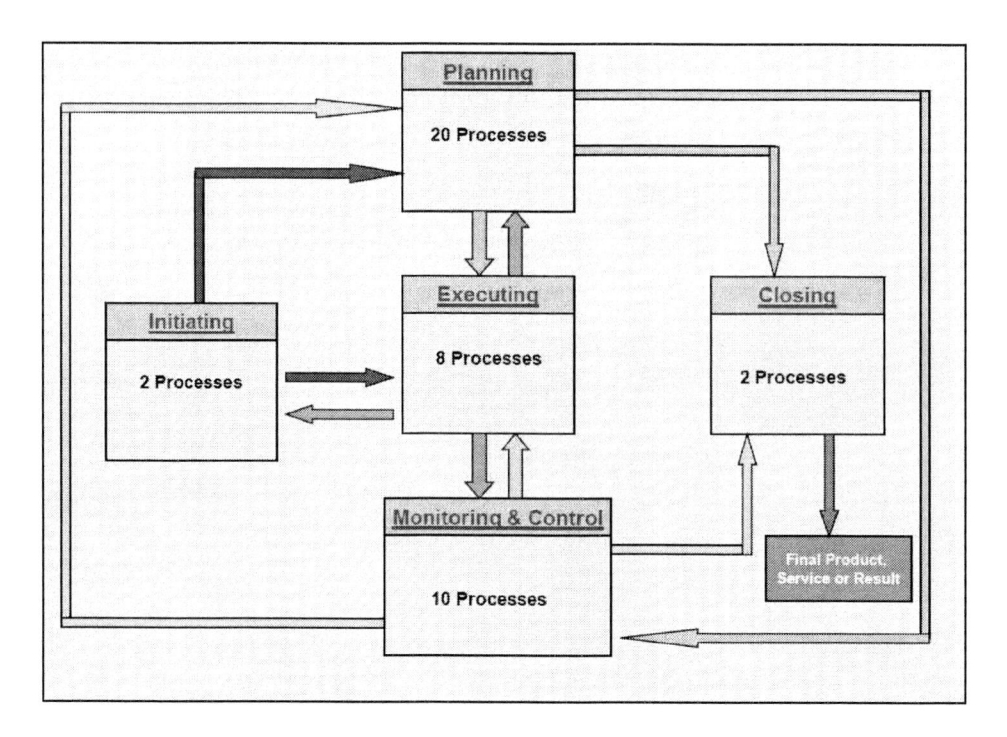

Figure 6.1: The process groups

## 6.3 Processes

> **To live means to finesse the processes to which one is subjugated.**
>
> *Bertolt Brecht*

The PMBOK defines 42 processes.[6] The PMBOK defines a process as follows:

[6]This number changed in the current version of the PMBOK (4th Edition), so one should consider the PMBOK still in flux. In particular, the entire *Integration Management* knowledge area changed drastically. Our view is that PMI still hasn't quite figure out this knowledge area!

*A process is a set of interrelated actions and activities performed to achieve a pre-specified product, result, or service. Each process is characterized by its inputs, the tools and techniques that can be applied, and the resulting outputs.*

For example, *Develop Charter* is a process. It is member of the **Initiating** process group and the *Integration Management* knowledge area.

## 6.3. Processes

More informally, a process is a project management step that helps you complete your project successfully. Processes fall into one of two major categories:

- *Project management processes:* These are selected, tailored, and followed to ensure a smooth and effective flow of work throughout the life of the project.

- *Product oriented processes:* These make up the product life-cycle and vary by application domain, i.e., construction, information technology, defense, pharmaceutical, entertainment, etc. It is the product life-cycle in which the product or service is created.

Processes have inputs, tools and techniques, and outputs, which are illustrated in Figure 6.2.

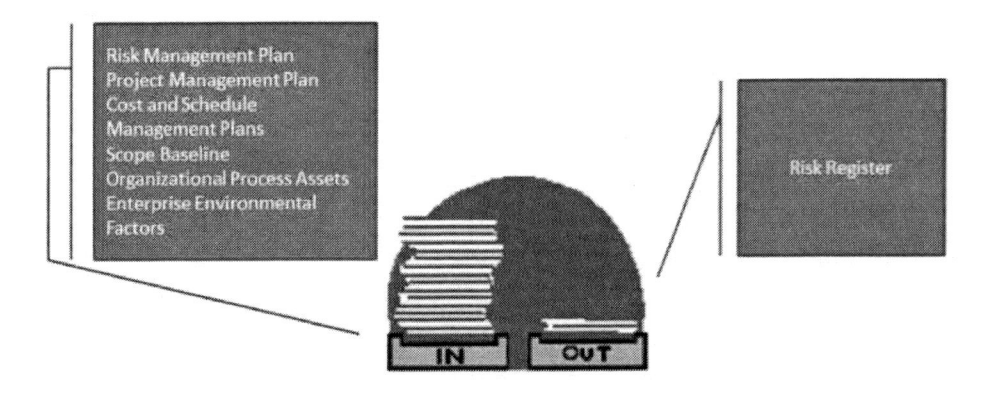

Figure 6.2: The inputs and outputs for the *Identify Risks* process.

As an example, we will focus on the process named *Identify Risks*. Before the project team can begin to identify the risks that may arise, they must have access to key information and data, which are the *inputs*.

The inputs to *Identify Risks* consist of examples of risks from historical projects and templates for their development. Risks may also exist as outputs from previous processes on the current project. For example, risks might have been identified in the *Define Scope* process.

Formally, the *Identify Risks* process requires the following information as inputs: Risk Management Plan, Project Management Plan, Cost and Schedule Management Plans, Scope Baseline, Organizational Process Assets, and Enterprise Environmental Factors.

The project team analyzes all of the above information and creates a *Risk Register*, which is the only output for this process, and consists of a list of risks that the team thinks might occur during the execution of the project.

Since developing and assessing the impact of risks is a creative process, the team uses a variety of tools and techniques to assist in the analysis. These might include interviewing stakeholders who might have experience on similar projects, brainstorming, and Delphi techniques.[7] Historical checklists from previous projects also help to identify risks and create the risk register.

### 6.3.1 The Knowledge Areas

> **If a man empties his purse into his head no one can take it away from him.**
> **An investment in knowledge always pays the best interest.**
>
> *Benjamin Franklin*

The PMBOK defines knowledge as understanding a process, practice, or technique, or how to use a tool. Each *Knowledge Area* is an identified skill of project management, defined by its knowledge requirements and described in terms of its processes, practices, inputs, outputs, tools, and techniques. In Part III, we have dedicated an entire chapter to each of the knowledge areas. The relations between *Knowledge Areas, Process Groups,* and the individual *processes* are shown in Tables 6.3 and 6.4.

The *Knowledge Areas* are:

1. Integration Management
2. Scope Management
3. Time Management
4. Cost Management
5. Quality Management
6. Human Resource Management
7. Communications Management
8. Risk Management
9. Procurement Management

---
[7] The Delphi technique is covered in section 17.2.2

Table 6.3: Project Management *Process Groups* mapped to *Knowledge Areas*. Page 1 of 2

| **Knowledge Area** | Initiating Process | Planning Process | Executing Process | Monitor and Control | Closing |
|---|---|---|---|---|---|
| **Integration Management** | Develop Project Charter | Develop Project Management Plan | Direct and Manage Project Execution | Monitor and Control Work | Close Project or Phase |
| | | | | Perform Change Control | |
| **Scope Management** | | Collect Requirements | | Verify Scope | |
| | | Define Scope | | Control Scope | |
| | | Create WBS | | | |
| **Time Management** | | Define Activities | | Control Schedule | |
| | | Sequence Activities | | Control Scope | |
| | | Estimate Activity Resources | | | |
| | | Estimate Activity Durations | | | |
| | | Develop Schedule | | | |
| **Cost Management** | | Estimate Costs | | Control Schedule | |
| | | Determine Budget | | Control Costs | |
| | | Estimate Activity Resources | | | |
| **Quality Management** | | Plan Quality | Perform Quality Assurance | Perform Quality Control | |

## 6. THE PROCESS GROUPS

Table 6.4: Project Management *Process Groups* mapped to *Knowledge Areas*. Page 2 of 2

| Knowledge Area | Initiating Process | Planning Process | Executing Process | Monitor and Control | Closing |
|---|---|---|---|---|---|
| **Human Resources Management** | | Develop HR Plan | Acquire Team | | |
| | | | Develop Team | | |
| | | | Manage Team | | |
| **Communications Management** | Identify Stakeholders | Plan Communications | Distribute Information | Report Performance | |
| | | | Manage Stakeholder Expectations | | |
| **Risk Management** | | Plan Risk Management | | Monitor and Control Risks | |
| | | Identify Risks | | | |
| | | Perform Qualitative Risk Analysis | | | |
| | | Perform Quantitative Risk Analysis | | | |
| | | Plan Risk Response | | | |
| **Procurement Management** | | Plan Procurements | Conduct Procurements | Administer Procurements | Close Procurements |

# INITIATING PROCESS GROUP

> **He who has begun has half done.
> Dare to be wise. Begin!**
> *Horace*

This is where we begin the project.[1]

The primary focus of the initiating process group is to authorize the project. A key point to note is that a project does not exist until the charter is created. Therefore, the charter is often developed by someone external to the project, such as the project sponsor. In reality, if a charter is not available, the designated project manager assists with its development.

A project is started by generating the charter and identifying stakeholders. The *Develop Charter* process is part of the *Integration Knowledge Area* and *Identify Stakeholders* is part of the *Communications Knowledge Area*. See Figure 7.1.

These processes begin after project selection occurs. A formal project selection process, as described in section 2.8, would produce most, if not all, of the required inputs to these processes. In the unlikely scenario that a statement of work or business case is not available, it is left to the sponsor and project manager to describe

## 7. INITIATING PROCESS GROUP

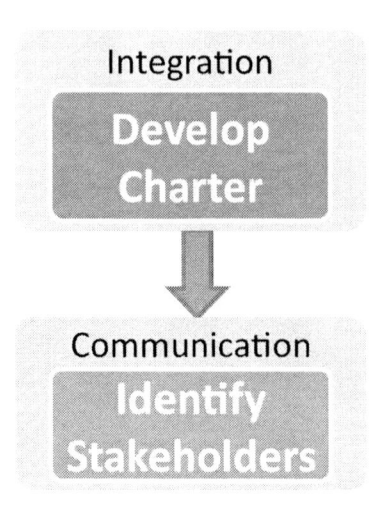

Figure 7.1: The *processes* contained in the *initiating* process group.

the nature of the new project, how the project maps to the organization's goals, and the business case, including a cost benefit analysis, .

## 7.1 Develop Charter

A project does not exist until its charter is created, so someone outside the project usually develops it. We now describe the inputs, outputs, and tools and techniques of the *Develop Charter* process, which are summarized in Figure 7.2. The goal of the process is, of course, to produce the project charter.

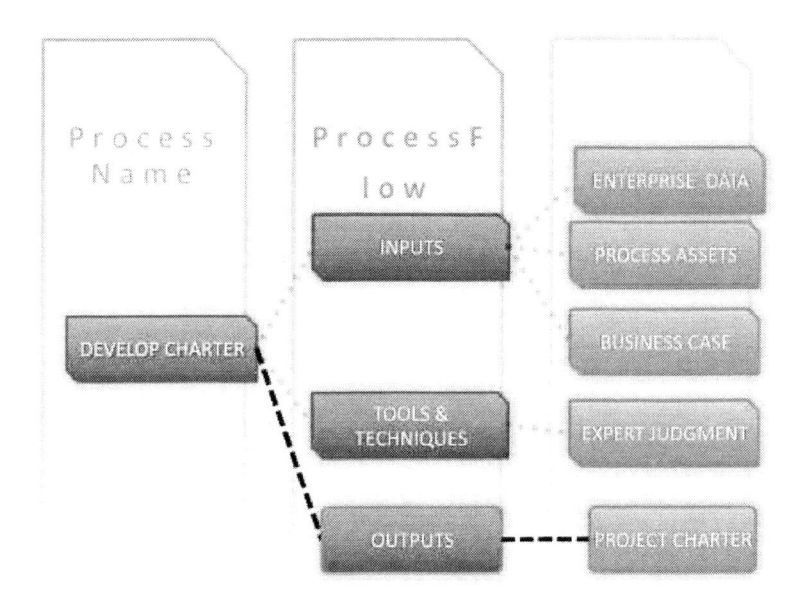

Figure 7.2: A summary of the *Develop Charter* process.

The *Develop Charter* process is defined in the PMBOK as:

> *The develop charter process formally authorizes the project (or phase), documenting initial requirements that satisfy the stakeholders' needs and expectations.*

The key point is that the charter grants to the project manager the authority to spend money and acquire staff. Therefore, without a charter the project does not exist.[1] No charter, no project.

[1] We often suggest that when your boss calls you in and congratulates you as the new project manager for project X, you should immediately request a copy of the charter. "I can't be the project manager for a project that does not exist!"

## 7. INITIATING PROCESS GROUP

### 7.1.1 Develop Charter Inputs

The inputs to the *Develop Charter* process are summarized in Figure 7.3. Before the sponsor develops the charter, the following inputs must be available:

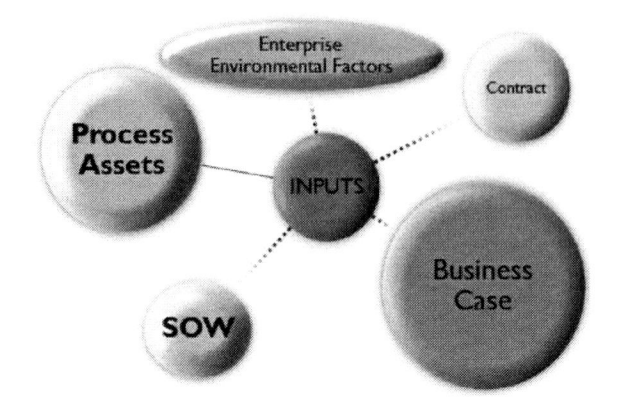

Figure 7.3: The inputs to the *Develop Charter* process.

1. *The Business Case.* Why should the project be done?[2]

2. *Enterprise Environmental Factors.* These answer the following questions:
   - How does the organization conduct the business?
   - What are the various departments and how do they operate?
   - What is the market place condition for the project?
   - What is the organizational environment in which the project exists?
   - What infrastructure exists?

3. *Organization Process Assets.* These are referred to as *process* assets. Some examples are:
   - Historical information, existing tools, and any templates for a charter from previous projects.
   - Lessons learned from previous projects, which are particularly valuable if available in a searchable knowledge-base.
   - Policies, Procedures, and standards.

[2] Every project manager should have an elevator speech that answers this question. You never know when you will run into your boss, who might ask, "Tell me again why are we doing that project?" Job survival depends on a really good answer!

- Data in a project management information system, particularly if supported by cost and schedule management tools.

4. *Statement of Work.* The SOW defines who is to do which tasks, and when. Often, there is no formal SOW when the charter is created. However, much of the the information usually exists elsewhere. e.g., the completion date for the project may be in the business case; products must be available before the holidays; and an Olympic stadium must be available before the Olympics begin.

5. *Contracts.* The sponsor may delegate aspects of the project to an external entity, in which case the contract is an input to the charter.

It is not unusual for the person creating the charter to have to troll through many existing company documents to assemble the required information. The above items can be used as a checklist to begin the search.

### 7.1.2 Develop Charter Tools and Techniques

The sponsor creates the project charter using existing assets, experience, and subject matter experts. A phrase used frequently in the PMBOK is *Expert Judgment*, and here this refers to any group or individual with specialized knowledge or training relevant to the creation of the charter. Such experts may include: stakeholders, potential customers, sponsors, professional organizations, subject matter experts, and staff from the project management office.

### 7.1.3 Develop Charter Outputs

There is only one output from this process, and that is the charter itself.

### 7.1.4 Charter Example

An example of a charter for the PMA website project is given in Table 7.1.

## 7. INITIATING PROCESS GROUP

Table 7.1: The charter for the PMA web site.

| | |
|---|---|
| **Project Title** | **PMA Web Site** |
| **Organization** | **Project Management Association** |
| **Start Date** | **June 14, 2011** |
| **End Date** | **June 14, 2012** |
| **Project Champion** | **Dr. Vijay Kanabar** |
| Purpose | The Project Management Association (PMA) is a networking group for current students and alumni of Boston University employed or interested in the Project Management profession. The PMA website project will create an environment for members of the community to share information, to be informed of current research, to obtain continuing education credits required to maintain certification, to learn about new employment opportunities and to get hints and tips on latest developments in the area of project management. |
| Description | The current Project Management website was implemented many years ago, and is not serving the needs of the PMA. The current website needs to be redesigned to keep up with new demands of the PMA, including access to research, changes in the project management profession, and improvements in tools and templates. This website project will create an environment that is both appealing and helpful to the project management professional, providing an equal balance of information sharing, tools and templates, and opportunities for networking. |
| Goals: | After installation, PMA should be able to: Increase the number of visits to the website by 50% over 2010 levels; decrease support costs of the website by 25%; and provide user friendly mechanisms to post, manage, update and remove content. |
| Success Criteria | 1) Build a community of PMs.<br>2) Membership > 500 in the first year.<br>3) Analytics reveal popularity of site. |
| **Project Budget:** | $15,000 |
| **Milestones:** | Initial Prototype to Stakeholders: 6/28/2011<br>Project Complete: 8/2/2011 |
| **Signatures:** | Champion:<br>PM:<br>Stakeholders |

## 7.2 Identify Stakeholders

**We must, indeed, all hang together,**
**or most assuredly we shall all hang separately.**

*Benjamin Franklin*

## 7.2. Identify Stakeholders

The *Identify Stakeholders* process begins the identification of stakeholders: anyone who can influence the project. Stakeholders exist both within the organization (e.g., the team, upper management) and external to it (e.g., users, trainers, sponsors).

Managing the interests of stakeholders is a vital activity for the project manager. A major risk to project success comes from not realizing who all the stakeholders are, or neglecting an important stakeholder. In fact, mismanagement of any single stakeholder can lead to a disaster because an angry or disillusioned stakeholder can hold up deliverables, make trouble for other interest groups, and generally cause havoc.

The definition of a stakeholder is:

> *A stakeholder is anyone actively involved in the project whose interests may be positively or negatively affected by the performance or the completion of the project.*

Stakeholders are involved!

It is important to realize that not everyone will have a positive attitude to the project. Some individuals or advocacy groups might prefer that the project not be done at all. Such people are stakeholders because they have an *interest* in the project, but their negative interest can be really challenging. Also, some stakeholders may be in favor of the project once it is completed, but they may hold a negative view *during* the project.

For example, a project to repave a street might be viewed quite differently by the different stakeholders. A clean, modernized street is a goal supported by almost everyone. However, digging up the street may make a mess in front of stores and houses, angering the people who live and work there, creating a challenge to the project manager.

During the *Identify Stakeholders* process, the project manager and the team identify both the stakeholders and their expectations. It is vital that the project manager actively manages stakeholder expectations, reduces conflict over competing requirements, and establishes unambiguous acceptance criteria for the project's deliverables.

Most likely, the process of stakeholder identification will continue throughout the planning process. This is a characteristic of project management: Processes are seldom completed in one pass, but are continually refined as more knowledge about the project is accumulated. This is an example of *progressive elaboration,* an important feature of project management.

*Identify Stakeholders* is a critical activity, and it is quite easy to overlook some of them. Let's consider a relatively simple project to repave the street in front of the classroom in which we teach the project management course. Table 7.2 lists the stakeholders and their issues.

Table 7.2: Stakeholders for the repaving project outside the classroom.

| Stakeholder | Interest |
|---|---|
| Sponsor | Who pays for the project |
| Customer | The end user of the project. The customer (the city) may be different from the requesters of the project (the residents). |
| Project Manager | Wants to get the project done on time, on budget. Wants to keep the stakeholders happy. |
| Technical Director | Wants to get the project done right. |
| Project Team | Their jobs depend on the project. Even a simple construction project consists of many different subcontractors. |
| Trainers | Will train users when the project is over. |
| Students | During the project, are affected negatively by the disruption. Once completed, they will like the result. |
| Faculty | Hate the noise outside their window. |
| Police | Make extra money during construction. |
| Deans | Feel obligated to explain that construction will result in a better looking university. |
| The Mayor | Is happy the university will stop complaining about the poor street condition. |
| Shopkeepers | Complain business is down during construction |
| Residents | Complain there is less parking during construction. |
| Red Sox Fans | Miss the first inning because of the mess. |

### 7.2.1 How Stakeholders Influence the Project

Stakeholders have varying levels of influence. Many stakeholders have specific requirements they want included in the project, and the team must strive to meet those needs. It is up to the team to decide which stakeholder requirements can be fulfilled, and the failure to meet a particular stakeholder's expectations is a major risk factor. At the least, by not meeting a particular stakeholder requirement, you run the risk of failing an acceptance test. The key concept is "stakeholder expectations," and managing them is a key role for the project manager.

Project managers spend a lot of time dealing with stakeholders. When conflicts arise, the project manager must take the long term view, and stakeholders more as as partners than adversaries. Short-term wins only make losers try harder in the future, they become better adversaries.[2]

### 7.2.2 Identify Stakeholders Inputs

Many of the process inputs are the same as for the *Develop Charter* process. The inputs to the *Identify Stakeholders* process are illustrated in Figure 7.4.

Quite frequently in project management, an output from a previous process is an input to the next process. That is true here: The *Charter* was an output from the *Create Charter* process and it is a key input the the *Identify Stakeholders* process.

### 7.2.3 Identify Stakeholders Tools and Techniques

Many analysis tools are useful in helping the project manager identify stakeholders and their influence. Not all stakeholders have the same vested interest in the outcome of the project. Not all stakeholders have the ability to influence the outcome of the project or override the interests other powerful stakeholders.

The first step is the development of a list of stakeholders, which is called the *Stakeholder Register*. The next step is to identify stakeholder influence, and a tool to accomplish this is illustrated in Figure 7.5. The goal is to create a strategy for managing the various stakeholders, which is a major output of the *Identify Stakeholders* process.

In Figure 7.5, stakeholders are classified in two dimensions: The vertical axis indicates their power to influence the project and the horizontal axis indicates their interest in the project, i.e. their desire to take part in meetings and evaluate out-

## 7. INITIATING PROCESS GROUP

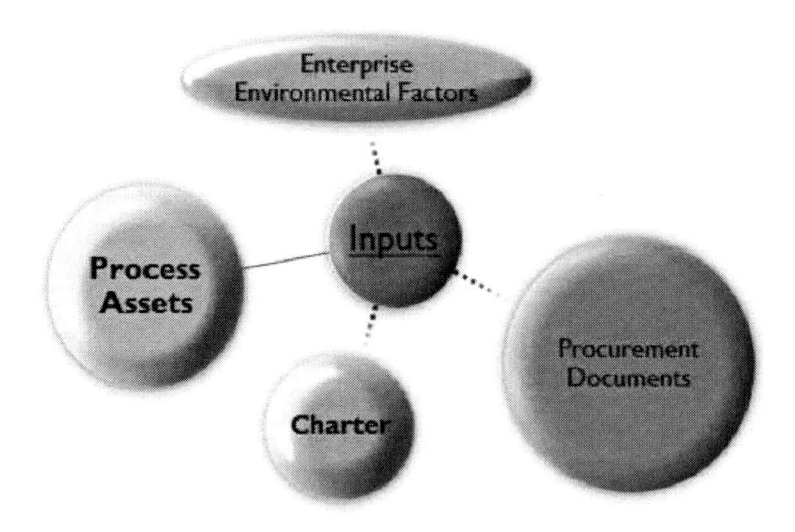

Figure 7.4: The inputs to the *Identify Stakeholder* process.

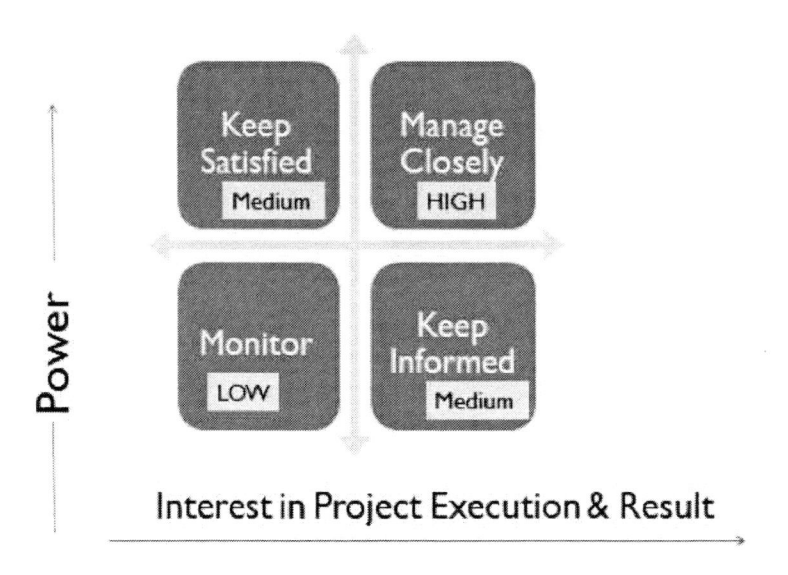

Figure 7.5: The tool to create the stakeholder management *strategy*.

puts. Stakeholders are ranked as either "Low" or "High" in both categories. Every entry in the *Stakeholder Register* Is assigned to a box in Figure 7.5.

The actions of the project manager towards the stakeholder groups are also shown in each of the four boxes. This constitutes the *Stakeholder Management Strategy*.

For example, stakeholders with high power and high interest are assigned: *manage closely*. They should be frequently consulted, their opinions weighed, and their views acknowledged, particularly with respect to deliverables. On the other hand, stakeholders with low power and low interest should be assigned: *monitor*.

Note that stakeholder analysis takes place continually, and the *Stakeholder Register* is likely to be updated frequently.

### 7.2.4 Identify Stakeholder Outputs

The important outputs from the *Identify Stakeholders* process are the *Stakeholder Register* and the *Stakeholder Management Strategy*. In Table 7.3, we provide a tool that can be used to manage the important stakeholders.

Table 7.3: Stakeholder Register & Management Strategy: A tool for identifying the expectations and creating a strategy to manage stakeholders.

| Stakeholder | Role | Goal | Expectations |
|---|---|---|---|
| Joe Brown | President, PMA | Web site to promote social network and organization growth. | Complete before the conference. |

### 7.2.5 Summary

In this chapter we provided a detailed anatomy of a the *initiating* process group. However, we have covered just two of the forty two processes!

The *inputs* referred to information that the project manager uses to create the process outputs. Using tools and templates, we illustrated how to create the process outputs: Charter, Stakeholder Register & Management Strategy.

Throughout Part II of the book, we repeat this approach: defining the inputs, tools and techniques, and outputs. By covering this simple Process Group in considerable detail, we hope that when covering the more complex process groups,[3] the reader will be familiar with the approach.

---

[3] Planning has 20 processes!

# CHAPTER 8

# PLANNING PROCESS GROUP

> **Give me six hours to chop down a tree and
> I will spend the first four sharpening the axe.**
>
> *Abraham Lincoln*

In this chapter we focus on the *planning* process group, which is the largest group the project manager must deal with[1]

An overview of the *planning* process group is shown in Figure 8.1. The technical aspects of the documents (e.g., how to write the scope, the technical details of the network diagram) are covered in the knowledge area chapters.

Planning begins by carefully defining the scope of the project in concert with the stakeholders, and then developing the cost and schedule estimates. Planning also involves: analyzing the risks to the project; defining how to assess the quality of the deliverables; establishing the communications between all parties; acquiring and training the team; and finally, deciding on the approach to sub-contractors.

The technical aspects of the planning processes are extensive, and include: collecting the requirements and writing the project scope; evaluating constraints and creating the work breakdown structure; estimating costs, identifying resources, and developing the network diagram; and determining the project schedule.

[1] We might also suggest that these are the most important processes for the project manager. Maybe not for the project, but for the project manager. A badly planned project is doomed.

# 8. Planning Process Group

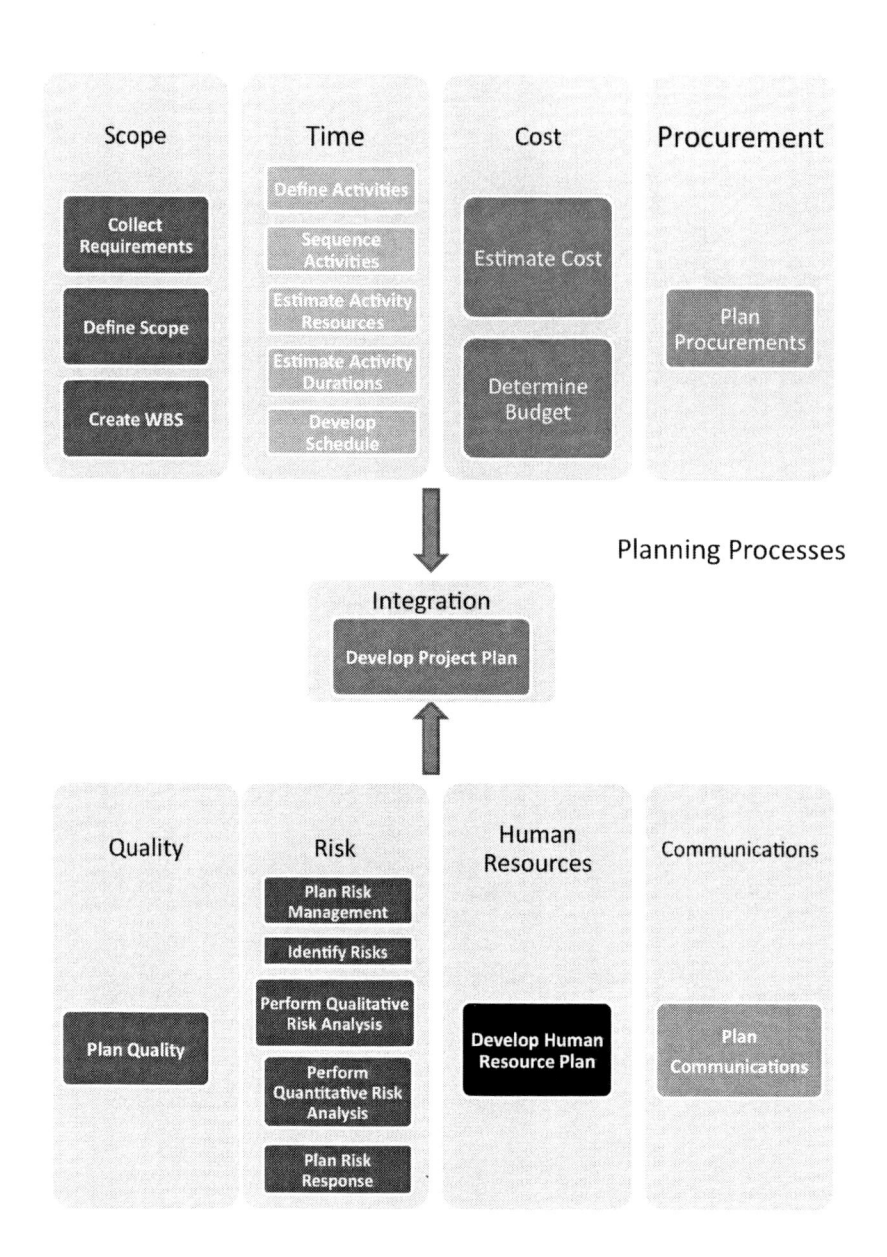

Figure 8.1: Overview of the *planning* process group, and the processes within it.

The primary outputs of the planning process group are the components of a comprehensive Project Management Plan, which consists of multiple sub-documents.

It is important to realize that planning is inherently iterative in nature. As stakeholder needs are refined, changes to the plan will be proposed, and not just technical or content requests, but also the real-world demands of cost and schedule. The progressive nature of the evolution of planning is referred to as *rolling wave planning*.

For each process we identify the key inputs, because you can only start a new document when all the preceding documents (the inputs) are completed. We also identify the outputs, because future processes can only be started when the key deliverables (the outputs) are complete.

Since planning covers so many disciplines, we divide our discussion into the following major sections:

- *The Project Management Plan*: This defines the entire plan, both technically and managerially.

- *Scope Planning*: The *scope* contains the user requirements and is the most important document in the project: .

- *Time Planning*: Here the project schedule is developed, and the *critical path* emerges, the most important concept in project management.

- *Cost Planning*: These are the steps required to develop the project cost estimate, and the budget.

- *Risk Planning*: The risks are identified, their impacts assessed, and how to mitigate them.

- *The Sub-Plans*:

    - *Quality Plan*: This defines the quality standards for the project, both the process and the content.

    - *Human Resources Plan*: This defines how the project team is to be acquired and developed.

    - *Communications Plan*: This defines the distribution of information to stakeholders.

    - *Procurement Plan*: This defines the role of sub-contractors.

# 8. Planning Process Group

## 8.1 Develop Project Management Plan

The *Develop Project Management Plan* process is where the *Project Management Plan* is created. It is the major document used throughout the project to explain precisely how the project will be planned, managed, executed, assessed, and eventually, closed.

Table 8.1 shows the inputs and outputs to the *Develop Project Management Plan* process. The inputs consist of the *charter*, the preliminary, pre-project work (rationale, business case, the desired cost and schedule, etc.), and any existing assets (the company's tools, technology, and templates) and environmental factors. The output is the *project management plan*.

Table 8.1: The *Develop Project Management Plan* process inputs and outputs

| Input | Output |
| --- | --- |
| Project Charter | Project Management Plan |
| Outputs from project planning | |
| Environmental factors | |
| Organizational assets | |

## 8.2 Scope Planning

> **By looking at the questions the kids are asking, we learn the scope of what needs to be done.**
>
> *Buffy Sainte-Marie*

Once the project charter has been created and the stakeholders have been identified, the project manager can begin the three scope planning processes: *Collect Requirements*, *Define Scope*, and *Create WBS*. Each of these processes is described, along with the required inputs and outputs. Major documents are also defined.

### 8.2.1 Collect Requirements

*Collect Requirements* is the process of clearly defining and documenting all stakeholder's goals, objectives, and needs for the project. The key inputs and outputs associated with this process are shown in Table 8.2. The outputs—the deliverables from the process—are described in the following sections.

## 8.2. Scope Planning

Table 8.2: The *Collect Requirements* process inputs and outputs

| Input | Output |
|---|---|
| Project Charter | Requirements Document |
| Stakeholder Register | Requirements Management Plan |
| Stakeholder Management Strategy | Requirements Traceability Matrix |

**Requirements Document**

An easy way to begin thinking about the stakeholders' requirements is to answer the following questions:

- *What?* What do the stakeholders want?

- *When?* When do the stakeholders want it?

- *Who?* Who is going to do what?[2]

Other information included in the requirements document might include:[3]

- *Traceability information.* The name of a stakeholder is associated with each key functional requirement.

- *Acceptance criteria.* These are the specific, measurable properties of the delivered project. They form the basis of the tests to ensure that the stakeholder requirements have been met. One has to be able to answer questions such as: What are the criteria for satisfying the stakeholder? How are the requirement to be tested?

- *Priority of the Requirement.* Different stakeholders have different priorities, which can be classified as "must have" or "nice-to-have." This is a useful way to separate the priorities.

- *Non-Functional Requirements.* These include such items as security, performance, and supportability issues. Specific examples of non-functional requirements are:

    - *Usability*, e.g., the system should be compliant with U.S. Department of Justice Americans with Disabilities Act (ADA).

    - *Availability*, e.g., the website should be hosted with a reliable provider that ensures access 99.9% of the time.

---

[2] Another question might come to mind: How? This question is not answered here, because How? answers the design question, i.e. how are the requirements to be met. We will discuss the difference between requirements and design in Chapter 13–Scope.

[3] For small projects, these should be considered as a checklist. That is, a simple one line statement may be all that is necessary to explain the role of these issues in a small project.

As an example, we present the requirements document for the PMA web site in Table 8.3.

Table 8.3: *Requirements document* for the PMA case study.

| Category | Requirement | Stakeholder | Acceptance Criteria |
|---|---|---|---|
| Functional Requirements | A form to register new members | PMA Director | Should be user friendly form |
| | Email Newsletter to members | Marketing Director | Ability to send up to 3,000 emails to members |
| Maintainability Requirements | Edit Registration form | IT Staff | Easy to add and edit fields in registration form |
| | Update web site | IT Staff | System easily updated by IT staff |
| Security | Membership data will be encrypted in the database | Information Assurance Staff | Membership data secure against hacking tests |

**Requirements Management Plan**

The *Requirements Management Plan* is the document that specifies the way in which requirements will be *managed* throughout the life of the project. It describes attributes such as requirements collection, traceability, and configuration management. The configuration management of the requirements is important, as it specifies the process to be followed when someone proposes to change a requirement.

As projects evolve, there is an overwhelming temptation to give in to user requests to add functionality.[4] The impact of any change on both cost and schedule must be weighed against the proposed functionality improvement.

In this context, it is important to distinguish between refinements (good) and enhancements (bad). Enhancements usually increase the cost and delay the project. This process is described in more detail in Chapter 13—Scope.

---

[4]"Can we *please* just add this minor function?"

## 8.2. Scope Planning

**Requirements Traceability Matrix**

After the Work Breakdown Structure (WBS) is completed a *Requirements Traceability Matrix* can be constructed. This matches the attributes in the *Requirements Document* to the WBS deliverables. and allows for Verification and Validation of the requirements. Verification is the process that tests the *technical* validity of the requirements. Validation is the process that ensures the *value* of the individual requirements to the stakeholders.

For the PMA case, Table 8.4 shows a *Requirements Traceability Matrix*, which links the requirements to the WBS items.

Table 8.4: *Requirements Traceability Matrix* for the PMA case study

| Requirement | Status | Acceptance Criteria | WBS ID |
|---|---|---|---|
| Form to register new members | Completed | Form tested and approved by QA department | 2.1 |
| Email Newsletter to members | Not Started | Test designed for 3,000 emails | 2.2 |

### 8.2.2 Define Scope

As expected, the *Define Scope* process defines the scope of the project and produces the *Scope Statement*, one of the most important documents that the project team will produce. The scope can be started once the *charter* and *requirements document* are completed.

The *Scope Statement* is the fundamental document that describes all aspects of the project, both the managerial process and the desired content to be delivered. The *Scope Statement* is also the basis for a macro (or top-down) cost estimate.

The inputs and outputs—the deliverables—are shown in Table 8.5.

**Project Scope Statement**

Typically, the scope includes the following sections: Description of the project; its justification; the business case, including return on investment arguments; deliverables; acceptance criteria; exclusions; constraints; and assumptions. The de-

Table 8.5: The *Define Scope* process Inputs and Outputs

| Input | Output |
| --- | --- |
| Project Charter | Project Scope Statement |
| Requirements Documentation | Project Document Updates |
| Process Assets | |

tailed contents and the technical aspects of preparing a scope statement are covered in Chapter 13—Scope. A major section of the scope defines what the project will do, and is referred to as the *specification*, or "spec."

**Project Document Updates**

While developing stakeholder requirements, it is expected that changes to previous documents will occur. For example, as requirements are refined, new stakeholders may be identified, requiring updates to the *Stakeholder Register*. Therefore, one should expect *Project Document Updates*, which is an output from this process. Also, one may need to refine the *Requirements Traceability Matrix*.

This is a clear illustration of the iterative nature of project planning. Planning is not a one-time-through, cascading waterfall process. Project planning requires the project team to iterate: to continually examine the existing documentation, and as required, to carefully update all the previously published documents. In particular, each time a new plan or sub-plan is created, the project team should revisit all related documents and assess the wider impact of the new plan.

### 8.2.3 Create WBS

The *Work Breakdown Structure* (WBS) is created once the project scope statement is complete. The WBS is derived from the scope baseline and generates individual *activities*, as well as the elements of the WBS dictionary.

The key inputs and outputs associated with this process are shown in Table 8.6. The outputs—the deliverables—are described in the following sections.

**WBS**

The WBS is a deliverable-oriented hierarchy and defines each deliverable. The WBS further decomposes major deliverables into smaller work packages.

## 8.2. Scope Planning

Table 8.6: The *Create WBS* process inputs and outputs

| Input | Output |
|---|---|
| Project Scope Statement | WBS |
| Requirements Documentation | WBS Dictionary |
| Process Assets | Scope Baseline |
|  | Project Document Updates |

The high level WBS is typically presented in graphical form, and an example is given in Figure 25.5. This is suitable for managing the project and tracking the costs. The low level WBS is usually presented in outline form (see Figures 14.4 and 14.5). The low-level WBS is also the foundation for a bottom-up estimation of the project cost. The detailed contents and the technical aspects preparing the WBS are covered in Chapter 14–WBS.

A sample WBS for the PMA project is given in Figure 8.2.

**WBS Dictionary**

The *WBS Dictionary* is a repository that contains the detailed description and data for the work required for each element of the WBS. The *WBS Dictionary* includes: activities, milestones, start and end dates, the organization responsible for the element, quality requirements, performance measurement criteria, resource requirements, cost estimates, and contact information. For the PMA project, we provide an example of a *WBS Dictionary* in Table 14.1.

**Scope Baseline**

The approved combination of the project scope statement, the WBS and the WBS dictionary constitute the *Scope Baseline*. You can expect the *Scope Baseline* to be updated often. Therefore, *Update Scope Baseline* appears frequently as a process output as changes to the project scope emerge.

## 8. Planning Process Group

Figure 8.2: The graphical *WBS* for the PMA case.

### 8.3 Time Planning

**Lost time is never found again.**

*Benjamin Franklin*

[5] The PMBOK uses "time," but we believe that a more appropriate word is "schedule." After all, who can plan *time*? One is really developing the *schedule*.

*Time Planning* covers the processes required to manage the timely completion of the project.[5] There are five processes associated with time (or schedule) planning, and these are shown in Table 8.7, along with the inputs and outputs. The impor-

## 8.3. Time Planning

tant outputs are in bold. It is clear from Table 8.7 that the outputs from one process are often the inputs to the next process.

Table 8.7: The *Time Planning* processes with their associated inputs and outputs. Important outputs are in bold.

| Inputs | Process | Outputs |
|---|---|---|
| Scope Baseline<br>Environmental Factors<br>Process Assets | Define<br>Activities | **Activity List**<br>Activity Attributes<br>Milestone List |
| Activity List<br>Activity Attributes<br>Milestone List<br>Activity List | Sequence<br>Activities | **Schedule Network Diagram**<br>Project Document Updates |
| Activity List<br>Activity Attributes<br>Resource Calendars<br>Environmental Factors<br>Process Assets | Estimate<br>Activity<br>Resources | Activity Resource Requirements<br>**Resource Breakdown Structure**<br>Project Document Updates |
| Activity List<br>Activity Attributes<br>Activity Resource Requirements<br>Resource Calendars<br>Activity duration estimates<br>Project Scope Statement<br>Environmental Factors<br>Process Assets | Estimate<br>Activity<br>Durations | **Activity Duration Estimates**<br>Project Document Updates |
| Activity List<br>Activity Attributes<br>Schedule Network Diagram<br>Activity Resource Requirements<br>Resource Calendars<br>Activity duration estimates<br>Project Scope Statement<br>Environmental Factors<br>Process Assets | Develop<br>Schedule | **Project Schedule**<br>Schedule Baseline<br>Schedule Data<br>Project Document Updates |

*Time Planning* is a complex and important activity, as it results in an estimate of the project schedule which is one of the most important aspects of project planning. Everyone wants to know: When will it be finished?

The data for *Time Planning* is most conveniently captured, documented, and reported in a software system that includes project management scheduling, such as *Microsoft Project®*, *GANTTER®*, or *Primavera®*. We illustrate this by providing

## 8. PLANNING PROCESS GROUP

samples from the PMA case study using *Microsoft Project*.

The technical aspects of developing the project schedule are covered in Chapter 16.

**Activity List**

The *Activity List* is created from the WBS. An *activity* is any task that takes time, and you start by generating an activity from each element of the WBS. An illustration of the *Activity List* for the PMA project is presented in Table 8.8.

Table 8.8: *Activity List* for the PMA Case

| **Initial Design of Membership Form** |
| --- |
| Create the Requirement Specification |
| Create User Interface Design |
| Create Database Table to Store Membership Data |
| Review Specification and Prepare Test Cases |
| Review User Interface Design documentation |
| Documentation of all Systems Documentation |
| Update Project Management Documentation |
| Completion of Initial Design Phase |

**Activity Attributes**

*Activity Attributes* are the properties and characteristics of the activities, such as predecessor and successor activities, logical relationships between activities, leads and lags, constraints, resources, and assumptions. The activity attributes develop as the planning process matures.

The most important *Activity Attributes* are:

- *Identification:* The name of the activity (and perhaps, its number).

- *Duration:* How long it will take to complete.

- *Predecessors:* The activities required to be completed before it can start.

Once these attributes are determined, they can be entered into a project scheduling system, such as *Microsoft Project*, and the schedule drops out.

## Milestone List

The *Milestone List* describes the important project milestones. Milestones play a key role in assessing the actual schedule against the plan as the project progresses. The accomplishment of major deliverables at specific milestones shows whether the schedule agrees with the stakeholders' planned expectations. It is useful to provide additional attributes for milestones, such as clarifying if the milestone date is Internal or External, and if it is Mandatory or Flexible.[6]

Table 8.9, gives an example of a *Milestone List* for the PMA project.

Table 8.9: *Milestone List* for the PMA case.

| Milestone | Date | Type |
|---|---|---|
| Initiation Phase Complete | 1/15 | Internal, Flexible |
| Project Planning Complete | 2/1 | Internal, Flexible |
| Initial Design Phase Complete | 2/15 | Internal, Flexible |
| Prototype Implementation Complete | 2/28 | External, Flexible |
| Full Website Complete | 3/10 | External, Mandatory |
| Closing Processes Complete | 3/15 | Internal, Mandatory |

## Project Schedule Network Diagram

Once we have a list of activities and milestones, they can be entered into a software scheduling system to produce a visual network diagram. The network diagram displays the timing relationships between the activities, identifies the critical path, and shows which activities can be worked in parallel. We can also include additional information such as leads and lags. The network diagram is the fundamental tool used to generate an accurate estimate of the project schedule.

We illustrate the high level portion of a network diagram in Figure 8.3 for the PMA case.

### 8.3.1 Estimate Activity Resources

In the *Estimate Activity Resources* process you estimate the types and quantities of resources required for each activity. Resources include people (the team, external consultants, subject matter experts, etc.), material, equipment, and supplies.

[6]The technical details of these terms are covered in Chapter 14—WBS.

## 8. PLANNING PROCESS GROUP

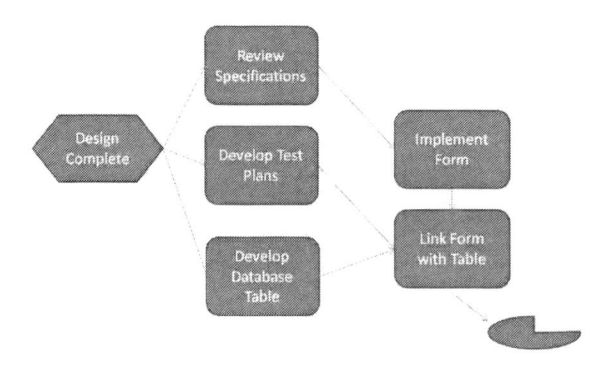

Figure 8.3: A portion of the high level network diagram for the PMA case.

Table 8.10 shows examples of resource estimation for the PMA project. Note that the resource types are matched with the activities using them.

Table 8.10: Some examples of *Estimate Activity Resources* for the PMA case.

| Activity | Resource Type | Quantity |
| --- | --- | --- |
| Create Requirement Specification | Business Analyst | 2 |
| Create User Interface Design | Systems Analyst | 1 |
| Create Database Table | Database Developer | 1 |
| Review Specification and Prepare Test Cases | Test Developer | 1 |
| Review User Interface Design Documentation | Design Specialist | 1 |
| Writing Systems Documentation | Programmer | 1 |
| Update Project Management Documentation | Project Manager | 1 |
| Database & Programming Activities | High End Work Stations | 6 |

**Resource Breakdown Structure**

The *Resource Breakdown Structure* (RBS) hierarchically categorizes the available resources according to different functions, types, or categories. As an illustration, Table 8.4 presents an RBS in hierarchical format for the PMA project.

```
    0   Project PMA RBS
    1.    Personnel Resources
          1.1   Business Analyst (2)
          1.2   Database Developer (1)
          1.3   Test Developer (1)
          1.4   Design Specialist (1)
          1.5   Programmer (4)
          1.6   Project Manager (1)
    2.    Equipment
          2.1   High End Workstations (6)
          2.2   Printers (3)
    3.    Materials
          3.1   DVDs, USBs, etc.
          3.2   Books, Online Tutorials, etc.
    4.    Services
          4.1   Web Hosting
          4.2   High Speed Networks
```

Figure 8.4: *Resource Breakdown Structure* for the PMA case.

### 8.3.2 Estimate Activity Durations

*Estimate Activity Durations* is the process in which the time to complete an activity is estimated. The required resources are considered to be an input.[1]

Many techniques are available for estimating the duration of an activity, including both top-down and bottom-up. Popular methods for estimating durations include parametric estimating, analogous or experience-based estimating, the three-point (PERT) method, and the Delphi approach.[7]

An example of *Activity Durations* is shown in Table 8.11 for the PMA case.[8]

### 8.3.3 Develop Schedule

> **The sooner you fall behind, the more time you'll have to catch up.**
>
> *Steven Wright*

[7] This is an important knowledge area and we have dedicated an entire chapter to duration (and cost) estimating–Chapter 17—Cost.

In the *Develop Schedule* process, the scope statement, activity list, milestone list, activity resource requirements, and duration estimates are all analyzed to produce

[8] Note that activities with zero durations are considered to be *milestones*.

Table 8.11: *Activity Durations* for the PMA case

| Activity | Duration (days) |
|---|---|
| **Design** | |
| Review preliminary software specifications | 2 |
| Develop functional specifications | 5 |
| Develop prototype based on functional specifications | 4 |
| Develop prototype based on functional specifications | 4 |
| Review functional specifications | 2 |
| Incorporate feedback into functional specifications | 1 |
| Obtain approval to proceed | 0.5 |
| Design complete | 0 |
| **Development** | |
| Review functional specifications | 1 |
| Identify modular/tiered design parameters | 1 |
| Assign development staff | 1 |
| Develop code | 15 |
| Developer testing (primary debugging) | 15 |
| Development complete | 0 |

the *Network Diagram*.

The single most important concept that emerges from the *Network Diagram* is the *critical path*. An example of a piece of the network diagram is shown in Figure 8.5 for the PMA case, and we can immediately see that the activity *Review Functional Specification* is on the critical path. Critical path boxes are bold.

Further, three activities can start upon completion of the design phase, and we can now see their start and completion times, their durations, and the resources required. As the start and completion times for the activities emerge, we can add these dates to the WBS Dictionary.

Modern software systems make it relatively east to generate such network diagrams.[9] The project schedule shown in the network diagram is called a GANTT chart, and it is widely used to communicate the schedule information.

A GANTT chart is easily understandable by anyone, even if they have no formal training in network diagrams. An example of a GANTT chart is shown in Figure 8.6 for the PMA project.

[9]We insist there is no excuse for not using them.

8.3. Time Planning

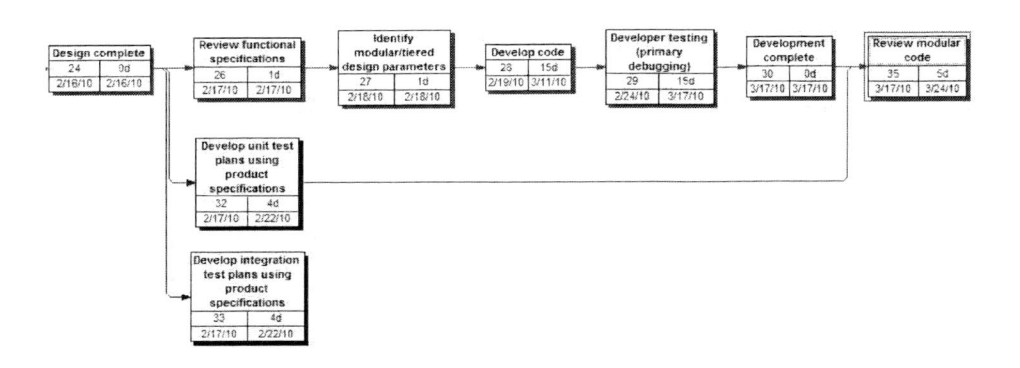

Figure 8.5: A portion of the network diagram for the PMA case.

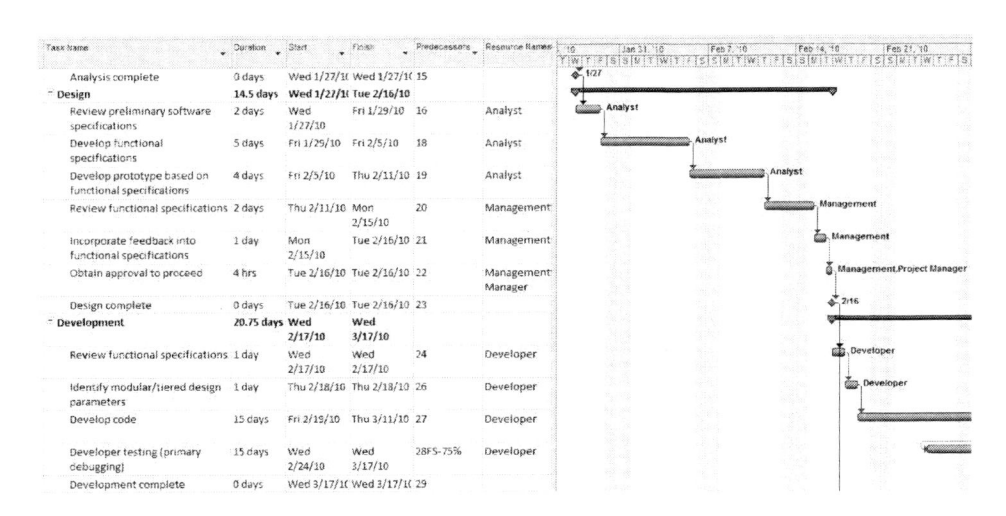

Figure 8.6: A portion of the GANTT chart for the PMA case.

**Schedule Baseline**

Once the project schedule has been estimated, we can save it as a *Schedule Baseline*.

> *The Schedule Baseline is a specific version of the project schedule that is accepted and approved by the team, with baseline start and finish dates.*

105

## 8. PLANNING PROCESS GROUP

This baseline, which is a component of the *Project Management Plan*, must be communicated to all stakeholders. Before project execution starts, an official sign-off on the baseline is recommended.

In Figure 8.7 we illustrate the schedule baseline graphically using the Timeline Tool from Microsoft Project. Typically, however, it is the GANTT chart that is submitted to stakeholders to communicate the schedule baseline.

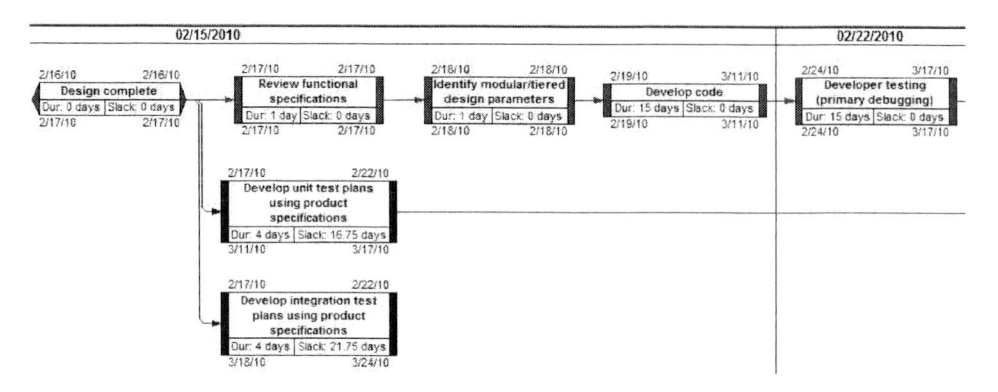

Figure 8.7: A portion of the Timeline diagram for the PMA case.

Before we continue to *cost planning*, we summarize in Figure 8.8 where we are in the planning process. The figure highlights the important processes and deliverables that most project teams would have completed at this point. We have completed the user requirements and the project scope; we have designed the WBS; and we have developed the network diagram, which gives us the schedule. The next step is *cost planning*, in which we develop the project cost estimate.

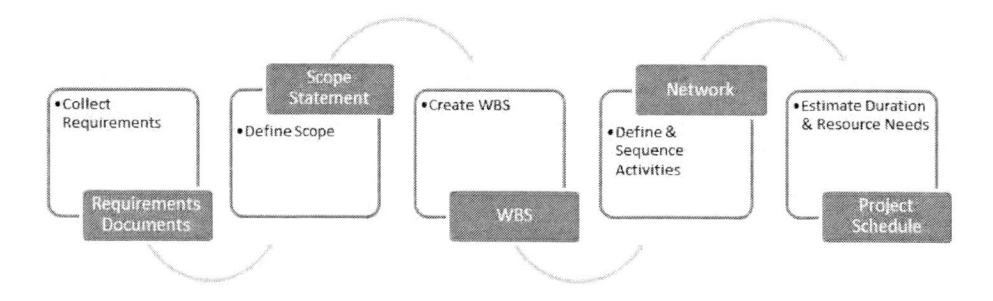

Figure 8.8: A summary of the status after completing *Scope* and *Time* planning.

## 8.4 Cost Planning

> **The cost of living has gone up another dollar a quart.**
>
> *W. C. Fields*

After the project schedule is created we progress to *Cost Planning*. Cost plans can range from being formal and highly detailed to informal and general in nature. While the team hopes to produce accurate estimates of the cost and schedule, the reality is that these will contain uncertainty, depending upon the quality of the scope and the chance of unknown risks materializing.

The accuracy of the cost and schedule varies over time. Early on, the accuracy may be quite low, but it should improve as the project proceeds.[10] It is important, therefore, to establish a good communication framework that clearly disseminates to the stakeholders the cost and schedule estimates, the current views on their accuracy, any variances, and the assumptions involved. Chapter 17—Cost is dedicated to cost estimation, a very important knowledge area.

The processes associated with cost planning include: *Estimate Costs* and *Determine Budget*. The inputs and outputs are presented in Table 8.12.

Table 8.12: *Cost Planning* processes, inputs, and outputs.

| Inputs | Process | Outputs |
|---|---|---|
| Scope Baseline<br>Project Schedule<br>Human Resource Plan<br>Risk Register<br>Environmental Factors<br>Organizational Assets | **Estimate Costs** | Activity cost estimates<br>Basis of estimates<br>Document Updates |
| Activity cost estimates<br>Basis of estimates<br>Scope Baseline<br>Project Schedule<br>Resources Calendars<br>Contracts<br>Organizational Assets | **Determine Budget** | Cost performance baseline<br>Funding Requirements<br>Document Updates |

[10] A useful rule of thumb is that the project cost is known to within 20% once the project is 20% complete. The interesting issue is that the internal team almost always knows this. Whether the customer is informed is an ethical and political issue!

### 8.4.1 Estimate Costs

> **Large increases in cost with questionable increase in performance can be tolerated only for racehorses and fancy women.**
>
> *Lord Kelvin*

The first step in *Estimate Costs* is to develop a rough, approximate estimate of the resources needed to complete **each activity**.[11] This requires the project manager to consider alternative implementation approaches in both the technical approach and the management process.

An example of technical alternatives might be: Should a prototype be developed, and the project requirements incrementally developed in concert with user feedback, or, is the scope to be carefully defined, and the project developed using the waterfall approach? There are also options for the management approach: Which activities can be processed in parallel? Should we build the activity in-house or outsource the development?

For example, for the PMA project, we might analyze whether to outsource the website development to an experienced engineer or build the website in-house. This is a classic "make versus buy" decision.

Like many processes, *Estimate Costs* is an iterative process, and the accuracy increases as time goes by. Early on, it is important to label the the cost estimate clearly as an *Order of Magnitude* estimate. History suggests that the variation in early cost estimates is often ±50%![12]

As the project proceeds, and the scope is refined, the cost estimate becomes more reliable. As the accuracy improves, the estimate may be relabeled as a *Budget Estimate*. Eventually, when the project manager is confident about the project scope and potential risks, the cost estimate becomes a *Definitive Estimate*.[13]

Cost estimates are expressed either in units of currency or in units of effort, such as staff hours or staff months. Estimates in units of effort are more useful, as they are not subject to inflation.

Cost estimates also include the costs associated with materials, equipment, and services. Finally, there is the entire issue of the overhead costs (benefits, office, utilities, etc.), and these are also covered in Chapter 17–Cost.

Finally, cost estimation should include an allocation for risks, which is called a *contingency*. Risk analysis is the topic of Chapter 22—Risk.

---

[11] Note that at this point, we are estimating the costs of the **individual activities**, not the entire project. In reality, one may estimate the entire project cost from the scope parameters.

[12] Data also to suggests that the larger the project, the larger the initial error. Beware though, this is often a political error, in that people, particularly politicians, are often reluctant to release the true cost.

[13] Only a foolish project manager would be so confident.

Depending upon the industry, worksheets may be available to help the team estimate the costs of activities. For example, for a construction project in the City of Boston, there are detailed worksheets available.[2]

**Basis of Estimates**

The *Basis of Estimates* document contains a description of how the cost estimate was obtained for each WBS element. Such details are important to note, and if detailed, may be listed in a separate appendix to the cost estimate.

### 8.4.2 Determine Budget

After completing the cost estimate, the *Determine Budget* process occurs. This is defined as:

> *Determine Budget is the process of aggregating the estimated costs of the individual activities, or work packages, to establish an authorized cost baseline.*

There are two outputs: The *Cost Performance Baseline* and the *Project Funding Requirements*.

**Cost Performance Baseline**

This is defined as:

> *The cost performance baseline is the time-phased budget that is used to measure, monitor, and control the cost performance for the project.*

The inputs to the *Cost Performance Baseline* are the scope baseline, project schedule, and the cost estimates.

In order to create the *Cost Performance Baseline*, we must add up both direct and indirect costs. (Direct and Indirect Costs are covered in chapter 17—Cost.) A typical baseline consists of the following information: Work Package ID and name, cost per time period, and cumulative cost.

Microsoft Project can output the time phased costs by resource, and an example is shown in Table 8.13 for the PMA project.

## 8. PLANNING PROCESS GROUP

Table 8.13: *Time Phased Costs by Resource* for the PMA project. Output from Microsoft Project

| Resource | 1/3/10 | 1/10/10 | 1/17/10 | 1/24/10 |
|---|---|---|---|---|
| Management | $1,200 | | | $400 |
| Project Manager | $1,60 | | $2,000 | $2,000 |
| Analyst | $840 | $2,800 | $1,680 | $1,400 |
| Tester | $2,800 | $2,800 | $2,800 | $2,800 |
| **Total** | $6,440 | $5,600 | $6,480 | $6,600 |

This is only part of the cash flow analysis. It is only the outflow of cash that comes from paying the team. The incoming cash payments from the sponsor must also be added. As an example, we have aggregated the project budget (costs and payments) for the PMA project website which are shown in Figure 8.9.

The next step in cost budgeting is to add all of the cash inflows and outflows, since workers, subcontractors, and suppliers need to be paid in a timely fashion. On most projects this requires a detailed cash-flow analysis, as the customer may not pay until specific milestones are completed. Meanwhile, bills and invoices may accumulate and may require the project manager to borrow funds to pay the bills. Therefore, synchronizing cash-flow is as important an issue as the total amount of money required.

Figure 8.9 shows the outflow of cash as payments are made to the team (black). It also shows the inflow of cash from the sponsor (grey). The inflows are separated in time because they are tied to deliverables. For example, there is a payment from the sponsor in week 0, representing a payment upon signing of the contract. The payment in week 4 is for the successful completion of the scope.

In Figure 8.10, we have added the weekly cash flows to produce the cumulative net cash position over the life of the project (shaded). The cash flow is initially positive due to the payment in week 0, at contract signing. The net cash position fluctuates as team members are paid, deliverables are completed, and sponsor payments are received.

In weeks 7 and 10, the net cash position turns negative, representing a situation where the project manager will have to borrow money to pay the bills. In weeks 12-17, the project manager will need a line of credit approaching $20,000. Note that the project will eventually end up in a positive situation, but not until well after week 20.

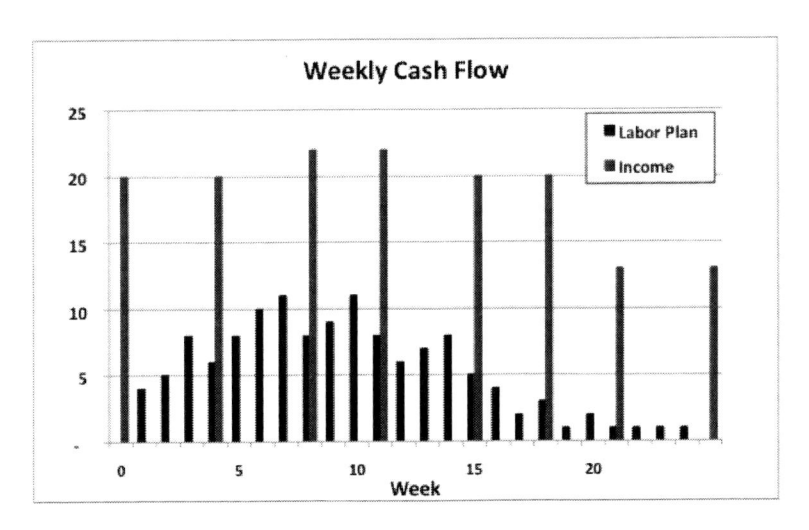

Figure 8.9: The time-phased budget for the PMA project

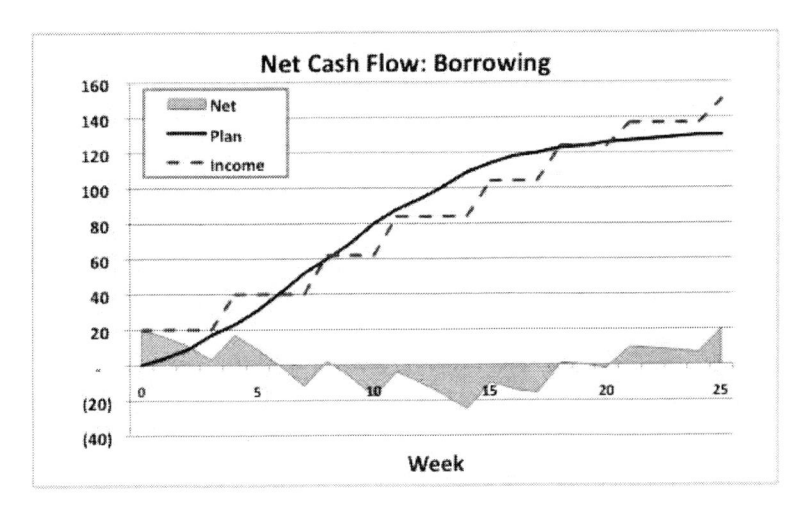

Figure 8.10: The cumulative net cash position for the PMA project

The occurrence of risk events can impact the project cost and schedule. There are usually considered to be two types of risks: *Known-unknowns* and *unknown-unknowns*. The known-unknowns are listed in the *Risk Register* and can be quantified.[14] The unknown-unknowns are those events that are totally unexpected, and are much more difficult to deal with.[15]

[14]Well, it is assumed that they can be quantified.

[15]"No one could have expected that .... (insert your favorite event here)."

During the process of risk quantification the team calculates and sets aside contingency reserves for known-unknowns. These reserves can be integrated into the project budget baseline. The PMBOK suggests that funds also be allocated for unknown-unknowns, depending upon the risks and uncertainty existing in the project.[16] A project manager may keep a separate account with the contingency funds to be spent as needed.

## 8.5 Risk Planning

> **Risk comes from not knowing what you're doing.**
>
> *Warren Buffett*

Risk management is a large component of the project management plan, with several processes and outputs, and significant technical work. The technical aspects of risk management are covered in Chapter 22—Risk.

Risk management is both an art and science, and deals with planning for the management of the risks; identifying risks; quantifying them; and planning a response in case the risk occurs.[17]

An overall view of risk management is given in Table 8.14, which lists the risk processes, as well as their inputs and outputs.

### 8.5.1 Plan Risk Management

IN this process, the overall plan for risk management is developed. The inputs and outputs to the *Plan Risk Management* process are given in Table 8.14. The major deliverables are described below.

**Risk Management Plan**

The *risk management plan* documents the project team's approach to managing uncertainty, threats or opportunities, stakeholder risk tolerance, resources for assisting with risk analysis, identification of risk categories, assigning weights for risk probabilities and their impact, details about risk management funding, and risk audit approaches.

---

[16] Unfortunately, it is very difficult to convince upper management to set aside funds for things you don't know anything about.

[17] It should be noted that in the PMBOK, the risk processes come after quality and before procurement. We have combined the HR, quality, and procurement processes into the *Sub-Plans* to make what we think is a more organized and easily understood approach.

## 8.5. Risk Planning

Table 8.14: The Risk Management Processes, Inputs and Outputs.

| Inputs | Process | Outputs |
|---|---|---|
| Scope Statement<br>Cost Mgmt Plan<br>Environmental Factors<br>Process Assets | **Plan Risk Management HR Plan** | Risk Management Plan |
| Risk Management Plan<br>Cost Estimates<br>Environmental Factors<br>Scope Baseline<br>Stakeholder Register<br>Cost Mgmt Plan<br>Schedule Mgmt Plan<br>Quality Mgmt Plan<br>Project Documents<br>Environmental Factors<br>Process Assets | **Identify Risks** | Risk register |
| Risk Register<br>Risk Mgmt Plan<br>Scope Statement<br>Process Assets | **Perform Qualitative Risk Analysis** | Risk register updates |
| Risk Register<br>Risk Mgmt Plan<br>Cost Mgmt Plan<br>Schedule Mgmt Plan<br>Process Assets | **Perform Quantitative Risk Analysis** | Risk register updates |
| Risk Register<br>Risk Mgmt Plan | **Plan Risk Responses** | Risk register updates<br>Risk related<br>  contract decisions<br>Project Mgmt Plan updates<br>Document updates |

Before you can create the *risk management plan* you must have access to the project scope statement, the schedule, the cost management plan, the communications management plan, and the enterprise and organizational assets. The risk management plan is a key input to the risk register.

A sample *Risk Management Plan* is shown in Figure 8.11 for the PMA web project case study.

---

**Risk Management Plan**

Project Title: **PMA Website**   Version: **1.2**   Date: **4-15-2011**

**Methods and Approaches:**
1. The PMI methodology and best practices will be followed for risk management, including the adoption of identifying, quantifying, identifying responses, and monitoring and controlling risks.
2. The team will use an Agile approach to reduce risk by breaking the project into small modules and iterating, with each iteration each lasting only a week.
3. Escalation of risk to senior management shall occur promptly.

**Tools and Techniques:**
Risks will be classified in the Risk Breakdown Structure (RBS), which is illustrated in the Risk Categories section below. Techniques used to identify risks will include: Brainstorming, risk auditing, the Delphi technique, interviewing experts, and survey of like projects.

**Risk Categories:**
From our experience with similar projects, we have identified the following categories of risks:

| Category | Risks |
|---|---|
| Schedule | Tight Schedule, Scope Creep, Poor Estimation |
| Resource | |
| Communication | Communication skills, Previous Experience |
| Budget | |
| Technical | Software quality and browser compatibility risks |

**Stakeholder Risk Tolerance:**
High tolerance=3; medium=2; and low tolerance=1

| Issue | Sponsors | Project Manager | Team Members |
|---|---|---|---|
| Performance | 1 | 0 | 1 |
| Budget | 1 | 1 | 1 |
| Schedule | 2 | 0 | 1 |

**Definitions of Probability:**
Fuzzy labels of High (H), Medium (M) and Low (L) will be used. High will imply risks above 80%, Medium will be risks at 40% to 80% and Low will be risks below 40%.

**Risk Management Funding and Contingency:**
Upon completion of risk analysis and contingency planning, contingency funding may be requested. If the project risk is high, we will request senior management to set aside management reserve as well. We plan to set aside a 5% contingency for budget risks and 10% for schedule risks. The technical risks are assumed to be low.

**Frequency and Timing:**
Risk Analysis will be conducted every week at the project team meeting.

---

Figure 8.11: *Risk Management Plan* for the PMA case.

## Risk Register

The *Risk Register* plays a key role in the risk management planning process. Creating the *risk register* is the first step in the process, and evolves as more activities are completed. During the *Identify Risks* and *Quantify Risks* processes, the risk register might simply consist of the worksheet, as in Table 8.15:

Table 8.15: *Risk Identification* for the PMA case.

| Risk ID | Risk | Rating (H, M, L) |
|---------|------|------------------|
| 1 | Technical Risk: Lack of WordPress programming knowledge | M |
| 2 | Communication Risk: Various stakeholders geographically separated. | H |

**Risk Register Updates**

The risk register is updated as the risk management activities evolve. The register is updated as plans for dealing with the identified risks emerge. These typically involve the following approaches: Prevent/Avoid the risk, Transfer the risk, Mitigate the risk, or Accept the risk, i.e., absorb the risk and do nothing for now, just monitor the situation. Once the strategy for dealing with the risks is assigned, Table 8.16 can be updated as follows:

Table 8.16: *Risk Identification Updates* for the PMA case.

| Risk ID | Risk | Rating (H, M, L) | Response |
|---------|------|------------------|----------|
| 1 | Technical Risk: Lack of WordPress programming knowledge | M | Training will be provided to mitigate risk. |
| 2 | Communication Risk: Various stakeholders geographically separated. | H | Accept risk–we are unable to do anything about this. Mitigate by providing virtual teaming skills |

The technical aspects of risk management are described in chapter 22–Risk.

### 8.5.2 Identify Risks

The goal of this process is simply to identify risks and add them to risk register. A preliminary list of risks can be derived from existing resources: experience with comparable projects, brainstorming, or a formal search though a knowledge-base from historical projects.

As with cost estimation, we can identify risks using either a top-down or bottom-up approach. Early in the project life cycle, we capture risks using top-down risk identification. The advantage of the top-down approach is that it is conducted early in the planning process, and the team has time to change the scope of the project to mitigate or eliminate risks. This technique is called *Risk Prevention*, and mitigating risks early on can make the project significantly less costly.

We recommend the Post-It® approach to risk identification: Provide each member of the project team Post-It® notes and ask them to write down all the risks they can come up with. They should be encouraged to briefly document the risk, and add attributes such as: Risk Category (e.g., Technical, Scope, Communication); and Project Impact (e.g., Cost, Schedule). The risks are then entered into the *Risk Register*, which at this stage may simply appear as:

1. Lack of programming knowledge. Risk Category: Technical

2. Some team members are geographically separated. Risk Category: Communication

There are many popular methods to help identify risks:

- *Historical databases* and *Lessons learned:* These are typically recorded in a debriefing at the end of projects. They identify "What worked?" and "What did not work?" The former is a good source for the under-appreciated *good risks*, while the latter is a source for threats (bad risks).

    For example, on the PMA project we identified a good risk called "Expedite purchase of new hardware and software." The team identified this as a way to enhance both the cost and schedule.

- *Checklists:* These provide a useful starting point in risk identification.[18] Typically, a checklist will stimulate the team to come up with useful ideas.

    Checklists have received a huge boost in popularity, thanks to a best-seller entitled *The Checklist Manifesto* by Dr. Atul Gawande.[3][11]

- *Risk Breakdown Structure (RBS):* The RBS is a tool to classify risks according to their category, e.g., technical, scope, etc. Several RBS templates are available in the public domain and can be used as a starting point.

---

[18] Of course, anything missing from the checklist is also a risk!

Table 8.17: Definition of of *impact* of risks for the PMA case.

| Value | Definition | Examples |
|---|---|---|
| 1 | Unacceptable, or Catastrophic Risk: | The system is compromised, and data is visible to hackers. |
| 3 | Minor Damage, or Acceptable Risk: | Project completion date slips by a week. Delay in receiving hardware by a week. |

- *Cause and Effect Diagrams:* These are also called Ishikawa diagrams, or Fishbone diagrams. They provide a useful method of identifying and classifying risks, as well as the responses. This tool is described in Chapter 19—Quality.

### 8.5.3 Perform Qualitative Risk Analysis

In this process we assesses the risks listed in the risk register and prioritize them *qualitatively*. For each risk, this requires determining the likelihood that the risk will occur, and the impact upon the project objectives.

Our preferred approach is to use a scale from 1-5, for both the likelihood and the impact.[19] The risks are then plotted on a grid. The advantage of using a 1-5 scale is that it provides useful bands in the grid—see Figure 22.1. The project manager needs to establish agreed-upon definitions for both the likelihood and the impact. Examples help to clarify categories, such as those shown in Table 8.17 for the PMA project.

At this point in the PMA project we could extend the Post-It® approach as follows: The risks the team identified earlier using Post-It notes can now be placed on a flip chart to create the likelihood/impact chart. The results are then transferred into the risk register.

### 8.5.4 Perform Quantitative Risk Analysis

This process provides a numerical, or quantitative, estimate of the impact of the risks under discussion. The impact is usually measured in dollars, although the same techniques can be used for schedule slippages.

For example, we might be interested in identifying a contingency budget reserve for the risks associated with the Lack of Programming Knowledge on the PMA project. We would perform the quantitative risk analysis calculations as follows:

[19] We prefer to use the term *likelihood* rather than probability. Using the term probability tempts people to assign numbers such as 73% which, at this stage, are meaningless.

| Risk: | Probability | Impact |
|---|---|---|
| Lack of Programming Knowledge: | 50% | $10,000 |

If the risk occurs, the estimated contingency fund that must be set aside to pay someone to finish the project is:

$$Contingency\ Fund = 0.5 * \$10,000 = \$5,000. \quad (8.1)$$

### 8.5.5 Plan Risk Responses

In this process we develop a plan for what to do if the risk actually occurs. We attempt to reduce the impact of the risk by planning a smart response. Risk responses typically fall in the categories shown in Table 8.18:

Table 8.18: Risk response categories.

| Risk Response | How |
|---|---|
| Prevent | Changing the scope of the project. |
| Mitigate | Reducing the likelihood or impact., Or both! |
| Transfer | Passing the risk on to a third party. |
| Accept | Do nothing. Set aside a budget to deal with the risk. |

## 8.6 The Sub-Plans

Here we cover the sub-plans that make up the final pieces of the Project Management Plan: Quality, HR, Communications, and Procurement.

### 8.6.1 Plan Quality

> **The quality, not the longevity, of one's life is what is important.**
>
> *Martin Luther King, Jr.*

The output of the *Plan Quality* process is the *Quality Management Plan*, which describes how the quality requirements for the project will be met. The definition is:

## 8.6. The Sub-Plans

*Plan Quality is the process for identifying quality requirements and standards, and documenting how to demonstrate compliance.*

The inputs and outputs, are listed in Table 8.19.

Table 8.19: The *Plan Quality* inputs and outputs.

| Inputs | Outputs |
| --- | --- |
| Scope Baseline | Quality management plan |
| Stakeholder Register | Quality metrics |
| Cost Performance Baseline | Quality checklists |
| Schedule Baseline | Process Improvement Plan |
| Risk Register | Document Updates |
| Environmental Factors | |
| Process Assets | |

### Quality Management Plan

In order to create a *Quality Management Plan*, you must have completed the all of the input documents listed in Table 8.19. This plan is used in all subsequent quality management processes and is also consulted when creating the *Project Management Plan*.

As an example, we present a sample quality management plan for the PMA project, which is shown in Figure 8.12.

### Quality Metrics

*Quality Metrics* provide specific measurements of project attributes, and are identified in the *Plan Quality* process. Every industry has its own metrics, e.g., many companies have "customer satisfaction" metrics that are tracked over time.

For service-oriented applications, such as call-centers, metrics might include the time to answer the call, average time to satisfy the customer, percent of 'very satisfied' customers, etc. For software industries, metrics of interest are: Software code defects per thousand lines; mean time to failure; mean time to repair; and test set coverage.

As an example, for the PMA website project, response time was identified as a key metric. Response times to a user request for information was demanded to be less

## 8. PLANNING PROCESS GROUP

---

**QUALITY MANAGEMENT PLAN FOR THE PMA PROJECT**

**A. Overview:**
This plan describes the information required to effectively manage PMA project quality from planning through delivery. It defines quality policies, procedures, roles, responsibilities and the authorities involved.

**B. Quality Responsibilities and Quality Roles:**
    Design and User Interface
        Test User Interface specification – Design Team
    Development Environment
        Unit Testing – Development Team
        Functional testing – Test Team
    Staging Environment
        Testing – Test Team
        Compliance Testing – End User including an Impaired End User
        Performance Testing – Performance Tester
        Execute Training Exercised– Trainers, End Users
    Production
        Production Testing – Test Team

**C. Quality Assurance Approach:**
Validate: Requirements & functionality of the system; the transition from the requirements specifications to functional & detail designs; and the application is correct and accurate. Adhere to DoJ ADA Compliance Requirements. Customer satisfaction will be measured by industry standard usability practices.

**D. Quality Control Approach:**
The Test Plan will describe the processes, methods, tools and techniques to be used in performing quality control, specifically supporting the following objectives:
  Metrics:       Identify the items that should be targeted for testing.
  Types:        Outlines the testing types that will be executed.
  Resources:   Identifies the required resources and estimates test efforts.
  Deliverables:  Lists the deliverable elements of the test project.

**E. Quality Improvement Approach:**
Proactively identify approaches to improve processes, and techniques, and provide training to all resources.

**F. Tools, Environment and Interfaces:**
List tools, tool description, and industry recognized benchmarks.

**G. Quality Reporting Plan**
The communication matrix will identify all stakeholders, who will be informed continually about all aspects of quality and performance.

---

Figure 8.12: PMA Quality Management Plan.

than 2 seconds for all minor requests, and less than 5 seconds for major database-oriented requests. These are examples of specific, measurable attributes of the web site, and make excellent metrics.[20]

**Quality Checklists**

Quality is enhanced if *Quality Checklists* are used to ensure that the project team produces all documents and does not miss a process. Well-designed checklists actually simplify the project manager's life. For example, for a small project full-scale plans may not be required in all areas. In that case, a checklist can function as a reminder that all issues have been covered without writing a long bureaucratic plan.

Organizational process assets will typically include checklists that can be tailored for the current project. Some examples of checklist items are listed below. For each item, the project manager can simply indicate whether the issue has been considered with a 'Yes' or 'No', and a brief comment.

- Are project management activities identified for the project?

- Do we have measurable and prioritized goals for managing the quality of the products?

- Have the following been considered: Functionality, reliability, maintainability, and usability?

- Has the project team received training in project management, quality management, and risk analysis?

### 8.6.2 Develop Human Resources (HR) Plan

**The human mind is our fundamental resource.**

*John F. Kennedy*

Human Resources (HR) Management deals with processes for organizing, managing, and leading the project team. There is one key output from this process: The HR Plan. However, it is a comprehensive document made up of several subsidiary plans, including such items as: Roles and Responsibilities; Project Organization; and Staffing Management.

[20] Of course, there is an issue here: Does fast response make the web site friendly? Obviously not. More metrics would be needed to measure "user friendly,"

## 8. Planning Process Group

The HR Plan identifies the people with the necessary skills to complete the activities, and documents their roles and responsibilities. This is often accomplished with a project organization chart. The staffing plan includes timetables for staff acquisition and release; identifies any training needs, or team building strategies; plans for recognition and rewards; and covers compliance considerations, and safety issues.

The inputs and outputs to the *Develop HR Plan* process are shown in Table 8.20.

Table 8.20: The *Develop HR Plan* inputs and outputs

| Inputs | Outputs |
| --- | --- |
| Activity Resource Requirements | HR Plan |
| Environmental Factors | |
| Process Assets | |

We present a sample *Organizational Chart* for the PMA project in Figure 8.13. We also present a sample *HR Management Plan* in Figure 8.14.

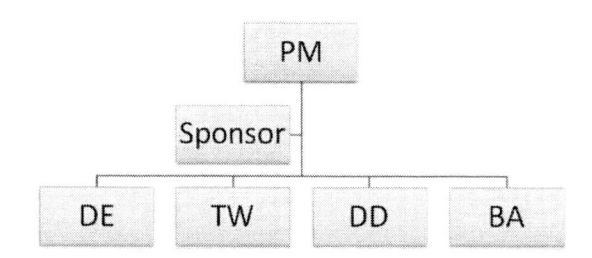

Figure 8.13: The organizational chart for the PMA project.

### 8.6.3 Plan Communications

> **The single biggest problem in communication is the illusion that it has taken place.**
>
> *George Bernard Shaw*

Project communication is essential for successful project management. Communication ensures timely and appropriate generation, collection, distribution, storage, retrieval, and disposition of project information. The project manager must

## 8.6. The Sub-Plans

---

**HUMAN RESOURCES PLAN.**

**ROLES AND RESPONSIBILITIES**
The Project Manager (PM) is responsible for the success of the PMA Website project. The PM must authorize and approve all project expenditures and communicate with the stakeholders. The team members will be responsible for timely execution of the assigned activities and the quality their work (the activities) should meet established acceptability criteria.
The Design Specialist (DS) is responsible for the design specification & gathering coding requirements.
The Technical Writer (TW) is responsible for training users and the sponsoring IT staff in how to maintain the website. The TW will produce the training manuals, and document configuration changes to the software.
The Database Developer (DD) will implement the backend database connections to the website and will design and build the data tables. The DD must be proficient in PHP and MySQL.
The Business Analyst (BA) is responsible for: Gathering website requirements; building the test cases; and the test plan.
**ORGANIZATIONAL STRUCTURE**
STAFF ACQUISITION
The project staff will consist entirely of internal resources. No procurement or contracting will be performed. The PM will identify and assign resources in accordance with the organization structure.
STAFF RELEASE
The project staff will be released from the project upon completion and all accounts will be disabled according to information assurance procedures.
TRAINING
Training will be scheduled during the implementation phase and will be documented in the project schedule.
PERFORMANCE REVIEWS
The Project manager will review each team member's assigned work activities at the onset of the project and communicate all expectations of work to be performed. A bonus of 15% of the project cost will be distributed as bonus to recognize team member performance for timely completion of all deliverables within the quality benchmarks.
REGULATION AND POLICY COMPLIANCE
The Department of Justice, American Disabilities Act, will be strictly adhered to. This will require effort in human resources for both development and testing.

---

Figure 8.14: HR Plan for the PMA case.

communicate effectively with internal and external stakeholders, and with personnel from different cultural and organizational backgrounds. There is only one process: *Plan Communications*, which has one deliverable: The *Communications Management Plan*.

The inputs and outputs to the *Plan Communications* process are shown in Table 8.21.

## 8. Planning Process Group

Table 8.21: The *Plan Communication* inputs and outputs.

| Inputs | Outputs |
|---|---|
| Stakeholder Register | Communications Management Plan |
| Stakeholder Strategy | Document Updates |
| Environmental Factors | |
| Process Assets | |

The communications management plan describes the communication needs of the project, including audiences, messages, methods, and other relevant information. It also defines the approach to be used for those communications. Typical information includes: The sender; the messages to be communicated, and the frequency with which they will be distributed; the audience; and the media or method to be used.

A sample communication management plan for the PMA project is illustrated in Table 8.22.

Table 8.22: The PMA *Communication Management Plan*.

| Message | Description | Audience | Method | Frequency | Sender |
|---|---|---|---|---|---|
| Kickoff Meeting | Introduce team Review goals objectives & processes | Sponsor Project Team Stakeholders Sponsor | Video Conf. | Once | PM |
| Team Meetings | Review project status | Project Team | Conf. Call | Weekly | PM |
| Technical Meetings | Status of deliverables | Project Staff | Conf. Call | Weekly, or as required | Project Lead |
| Monthly Project Status Meetings | Report status of project & technical deliverables | Customer Stakeholders PMO Staff Upper Mgmt | Face to Face | Monthly | PM |

The project manager may want to tailor the above plan by adding communication guidelines, including the reason for the communication. For example:

> *Kick Off Meeting.* This is an important meeting, and the objective is to get to know the stakeholders and communicate the project objectives.

*Meeting Agenda.* The Agenda will be distributed two days ahead of the meeting, and will specify the presenter for each subject, along with a time limit to prevent meeting overruns. Meeting minutes will be recorded by a team member on a rotating basis, and emailed to all members who attended the meeting within 48 hours.

### 8.6.4 Plan Procurements

> **The universe never did make sense;**
> **I suspect it was built on government contract.**
>
> *Robert A. Heinlein*

Procurement planning is all about contracts and their administration. This is a highly specialized area and a good example of the diverse knowledge required by a project manager. The project manager does not need to know all the legal details, but does need an understanding of the risks of the various contract types (covered in Chapter 23—Procurement). Also, a project manager needs to pay special attention to what is to be delivered by whom, which is detailed in the Statement of Work (SOW), which is the most important contractual document.

There is only one process: *Plan Procurements.*

The important output from the *Plan Procurements* process is the *Procurement Management Plan*, which typically includes the following items of information: contract type, statement of work, procurement role and responsibility, procurement documents, seller lists, selection criteria, bonding and insurance requirements, and constraints and assumptions. The outputs are shown in Table 8.23

The PMA case study does not have any procurement–all the project work is done with internal resources. This is an example where the item could be checked off with no further work required.

## 8. Planning Process Group

Table 8.23: *Plan Procurements* Inputs and Outputs

| Inputs | Process | Outputs |
|---|---|---|
| Scope Baseline | **Plan** | Procurement Mgmt Plan |
| Requirements Doc. | **Procurement** | Procurement SOW |
| Teaming Agreements | **Management** | Make-or-buy decisions |
| Risk Register | | Procurement documents |
| Risk-related contract decisions | | Source selection criteria |
| | | Change Requests |
| Activity Resource Reqs. | | |
| Schedule | | |
| Activity Cost Estimates | | |
| Cost Perf. Baseline | | |
| Environmental Factors | | |
| Process Assets | | |

# CHAPTER 9

# EXECUTING PROCESS GROUP

**Everything should be made as simple as possible, but not simpler.**

*Albert Einstein*

The *Executing Processes Group* is where you actually implement the project.[1] A summary of the executing processes is given in Figure 9.1, which shows that besides actually executing the project, the bulk of the work for the project manager is to manage:

- *People and resources:* Acquire, develop and manage the project team.

- *Communications:* Distribute information and manage the expectations of the stakeholders.

- *Changes:* Manage updates to project documents through change requests.

- *Quality:* Audit the quality requirements and quality control measurements.

- *Procurements:* Evaluate subcontractors and award contracts.

[1] Phew, finally!

# 9. EXECUTING PROCESS GROUP

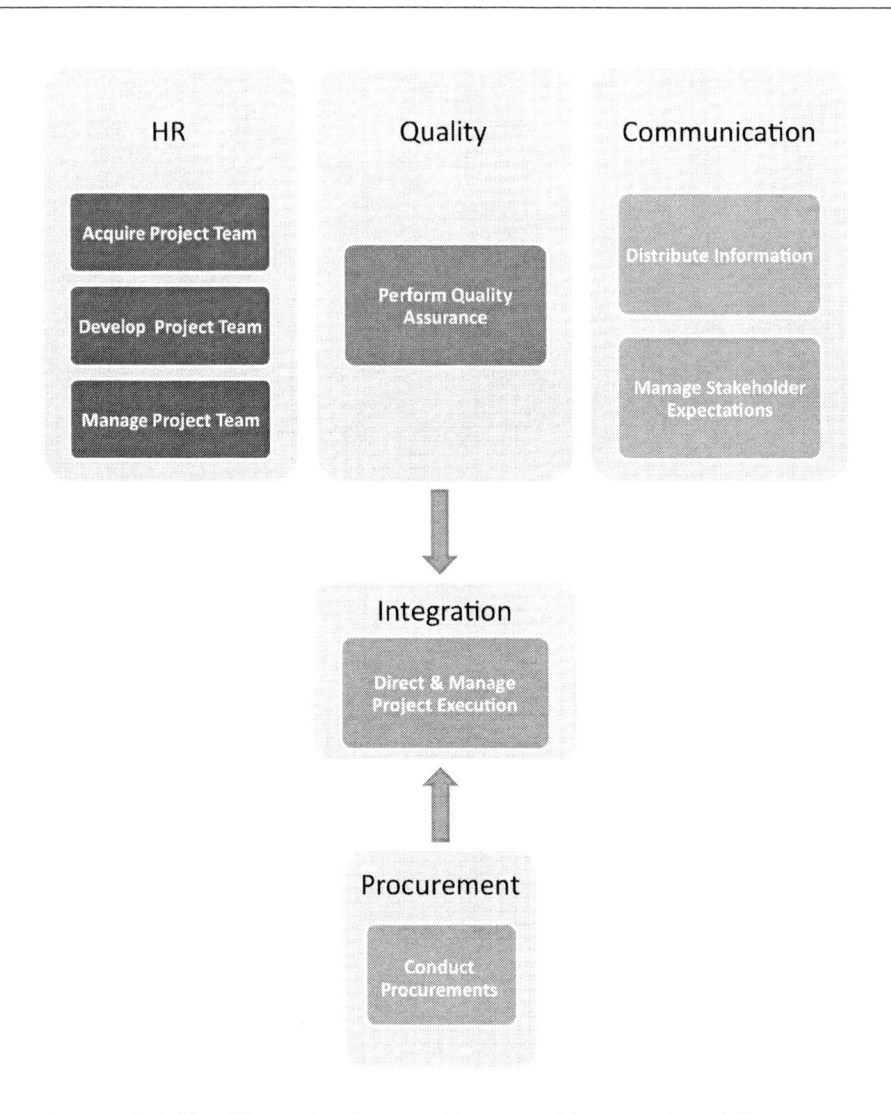

Figure 9.1: The *Executing Process Group* and its associated *Processes*.

## 9.1 Direct and Manage Project Execution

> **We cannot direct the wind, but we can adjust the sails.**
>
> *Unknown*

The key process in the *executing* process group is *Direct and Manage Project Exe-

*cution.* The primary inputs are from the *project management plan* and the outputs are the actual project deliverables. A vitally important output is the project performance information: whether the project spending is on track, and whether the project is on schedule.

The inputs to and outputs from the *Direct and Manage Project Execution* process are shown in Table 9.1.

Table 9.1: The *Direct and Manage Project Execution* process inputs and outputs.

| Inputs | Outputs |
| --- | --- |
| Project management plan | **Deliverables** |
| Approved Change Requests | Work performance information |
| Environmental factors | Change Requests |
| Organizational assets | Project Mgmt Plan updates |
|  | Document Updates |

## 9.2 Perform Quality Assurance

> **Excellence, then, is not an act but a habit.**
>
> *Will Durant*

Many organizations use the term quality assurance to describe the activities that are undertaken to ensure quality results. The *Perform Quality Assurance* process therefore deals with auditing the quality of deliverables and analyzing the results from quality control measurements. The goal is to ensure that the project meets all appropriate standards.[2]

Quality Assurance (QA) is typically conducted through a series of audits, and what results from the audit is a description of good practices to share, deficiencies or defects, and areas for improvement. This generally results in change requests and updates to project documents.[3]

The inputs to and outputs from the *Perform Quality Assurance* process are shown in Table 9.2.

As an example, a QA audit for the PMA case might go as follows: The motivation for the audit is that the PMA project manager is concerned that the quality standards in place for the website under development might result in a product that is

[2] Essentially, this process is an audit of the quality standards and processes themselves. Remember also that quality assurance covers every stage of project development, not just the implementation phase.

[3] Quality control is technically different from quality assurance. Quality control involves monitoring project results, while quality assurance is about compliance to the customer's needs. It is best to keep the two terms separate, as they have very specific definitions.

Table 9.2: The *Perform Quality Assurance* process inputs and outputs.

| Inputs | Outputs |
|---|---|
| Project management plan | QA Change Requests |
| Quality metrics | Areas for Improvement |
| Quality control measurements | Organizational Process Updates |
| Information on completed Deliverables | Updates to project documents |

vulnerable to cyber-security threats. Therefore, with the assistance of the QA team, a quality audit was conducted. The results are presented in Table 9.3:

Table 9.3: PMA Quality Assurance Audit Results

| QUALITY ASSURANCE AUDIT ||| 
|---|---|---|
| ☐ Project | ☐ Project processes | ☐ Project documents |
| ☐ Product | ☐ Organizational Policies | ☐ Quality Management Plan |

As a consequence of the audit, quality assurance updates were made to the organizational processes and the project management plan. Also, areas for improvement were suggested:

**Software Design:** Focus on best practices to ensure that design specification produces secure website code.

**Hosting Environment:** Ensure that the website hosting site is secure.

**Software Development Life cycle:** Introduce software quality assurance steps, including maintenance recommendations.

**Personnel:** Schedule constraints on programmers will be watched. Training will be provided to ensure that software used is properly configured and that the product is secure.

**Process:** A layered system of security will be introduced into the existing plan.

## 9.3 Acquire Project Team

**Talent wins games, but teamwork and intelligence wins championships.**

*Michael Jordan*

When the project schedule was developed, a resource plan was created to ensure that adequate staff will be available to perform all required activities. During the execution phase, the project manager must identify the required resources and ensure that they are available, a process known as *Acquire Project Team*.

For example, the project manager for the PMA case study consulted the resource plan, which contained information about team skills, an assessment of their capabilities, roles and responsibilities, and their availability. Using this information, the project manager completed the project *staffing assignment* form shown in Table 9.4:

Table 9.4: PMA Staffing Assignments

| Calendar | Resource | Committment |
|---|---|---|
| Quarter 1, 2012 | Project Manager | 1 – Full time |
| Quarter 2, 2012 | Business Analyst | 2 – Half time |
| Quarter 3, 2012 | Programmer | 2 – Half time, 1 – Full time |

Like many software scheduling systems, Microsoft Project supports Resource Calendars. The above information could be entered into such a tool as soon as the project staffing assignments have been agreed to by the functional managers and the commitment information is available.

## 9.4 Develop Project Team

> **A person will sometimes devote all his life to the development of one part of his body — the wishbone.**
>
> *Robert Frost*

Some of the assigned staff may not have the required technical skills, and so the project manager is responsible for providing training.[4]

Once the team is assigned, the job of the project manager is to develop it. This is accomplished in the *Develop Project Team* process, where the goal is to improve the competency of the various individual team members and to generate team cohesion. The inputs and outputs for the *Develop Project Team* process are shown in Table 9.5.

[4] Did you squirrel away training funds for this eventuality? You didn't assume that all of the staff would be exactly what you needed, did you?

## 9. Executing Process Group

Table 9.5: The *Develop Project Team* process inputs and outputs.

| Inputs | Outputs |
|---|---|
| Project staff assignments | Team performance assessments |
| Project Mgmt Plan | Environmental factors updates |
| Resource Calendars | |

Typical examples for the team directory, operating agreement, and performance assessment are shown in Tables 9.6, 9.7, and 9.8. Each team member should complete all of these forms.

Table 9.6: PMA Team Directory

| | |
|---|---|
| **Name:** | Victor King |
| **Role:** | Project Manager |
| **Contact Information:** | 617-555-1212 |
| | vking@somewhere.com |
| **Name:** | Mary Contrary |
| **Role:** | Systems Analyst |
| **Contact Information:** | 780-111-1212 |
| | mcontrary@somewhere.com |
| **Name:** | Bruce Lee |
| **Role:** | Web Programmer |
| **Contact Information:** | 978-555-1212 |
| | blee@somewhere.com |
| **Name:** | Maya Banker |
| **Role:** | Cost Analyst |
| **Contact Information:** | 977-555-1212 |
| | blee@somewhere.com |

Table 9.7: PMA Team Operating Agreement

| | |
|---|---|
| **Purpose:** | This team operating agreement provides ground rules to help the project team work productively together. Any updates to this agreement will be discussed by the project team members after obtaining consent from all participants. |
| **Guidelines:** | Identify guidelines such as how the project team members will report status at each team meeting.<br>Frequency of team meetings including location of meetings<br>The preferred platform for meeting as well as the storage medium for sharing documents<br>Procedure for managing issues and change requests<br>Procedure for reviewing action items and updating them at each meeting<br>What is the responsibility of each team member in case they miss a meeting |
| **Communication & Decision Making:** | Each team member will be encouraged to bring their area of expertise to the table and communication will be encouraged. All team members will be empowered to make decisions. Also any voting procedures will be covered here to resolve a conflict. |

Table 9.8: PMA Team Performance Assessment

| | |
|---|---|
| **Technical Performance:** | Rated as *Meets Expectations* or *Needs Improvement*.<br>Example: Programmers: Need Improvement. They do not have experience with WordPress programming and customization. |
| **Interpersonal Skills:** | Rated as *Meets Expectations* or *Needs Improvement*.<br>Example: The team members will benefit from some exposure to communication, collaboration, and conflict resolution. |
| **Areas for Development:** | *Describe the approach and actions for improvement:*<br>Example: The team will be given half day training in the area of project communication. Programmers will be provided three days worth of training, either online or at a local company, in the areas of WordPress, PHP, and MySQL. |

## 9.5 Manage Project Team

> **As a coach, I play not my eleven best, but my best eleven.**
>
> *Knute Rockne*

Once the project team is developed, the ongoing process of *Manage Project Team* begins. This process deals with tracking each individual team member's performance, providing feedback, and resolving any issues that arise. Updates to project documents need to be made to reflect any changes.

An individual team member's performance assessment should be documented in a form that includes their strengths, weaknesses, areas for development, and actions to be taken. Actions may be required by both the project manager and the team member.

The inputs and outputs to the *Manage Project Team* process are shown in Table 9.9.

Table 9.9: The *Manage Project Team* process inputs and outputs.

| Inputs | Outputs |
| --- | --- |
| Project staff assignments | Environmental factors updates |
| Project Mgmt Plan | Organizational asset updates |
| Team performance assessments | Change requests |
| Performance reports | Project Mgmt Plan updates |
| Organizational assets | |

## 9.6 Distribute Information

**The speed of communications is wondrous to behold. It is also true that speed can multiply the distribution of information that we know to be untrue.**

*Edward R. Murrow*

*Distribute Information* is where information is sent to all stakeholders on a regular, planned basis. The process inputs and outputs are shown in Table 9.10.

Table 9.10: The *Distribute Information* process inputs and outputs.

| Inputs | Outputs |
| --- | --- |
| Project Mgmt Plan | Organizational asset updates |
| Performance reports | |
| Organizational assets | |

## 9.7 Manage Stakeholder Expectations

> **Oft expectation fails, and most oft there where most it promises; and oft it hits, where hope is coldest; and despair most sits.**
>
> *William Shakespeare*

*Manage Stakeholder Expectations* deals with the process of communicating with both internal and external stakeholders. The project manager must keep stakeholders informed about project progress and issues that arise. What comes out of these efforts are changes in the implementation which require updates to documentation.

The inputs and outputs for *Manage Stakeholder Expectations* are shown in Table 9.11.

Table 9.11: The *Manage Stakeholder Expectations* process inputs and outputs.

| Inputs | Outputs |
| --- | --- |
| Stakeholder Register | Asset updates |
| Stakeholder Mgmt Strategy | Work performance information |
| Project Mgmt Plan | Change Requests |
| Issue Log | Project Mgmt Plan updates |
| Change Log | Document Updates |
| Organizational Assets | |

A *Stakeholders Issues Log* can be used to document communications from stakeholders, and an example of for the PMA case is given in Table 9.12.

Table 9.12: The PMA *Stakeholders' Issues Log*.

| | |
|---|---|
| Issue # | 103 |
| Date Reported: | 02/10/2012 |
| Reported By: | Bruce Lee, Programmer. |
| Issue Description: | Web site assets such as videos and images not provided to project team in a timely manner. |
| Ranking & Classification: | High: Impacts the critical path. Programming phase concludes in one week and we need access to the media urgently. |
| Impact to Project: | Delay of project schedule. |
| Resource Assigned To: Assignment: | Systems Analyst, Mary Contrary. Investigation & Resolution |
| Current Status: Date Resolved: | Team plans to put some placeholder graphics and media as an intermediate step. It may require redesign of website if the media quantity is either less or more than we anticipate Open. We hope to have this issue resolved by 02/17/2012 |
| Resolution, Comments | Systems analyst Mary Contrary has been assigned to work with the sponsor to get the required media urgently. If sponsor does not respond within three days, the Project Manager will escalate this issue. |

## 9.8 Conduct Procurements

> **I'm not going to buy my kids an encyclopedia.
> Let them walk to school like I did.**
>
> *Yogi Berra*

This final *executing* process is *Conduct Procurements*, which deals with obtaining seller responses, selecting a seller, and awarding a contract. The inputs and outputs are presented in Table 9.13.

## 9.8. Conduct Procurements

Table 9.13: *Conduct Procurements* Inputs and Outputs.

| Input | Output |
| --- | --- |
| Project management plan | **Selected sellers** |
| Procurement documents | **Procurement Contract award** |
| Source selection criteria | Resource calendars |
| Qualified seller list | Change requests |
| Seller proposals | Project Mgmt Plan updates |
| Project documents | Project document updates |
| Make or buy decisions | |
| Teaming agreements | |
| Organization assets | |

# CHAPTER 10

# MONITORING AND CONTROLLING

**Kirk:** You're not exactly catching us at our best.
**Spock:** That much is certain.

*Star Trek IV*

In the *Monitoring and Controlling* process group, the project's deliverables are reviewed, which means they are compared to the established baselines. The project manager monitors the big three: cost, schedule, and scope. However, the project manager must also continually check the status of risks and review quality.[1]

An important part of the *Monitoring and Controlling* process group is the management of changes. Each time a change is proposed, the project team should revisit all related documents, which is accomplished in the *Perform Integrated Change Control* process.

If there are significant variances from the plan, the project manager must take immediate corrective action, following the established change control process. The important question, as always, is: Are the required changes refinements or additions? Changes are submitted to the change control board to determine if they are to be implemented or not.

Monitoring and controlling also involves forecasting. For example, using earned value analysis techniques, the project manager can estimate a revised cost and

[1] Questions to ask here include: How is the project progressing against objectives? Milestones? Schedule? Budget?

# 10. MONITORING AND CONTROLLING

schedule for completing the project. The work in the monitoring and controlling processes includes:

Validate and Verify Deliverables.
Measure deliverables against the cost and schedule baselines
Determine Variances and return to cost and schedule
Respond to threats and opportunities
Manage changes through established change control procedures
Leverage tools and techniques such as Earned Value
Monitor and control procurements and sub-contractors
Use Configuration Management and Integrated Change Control systems

A summary of the processes in this group are given in Figure 10.1.

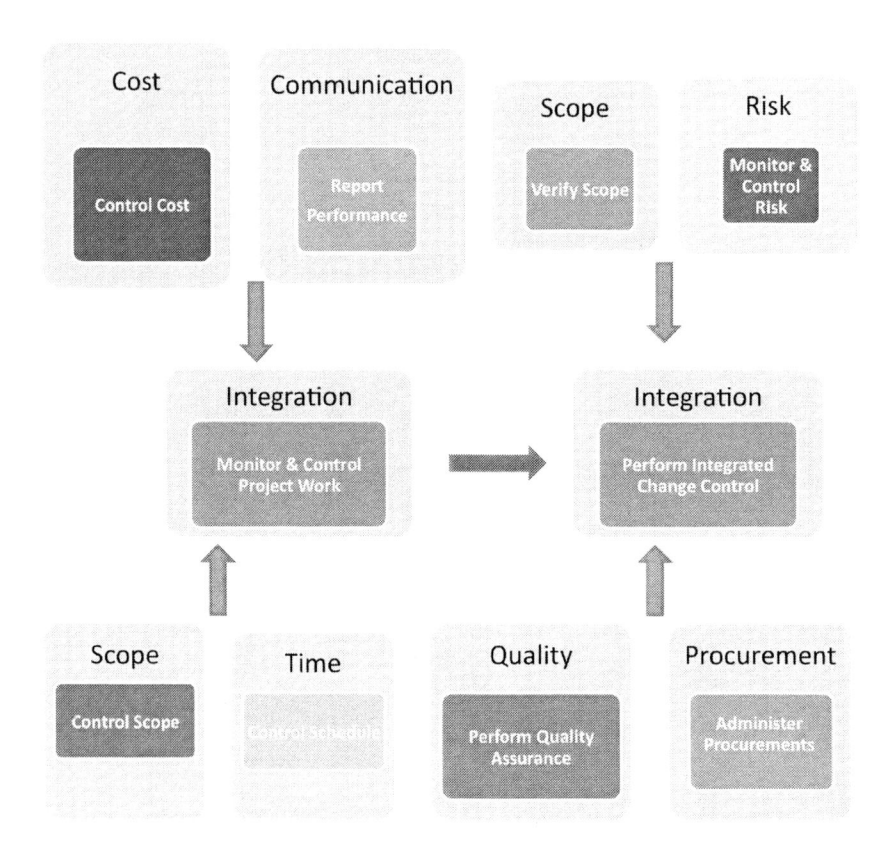

Figure 10.1: The *Monitoring and Control* process groups and the associated *Processes*.

## 10.1 Monitor and Control Project Work

**If everything seems under control, you're just not going fast enough.**

*Mario Andretti*

The *Monitor and Control Project Work* process is where the tracking, reviewing, and regulation of progress occurs. This involves determining the status of the project, which is documented in the status reports. These reports are analyzed to determine actual vs. planned progress, and if required, revised forecasts of the cost and schedule are generated.

A common theme throughout the monitor and controlling process is the tracking of the scope, cost, and schedule, and reporting on the performance, which is illustrated in Figure 10.2. The inputs and outputs to *Monitor and Control Project Work* are shown in Table 10.1.

Figure 10.2: Monitoring and controlling project work is about tracking, reviewing, and regulating project progress.

Table 10.1: The *Monitor and Control Project Work* inputs and outputs

| Inputs | Outputs |
| --- | --- |
| Project Mgmt Plan | Change Requests |
| Performance Reports | Project Mgmt Plan updates |
| Environmental Factors | Document updates |
| Process Assets | |

## 10.2 Perform Integrated Change Control

> **Change is inevitable....except from vending machines.**
>
> *Steven Wright*

*Perform Integrated Change Control* is the process that describes how changes are documented, approved, and managed. This is accomplished through a *Change Control System*, CCS, which is summarized in Figure 10.3.

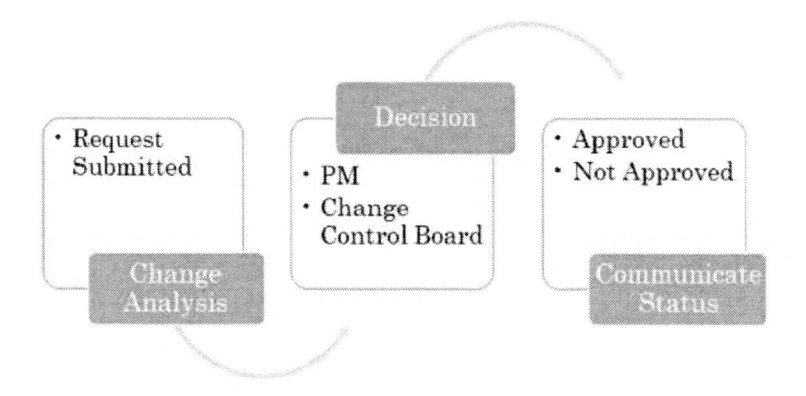

Figure 10.3: The Change Control System (CCS).

*Why do changes occur, and what causes them?*

Changes occur for many reasons and, typically, by stakeholders requesting additional functionality. This results in scope creep, which is the uncontrolled growth of the project.

Even the project team can be responsible for scope creep as they implement improvements to the project by providing features that the sponsor did not request.[2] Sometimes, changes occur due to some unknown risks materializing and these may result in changes to the project cost or schedule.

*What happens when we need to make a change?*

In practice, before changes are made, they need to be approved by the stakeholders. A formal process is required, as documenting the change helps the various stakeholders understand the nature of the request and the potential impact. The

---
[2]This is often called gold plating.

## 10.2. Perform Integrated Change Control

change is documented in a *Change Request*, which is the initiator of the *Perform Integrated Change Control* process.

Usually, a project has a Change Control Board that analyzes the *change request*, and decides whether to approve it or not. [3]

Once the change is approved, the project manager performs a variance analysis, which will document how significant the impact of the approved change is. The project manager will need to revise the scope based on the approved change, and create a new baseline. Once the new baseline is created, all relevant project documentation must be updated, especially cost and schedule baselines.

The definition of the *Perform Integrated Change Control* is:

> *The process of reviewing all change requests, approving and managing changes to the deliverables, organizational process assets, project documents and the project management plan.*

The word "integrated" reminds us that any changes have to be considered from a global project perspective, since even a small change can affect many different areas. Therefore, a change control system is employed to ensure that changes do not result in chaos.

The first requirement for any proposed change is to determine if it is a refinement or an addition. Refinements are desirable, and a natural part of the progressive elaboration process. Additions however, require a totally different attitude. Any proposed change that will add to the scope should be immediately halted, and thoroughly evaluated.

Formally, the group responsible for approving or rejecting a change is the *Change Control Board* (CCB). The stakeholders should be informed of the potential cost and schedule impacts, and in particular, the customer and sponsor, who will have responsibility for the cost and schedule. These constituencies are represented on the CCB.

The inputs and outputs are shown in Table 10.2 and an example of change management in the PMA case is given in Figure 10.4.

---

[3] If the scope change was not documented then it was not requested.

Table 10.2: The *Perform Integrated Change Control* inputs and outputs.

| Input | Output |
|---|---|
| Project management plan | Change request status updates |
| Work performance information | Project Mgmt Plan updates |
| Change Requests | Document updates |
| Environmental Factors | |
| Organizational assets | |

---

**Change Requests**

During the PMA project, changes will be requested through a formal system. A standard *Change Request* document will be prepared, which contains the proposed change; its rationale; and the potential cost and schedule impacts. The process for reviewing potential changes is outlined below.

- Change Request submitted formally using a form.
- Project Manager performs initial triage and studies impact.
- Stakeholders review the proposed change and assessed impacts.
- Change is either accepted, rejected or deferred by CCB.
- All stakeholders are notified.

---

Figure 10.4: The *Change Management Plan* for the PMA web site

## 10.3 Verify Scope

The *Verify Scope* process is where the scope is formally accepted as a completed deliverable. Accepting completed deliverables requires the project team to interact with stakeholders, and have them formally declare that the requested work has been satisfactorily accomplished.[4]

The inputs and outputs are shown in Table 10.3.

Table 10.3: The *Verify Scope* process inputs and outputs.

| Input | Output |
|---|---|
| Project management plan | Accepted deliverables |
| Requirements documentation | Change requests |
| Requirements traceability matrix | Project document updates |
| Validated deliverables | |

[4]Note that the customer's needs and wants were validated previously, so now we are verifying their elaboration in the scope.
In reality, of course, new desires will show up here!

The only tool used to verify scope is inspection: That is, the team determines whether the deliverables meet the acceptance criteria. Inspections are described by other keywords, such as reviews, audits and walks-through. Whichever words are used, stakeholders and sponsors examine the work produced by the team, and indicate if it is satisfactorily completed.

The *Requirements Traceability Matrix* can be used as a baseline to help verify the scope. The *Configuration Management System* (CMS) documents the results of scope verification. For example, the CMS documents project updates, and specifies if the scope has been verified; whether the deliverables were accepted, and how the change requests were processed.

For the PMA case, we present a simple example of the *Scope Verification* process and results in Table 10.4.

Table 10.4: PMA Scope Verification

| ID | Requirement | WBS ID | Verification | Validation |
|----|-------------|--------|--------------|------------|
| 1 | Home Page useful information to members & non-members | 1.2.2<br>1.2.2 | Review of page with Sponsor | Sponsor acceptance |
| 2 | Section to increase social networking capability of BUPMA | 1.3.2.1.7<br>1.3.2.1.8<br>1.3.2.1.10 | Walkthrough | Sponsor acceptance |

## 10.4 Control Scope

The *Control Scope* process is where the scope is controlled, i.e., changes to the scope baseline are carefully managed.

The principle method used to analyze a deliverable is *Variance Analysis*. The team analyzes the deliverables for compliance with customer requirements, while also assessing if they are within the planned cost and schedule. If changes need to be made to the scope baseline, *Change Requests* are generated. Variances between the planned and actual cost and schedule may also require corrective actions, and those too may result in *Change Requests*.

The inputs and outputs to *Control Scope* are shown in Table 10.5.

Table 10.5: The *Control Scope* process inputs and outputs.

| Input | Output |
|---|---|
| Project management plan | Work Performance measurements |
| Work performance information | Organizational assets updates |
| Requirements documentation | Change requests |
| Requirements traceability matrix | Project Mgmt Plan updates |
| Organizational assets | Document updates |

## 10.5 Control Schedule

In the *Control Schedule* process, you monitor the project schedule, producing updated progress reports, which may result in changes to the schedule baseline. The approach is similar to that of the *Control Scope* process, but the focus is on the schedule: Updating changes to the schedule baseline after the impact of the change has been considered by the Change Control Board.

The project manager uses variance analysis (for technical assessment) and performance reviews (for cost and schedule assessment) to determine and report project progress. The project management information system can be used to determine an updated schedule.

Table 10.6: The *Control Schedule* process inputs and outputs

| Input | Output |
|---|---|
| Project management plan | Change requests |
| Project Schedule | Work performance measurements |
| Work performance information | (eg., Update all EV metrics) |
| Scope baseline | Work Performance Metrics |
|  | (e.g., updated SPI) |
|  | WBS and related documentation updated |
|  | Change requests |

For the PMA case study, we illustrate a *Variance Analysis* with a sample report shown in Table 10.7.

Table 10.7: Variance Analysis and Work Performance Results

| Project: | PMA | |
|---|---|---|
| Date: | 05/20/2011 | |
| **Planned: Schedule:** | **Actual Schedule** | **Variance** |
| **Package 1:** 20 out of 47 project deliverable reports, documents expected completed by 4/15 | Only 13 deliverables were completed by 4/15/2011 | |
| Planned Value: $PV = \$4,000$ | Earned Value: $EV = \$3,000$ | Schedule Variance: $SV = -\$1,000$ |
| **Package 2:** First iteration of website scheduled to be completed by 4/15 | Only 80% of the site pages complete | |
| $PV = \$2,500$ | $EV = \$2,000$ | Schedule variance: $SV = -\$500$ |
| Total PV = \$6,500 | Total EV = \$5,000 | Variance: \$1,500 $SPI = 0.77$ **Behind schedule.** |

**Root Cause:**
(#1) One member of the team was on medical leave of absence.
(#2) Detailed Design delayed by team member on a different page

**Planned Response:**
New team member requested to pick up the slack.
All documents will be updated to reflect this change.
Existing team will work extra hours until the new resource is up to speed.

## 10.6 Control Costs

Project costs are monitored in the *Control Cost* process, which involves updating the project budget and managing changes to the cost baseline. The process is similar in nature to the *Control Schedule* process, except the focus here is on costs. Both involve following the flow of events: review of reports and analyze performance data, such from earned value analyses. The inputs and outputs to the *Control Costs* process are shown in Table 10.8

Using tools such as Earned Value Management (EVM), an estimated budget is generated, along with any necessary changes to the the *Project Management Plan*.

For the PMA case study, we illustrate this process with the sample report that was

## 10. Monitoring and Controlling

Table 10.8: The *Control Costs* process inputs and outputs.

| Input | Output |
|---|---|
| Project Mgmt Plan | Work performance measurements |
| Project Funding Requirements | Budget forecasts |
| Work performance information | Organizational assets updates |
| Organizational assets | Change requests |
|  | Project Management Plan updates |
|  | Document updates |

shown in Table10.7. Thisis an example of using one report to cover multiple topics. This is efficient and helps eliminate errors by reducing redundancy.

## 10.7 Perform Quality Control

In the *Perform Quality Control* process, the team monitors the deliverables to assess the performance of the project. Project deliverables are monitored for quality and any technical defects or deviations from planned cost and schedule will necessitate recommendations for corrective action.

The inputs and outputs are shown in Table 10.9.

Table 10.9: The *Perform Quality Control* process inputs and outputs.

| Input | Output |
|---|---|
| Project Mgmt Plan | Quality control measurements |
| Quality metrics | Validated changes |
| Quality checklists | Validated deliverables |
| Work performance measurements | Organizational assets updates |
| Approved Change Requests | Change Requests |
| Deliverables | Project Mgmt Plan updates |
| Organizational assets | Document updates |

In the PMA case study, the project team conducted *Verification and Validation*. The purpose verification was to find defects in documents such as specifications or test cases, but not to fix them. Verification was accomplished through reviews, meetings, inspections, and walks-through.

Validation occurred after verification. Validation was the testing of the functionality of the product, i.e. does the product meet the customers' requirements. The output of the *Verification and Validation* was the *Quality Control Measurements* document, which is shown in Table 10.10.

Table 10.10: PMA Quality Control Measurements.

| Planned Result | Actual Result | Variance |
|---|---|---|
| Page load 3 seconds. | Average Page Load 10 seconds | 7 seconds |
| Link Navigation 5 seconds. | Average Link Navigation 15 seconds | 10 seconds |
| **Root Cause:** | | Slow response time attributed to the hosting provider. |
| **Planned Response:** | | Communicate with hosting company. Contingency: Investigate new hosting company immediately. |

## 10.8 Report Performance

*Report Performance* is a communications process, where the project manager is responsible for collecting and disseminating status reports, forecasts, and technical performance information. The inputs and outputs are shown in Table 10.11.

Table 10.11: The *Report Performance* process inputs and outputs.

| Input | Output |
|---|---|
| Project Mgmt Plan | Performance reports |
| Work performance information | Organizational assets updates |
| Work performance measurements | Change Requests |
| Budget Forecasts | |
| Organizational assets | |

There are two kinds of reports: A *Performance Report* and a *Forecast Report*. Examples of these are given for the PMA case: The performance report is the *Earned Value Status Report*, which is shown in Figure 10.5. The *Forecast Report* for the PMA case is a calculation of the new *Estimate at Completion*, which is shown in Figure 10.6.

10. MONITORING AND CONTROLLING

The initial budget for the PMA project was estimated at $12,500. The reports show we have a revised forecast for the final cost of $12,900. The project is over budget, as indicated by the $CPI = 0.97$.

**EARNED VALUE STATUS REPORT**

Project Title: BUPMA    Date Prepared: 4/20/

Budget at Completion (BAC): $ 12,500.00    Overall Status: Almost on budget, behind schedule

|  | Current Reporting Period ($) | Cumulative ($) | Past Period Cum |
|---|---|---|---|
| Planned value (PV) | 6,500 | 10,000 |  |
| Earned value (EV) | 5,000 | 8,500 |  |
| Actual cost (AC) | 5,250 | 8,750 |  |
| Schedule variance (SV) | (1,500) | (1,500) |  |
| Cost variance (CV) | (250) | (250) |  |
| Schedule performance index (SPI) | NA | 0.850 |  |
| Cost performance index (CPI) | NA | 0.971 |  |

Root Cause of Schedule Variance:
(#1) One member of the team was on medical leave.
(#2) Team not on same page on design and implementation issues.

Impact on Deliverables, Milestones, or **Critical Path**:

There is a chance that project deliverables for this week and subsequent weeks will get dela[...]

Figure 10.5: A *Performance Report* showing the status of the PMA project, which uses Earned Value to determine that the project is over budget.

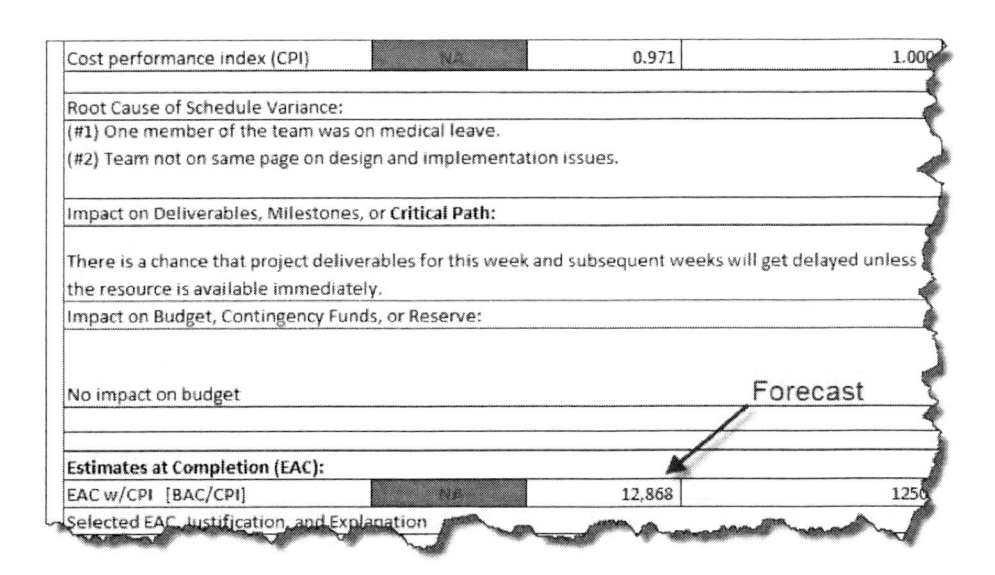

Figure 10.6: A *Forecast Report* showing the revised forecast for the estimate at completion (EAC).

## 10.9 Monitor and Control Risks

In the planning phase we covered the risk planning processes: *Plan Risk Management, Identify Risks, Perform Qualitative Risk Analysis, Perform Quantitative Risk Analysis,* and *Plan Risk Responses*. Once the project begins executing, the *Monitor and Control Risks* process describes how the project team will track and manage the risks that have already been identified.

The process also describes how to deal with any new risks that appear in the execution phase of the project. Finally, the team evaluates the effectiveness of the *Risk Management Plan*. The inputs and outputs to the *Monitor and Control Risk* process are shown in Table 10.12

The activities associated with this process require the team to monitor residual risks through the risk mitigation process, as well as to identify, quantify, and respond to new risks. The project manager also has to ensure that risk policies and procedures are followed and that all project assumptions remain valid.

For the PMA case study we show an updated *Risk Register* in Table 10.13. This is an extension of the *Risk Register* illustrated in the Planning phase.

## 10. Monitoring and Controlling

Table 10.12: The *Monitor and Control Risks* process inputs and outputs.

| Input | Output |
|---|---|
| Risk Register | Risk Register Updates |
| Project management plan | Process Assets Updates |
| Work Performance information & reports | Change requests |
|  | Project Document Updates |

Table 10.13: Updated Risk Register

| Risk ID | Risk | Response | Responsible Resource Mitigation | Rating (H,M,L) | Current Status (Traffic Light) |
|---|---|---|---|---|---|
| 1 | Technical Risk: Lack WordPress programming knowledge | Training provided to mitigate | Mary | L | Green |
| 2 | Communication Risk: Various stakeholders geographically separated | Accept risk: Unable to do much. Mitigate with virtual team training | Mary | L | Green |
|  |  |  | Dave | M | Orange |

The *Risk Audit* is a tool that is used to monitor and control project risks, and it is illustrated in Table 10.14.

Table 10.14: PMA *Risk Audit* tool.

| Audit of Process | Rating | Actions to Improve |
|---|---|---|
| Risk Identification and Mitigation | Satisfactory | Risk analysis could be improved by the PMA agenda item at weekly team meetings and communicating to stakeholders |

## 10.10 Administer Procurements

The *Administer Procurements* process describes the relationship with sellers and how to monitor the contracts with them to assure appropriate performance. It also describes how changes and corrections can be made to a contract.

## 10.10. Administer Procurements

The inputs and outputs for the *Administer Procurements* process are shown in Table 10.15.

Table 10.15: The *Administer Procurements* process inputs and outputs.

| Input | Outputs |
|---|---|
| Procurement documents | Change requests |
| Contract Performance reports | Updated documentation |
| Project management plan | |
| Procurement documentation | |

In our PMA case study we do not have any external contracts or procurement relationships, so for this section of the plan, we can simply note: Not Applicable.[5]

---

[5] This is not unusual in project management, as not all processes apply to all projects. The processes are used as checklists, and if one is not needed, it is OK. Just be sure to note this in the PM plan.

# CHAPTER 11

# CLOSING PROCESS GROUP

> **Acceptance of what has happened is the first step to overcoming the consequences of any misfortune.**
>
> *William James*

In the *Closing Process* group, the project deliverables are formally *accepted* by the customer[1] and it is the job of the project manager to complete the project (or phase). Activities at this stage consist of:

- *Formal Acceptance of the Project.* The project manager must obtain final acceptance of the project.

- *Post Implementation Activities.* These include soliciting and documenting the lessons learned; releasing all project resources; archiving project materials; and conducting post-project reviews.

- *Closing Out Contracts.* If a seller was involved, the final procurement details are completed.

Projects come to an end when they have completed their deliverables and satisfied their stakeholders.[2] Sometimes projects are suspended or killed for busi-

---

[1] The deliverables were previously validated–an output of the *Perform Quality Control* process.

[2] Hopefully, successfully!

ness reasons or failure of the team to perform adequately. We will cover the scenario of early project termination when we discuss the *Close Procurements* process. Whether successful or not, the project manager must complete the project closure processes–see Figure 11.1.

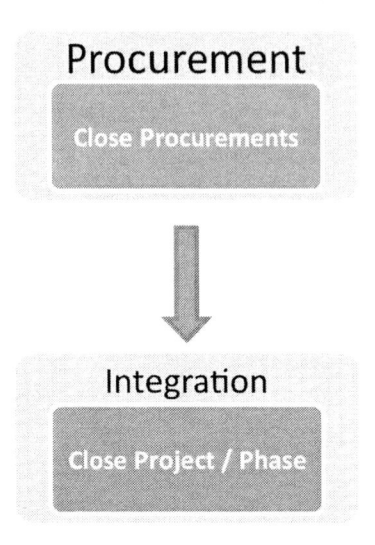

Figure 11.1: The *Closing* process group and its associated *Processes*.

The following questions need to be asked at the start of project closure:

- *Organizational Issues.* Who will be involved in the project closure phase? When and where will project closure be conducted?

- *Project Evaluation.* How did the project perform against its stated objectives? How did the cost and schedule compare against the plan?

- *Lessons.* What lessons were learned? What might be done differently next time?

A team meeting at this stage will be a good learning experience for everyone. Typically this meeting might involve asking questions such as:

- How well did the plan the project?

- How well did we execute the project?

- How well did we monitor and control the project?
- How well did we communicate internally and externally?
- How would you rate your satisfaction working on this project?
- How can we improve on the above aspects?

There are two processes: *Close Procurements* and *Close Project or Phase*. *Close procurements* is associated with the *Procurement* knowledge area, and *Close Project or Phase* is associated with the *Integration* knowledge area, as indicated in Figure 11.1.

## 11.1 Close Project or Phase

*Close Project or Phase* is the process of formally completing the project or phase. The formal name includes "close phase" because the project management process groups may be applied repeatedly in a multi-phase project.

*Close Project or Phase* involves administrative closure, which is the name given to the collection and archiving of project reports and documents; creating project archives; and the capturing of lessons learned from the project.

The inputs and outputs are illustrated in Table 11.1.

Table 11.1: The *Close Project or Phase* inputs and outputs.

| Input | Output |
| --- | --- |
| Project Mgmt Plan | Final product, service or result transition |
| Accepted Deliverables | Process assets updates |
| Organizational assets | Organizational assets updates |

First, what are accepted deliverables? This is the list of final deliverables accepted through the *Verify Scope* process, which is part of the *Monitoring and Controlling* process group. Process assets include documents such as the project audit guidelines, project evaluation requirements, and transition criteria.

The completion of the project results in a final product, service or result, and the outcome is described in the formal sign-off document.[3] This process is widely known as *Formal Acceptance*, and involves documenting the stakeholder comments that emerged during the acceptance process.

[3] The sign-off document does not refer to the physical project, only the process outcome.

## 11. Closing Process Group

The output *Organizational Asset Updates* refers to updates to the project management plan, risk registers, change management documentation, and the cost budget. Together with lessons learned, these documents constitute historical information, and should be transferred to the organizational knowledge base for use by future project managers.

Another useful document that the project manager may decide to write is the *Transition Plan*—a document to guide the sponsors in the use the product that was just accepted. This plan will help ensure satisfactory transition of the project into its operational role.

A final face-to-face meeting with the sponsor is desirable and it is where the final product and transition plan are discussed. This will create a positive lasting experience for the stakeholder.[4]

A key problem with this phase of the project is that the team members are very busy and they are released from the project to work elsewhere. Therefore, lessons learned from a project are frequently not captured. To resolve this problem, organizations should commit to continual improvements by budgeting time for the process of lessons learned and disseminating them.

The project manager may be responsible for some post-project activities, such as working with the functional managers in a matrix structure to release and re-assign personnel resources. Also, the project manager may want to write an honest performance assessment report for each project team member for consideration by the functional manager. The project manager should discuss such appraisals personally with each team member.

Another suggested post project activity is to follow up with the customer several weeks or months after the product or service is in use. Such interaction would generate goodwill with the business sponsor, as well as provide the project manager with opportunities to determine if the strategic business reason for undertaking the project materialized.[5]

### Lessons Learned

The project manager should create a *Closeout Report*, which includes an executive summary of the project and highlights of the scope. The report should also document the project management processes, commenting on any significant schedule, cost, quality and communication issues. The lessons learned should also be recorded here. Finally, the *Closeout Report* should be widely disseminated so that people in the organization can benefit from the accumulated wisdom.

---

[4] The last impression is the best impression!

[5] A good project manager would celebrate success and reward participants with a party.

## 11.1. Close Project or Phase

A sample project *closeout report* document containing some lessons learned from the PMA project is illustrated in Figure 11.2.

---

**Closeout Report containing lessons learned from the PMA project**

Project Name:    PMA    Date Prepared:    5/9/11    Project Manager:    V. Kanabar

**Summary:**
The PMA project was a successful project: It fully met its objectives. The scope and sponsor requirements were fully implemented and accepted. Product quality was verified and validated and the project stayed within the planned schedule and cost baselines.
The sponsors communicated during acceptance they were happy with the deliverables. The team members communicated that the project was a great learning experience for all. They attribute this in part to the excellent collegiality and communications among team members. They also observed that team members were willing to pick up slack for each other, especially when one of the team members was on medical leave of absence.

**Lessons learned:**

1. The project was well-planned and the team executed it very well.

2. The project team's focus on cost estimation and risk management paid off. Since the estimates were on target, the project schedule stayed on track. Since a comprehensive risk response plan was created, issues and risks were mitigated satisfactorily.

3. Very few technical risks materialized, which appeared due to good risk management.

4. We communicated with the sponsor about the project scope and requirements early on. This was very important for the final success of the project.

5. We created a code of conduct for the team which dictated how communications should take place, and how conflicts were to be resolved. This helped avoid conflicts.

6. We conducted team-building exercises early on. Since some team members were working virtually, it was very important to investigate and implement virtual team-building techniques. Personality issues were resolved early on according to the code of conduct.

7. We were honest about problems, and so we resolved many early before they became difficult issues.

8. We completed project deliverables in a timely manner and engaged stakeholders on a regular basis.

---

Figure 11.2: Project Closeout Report and Lessons Learned

## 11.2 Close Procurement

*Close procurement* involves the closure of contracts and procurement relationships with the various sellers. The inputs and outputs for the process are shown in Table 11.2.

Table 11.2: The *Close Procurement* inputs and outputs.

| Input | Output |
|---|---|
| Project management plan | Closed Procurements |
| Procurement documentation | Process assets updates |

The following options exist for closing a procurement:

- All deliverables have been completed and meet expectations.
- Termination of the project early by mutual agreement.
- Termination the project by default when the buyer has unresolvable problems with the seller.

Procurement is an area that is dominated by the legal implications. Therefore, the project manager must be aware of the contents of all contracts, as well as the financial and legal procedures, and follow them strictly. Two key inputs are needed: The procurement documentation and the project management plan. The procurement documentation is used to verify that all contractual requirements have been met.

Even if the project closes abruptly, either by mutual consent or otherwise, the *Close Procurement* process must occur. Typically, this is guided by the close procurement clause in the contract that the buyer and the seller agreed to.

What comes out of the walk-through, audits and final negotiations is the signing of the legal close procurement papers, which document procurement closure. [6]

Company assets are updated, and the following items are typically added to the repository:

- *Acceptance Notice.* This formally acknowledges the acceptance of the deliverables by the buyer.
- *Warranty.* Assurance of warranty is kept for future reference.

---

[6] When we remodeled our kitchen we conducted a walk-through with the contractor to inspect the finished construction. We had agreed to hold back $5,000 to be paid upon successful completion of the work. We went through the "punch list" to ensure that everything was indeed completed.

- *Contract Documentation.* This includes procurement documents such as closed contracts.

- *Lessons Learned.* Experience with the project, deliverables, and the vendors are documented for future reference by the organization.

**PMA Closure Example**

Suppose during the PMA case study, the design of the database of member information was subcontracted out to a database expert. Below is a sample of some issues to be included in the contract closeout document, evaluating the services that were procured:

- Vendor performance analysis: What worked well and what can be improved?

- Record of contract changes.

- Record of contract disputes.

# Part III

# The Knowledge Areas

# CHAPTER 12

# INTEGRATION

**I'm not for integration and I'm not against it.**

*Richard Pryor*

The *Integration* knowledge area is the least understood part of project management. Partly, this is because PMI keeps changing its mind about what is in it, and partly it is because it is hard to figure out what is actually meant by *Integration*.[1]

One way to understand this knowledge area is to view it as consisting of the activities that a project manager must perform in order to coordinate the project. That is, one of the jobs of the project manager is to keep an eye in the interactions between the various pieces. Integration, therefore, demands a global view of the project and strong communication skills.

For example, any technical changes to the scope will probably introduce new risks, impact the quality, and require new team skills. It will also affect the project management in that it will require: a new estimate of the cost and schedule; a modified communications plan if the change introduced new stakeholders; and possibly a sub-contract if the work needs to be out-sourced. It is the project manager's responsibility to make sure that all aspects of the scope change are analyzed and considered.

[1] After you've said "this is where you put all the parts together," it quickly gets fuzzy.

## 12. INTEGRATION

Each process produces deliverables. The expertise in the knowledge area is the skills, tools and techniques that a project manager needs to produce the deliverables effectively. Therefore the knowledge area chapters focus on the technical aspects of actually producing the deliverables.

Processes are associated with both *knowledge areas* and *process groups*, and their relationship for the *Integration* knowledge area are shown in Table 12.1:

Table 12.1: The *Integration* knowledge area processes and their associated *process groups*.

| Initiating | Planning | Executing | Monitoring & Controlling | Closing |
|---|---|---|---|---|
| Develop Project Management Plan | Develop Project Charter | Direct & Manage Project | Monitor & Control Project | Close Project or Phase |
| | | | Perform Integrated Change Control | |

There are two major deliverables from the *Integration* knowledge area, the *Charter* and the *Project Management Plan*. During execution of the project, the major responsibility of *Integration* is to manage the *Change Requests*. The complete set of deliverables associated with the *Integration* knowledge area are shown in Table 12.2.

Table 12.2: The deliverables (outputs) from the processes in the *Integration* knowledge area.

| Process | Deliverable |
|---|---|
| Develop Project Charter | The Charter |
| Develop Project Mgmt Plan | Project Management Plan |
| Direct & Manage Project Execution | Deliverables, Change Requests |
| Monitor & Control Project | Change Requests |
| Perform Integrated Change Control | Change Requests Status Updates |
| Close Project or Phase | The final project, Lessons Learned |

## 12.1 The Charter

The *Charter* is the document that formally authorizes the project. It is often developed as a partnership between the sponsor (who pays), the customer (who specifies performance), major stakeholders (users), and the performing organization. Usually, the project manager is specified very early in this process.

In section 7.1 we specified the inputs and outputs for the *Develop Charter* process. Here, we concentrate on the technical details: What goes into the *Charter*?

The charter is often a short document that kicks off the project.[2] The key is to make sure that the charter accurately represents the goals of the stakeholders.

As a first example, we present in Figure 12.1 a charter developed by one of our students for a party project.[1]

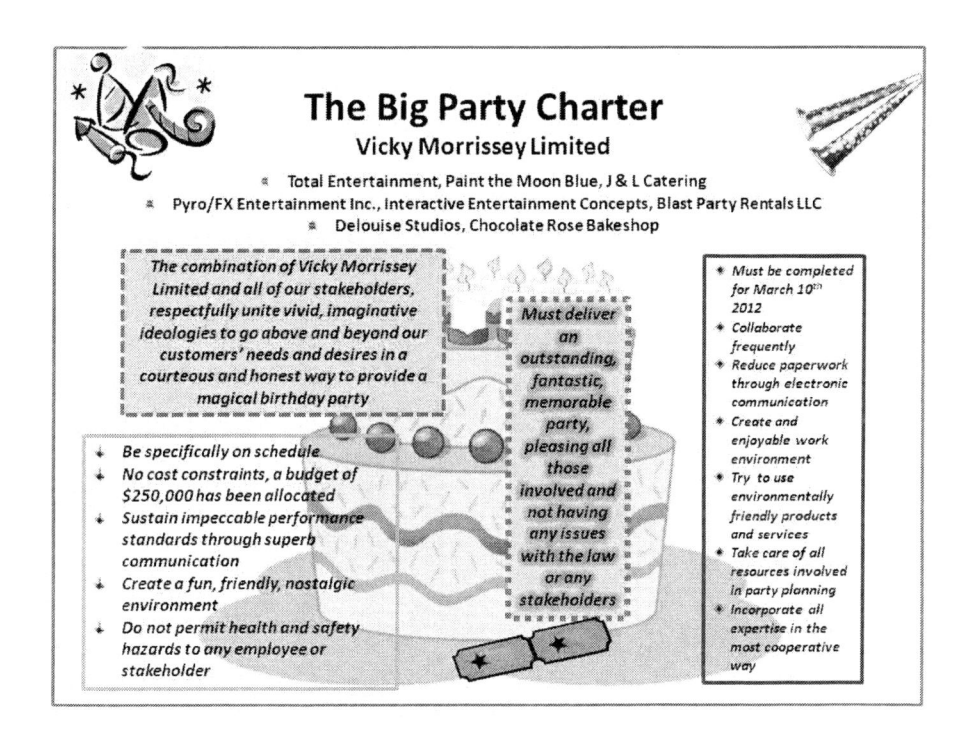

Figure 12.1: Vicky's Party Charter!

What we like about this charter is that while all of the information is there, it is also fun! As *fun* is an important theme and an attribute of the party, it is perfectly

[2] We once saw a one page charter that authorized a $120 million dollar project!

## 12. INTEGRATION

appropriate to feature it in the charter.

Don't be fooled by the presentation, there is a lot of important information here. The stylish format matches the stakeholder goals: "a vivid, imaginative ideology." There are cost and schedule details (a budget of $250,000 and completed for March 10th), but even the technical constraints match the party's philosophy: reduced paperwork, environmentally friendly products.

The entire ethos of the party is clearly communicated throughout this innovative charter![3] The bright colors and graphics all communicate the ambiance and style of the party to the stakeholders.

As a second example, we present a more traditional charter for the PMA case in Table 12.3. The charter first identifies the project champion and the project manager. It then describes the project's purpose, description and goals, all requirements established by the stakeholders. Next comes the budget and key milestones. Finally, the major stakeholders sign the charter to acknowledge their commitment to the project.

Some of the preliminary work on customer requirements may have been contracted out. This often happens on large projects where specific technical expertise is required to specify the performance. The data from such contracts are an input to the charter, and the Statement of Work (SOW) will be particularly useful, as it contains a concise summary of the project deliverables, the business need for the project, a preliminary scope, and the value of the project from a strategic perspective.

The charter usually specifies what the project will accomplish, the funding required, and an overall schedule. A good use for the charter is to focus agreement on the key features of the preliminary specification.

Many organizations require a *Business Case* to be completed before the charter is created. The Business Case identifies the needs or problems that the project will address. It should identify related projects undertaken in the past to resolve the same or similar business problem.

There are two important inputs to the charter: *Enterprise Environmental Factors* and *Organizational Process Assets*. These are not so much individual documents as collections of information. Since they are inputs to many of the project management *processes*, they are briefly described here.

---

[3] If you do not know how to proceed on this project, you are not paying attention. Read the charter again.

Table 12.3: The charter for the PMA web site.

| Project Title | PMA Web Site |
|---|---|
| Organization | Project Management Association (PMA) |
| Date | June 14, 2011 |
| Champion:<br>PM: | Dr. Roger Warburton<br>Dr. Vijay Kanabar |
| Purpose | PMA is a networking group for current students and alumni of Boston University employed or interested in the project management profession. The PMA website will create an environment for members of the community to share information, to obtain continuing education credits required to maintain certification, to learn about new employment opportunities, and to learn about the latest research and practical developments in the field of project management. |
| Description | The current website, implemented many years ago, is not serving the needs of the PMA, and must be redesigned to keep up with new demands of PMA, changes in the project management profession, and improvements in tools, techniques, and templates. The website will create an environment that is both appealing and helpful to the project management professional, providing an equal balance of information sharing, tools and templates, and opportunities for networking. |
| Goals: | After installation PMA should be able to increase the number of visits to the website by 50% over 2010 levels and decrease the support costs of the website by 25% by providing a user-friendly mechanism to post, manage, update and remove content. |
| Project Costs: | $15,000 |
| Milestones: | Initial Prototype to Stakeholders: 6/28/2011<br>Project Complete: 8/2/2011 |
| Signatures: | Champion:<br>PM:<br>Stakeholders |

## 12.1.1 Enterprise Environmental Factors

Examples of *Environmental Factors* include:

- Industry and government standards, such as ISO 9000, which specifies the fundamentals of quality management systems.

- Marketplace data and business intelligence.

## 12. INTEGRATION

### 12.1.2 Organizational Process Assets

Examples of *Organizational Assets* include:

- Company assets useful to the project, such as standards, procedures, tools, templates, and information systems.

- Historical information, lessons learned, and any knowledge bases relevant to project management.

- Past project files, data, documents, templates, measurement guidelines, and procedures.

## 12.2 The Business Case

The *Business Case* provides the data to establish that the project is worth its investment. There are many reasons to do a project:

- *Core Mission:* The development of a new product may be viewed as essential to maintain the company's position in the market space.

- *Market:* The company believes that there is an untapped market they can satisfy.

- *Exclude Competition:* The company believes they can position the project to prevent others from gaining entry into their market.

- *Core Technology:* The company wants to invest in a technology they believe will soon become important, and that will create a platform for future projects.

- *Image and Citizenship:* The project will present the company in a good light.

- *Unreliable Suppliers:* The project will diversify its suppliers and make deliveries more dependable.

- *Changing Regulations:* Upgrades to the company's information system are necessary to comply with changes to tax, environmental, or legal regulations.

As an example, we present the business case for the PMA project in Table 12.4. It specifies the key benefits of the project, and makes a strong case to senior management to fund the project. It could also discuss the following topics: Problem the project is designed to address; a cost/benefit analysis; risks, including the impact of not doing the project; and an implementation strategy.

Table 12.4: The *Business Case* for the PMA web site.

| Key Project Benefits |
|---|
| Provide a comprehensive site for project management activity and collaboration, which will include the latest news, tools to assist the project managers, PMI resources, introductions to research, evaluations of new practical tools, and employment postings from both employees and employers. |
| To become an online resource for the project management community. |
| Increase awareness of the BU Graduate programs in Project Management and increase exposure to new companies. |
| Attract potential students to the BU Graduate program in Project Management by showing our leadership position in the project management community. |
| Further the *state of the art* of project management by providing access to research, tools, templates, hints and tips to visitors to the site. |
| Provide a resource for BU students and alumni to receive and post available jobs from companies looking for highly skilled project managers. |
| Increase visibility and cooperation between the BU and the Project Management Institute to foster a better working relationship and more visibility for BU. |

It is important for the project manager to periodically review the business case, particularly after major milestones. For example, when the scope is complete, it should be checked to ensure that it implements requirements that reflect the business case.[4]

## 12.3 The Project Management Plan

The writing of the *Project Management Plan* is a massive undertaking, as it contains dozens of sections. The plan documents the actions necessary to define, prepare, integrate, and coordinate all subsidiary plans. In the *Integration* knowledge area, the focus is on making sure that all of the plans are coordinated and consistent.

The Project Management Plan has many sub-components:

[4] It is easy to get carried away in scope development and end up with a great project that does not satisfy the business case! Also, changing market conditions can invalidate the need for the project, so checking the business case is project management job security.

## 12. INTEGRATION

- **Management:**
  - *Processes to be followed:* How much detail is required.[5]
  - *The Life Cycle:* The various phases.
  - *Tools and Techniques:* Company assets, and references to existing documentation is appropriate.
  - *Change Control:* This is an important aspect of project management, and so it is important to explicitly lay out the rules and tools.

- **Cost and Schedule:**
  - *Earned Value Management:* This is a vital component of project management, and so it is important to explicitly lay out the approach to be followed and the tools to be used.
  - *Reviews:* Who and when? What information is distributed?

- **Sub-Plans:**

  These include management plans for: Scope and requirements; schedule and cost; quality; human resources; communications; risks; and procurements.

## 12.4 Direct and Manage Project Execution

As described in section 9.1, during this process the project manager manages the creation of the deliverables, and ensures that they meets project objectives. The project manager also measures the cost and schedule performance against the plan, and manages all communications, risks, quality, and human resources.

A key thread that occurs in all activities is the management of change. When the need for a change is detected, there are three possible actions:

- *Corrective action:* The project manager needs to bring the performance of the project into line with established objectives.
- *Preventive action:* The project manager can take action to reduce the probability of negative consequences arising from risks.
- Defect repair: The project manager needs to fix the problem.[6]

---

[5] For small projects, a check-off of the issues might be all that is required.

[6] There will inevitably be a lot of debate about whether it is really a defect or the customer's mistake in specifying the requirement. In other words, who is going to pay for it?

As an example, in the PMA project, the project manager directs and manages activities such as:

- Creating web pages.

- Training staff in web technology.

- Reassigning best staff to the critical path.

- Managing communications with the project champion, business units, and other stakeholders.

- Generating project reports.

- Managing risks.

- Updating the project notebook with lessons learned.

## 12.5 Monitor and Control Project Work

The project manager monitors and controls project work throughout the project.

As an example, for the PMA project, the project manager conducts activities such as:

- Producing cost and schedule variance reports using Earned Value.

- If there is a significant variance, a change request is made and the plans are updated and approved by sponsors and stakeholders.

- Using earned value techniques, revised forecast estimates are made for the cost (e.g., a new estimate to complete) and schedule.

As an example, consider the PMA case. Suppose a key programmer left the project, and this required corrective action. This would be uncovered during the *monitor and control project work* process. In the PMA project, keeping to the schedule is important, and the project manager proposed a thorough analysis of the issues, which were documented in a change request. [7]

[7] Notice that the analysis of the change request is not conducted here, it is performed in the *Perform Integrated Change Control* process.

## 12.6 Perform Integrated Change Control

This is the process of reviewing all change requests, which may apply to either the deliverables or the documentation. All change requests must be formally documented, approved by stakeholders, carefully implemented, and monitored.

Each proposed change is reviewed for its cost and schedule impact, and then either rejected or approved. Only *approved changes* are incorporated into a revised baseline.

As an example, again consider the above PMA case, where a key programmer left the project. The project manager created a *change request* during the *monitor and control project work* process. In the *Perform Integrated Change Control* process, the *change request* is reviewed and analyzed in consultation with stakeholders. The team came up with the following proposed solutions:

1. Hire and train a new team member.
2. Move team members to different activities.
3. Change the scope slightly to reduce the effort.

Keeping to the schedule is most important, and the first two proposed solutions will result in a delay. Only the third option will maintain the schedule, and so it was selected. After everyone agreed to the reduction in scope, the change was approved. The project manager documented all of the potential impacts of the change request, in all relevant plans, and also requested that the team members update the baseline configuration of the system.

## 12.7 Close Project or Phase

As described in section 11.1, during the closing phase the project manager reviews all project work, makes sure the deliverables are complete and that the objectives have been met.

For example, for the PMA case, this involved final updates to all documentation, and migration of the new website to the production server for live use.

# CHAPTER 13

# SCOPE

**If you can't explain it simply,
you don't understand it well enough.**

*Albert Einstein*

## 13.1 Scope Definition

The scope document describes both the project, as well as how it is to be accomplished. As such, it is by far the most important document in the entire project. Bar none.

*The scope document is a complete description of all the products and services in the project.*

The scope has two functions. First, it describes the features and functions that define and characterize the project. We will reserve the word *specification* for the document that precisely defines what the project is supposed to do.

A good example of a *specification* is an architect's conceptual drawing of a building. Stakeholders can evaluate the proposed structure to determine if it satisfies their needs (The "What"). At this stage, it is quite normal for the discussion to include all sorts of non-construction issues, such as: Is there enough space for the proposed functions? Does it fit in its surroundings? Is it energy efficient?

Once the conceptual requirements are agreed to, the architect will create the detailed design (the "How").[1] The specification is usually developed by asking stakeholders what they want. Unfortunately, a stakeholder will tell you anything you ask about, but nothing more.[1]

Second, the scope contains organizational and managerial information, such as milestones and deliverables, limits and constraints, the requirements for communicating with customers and stakeholders, and a Statement of Work (SOW).

The scope is the foundation document—it describes everything in the project, both the precise definition of what it is or will do, and how it will be executed. It therefore functions as the primary communication tool between the project team and the stakeholders. If you mess up the scope, the project is doomed.

The SOW describes *how* the project will be performed, and in particular, who will perform which activity. The SOW is usually defined by the customer, who establishes the cost and schedule, the deliverables and milestones, and wants regular reports about the status of the project.

For completeness, we provide the PMBOK definition of the scope:

> *The project scope describes the deliverables and work required to create those deliverables.*

The problem with the PMBOK definition[2] is that there is more to the scope than deliverables. The scope also includes *services*, such as monthly meetings with the customer. While there might be deliverables from such a meeting (e.g., the minutes), the actual entity being specified in the scope is the *meeting*, its frequency and attendees, not just the minutes.

### 13.1.1 What? How? When? Who?

These questions are useful in determining what goes into the the scope. For example, suppose our project is to build a web site that registers students for courses.

- *What?*

    These are the requirements. For example, a web site that registers students would include details such as the response time, the number of students

[1] Notice there is still no project management information here, e.g., no cost or schedule.

[2] We might be considered to be splitting hairs here.

that can be handled simultaneously, the general look and feel of the site, testing criteria, etc. There would also be technical and legal requirements, e.g, there are legal privacy issues and parental rights associated with personal student data.

- *How?*

This is the design for the project: For example, the details of how the above web site is to be constructed. One could expect to see the user interface defined (perhaps by screen mockups), the database design, and details about networking and communications with the server.

- *When?*

This is the schedule for the project: For example, the web site should be up and running by the beginning of the next Fall semester.

- *Who?*

Who will do what? The document that defines this is known as the Statement of Work (SOW), and for the web site project would consist of a list of tasks to be performed and the person responsible for each task.

### 13.1.2 The Theme

If you are planning a party, what is the theme? Suppose you specified the purpose (Mom's birthday), the time and place, as well as the guest list, budget, milestones and deliverables. You are still missing an important piece: The Theme!

What kind of party is it going to be? Establish the theme early on, it will guide the rest of the planning.

### 13.1.3 Complete and Precise

The scope must be both complete and precise. If you are building a new web page, the scope document defines exactly what the web page is supposed to do. If the scope does not include how to login, the scope document is incomplete—there is something missing. If the scope specifies that a user name is required, but not the number of allowed characters, then the scope is imprecise.

The scope should have only enough material to be complete and precise. Clear and precise writing is essential.[3] Tables, charts and diagrams accomplish this effectively. Resist the urge to describe a diagram, it duplicates information.

[3] We make no excuse for demanding excellent writing of project managers. Clear communication is an essential skill and good writing is paramount.

The scope must be complete. Forgetting to define the number of bathrooms will lead to a big problem later.

The scope must also be precise. Specifying 2 bathrooms is not precise enough. Do they include baths and/or showers?

One of the most useful phrases a project manager can use in meetings is "What does the scope say?" This immediately focuses energy on what is *required*, not what someone would like to implement. Also, there is no arguing with the scope, it is what the customer wants.[4]

## 13.2 The Specification

The definition of the specification, which is often referred to as the "spec," is:

> *The specification completely and precisely defines the required features and functions that characterize the project.*

Let's examine the some of the issues in the construction of the specification.

**Design vs. Requirements**

> **Sometimes I can't figure designers out.**
> **It's as if they flunked human anatomy.**
>
> *Erma Bombeck*

The first thing to emphasize in the definition is the word *required*. The specification says *what* is required, not *how to do it*. Unfortunately, it is sometimes hard to distinguish the "what" from the "how."

In fact, it is naive to think that one can completely specify *what* is to be done without some notion of *how* it is to be accomplished. Suppose you ask a contractor to build a house. You can specify the requirements for the house: a kitchen, 3 bedrooms, 2 bathrooms, etc. However, the cost will certainly depend on how it is built: One floor or three?

Requirements cannot be specified without a context. Most projects have a requirements definition phase, and part of that work is preliminary design. This design work is not to define how to do the job, but to demonstrate the project's feasibility.[5]

---

[4] Maybe it's not what they want, but at least it's what they agreed to.

[5] The PMBOK defines this as *Collect Requirements*.

"Feasibility" applies to a multitude of issues: Scope performance, cost and schedule. For example, the preliminary design might demonstrate: that performance requirements are achievable (a web site's response time, the span of a bridge); that the cost is appropriate (the design allowed you to conduct a parametric cost analysis); and that the schedule is achievable (a preliminary network diagram resulted in a reasonable schedule).

The primary responsibility of the requirements definition phase is to produce a *realistic* specification.[6]

As you try to refine the requirements, it becomes harder and harder without including design details. For example, suppose you require 25% more kitchen cabinet space in a new kitchen. This is a clear requirement. But it becomes difficult to specify it more precisely without explaining what the new kitchen will look like (i.e., you are specifying a design).

For example, suppose that in a kitchen project, you specify: "The new kitchen should have 25% more cabinet space." Then, as the project manager, you have the responsibility to demonstrate that it is feasible both technically (in a suggested plan) and practically (via preliminary cost and schedule estimates). If the only way to get the 25% more space is to knock down walls, then a cost estimate for that activity should be developed. You can then determine if the cost of knocking down walls is prohibitive or not.

## 13.3 Scope Contents

Below we list the topics that should be included in a scope document. We emphasize that this is a checklist, not an outline. The scope for each project is different, and may have the information laid out in any appropriate format. On small projects it is efficient to combine several sections.

### 13.3.1 The Project's Justification

Why are you doing the project? The project might be justified as a new business opportunity. Often, a project is required by changing regulations (tax, privacy, environmental, etc.) In this case, the motive is not profit, but compliance. Whatever the project's justification, it is important to demonstrate that the project is *essential* to the company's business goals.[7]

[6] It's easy to specify an unrealistic and impossible system with everything in it that you could possibly want. You just won't get it.

[7] Otherwise, why do it?

### 13.3.2 Deliverables and Milestones

For a complete discussion of deliverables and milestones, see Chapter 3. Examples of deliverables for a party are listed in Table 13.1. Note that we have divided them into the major milestones and intermediate milestones. We have also added dates, which is an example of combining information from different sections of the scope. If a change occurs, you will only have to change the information in one place.

Table 13.1: *Deliverables and Milestones* for a party.

| Major Milestones | Date |
|---|---|
| Birthday Party | Aug 15, 2012 |
| Planning Complete | June 30, 2012 |
| **Intermediate Milestones** | **Date** |
| Select Venue | February 1, 2012 |
| Contract with Venue | February 15, 2012 |
| Invitations Designed | May 15, 2012 |
| Invitations Sent | June 1, 2012 |

### 13.3.3 Budget

Customers almost always have a budget, or a target cost for the project, and so it is useful to identify this in the scope.

If possible, the cost drivers should be established, so that a range of costs can be considered. For example, when planning a party, you determine that the major factor driving the cost is the food and drink, estimated at $20 per person. You are planning to invite 50 people, so you might establish a preliminary food and drink budget of $1,000, and an overall party budget of $1,500.

### 13.3.4 Acceptance Criteria

What will satisfy the stakeholders? How will you know when you are done?

Some thought about the acceptance criteria helps to clarify the scope. For example, for the PMA website, specifying response times will help to define ease of use.

### 13.3.5 Risks

While developing the scope, it is useful to list some major risks, the details of which are discussed in detail in Chapter 22—Risk.

### 13.3.6 Constraints

It is important to identify the constraints, so they can be analyzed and negotiated.

*A constraint is any factor that limits the options for the project.*

Some examples of constraints are:

- *Personnel Constraints:* The unavailability of a key technical person will hold things up. For example, in the kitchen project, the architect was the only one who had the skills to use the software program that analyzed beam loading. All changes to the structural design had to be checked by the architect. When he wasn't around, the project suffered a delay.

- *Equipment Constraints:* On construction projects, the availability of bulldozers and earth moving equipment is often a constraint, becasue they cannot be moved quickly from job to job.

- *Contractual Constraints:* The contract often contains provisions, such as the specification of a particular person by name. It is not unusual for the customer to demand a "right of approval" for the assignment of a new project manager.

- *Financial Constraints:* Cash flow and borrowing can impose financial constraints.

- *Schedule Constraints:* These may arise from several sources. For example, in the PMA web site, upgrades must be operational at the beginning of each semester. In the City of Boston, construction of roads cannot continue after October 31st.

- *Legal Constraints:* Projects are subject to many laws and regulations, which must all be followed: Accounting, environmental, and human resources. Such constraints are found in industry standards, such as environmental regulations, building codes, and ANSI standards.

Constraints are not included in the scope, but are incorporated "by reference." This means that the all applicable documents are referenced in the scope, and all of their conditions must be upheld.

Every constraint involves an associated risk because it limits one's options. Therefore, project managers should proactively manage constraints.

For example, suppose a deliverable must be available by a specific date. This is a schedule constraint, and if it proves problematic, the project manager may conduct a trade-off analysis to analyze options.

For example, the schedule might be accelerated by hiring an outside consultant, but at increased cost. Adding a consultant may also introduce a new risk because, as an outsider, he or she may not be familiar with critical technical details. On the other hand, if the deliverable is a low priority, the project manager may propose to the customer that it be delayed, or perhaps even deleted altogether.

This example shows how constraints affect projects, and how trade-offs allow the project manager to examine carefully the different aspects of the issue and propose appropriate solutions.

### 13.3.7 Limits and Exclusions

It is useful to define what the project will *not do*. This often provokes interesting discussions with the customer.[8]

### 13.3.8 Assumptions

Project managers and teams must understand how assumptions affect the project.

*An assumption is any factor considered to be true.*

All projects contain assumptions, and they are sometimes hidden or not obvious. Assumptions can arise from diverse issues: The customer's desire to review documents; interactions with company management; technical issues; availability of personnel; and external events.

An example of a *Technical Assumption* is: The specification of a particular piece of hardware by the customer.

---

[8] Particularly when they discover that their favorite requirement is excluded.

The project manager would then explicitly define the assumption in the scope document, along with relevant details: "The hardware shall be provided by the customer, and the selected model shall be sufficient to process all transactions in the required time frame."

We see immediately how important it is to have the assumption explicitly documented. In the above case, the project manager may seek schedule relief or additional funds from the customer. If the assumption were not explicit, it is not clear who would have to pay for the hardware upgrade.

If the hardware provided by the customer turns out not to meet the throughput requirement, the project manager may offer the following options to the customer:

1. The current throughput is close to the specified performance, and might be acceptable to the users, so the throughput requirement may be relaxed. Some minor modifications to the user manual and training may be required. This is low risk, and will incur no additional cost.

2. Upgrade the server at a cost of $5,000. This is considered a low risk solution that will work.

3. Redesign the database to speed up the transactions at a cost of $8,000. This is considered high risk, and may not accomplish the throughput goals.

Other examples of assumptions are:

- *Schedule Assumptions:* The approval date of permits by city or state governments; the availability of plans from an architect; the availability of hardware or software by certain dates.

- *Personnel Assumptions:* When redecorating, we all know how frustrating it can be to wait on plumbers, electricians, carpenters, and painters, who never seem to be available when you are, or when they were scheduled.

- *Financial Assumptions:* This may involve the availability of funds for equipment, or cash to pay people.

### 13.3.9 Technical Requirements

A project is usually subject to external standards, which are called *technical requirements*. Many technical requirements are found in industry standards, such as plumbing and electrical codes, environmental regulations, and tax laws.

For example, if you decide to include fireworks in your party project, you must satisfy the local fire department regulations, and maybe even have to pay for an on-duty fireman. Another example is the legal implications of serving alcohol.

## 13.4 Statement of Work (SOW)

The SOW is the basis of the *contract* between the customer and the organization performing the project. The length and complexity of the SOW will depends on the size of the project. There may be several versions of the SOW as the project evolves: A short SOW for a request for proposal; the winning bidder may then develop a detailed SOW.

> *The statement of work (SOW) is a description of the products and services to be supplied during the project.*

Whatever the stage of the project, and whatever its size, the SOW contains the following type of information:

- Tasks to be performed, and by whom.
- Deliverables and Milestones (with dates).
- Schedule of reviews with customers and stakeholders.
- Cost and schedule reporting criteria.
- Payment terms and the payment schedule.
- Legalities, like cancellation clauses, Force Majeure,[9] etc.

An important part of the SOW is the *Customer Interface.* This specifies how often the project manager will meet with the customers and stakeholders, and what information will be reported. As a minimum, the project manager reports progress on deliverables, costs and the schedule.

The project manager must be careful not to introduce overlap and repetition between the sections of the scope. The SOW, in particular, is liable to contain duplicate information, such as task assignments and deliverable dates. We emphasize therefore, that the sections described here should be regarded as a checklist, not a document outline.

---

[9] All contracts have one of these clauses, but few of us actually understand them.

The job of the project manager is to find creative ways to include all the information without repetition. For example, combining Milestones, Deliverables, and Responsibilities into a table can avoid duplication and make the important information clear.

## 13.5 The Triple Constraints

Projects change, and so does the scope. A key to managing the scope is to realize that any change will induce ripples throughout the project, which is indicated in Figure 13.1, as the "Jello® Triangle."[10]

This is a visual device used to communicate the idea that changing any one of the three aspects of the project (scope, time, cost) will result in changes to the other two. For example, if the customer suggests adding an activity to the project, then the cost will probably increase and the schedule will lengthen. Similarly, a reduction is cost can usually only be accommodated by a reduction in scope.

Sometimes, *quality* is inserted in the center of the triangle to indicate that quality

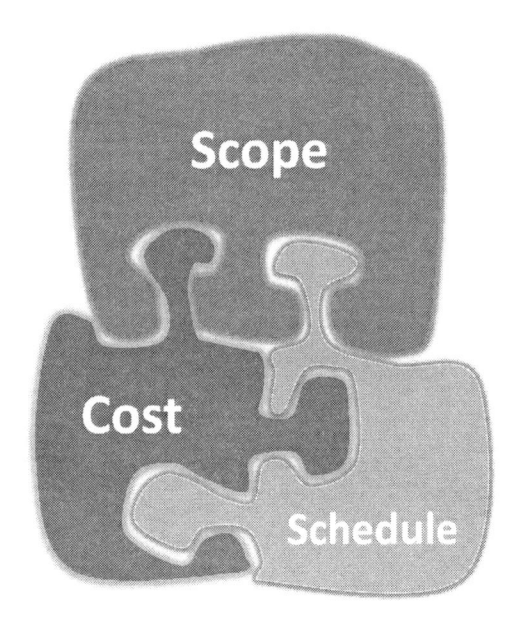

Figure 13.1: The Jello® Triangle: The triple constraints of scope, cost and schedule.

[10] This is sometimes referred to as the *Iron Triangle*, but we prefer to think of it as the *Jello* triangle. Frankly, we can't think of anything less like iron.

is affected by the balancing the other three factors. In other words, quality is affected by changes in the scope, cost, and schedule. Actually, everything is affected by such changes, including risks, the team, contracts, etc. So why just quality in the middle?[11]

## 13.6 The Priority Matrix

Figure 13.1 illustrates that when a change is proposed, it is likely to affect the scope, cost and schedule. But which one has priority? Is holding the budget more important than keeping to the schedule? Complicating the decision is that different stakeholders will have conflicting views of priorities, making it difficult to impartially propose a uniformly acceptable approach.

The tool to help manage this issue is called the *priority matrix*, which is shown in Table 13.2. The *priority matrix* is created during scope development, but its real purpose is to manage changes during implementation. The idea is to establish the relative priorities between scope, cost, or schedule.

Table 13.2: The *Priority Matrix* for a fighter jet.

|           | Scope | Schedule | Cost |
|-----------|-------|----------|------|
| **Constrain** | ■     |          |      |
| **Enhance**   |       | ■        |      |
| **Accept**    |       |          | ■    |

To do that, we first pick either the scope or the cost or the schedule, and assign it to one of three categories:

[11] Personally, we think this is dumb!
What is quality? The formal definition in the PMBOK is *conformance to requirements*. Requirements are in the specification, which is in the scope. But if quality is in the scope, why is it in the middle of the figure? That is just fuzzy thinking, and we hate fuzzy thinking.

- *Constrain:* If we constrain the scope, we are saying that the maintaining the scope is more important than cost and schedule, and that we refuse to compromise on the performance characteristics.

  An example of this situation occurs when developing a military system, such as a fighter jet. The scope specifies the requirements for the jet, which are not negotiable. For example, the maximum speed may be defined by the requirement that the jet be faster than all potential adversaries. During the development of the jet, changes might be proposed, but they will be rejected if they compromise the speed requirement.

## 13.6. The Priority Matrix

If changes are required to ensure the speed requirement is met, they will be implemented, even if they result in cost overruns or schedule delays.

- *Enhance:* Once we accept that the scope is constrained, we next chose between cost and schedule to enhance it as best we can, given that we cannot compromise the scope.

  Continuing the example of the jet, we might chose to enhance the schedule. That is, we take all opportunities to deliver early without compromising the scope.

- *Accept:* Once we accept that the scope is constrained, and that the schedule is enhanced, we must accept the cost implications.

  Continuing the example of the jet, when a change is proposed, we only accept it if it does not compromise the scope, and we will take all opportunities to enhance the schedule. We must also accept the cost (usually overrun!) implications.

This is documented in Table 13.2, where the bullet in the *constrain* row is in the scope column. This indicates that the scope is constrained—we accept no compromises on the performance. The bullet in the *enhance* row is in the schedule column, denoting that we will take all opportunities to enhance the schedule. The bullet in the *accept* row is in the cost column, denoting that we will accept the cost implications.

The *priority matrix* is filled out with exactly three bullets, with only one bullet in each row, and only one bullet in each column.

As another example, consider the project of organizing a party for my Dad's 85th birthday. The *priority matrix* is shown in Table 13.3. Here, we have stated that the schedule is constrained. That is, once we have fixed the date, it cannot change.[12] We decide that we are on a very firm budget, so we take all opportunities to save money. If that results in a slightly less fancy party, we will accept that.[13]

Table 13.3: The *Priority Matrix* for my Dad's birthday party.

|            | Scope | Schedule | Cost |
|------------|-------|----------|------|
| **Constrain** |       | ■        |      |
| **Enhance**   |       |          | ■    |
| **Accept**    | ■     |          |      |

[12] My Dad's 85th birthday is August 21st. We can save money by having the party in September. Ain't gonna happen!

[13] Dad will be so happy we are having a party, that he won't care where it is.

The project manager should establish the priority matrix during the development of the scope, and put it on the wall for everyone to see.[14] When changes are proposed, the project manager can look to the *priority matrix* to help referee between stakeholders.

### 13.6.1 Scope Creep

The customer comes first! Keep the customer happy!

Simply following these admonitions, leads to a serious problem: *scope creep*.

*Scope creep is the tendency of the requirements to grow over time.*

*Gold Plating* is a phrase used to describe the process of adding things into the scope that are merely nice to have. The key is for the project manager to focus on *refining* the scope, not *embellishing* it.

Stakeholders and customers often try to add requirements to the scope, and the project manager must guard against this. One way to do this is to manage changes very carefully: separately list each proposed change; evaluate the risks; develop the cost and schedule impact; and review all the information with the customer and stakeholders.

Most projects are under cost or schedule constraints and presenting the impact of changes will immediately force the customer to assess the true value of the changes and to prioritize them.

Most of the time scope creep results in cost overruns and delays. Despite this, scope creep is a common project affliction because there is relentless pressure on the project manager to satisfy the customer.

It is important to realize that changes are inevitable. Clarifications and refinements are OK, in fact are necessary. It is enhancements that must be ruthlessly rejected. Each proposed change should be analyzed to determine its impact on scope, cost, and schedule. This is the subject of *Integrated Change Control*—see Chapter 10.

A clear, well-defined specification immediately allows the project team to determine when extra work is being proposed. A clear specification is an insurance policy against scope creep. A specification that is broad and imprecise is an invitation for scope creep.

---

[14] We suggest that there are two things that every project manager needs on the wall: The priority matrix and the network with the critical path.

The tension between satisfying the customer and staying within cost and schedule is nicely illustrated by the practices of builders of super yachts.[2] A super yacht is a boat over 40 meters in length, and they are typically built under a fixed cost contract. A 40m power boat costs around $60 million!

When the customer asks for a change, it is hard to justify asking for an extra few thousand dollars, when the bill is already in the millions. Therefore, doing "small favors" for the customer is good business.

However, when a major change is requested, then the builder "opens up" the contract, and negotiates a major add-on.[15]

## 13.7 Writing the Scope

> **The most essential gift for a good writer is a built-in, shock-proof sh\*\*t-detector.**
>
> *Ernest Hemingway*

Good writing is essential in project management.

One might be tempted to think that the scope is always a long and complicated document. That would be wrong![16] The scope must be complete and precise, but that does not necessarily mean it has to be long. In fact, one should ruthlessly work to cut it.[17] Clarity is the objective, not length.

We listed the information to be included in the scope document, but you should regard this as a check list, not an outline. For example, if you construct a table of deliverables, you can satisfy the milestone requirement by simply adding a date column to the deliverables table. This is an example of specifying information in only one place.[18] If an additional table of milestones were included, then when a deliverable changed, that information would have to be changed in two places. This is inefficient, a source of errors, and to be avoided at all costs.

The scope contains assumptions, constraints, limits, and exclusions, which are interrelated. For example, if a permit is required to start construction, then this may involve an assumption (the customer will obtain the permit), a schedule constraint (the permit will be obtained in 30 days), and an exclusion (the construction permit does not include an environmental permit).

This can all be combined into a table so that the information about the permit is in one place. That way, if anything about the permit changes, only one part of the

---

[15] And attempts to make up for previous favors.

[16] I have only made this letter rather long because I have not had time to make it shorter—Blaise Pascal

[17] There is but one art, to omit—Robert Louis Stevenson.
   An elegant commandment that I have disobeyed to get you to obey it. How ironic.

[18] A friend of mine has as sign over his desk that says, **OHIO**—only handle it once.

## 13. Scope

scope need change. If the information were scattered among multiple sections, a change to the permit would required multiple changes to the scope, an error-prone process.

To become a good project manager, practice writing.[19]

> *Do not put statements in the negative form.*
> *And don't start sentences with a conjunction.*
> *If you reread your work, you will find on rereading that a*
> *great deal of repetition can be avoided by rereading and editing.*
> *Never use a long word when a diminutive one will do.*
> *Unqualified superlatives are the worst of all.*
> *De-accession euphemisms.*
> *If any word is improper at the end of a sentence, a linking verb is.*
> *Avoid trendy locutions that sound flaky.*
> *Last, but not least, avoid cliches like the plague.*
>
> "Great Rules of Writing"—*William Safire.*

---

[19] The difference between the right word and the almost right word is the difference between lightning and the lightning bug—Mark Twain

# Chapter 14

# The WBS

> **The secret of getting ahead is getting started.**
> **The secret of getting started is breaking your complex**
> **overwhelming tasks into small manageable tasks,**
> **and then starting on the first one.**
>
> *Unknown*

The WBS is part of the *define scope* process.

## 14.1 The Work Breakdown Structure (WBS)

Once the scope is complete and approved, the next step is to create the Work Breakdown Structure (WBS), and it is the foundation for all the steps to follow, particularly the development of the cost and schedule.

The WBS is a reorganization of the information in the scope, and we emphasize immediately that its creation is a *creative* process. There is no automated way to generate a good WBS.

## 14. THE WBS

Organizations often have templates for a WBS, which saves work, and helps not to forget pieces. But a template is not the answer, as all projects are unique, and the WBS will require tweaking and tuning.

*The WBS is a deliverable-oriented hierarchical decomposition of the work to be accomplished, with each descending level representing an increasingly detailed definition of the work.*

Suppose we have a project to design invitations for a party. To begin the explanation, a simple WBS for this project is shown in Fig. 14.1.

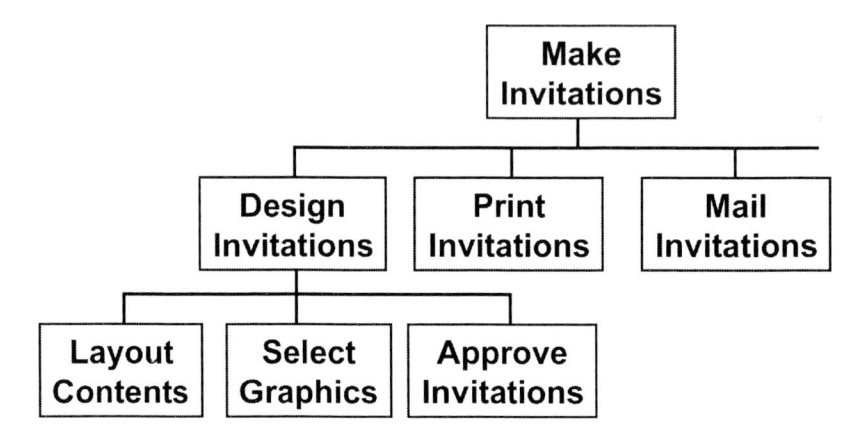

Figure 14.1: A portion of the WBS for a *Make Party Invitations* project.

The first thing to observe is that the WBS is hierarchical, which means that it is decomposed into in layers. At the top, we have a box, or node, that represents the entire project (Make Invitations). As one proceeds downwards, the layers contain more detail.

The second level contains three activities (Design, Print, and Mail). The Design Invitations box is decomposed further into Layout Invitations, Select Graphics, and Approve Invitations.

Decomposition is the subdivision of project deliverables into smaller, more manageable deliverables, until the work is defined at the *work package* level.

*Work packages are the lowest level items in the WBS, and represent the level at which cost and activity durations can be reliably estimated and managed.*

## 14.1. The Work Breakdown Structure (WBS)

There are several rules to follow in the construction of a WBS:

**WBS Rule #1**

*Each WBS activity is derived explicitly from, and traceable back to, the scope.*[1]

The relation from scope → WBS ensures that nothing is left out of the project.

WBS activities can come from many sources. Obviously, work is necessary to create the project deliverables. However, there are also project activities that have to do with the *process*, and these need to be in the WBS to ensure that all activities are in the Statement of Work.

For example, a scope assumption may define that the home owner will obtain the permit for construction. In which case, the WBS should contain an activity called *Get Permit*. The deliverable is clear (the Permit). Project management activities also go into the WBS, e.g., *Produce Monthly Reports*.

**WBS Rule #2**

*WBS components are defined by active verbs.*

Note that the top level box says *Make Invitations*. The verb "make" is important, it immediately expresses the idea that we are going to make the invitations—we are not going to purchase ready-made invitations. If we had decided to buy ready-made invitations, then the top level box would say *Buy Invitations*. Notice how important the verb is.[2]

As another example, consider *Pour Foundation*. The verb "pour" clarifies that the foundation is to be, well, poured, and not dropped in as a completed entity. Pouring also implies the need for a form to pour concrete into, the scheduling and arrival of a delivery truck, a time to harden, etc. All that derives just from the verb "pour." The WBS is enhanced by strong, active verbs.[3]

**WBS Rule #3**

*The child components together make up the parent component, and only the parent component.*

When decomposing a node, it is easy to add things into the project. You should take care to see that the decomposition only implements the contents of the parent, and no more.

For example, *Design Invitations* only involves design activities, it should not include printing or mailing. If you feel the urge to add something into the WBS, you should first request a change to the scope. If the ruling is that the change is a clarification, then you can go ahead.

---

[1] Technically, the chunks of the WBS are components of the system and/or deliverables. They do not become activities until later in the project development cycle. However, since they will almost always turn into activities, we occasionally cheat and use the word here. It is clearer to talk about "activities" than components.

[2] The latest version of the PMBOK defines all activities in terms of verbs. We've been campaigning for verbs for years, and are delighted to see the world catch up with us.

[3] And unlike your English class, it is quite acceptable to repeat verbs. Always go for the precise and correct verb, even if you have to repeat it. For example, if you are planning a wedding, it is OK to *make invitations, make table settings*, etc.

14. THE WBS

**WBS Rule #4**

*The WBS is deliverable-oriented: all of the components must produce a deliverable.*

In Fig. 14.1, all of the nodes produce a deliverable, and it is easy to understand what they are. Even the *Approve Invitations*, which is not part of the design process has a deliverable: The Letter of Approval from the customer.

We have continually emphasized the idea that deliverables are tangible. Consider the *Pour Foundation* example above, it is clear that the deliverable is tangible–the concrete foundation. By concentrating on deliverables and their verbs, you remove all ambiguity about the activity. You will easily be able to tell when the activity *Pour Foundation* is complete.[4]

**WBS Rule #5**

*There is no time ordering in the WBS.*[5]

When developing the WBS, you should never say things like "Printing comes *before* Mailing." Neither should you say "Mailing comes *after* Design." The WBS is just a list of activities. When designing the WBS, stay away from words like *before, after,* and *first.*[6]

**WBS Rule #6**

*The 4 ± 2 Components Rule.*

Psychologists tell us that we can only hold about 4-5 ideas in our heads simultaneously. Since all of the components of a layer are related, that means we should not have more than 5 or 6 nodes in a layer. If you have more than that, you should combine them into more manageable pieces.

When developing a WBS, it is not unusual in the early stages for some layers to sprawl across the page. This is where creative design is required. What nodes should be grouped together? Why should nodes be combined? What will be the result of combining nodes? There are reasonable answers to these questions, which we explore below when we talk about WBS design.

**WBS Rule #7**

*The WBS is Progressively Elaborated.*

The first version of the WBS is at a high level. As project planning and project design proceed, more detail is added. Clarifying the design, and detailing the deliverables as time goes on is called *progressive elaboration..* Clarifying the planning of schedules and costs as time goes on is called *rolling wave planning.*

Excessive decomposition at inappropriate times or in low priority sections is unproductive. Therefore, not all levels need to be developed to the same level of detail—it is perfectly acceptable for the tree to be unbalanced.

---

[4]You won't be able to carve your initials in the concrete.

[5]Sequencing, as it is called, comes later; in the *Sequence Activities* process.

[6]It is quite acceptable, and even normal, to arrange the activities as we did in Figure 14.1, where the earlier stuff is on the left. It's just that you are not allowed to say it!

In Figure 14.1, the node *Design Invitations* is decomposed, but *Mail Invitations* is not. This is perfectly acceptable, since the design step needs more clarification and definition, but mailing the invitations is pretty straightforward and needs no more explanation and, therefore, no decomposition.

The early work on the WBS tends to validate the requirements, finding spec errors and missing pieces. The later work on the WBS moves towards design, and begins to refine the project *performance*.

## 14.2 Some Bad WBS Practices

In Figure 14.2, we have deliberately committed a number of WBS no-nos. First, there are no verbs. If we examine the *Software Applications* node, we know we need a word processor, spreadsheet and utilities (presumably because the scope required them). But we do not know whether we are to develop them or to buy them, which makes a huge difference! [7]

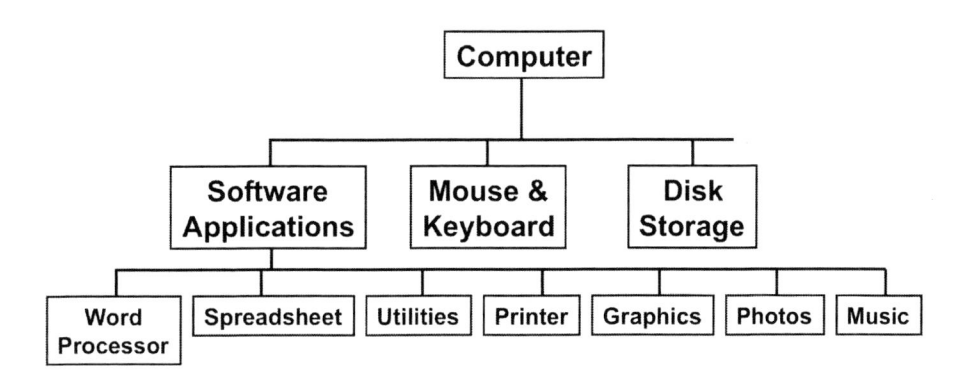

Figure 14.2: Some WBS No-nos.

Another poor aspect of this WBS is that the *Software Applications* node is decomposed into too many child nodes.

Also, the child nodes mix up apples and oranges: What is the *Printer* doing there? Since there is no verb, we do not know if it is printer software (in which case it might belong), or the physical printer (in which case it does not belong in the *Software Applications* node).

We might consider dividing the *Software Applications* node into *Applications* and *Utilities*. Then we have to decide which software goes where. Suppose the appli-

[7] We have deliberately selected an information technology (IT) example here because the IT folks frequently suggest that their systems are different. For example, IT folks use an *object oriented* design paradigm, and as long as they include active verbs, it's OK by us. After all, it's a WBS, not a design.

# 14. THE WBS

cations are expensive and require a careful evaluation of features vs. cost. On the other hand, suppose the utilities are generally low cost and we just have to select which ones we want. In that case, it makes sense in the WBS to separate the applications from the utilities.

That separation also improves the design because they are different types of activities requiring different expertise. Therefore, we would assign different people to the activities, since they require different skills: features and cost analysis for applications; simple collection for utilities. This separation is an example of a *design choice*. You should be careful with these, as they will haunt you for a long time.

This is an excellent example of how to go about the aggregating vs. decomposing process. It is about making the process easier to manage. Separating the complex software application evaluation from the simpler utilities acquisition puts like things together. Also, experts in applications may not be experts in utilities, so that is another reason to group them in separate entities.

We emphasize that the design of the WBS should facilitate the management of the project, not the design of the system.

## 14.3 Graphical vs. Outline WBS

### 14.3.1 Graphical WBS

Fig. 14.3 shows a first pass at a WBS for a kitchen remodeling project. In this form, it is called a *Graphical WBS*

We have the basics down, but it is now time to analyze it. The first step is to go back to the scope document and make sure that all of the requirements, features, and management processes are included in the WBS. Then we examine all of the other documentation (SOW, risk plans, etc.) and again ensure that all requirements are in the WBS.

If we did that, we would see that there is a large piece missing from the WBS. Can you figure what it is?[1]

The first layer decomposition has seven nodes. This is probably too many, so we should consider aggregating some.[8] There is no correct or right way to design a WBS, it is a creative process. So we will ask some questions and give suggestions as to how to proceed.

[8] Especially as there is a glaring omission.

## 14.3. Graphical vs. Outline WBS

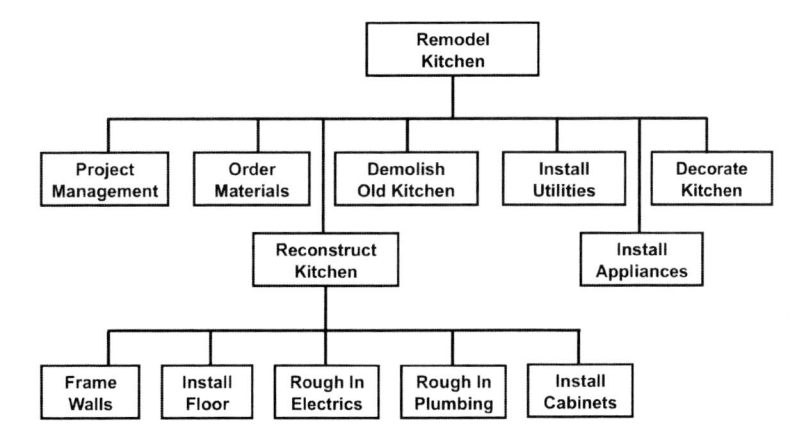

Figure 14.3: Preliminary WBS for a kitchen re-modeling project.

1. *Order Materials.* This has been separated out. This makes sense if one person orders everything, so that the project manager can find out the status of all orders by asking one person. On the other hand, if the appliances are to be ordered by the customer, and the plumber and electrician will order their own materials, then it does not make sense to separate this out at a high level.

2. *Utilities.* These are scattered throughout the WBS. We have *Install Utilities* at the top level, and plumbing and electrics at a lower level. We might consider moving the plumbing and electrics under utilities.

    There are two questions:[9] Can the utilities be better managed if they are under one unified *Install Utilities* node? Or, is it better to leave them under *Reconstruct Kitchen* next to the walls and floor nodes. Since the plumbers and electricians will almost certainly be separate sub-contractors, with their own skills, schedule and deliverables, perhaps it makes more sense to manage them under an *Install Utilities* node.

    The floor and framing are carpentry activities, and so belong together, and are probably OK where they are. Notice that we have learned something here: When we remove the plumbing and electric activities from the *Reconstruct Kitchen* node, what remains are activities for the carpenters. So a better name for the node might be *Do Carpentry*.[10]

As you start to add layers and nodes to the decomposition, the WBS quickly expands beyond the page. At this point, there are two approaches that help. First,

[9] At least two!

[10] We don't know the verb for *Carpentry*, so the boring "Do" will have to suffice

197

separate pages can be developed for nodes that are relatively independent. For example, we could separate out the carpentry node, and place it on a separate page. Since this is an important piece of the project, this page will make managing much easier.

To accomplish this, we need to add a numbering system to the WBS, so that when we view a subsystem, we know where it falls in the hierarchy.

### 14.3.2 Outline WBS

When the WBS gets too complicated for a graphical representation, then there is another option that works much better for presenting the details: The Outline WBS Format. An example of this is shown in Fig. 14.4 below.

```
0    Kitchen
  1.    Plan Project
     1.1      Obtain Loan
     1.2      Obtain Permit
  2.    Order Everything
     2.1      Select & Order Cabinets
     2.2      Select Appliances
  3.    Demolish Old Kitchen
  4.    Manage Utilities
     4.1      Install Plumbing
     4.2      Install Electrics
     4.3      Install Appliances
        4.3.1     Install Gas Range
        4.3.1     Install Refrigerator
        4.3.1     Install Electric Appliances
  5.    Do Carpentry
     5.1      Install Floor
     5.2      Install Frame Walls
  6.    Decorate Kitchen
     6.1      Plaster Walls
     6.2      Paint Walls
```

Figure 14.4: Outline WBS Format for the kitchen re-modeling.

## 14.3. Graphical vs. Outline WBS

You might object that the carpentry came after the utilities, which is illogical. However, we remind you that there is *no order* in a WBS. It is simply a list of activities.

There are several ways to number the WBS. The simplest is just to let *Microsoft Project* do it. Our preferred method is shown in Figure 14.4. Each major subsystem in numbered sequentially. Another method is to number the kitchen as 1.0, but then everything has a '1.' in front of it–see Fig. 14.5.

```
1.0    Kitchen
   1.1    Plan Project
       1.1.1    Obtain Loan
       1.1.2    Obtain Permit
   1.2    Order Everything
       1.2.1    Select & Order Cabinets
       1.2.2    Select Appliances
   1.3    Demolish Old Kitchen
   1.4    Manage Utilities
```

Figure 14.5: Outline WBS numbered starting with 1.0.

One can also use letters for the major subsystems, which is useful when a large system is being developed, both because there are more letters than numbers and you can use meaningful letters for subsystems.

For example, in Figure 14.6, activites at the top system level are labeled with an 'A'. The software subsystem activities are labeled with an 'S', the radar activities with an 'R', etc. This has the advantage on a large system of immediately indicating the area of expertise. When a staff member calls and says, activity R.2.6.4.3 is going to be late, the project manager at least knows the radar subsystem is involved.

```
A     Major System
    A.1     Collect System Requirements
    A.2     Design System
    A.3     Design Interfaces
S     Software
    S.1       Requirements Collection
    S.2       Design Software
    S.3       Code & Test
R     Radar System
    R.1       Design Radar subsystem
    R.2       Design Radar Hardware
    R.3       Build & Test Radar System
T     Test System
    T.1       Test System
    T.2       Test Subsystems
    T.3       Test Interfaces
U     Train Users
X     Conduct Acceptance Tests
```

Figure 14.6: Outline WBS using letters for major subsystems.

## 14.4 WBS Design

In Figure 14.2, we provided some excellent examples of the issues involved in the aggregating vs. decomposing process when designing a WBS. The decision to aggregate or separate is based on making the process easier to manage. That is separating the complex software application evaluation from the simpler utilities acquisition put like things together. Also, experts in applications may not be experts in utilities, so that is another reason to divide them into separate entities.

We emphasize that the design of the WBS should facilitate the *management* of the project. Note that we are not facilitating the design of the system, a subtle but important difference. The system designer has different goals from the project manager, and so the design may aggregate the software components for aesthetic design reasons, coherence (putting like things together), and de-coupling (reducing interdependencies).

The project manager structures the WBS completely differently from the design so as to make it easier to *manage* the project. The project manager focuses on deliverables, not design objects.[11]

[11]This incidentally, is why we think a Process Breakdown Structure (a PBS instead of a WBS) is a bad idea. The PBS focuses on processes, whereas the WBS focuses on deliverables. Deliverables are the basis of project management, not processes ... despite the fact that the PM-BOK is process oriented–but that's another discussion.

There are three parts to a WBS. Initially, one defines high-level deliverables, which give a broad overview of the project. In Figure 14.1, we established the high level actions of the Make Invitations project as design, print, and mail. These high level components will be used later to communicate the status of the project to the stakeholders. Since the major activities are designing, printing, and mailing, it makes sense to represent them in the WBS. When these activities are complete, they will indicate useful milestones.

### 14.4.1 Work Packages

The lowest level components in the WBS are called *work packages*; they are the leaves of the tree.

> *The work package represents the point at which cost and activity durations can be reliably estimated and managed.*

In the Make Invitations project in Figure 14.1, *Select Graphics* and *Mail Invitations* are work packages, since they are not decomposed further.

Initially, when the WBS is first constructed, the work packages identify:

- the outputs required, i.e., the deliverables
- the work with active verbs

As project planning proceeds, and information becomes available, the WBS work packages accumulate more information:

- the time to complete or the completion date
- a time-phased budget to complete the activity–the cost
- the resources (personnel time and equipment) required to complete the activity
- a single person who is responsible
- monitoring points (milestones) for measuring success
- quality requirements
- documentation, including scope references, technical requirements, etc.
- relevant contract information

### 14.4.2 Work Package Size

The WBS should be decomposed until the components are small enough to satisfy
**The 1 → 2 Rule**

*A work package should be completable by 1 – 2 people in 1 – 2 weeks.*

The rationale for this rule is that if something goes wrong, the project manager will learn about it quickly. The problem may still remain, but the project manager will have options, such as adding people, changing staff assignments, requesting clarification, etc.

### 14.4.3 Control Accounts

When people work on projects, their hours must be tracked.[12] To record the hours worked, a number or code is required to assign the work to.

For example, in the kitchen remodeling WBS (Fig. 14.4), someone working on the *Install Refrigerator* activity may report their hours with the code: 4.3.1. Or, more likely, the company's information system will assign a number code that maps to the WBS item 4.3.1.

However the cost accounting is tracked, there is a direct relation between the WBS components and the costs incurred while working on the project. Later, we will see how this information is used to compare actual performance with planned performance using *earned value*.

Control accounts are designated after the WBS has been constructed, and are selected to give the best way to track and manage the deliverables.

*The WBS component used for the project cost accounting is called the Control Account (CA). Each control account is assigned a unique code or number that links directly to the company's accounting system.*

Project costs are managed at the control account level. Control accounts may contain many work packages. For example, in Figure 14.4, the control accounts could be assigned at the level of *1. Plan Project, 2. Order Everything*, etc. It might be decided that tracking costs below this level is unnecessary work.

Control accounts are often associated with departments, who are then held responsible for the work. Using Figure 14.4 as the example again, *1. Plan Project* is

---

[12] Usually, this is so that they can be paid, but in non-profits and many other organizations, one tracks hours, not dollars.

assigned to the project management department; *2. Order Everything* is assigned to the purchasing department, etc.

### 14.4.4 WBS Dictionary

The definition of the WBS Dictionary is:

> *The WBS Dictionary is a detailed description of the work and technical documentation for each WBS element.*

For the PMA project, we provide an example of a *WBS Dictionary* element in Table 14.1.

Table 14.1: *WBS Dictionary Element* for PMA Case

| WBS Code | WBS Element |
|---|---|
| 2.1 | Create a Data Entry Form to Register New Members |
| | **WBS Element Description** |
| | The entry form should consist of the following essential attributes, first name, last name and email address. Additional information that can be captured includes education, college of graduation, current job title. The form should have email validation for format of the email and should test if the first name and last name fields are not blank. The QA department will test the form after it has been tested by the project team. They will also test for ADA compliance. |
| Milestone | Should be completed by November 30th of the current year. |
| Responsible | Joe Smith |
| Cost | 8 hours, $400 |
| Test | Add new member test. |

### 14.4.5 WBS and the Cost Estimate

The design of the WBS converts the scope into activities to be completed, and is the primary input to cost estimation process. The accuracy of the cost and schedule estimates depends directly on the quality of the WBS, because it is the foundation fo the bottom-up cost estimation. Therefore, when designing the WBS, it is important to highlight, or separate out, items with a significant cost.

## 14. THE WBS

A good example of this is shown in the New Kitchen project, where the appliances are separated out—See Figure 25.6: *4.3 Install Appliances*. The appliances were a major cost item, and so appear prominently in the WBS. The actual installation of the appliances turned out to be a minor activity from the scheduling perspective, just a few days of work.

The selection of appliances was also a major planning issue, because we knew it would take a long time to select them. As it turned out, this activity was not on the critical path. The delivery of the kitchen units took so long (12 weeks), and the selection of appliances activity was in parallel with it, so there was plenty of time to select appliances.[13]

The WBS is also the document used to report the status of the project to the customer, management and stakeholders. The *monitoring and controlling* processes will measure the progress of the WBS components. The WBS is also the link from the project to the company accounting system, and allows the assignment of work to specific team members.

The WBS is, therefore, a critical document, as it is the foundation of all planning to follow. Finally, we again emphasize that the design of the WBS is a creative process and a good design will make project planning better and go more smoothly. Templates help, but do not replace creative analysis.

---

[13] Which, incidentally, relieved a lot of pressure.

# CHAPTER 15

# TIME

> **Time is nature's way of keeping everything from happening at once.
> Space is what prevents everything from happening to me.**
>
> *John Wheeler*

Time management is really all about the *schedule*.[1] The PMBOK defines time management as consisting of:

1. *Define Activities.* The WBS work packages are turned into *activities*. Activities define the actions requires to produce the project deliverables.[2] High level WBS work packages may be further decomposed into lower-level activities in order to refine the deliverables. Activities are refined to the point where their cost and schedule can be *estimated*.

2. *Sequence Activities.* This defines the order in which activities must be carried out and the relationships between them.

3. *Estimate Activity Resources.* Resources include people and materials, such as cash, equipment, or supplies. The types and quantities of resources required to complete the activity are estimated.

---

[1] You can't really manage *time*, no one understands what it is, let alone explain how to manage it. But you can manage the schedule.

[2] An *activity* is anything that consumes time.

# 15. Time

4. *Estimate Activity Durations.* The time required to complete each activity is estimated.[3]

5. *Develop Schedule.* All of the above are combined to develop the project schedule. The schedule is an output of the network diagram, which is the focus of Chapter 16—Network. The critical path emerges.

6. *Control Schedule.* This is where the project manager *monitors* the status of the schedule as it evolves, and determines true schedule (vs. the planned schedule), and the impact of changes.

## 15.1 From WBS to Activities

The WBS is a deliverable-oriented list of activities. It is important to emphasize that there is no sequence to the activities in the WBS. The words "first" or "before" are not allowed when constructing the WBS. The order of activities is defined during *Sequence Activities* process: Which activities need to be completed before others can start? Which activities can be completed in parallel?

```
1.0   Build House
      1.1   Design House
      1.2   Initial Planning
      1.3   Hire Contractors
      1.4   Order Everything
      1.5   Construction
```

Initial Planning → Design House → Hire Contractors
                                → Order Everything

[3]The PMBOK defines this in terms of the rather cumbersome "number of work periods."

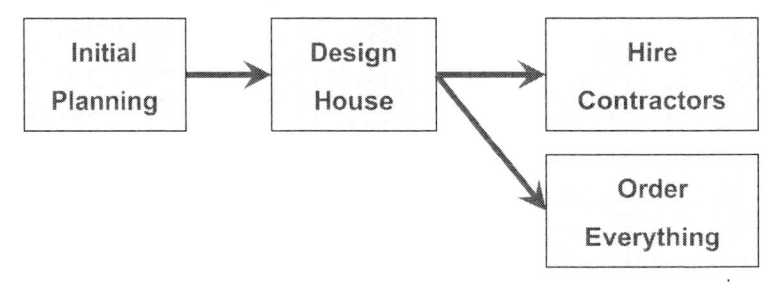

Figure 15.1: From WBS to ordered activities.

[4]An estimate of the durations is also required, but is ignored here to concentrate on the ordering.

Figure 15.1 gives an example of the process of going from the WBS to an ordered collection of activities ready to go into the network diagram.[4] After thinking about the activities in the WBS, it was decided that initial planning should come before the design of the house. Also, once the design is in place, the activities of hiring contractors and ordering stuff can be conducted in parallel.

# CHAPTER 16

# THE NETWORK DIAGRAM

> **Even if you are on the right track,
> you'll get run over if you just sit there.**
>
> *Will Rogers*

The WBS is a deliverable-oriented list of activities and we have continually emphasized that there is no sequence to the activities in the WBS. During cost estimation, the time to complete each of the activities (the duration) is estimated. With a list of activities and their duration as inputs, we can now construct the network diagram.

The goal of the network diagram is to produce the schedule for the entire project. The *critical path*, which is the most important concept in all of project management, emerges from the network diagram.

## 16.1  A Simple Example

This example contains everything you need to know about network diagrams. No matter what network you find yourself confronted with, no matter how large or complicated it looks, it will not contain any concepts that are not in the simple

## 16. THE NETWORK DIAGRAM

example presented here. If you understand this example, you need not be afraid of any network.

It's dinner time, and you decide to have chicken for dinner.[1] Some quick planning ensues, and you realize that you need to complete four activities, each with a time estimate (in minutes):

1. Marinate the chicken (15 min).

2. Cook chicken (20 min).

3. Microwave the vegetables (10 min).

4. Serve (5 min).

Next we must sequence the activities because they must be completed in the right order, e.g., cooking cannot happen before marinating. We also realize that cooking the chicken takes place in the oven, while the vegetables are microwaved. Therefore, these activities can happen in parallel. Finally, the 'serve' activity cannot take place until both the microwave and cooking activities are completed.

This is called activity sequencing, and the result is the determination of the *predecessor* activities. Predecessor activities are those that must be completed before an activity can start.

The next step is to create a table of activities, as shown in Table 16.1.

Table 16.1: Table of activities, durations, and predecessors.

| ID | Name | Duration | Predecessors |
|----|------|----------|--------------|
| A  | Marinate | 15 | None |
| B  | Cook Chicken | 20 | A |
| C  | $\mu$Wave | 10 | A |
| D  | Serve | 55 | B, C |

[1] A student paying attention will say, "Hey! This is not a project, it's routine! Quite correct. However, we have selected a *simple* example to illustrate the network digram, preferring clarity.

The first column identifies the activity, by giving it a label (or number), called the *activity identification* (ID). The *ID* is a unique number, and you can use any convenient system for numbering the activities. For example, in a complex diagram with sub-activities, you may use 1.1, 1.2, etc.

## 16.1. A Simple Example

The second column is the name of the activity, and the third lists its estimated duration. During the planning stage, which is where we still are in the project cycle, the durations are estimates. When the project moves into implementation, these will change to actual completion times.

The fourth column lists the predecessor activities. For example, activity D cannot begin until activities B and C are completed. Serving cannot happen until both $\mu$waving and cooking are finished.

### 16.1.1 Nodes

Using Table 16.1, we next construct a rough network diagram—see Fig. 16.1. This is a useful step, as it allows you to lay out the diagram and arrange the activities on the page. The circles in the diagram are called nodes.

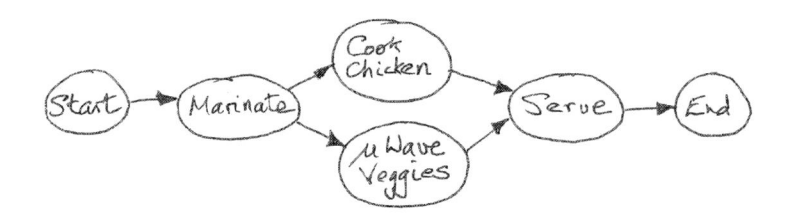

Figure 16.1: Rough Network Diagram.

Note that we have inserted start and end nodes. All projects should have start and end nodes. Sometimes an activity can be started at any time, but without a start node, it cannot be linked to the network. It is then what we call a dangling activity.

Later, the start and stop nodes will allow us to create milestones for the start and end of the project, so they are important planning tools. For example, we can add to the start node the idea that cooking begins at 6 pm. All projects need a start date, and the start node is a convenient place to put it.

### 16.1.2 Arrows and Predecessors

The arrows in figure 16.1 have a well-defined meaning:

*The arrow from A to B means that activity B cannot start until activity A is completed.*

B is said to be a *predecessor* of A. This definition of the predecessor is very precise. In fact, the entire network is constructed from this definition.

The start node has zero time (in fact, it is a milestone). Activity, A, the marinating activity, has one predecessor, the start node. Once we start the project, marinating starts.

As soon as marinating is completed, two more activities can start: cooking and microwaving. The arrows from A to B, and A to C have very specific, well-defined meanings: The arrow from A to B means that B cannot start until A has finished. The arrow from A to C means that C cannot start until A has finished.

The arrows from B to D, and C to D also have very specific, well-defined meanings. The two arrows going into the node D mean that D cannot start until *both B and C have finished*. That is, D cannot start until both B and C are complete.

We emphasize that all this is implied by the definition of the arrows. In practical terms, the two arrows going into D mean that serving cannot take place until both the chicken is cooked and the vegetables come out of the microwave.

These predecessor (or ordering) relations are shown in Table 16.1 in the "Predecessors" column. When the arrow is used in this way, it is called a finish-to-start constraint.

### 16.1.3 The Activity Properties Box

The definition of the activities properties box is shown in Table 16.2.

Table 16.2: The activity properties box.

| Earliest Start | ID | Earliest Finish |
|---|---|---|
| Slack | Description | Slack |
| Latest Start | Duration | Latest Finish |

Let's fill in this box for activity A. The ID is A, the description is "Marinate Chicken," and the duration is 15 minutes. The next box to be filled in is *Earliest Start*. A is the first activity and so it starts at time zero. Therefore, the earliest time that A can start is zero, so we put zero in the top left hand box.

We now ask the following question:

> If the earliest start for A is zero, and A takes 15 minutes to complete, what is the earliest finish for A?

It should be clear that the earliest finish for A is 15, which is shown in Table 16.3.

Table 16.3: Table of *earliest* properties for A.

| 0 | A | 15 |
|---|---|---|
|  | Marinate Chicken |  |
|  | 15 |  |

## 16.2 The Forward Pass

At what time will we serve dinner? Another way to look at this question is: How long is our project?

This question is answered by completing what is known as the forward pass. The definition of the arrow from A to B means that activity B cannot start until A has finished. Therefore, the earliest that B can start is the same as the earliest finish for A. Therefore, the earliest start for B is 15. We now ask the same question of B that we asked of A:

> If the earliest start for B is 15, and B takes 20 minutes to complete, what is the earliest finish for B?

It should be clear that the earliest finish for B is 35 = 20 + 15, which is shown in Table 16.4.

We now continue this *forward pass* process by completing the table for C, which is shown in Table 16.5.

A complication in the forward pass occurs when two arrows go into an activity, such as D—see Figure 16.2. The arrows from B to D and C to D mean that D cannot

## 16. THE NETWORK DIAGRAM

Table 16.4: Table of *earliest* properties for B.

| 15 | B | 35 |
|---|---|---|
|  | μWave Vegetables |  |
|  | 20 |  |

Table 16.5: Table of *earliest* properties for C.

| 15 | C | 25 |
|---|---|---|
|  | μWave Vegetables |  |
|  | 10 |  |

begin until both B and C have finished. In practical terms, the arrows represent the idea that serving cannot start until both cooking and microwaving have finished.

Therefore, the earliest start for serving is the latest of the earliest finishes for cooking and microwaving, i.e., after whichever activity is the *last to finish*.

The earliest finish for B is 35, and the earliest finish for C is 25. Therefore, B finishes last at 35, and D has to wait around for that, so the earliest start for D is 35. Since D takes 5, the earliest finish for D is 40. D is the last activity in the project, and since the earliest finish for D is 40, the earliest finish for the entire project is also 40.

*We know the earliest finish date for the project!*

When two arrows go into an activity, it is called a *merge activity*. The merge activity cannot start until both preceding activities are complete, and so the earliest start time for a merge activity is the latest of the earliest finishes of the preceding activities.[2]

This completes the forward pass. The only complication was that when two arrows entered activity D, and we took the latest of the earliest finish times as the earliest start time for D. Since B will take longer than C, there is some spare time between the finish of C and the beginning of D—the vegetables are going to be sitting around for a while.

The power of the forward pass is that it determines the earliest finish for the entire project. If we start cooking at 6 pm, the earliest we can expect to finish serving is 40 minutes later.

---

[2] This definition is almost impossible to remember, so when facing a test, we suggest you just draw Figure 16.4.

214

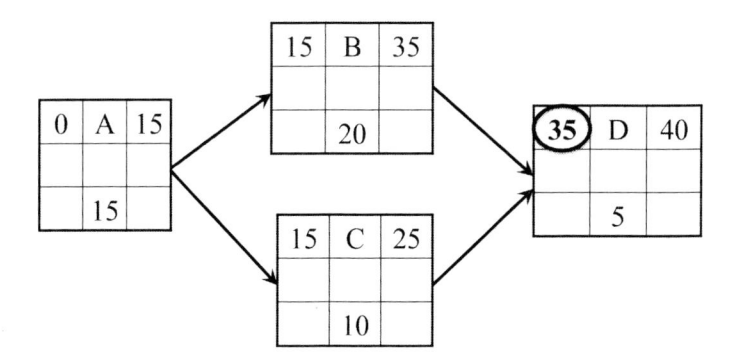

Figure 16.2: The completed *Forward Pass*.

## 16.3 The Backward Pass

> **Life can only be understood backward, but it must be lived forward.**
>
> *Søren Kierkegaard*

To start the backward pass, we go to the latest finish for the last activity in the network—node D in Figure 16.3. Note that D is the last activity in the project, so the latest finish for D is the *latest finish for the entire project*. To fill in the correct value for this box, we ask a deceptively simple-looking question:

*What is the latest finish for the project?*

Actually, this is a trick question, and you might want to think about it before continuing. The answer is below.[3]

For example, suppose you want to watch a TV show that starts at 6:30. Even if you are prepared to eat while watching TV, you will miss the start of the show, because the earliest time the serving will finish is 6:40. This is our best estimate for

[3] The end date for the project is .... *Whenever the customer wants it!*

215

## 16. THE NETWORK DIAGRAM

the project's finish time. We estimated the activity durations, and constructed the forward pass without knowing how long the project would take. The fact that we want to watch a show at 6:30 is now a problem.

In practice, this is not at all unusual. Customers always have a finish date in mind when they conceive the project. Some time later, the earliest finish time emerges from the forward pass, and often it is after the customer's preferred end date!

At this point, the project manager has several options, including doing more activities in parallel, reducing the time for activities, and re-negotiating the end date with the customer, but these are topics for a later discussion. For now, we will proceed with the backward pass by inserting 40 as the latest finish for D. In section 16.4.1, we will show what happens when another value is used.

We ask the question:

> If the latest finish for D is 40, and its duration is 5, what is the latest start?

It should be clear that the latest start for D is 35 (40 − 5 = 35), which allows us to complete the table for D—Table 16.6.

Table 16.6: Table of *latest* properties for D.

| 35 | D | 40 |
|---|---|---|
|  | Serve |  |
| 35 | 5 | 40 |

D can start as soon as both B and C have finished (this is the meaning of the arrows from B and C to D). Therefore, since the latest start for D is 35, the latest finish for both B and C is also 35. For B, the duration is 20, and since the latest finish is 35, the latest start is 15 (35 − 20 = 15). Similarly, the latest start for C is 25 (35 − 10 = 25). The latest start for B is 15 and for C is 25.

The arrows from A to B and A to C mean that activities B and C can begin once A is completed. B has the earliest of the latest starts of B and C. Therefore, since the latest start for B is 15, the latest finish for A must also be 15. (If the latest start for C (25) were inserted as the latest finish for A, this would violate the condition that B's latest start is 25.

For A, the duration is 15, and since the latest finish is 15, the latest start is 0 (15 − 15 = 0). Since A is the first activity, we have arrived at the latest start for the entire

## 16.3. The Backward Pass

project: The latest start for the project is at time 0. This completes the backward pass.

We can now complete the backward pass, which is shown in Figure 16.3.

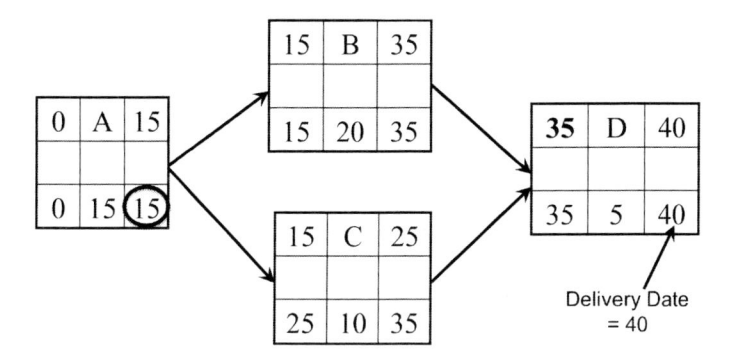

Figure 16.3: The completed backward pass.

A complication occurs when two arrows came out of an activity, which is called a burst activity. For the latest start time of a burst activity we used the earliest of the latest finish times as its latest start time.

### 16.3.1 Slack

The slack is defined as:

$$Slack = Latest\ Finish - Earliest\ Finish\ (LF - EF)$$
$$or$$
$$Slack = Latest\ Start - Earliest\ Start\ (LS - ES)$$

The easy way to remember the above formula is indicated in Figure 16.4 by the arrow to the left of the diagram: To calculate the slack, one subtracts the bottom number from the top number.

### 16. The Network Diagram

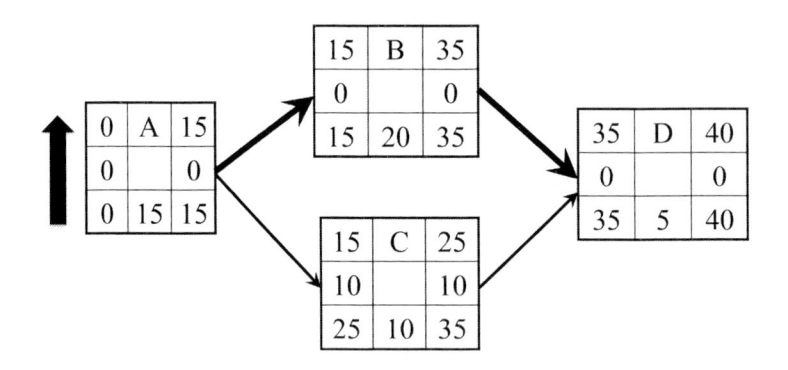

Figure 16.4: The slack and the *Critical Path*.

The values for the slack are shown in Figure 16.4. For example, for activity C, the latest finish, LF, is 35 and the earliest finish, EF, is 25, so the slack is $LF - EF = 35 - 25 = 10$. Similarly, the slack can be calculated from the latest start minus the earliest start, $LS - ES = 25 - 15 = 10$.[4]

The slack is also called the *float*.

## 16.4 The Critical Path

If we look at Figure 16.4, we note that there is something special about the path: $A \to B \to D$. All of the activities on the path have the *least* slack (in this case, the slack is zero). If any of the activities A, B, or D are delayed, the whole project will be delayed. There is slack in C, so if C finishes a little late, it will not delay the entire project.

The path $A \to B \to D$ is called the *critical path*.

**The Critical Path is the most important concept in project management!**

[4] We emphasize that you really should calculate both slacks, because when you make an error in the backward pass calculation (which is where most people err) the two slacks come out different. Making sure that the two slacks are the same eliminates a lot of errors.

## 16.4. The Critical Path

We can see in Figure 16.4, that the path $A \to B \to D$ has two very important properties:

- The critical path is the *longest path* through the network.

- The critical path is the *shortest time* in which the project can be completed.

The activities A, B, and D are critical because if anything delays any one of them, the entire project will be delayed. If the cooking takes 40 minutes, rather than the 30 that was planned, serving will finish 10 minutes later than scheduled.

Microwaving the vegetables does not lie on the critical path, and so it can be delayed without affecting the project schedule. If microwaving begins as soon as the marinating is done, and even if it takes an extra 8 minutes, it will still not delay the project. Activity C is said to have some slack.

The formal definition of the critical path is:

*The critical path is the path that has the least slack in common.*

Note that there may be more than one critical path. If the duration for activity C were 20 minutes, then there would be 2 critical paths: $A \to B \to D$ and $A \to C \to D$. This means that we should also allow the definition of the critical path to be ... *the path(s) that has (have) the least slack in common.*[5]

The microwaving activity has a slack = 10 minutes, and so it can be started up 10 minutes later and still not delay the serving activity. C can be started later or take longer, but as long as the combination does not exceed the 10 minutes of slack, the project will not be delayed.

Of course, if microwaving takes more than 10 minutes, it will now be on the critical path. If we forgot to turn on the microwave and only realized it after 15 minutes, then activity C ends up on the critical path and will delay the serving activity.

**Warning:**

A "task" is the word that MS Project uses for an activity. Tasks are essentially equivalent to *activities* as we have defined them. The word "task" is not used in the PMBOK.

[5] The inclusion of the plural form, as in "path(s)", makes the definition of the critical path so ugly that we have left it out of our definition. We know it is formally correct that way, so just remember that it might be "paths."

## 16. THE NETWORK DIAGRAM

### 16.4.1 Please Finish Earlier!

> **The show doesn't go on because it's ready.
> It goes on at 11:30.**
>
> *Lorne Michaels*

Our project started at 6 pm, and we now know that the earliest finish is 40 minutes later. Let's now suppose we want to watch a TV program that starts at 6:30. We simply insert 30 in the latest finish for D and repeat the process, i.e., we enter 30 into the latest finish for node D in Figure 16.5.

The latest finish for D is 30, and its duration is 5, so the latest start is 25.

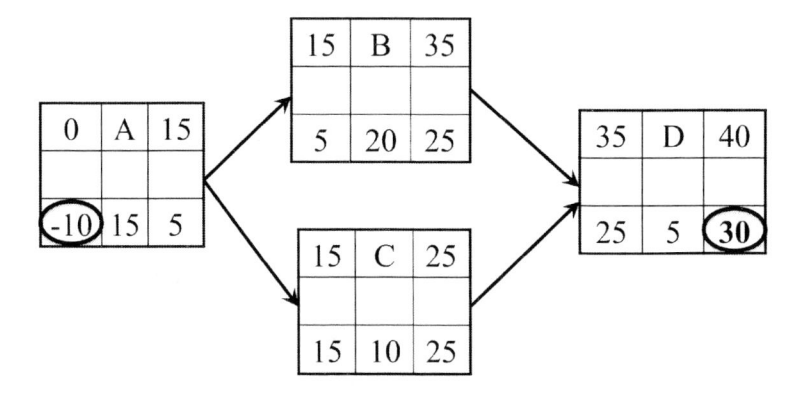

|   |   |   |     |   |   |    |   |   |    |
|---|---|---|-----|---|---|----|---|---|----|
|   |   |   | 15  | B | 35|    |   |   |    |
| 0 | A | 15|     |   |   |    |35 | D | 40 |
|   |   |   | 5   |20 |25 |    |   |   |    |
|-10|15 | 5 |     |   |   |    | 25| 5 |(30)|
|   |   |   | 15  | C | 25|    |   |   |    |
|   |   |   | 15  |10 | 25|    |   |   |    |

Figure 16.5: The completed backward with an earlier finish date.

Since the latest start for D is now 25, the latest finish for both B and C is also 25. For B, the duration is 20, and since the latest finish is 25, the latest start is 5 (25−20 = 5). Similarly, the latest start for C is 15 (15 − 10 = 15).

The latest start for B is 5 and for C is 15, so the latest finish for A is 5. For A, the duration is 15, and since the latest finish is 5, the latest start is −10 (5 − 15 = −10). The latest start for the project is at time *minus 10*

This simply says that to finish at 6:30 pm, we need to start 10 minutes earlier than 6 pm, i.e., at 5:50 pm. If the project has not started yet, then this is OK. If the project started at 6 pm, and you started the network diagram at 6 pm, then you are in trouble: You are going to miss the first 10 minutes of your TV show.

### 16.4.2 Milestones

Milestones, or events, denote important points in time in the project schedule, such as the completion of an activity or a deliverable. Examples of milestones are: The receipt of planning permission for a construction project; the delivery of the scope; the acceptance by the customer of a deliverable.

*Milestones are activities with zero duration.*

Milestones can and should be indicated on the network diagram, where they appear as triangles since they have zero duration. Milestones do not affect the flow of a project, even though they may appear along the critical path. In our cooking example, we might create a milestone called *Finished Cooking*, at the point at which the serving activity starts. If cooking is delayed, then the milestone will be delayed.

Explanations of project status to customers and upper management are usually clearer when presented in terms of milestones. This is because milestones represent the completion of important activities, and so are an excellent way to describe the project status. Also, presenting milestones rather than a complicated network diagram is a much less cluttered and clearer way to present the status of a project.[6]

### 16.4.3 Managing the Critical Path

By far the most important feature of any network diagram is its critical path. It is not at all unusual for the activities to change during a project, and their delivery may occur either earlier or later than originally planned. As soon as any change occurs on the project, the project manager should immediately check the impact on the critical path.

Suppose your immediate supervisor comes into your office and asks if he can borrow Mary for a few days. What do you do?

*Check the critical path!*

If Mary's assigned activity is not on the critical path, you can lend her out, and you gain credibility as a team player. If Mary's activity is critical, then you have an excellent excuse for declining to lend her out. On the other hand, you might suggest that Joe, whose activity is not on the critical path, would make a suitable substitute for Mary. You gain even more credibility as a smart team player.

[6] The PMBOK actually says that since milestones are easier to understand, it is better to present to upper management this way!

Many project management decisions are made easier when viewed in terms of their impact on the critical path. Consider the following recommendations:

- *Assign the best people to critical activities.* Often, this is **not** the case. Companies usually assign difficult activities to the most senior staff. Personally, we suggest assigning the most senior staff to the critical activities, even if they are the simplest. That way, they might finish early, and you pick up some valuable time.

- *Prioritize critical activities.* Every day when you come in, check the status of critical path activities. Smooth their way.

- *Conduct risk assessment on critical activities.* Once you start making up risks, it is easy to get carried away. Do the critical path activities first.

- *Regularly visit people working on critical activities.* Get them coffee. Keep them happy.

- *Assign the best computers and equipment to critical activities.* When a shiny, new, super-fast computer arrives, don't give it to the boss, give it to the person working on the critical path.

- *Roll up the non-critical activities.* An entire non-critical branch of the network can be lumped together as a single entity for management purposes. This unclutters the network diagram, and makes it easy to quickly pass over non-issues. Management typically prefers only to deal with problems.[7]

All of these management actions depend on knowing and understanding the critical path. The critical path typically includes only a small fraction of the activities in a project. This is useful, since it means the project manager can easily prioritize management decisions to ensure the critical path is not adversely affected.

### 16.4.4 Analyzing the Critical Path

The work on the critical path begins once it is created. Some issues are discussed below:

- *Is it sensitive?* When the majority of the activities fall on the critical path, the schedule is sensitive to any small delays. The project manager should try to move activities around, and break them up, to decrease the sensitivity.

---

[7]Of course, if any of those noncritical activities are late enough to affect the CP, they can quickly turn into real problems. Their impact on the critical path must be carefully assessed. Many late activities on a noncritical path can quickly turn it into a critical path.

- *A few long tasks dominate.* In this case, the long tasks should be divided into smaller activities. Many smaller activities can often be re-assembled in different ways, and often can be processed in parallel.

## 16.5 Activity Sequencing Relationships

Identifying activity relationships helps to describe the logical flow of work through the project. Predecessor and successor activities are constraints on the sequence in which activities must be performed. They dictate the order in which activities must be completed.

- *Predecessor Activities.* These must finish before any following activities can begin. (A is the predecessor to B in figure 16.4.)

- *Successor Activities.* These follow immediately after other activities. (B is the successor to A in figure 16.4.)

- *Concurrent, or parallel, activities.* These can be worked on at the same time, which shortens the schedule. (In figure 16.4, activities B and C can be performed in parallel—cooking the chicken and microwaving the vegetables can be performed at the same time.

- *Merge Activities.* These have at least two preceding activities on which they depend. In Figure 16.4, activity D is a merge activity (B and C merge into D).

- *Burst Activities.* These have at least two succeeding activities on which they depend. In Figure 16.4, activity A is a burst activity (B and C burst from A).

Dependencies dictate when or how an activity must be performed, and there are three types:

- *Mandatory Dependencies.* These are restrictions specific to one or more activities. Mandatory dependencies never change. Sometimes, mandatory dependencies are referred to as *hard logic.*

  For example, a mandatory dependency occurs in our cooking example, because we specified that marinating must be completed before cooking can begin. Many examples arise when building a house: The permit must be obtained before construction can start; the foundation must be finished before the walls can be started.

- *Discretionary Dependencies.* These are *preferred* ways of doing the project. Because they are *discretionary*, they may change as priorities change.[8]

  For example, in our cooking example, we may chose to complete the microwaving the vegetables activity after the chicken finished cooking. That way, the vegetables are still hot. We may equally well decide that the vegetables need to be cooked as quickly as possible, and so we would start them as soon as the chicken is marinated.

- *External Dependencies.* These are restrictions that result from activities outside the project itself. Usually, neither the project manager nor team members can control external dependencies. External dependencies may be either mandatory or discretionary.

  For example, obtaining a construction permit is an external, mandatory dependency. It is external, since the regulation comes from the town, and it is mandatory before construction can start.

Both mandatory and discretionary dependencies should be used with care, since they can affect the sequence of activities. Often there are assumptions involved, and these should be clarified and documented because the justification for the assumptions may change as the project evolves.

An example of an internal discretionary dependency is to insist that the vegetables and the chicken finish at the same time, so that they are hot.

## 16.6 Leads and Lags

The classic situation where a lag is used is in purchasing an item. Suppose you decide to buy a computer part and the delivery time is ten working days. The time estimate for the *Buy Part* activity might be one day (the time it would take to fill out the purchase request form, get signatures, etc.). Therefore the duration for the *Buy Part* activity should be 1 day.

Then you sit around for 10 days, waiting for the part. If you put 11 days in the network (1 to purchase the part and 10 for delivery), then the system will compute the cost of 11 days of work, when only one is really required. The 10 days of waiting should not be charged as a labor cost.

What is also important when adding up the costs, the *Buy Part* activity only consumes 1 day's worth of labor. The waiting activity costs nothing.

---

[8] Discretion is the better part of valor, and so the best way to perform the task is often the way that keeps the project manager happy.

However, waiting for the delivery takes 10 days, during which time no work is being performed. To properly handle this in the network diagram, you introduce a lag into the buying activity—see Figure 16.6.

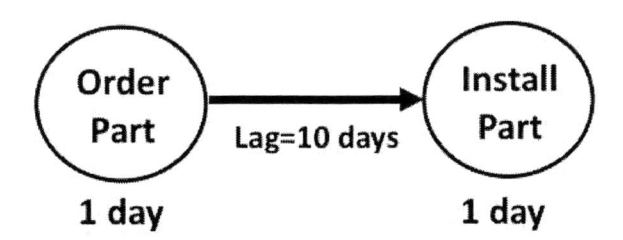

Figure 16.6: A classic Lag: Purchasing takes 1 day, but waiting for the part takes 10 days.

The time estimate for the *Buy Part* activity is 1 day, but the *Install Part* activity cannot start until after the lag period (10 days) has completed. More formally:

> *In a finish-to-start dependency, a lag is the time between the finish of a predecessor activity in a network diagram and the start of its successor activity.*

A *lead* says that an activity can begin early. (It can be thought of as a negative lag.) For example, in the preparation of a document, you might allow editors in the proofing department to start work a week before the document is complete and formally delivered. This is a risky action. The benefit is that some schedule compression might accrue because activities are being done in parallel. This must be balanced against the risk that the document might change substantially before delivery, and the editors might have to edit the document twice.

Leads and lags affect the timing of activities and so affect the critical path. In fact, they make the calculation of a critical path a bit tricky. While software packages can handle them correctly, the resulting critical path may not be easy to understand.

Our preference is not to use lags, but to explicitly put some sort of *Wait* activity in the network diagram. This clarifies the delay, and explicitly presents it to everyone. Especially if it is a significant item on the critical path, you would want everyone to know what the delay is. Also, you might not be able to affect the delay (e.g., manufacturing and shipping times), and so need to highlight it in the discussions.

### 16.6.1 Loops and Conditional Branches

A document that requires multiple drafts might be considered as an example of activities that could use loops in their sequencing. This might be described by Figure 16.7 as follows: Suppose Chapter #1 is written and delivered, so that the activity is complete.

The next activity is to review the Chapter #1 and create a second draft. This might be considered as a loop in the network diagram because *Write Chapter #1* is being re-executed. Such loops are not allowed in network diagrams. The arrow from *Edit* → *Write* in Figure 16.7 is considered an illegal construct.

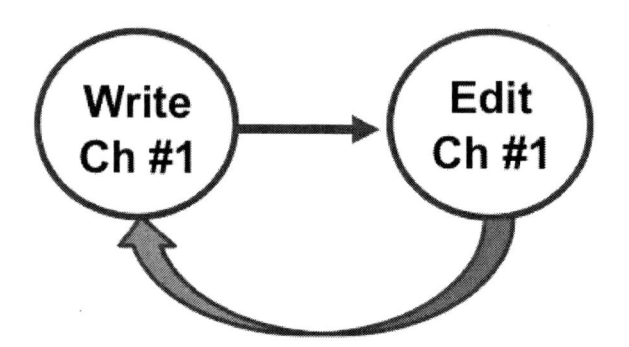

Figure 16.7: An illegal loop in a network diagram.

A much better way to describe the activities is the following:

1. Write Chapter #1

2. Edit Chapter #1

3. Re-write Chapter #1

Since the activities of writing, editing and even re-writing, require different skills, they can (and probably should) be assigned to different staff members. The initial writing may require an expert, and certainly, editing skills are quite different. After that, staff changes may require that the re-write be accomplished by yet another staff member. By not writing the activities in a loop, we more clearly define the work required and retain flexibility in assigning staff. So it is probably a much better option not to use the loop.

A conditional branch is one that has an "if" statement in it. An activity is completed "If something happens." Both loops and conditional branches tend to complicate the network. If you really want to include looping and branches, a technique called graphical evaluation and review technique (GERT) can be used.[9]

### 16.6.2 AOA and AON

Two approaches are used to describe project networks, and the one we have used so far is called *Activity on Node* (AON). AON is also called the *precedence diagramming method* (PDM), and is used by most project management software packages, and in practice, AON has come to dominate most projects.

So far, the diagrams in this chapter all used AON. Each activity is associated with a node (the circles in the diagram are nodes). The activities consume time[10] which is represented by the nodes.

There is another method called *Activity-on-Arrow*, (AOA) in which activities are denoted by arrows, so that if Figure 16.1 is rewritten in terms of AOA, it becomes:

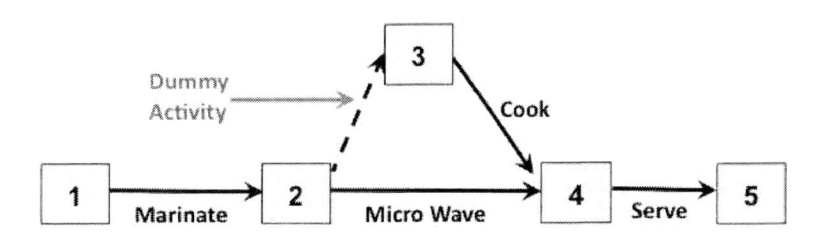

Figure 16.8: An *activity on arrow* (AOA) diagram, equivalent to Figure 16.1.

In an AOA diagram, the activities (and therefore, time) are denoted as arrows ans are labeled by the numbers of the nodes they connect. In the AOA diagram, the nodes consume no time. For example, the activity *Marinate* is 1 → 2, as it goes from node 1 to node 2. The activity *Cook* is 3 → 4.

The complication that occurs in an AOA diagram is the need for dummy activities. The *Cook* activity 3 → 4, and the *Microwave* activity is 2 → 4. In order to designate that *Cook* cannot start until *Marinate* is finished, the dummy activity 2 → 3, (the dotted line in Figure 16.8) must be added to the network.

Some analysts claim that the AOA form is easier to read and draw. We believe that the addition of the dummy activities tends to make AOA more difficult to under-

[9]Typically, both loops and conditional branches complicate the reading of network diagrams and confuse the readers more than they help. Like leads and lags, we avoid them like the plague.

[10]Remember, the definition of an activity is that it consumes time.

stand and construct.[11] What is true, however, is that AON has come to dominate the world of project management.

[11] Personally, we think that any system that requires adding something called a *Dummy* is pretty dumb! On the other hand, one of my colleagues thinks that AOA is the *only* thing to use. You decide.

# CHAPTER 17

# COST

> **The first 90% of the job took the first 90% of the money.**
> **The remaining 10% of the job took the other 90% of the money!**
>
> *Anonymous*

## 17.1 Cost Politics

Cost estimation is one of the hardest things to do on a project, for many reasons. First, it is technically challenging and quite difficult in its own right, but we will postpone this discussion until later in the chapter. Meanwhile, let's discuss the *perceptions* of a cost estimate.

### 17.1.1 It's an Estimate!

One of the problems that makes a discussion of cost difficult for the project manager is that once you have told the customer what the project cos is, that's it! No matter how many times you told them the number was "just a preliminary estimate," that number haunts you for ever.

We all behave the same way, no matter how enlightened we think we are. Does the following anecdote sound familiar? You ask the plumber for an estimate to unblock your sink drain. "About $150" the plumber says. Then plumber opens up the pipes under the sink and groans. Eventually, you get the bill: $250!

"But you said it would cost $150!" you cry.

Now magnify that by a thousand, and that is how your customer feels.[1]

In our experience, many people do not understand the concept of a draft document. Often people insist on correcting minor grammatical errors in something you clearly explained was a *Draft*. What you were hoping for was a high-level conceptual review of the ideas and concepts, you wanted to know if the project was feasible. They came back and said, "You should have asked if the project *were* feasible—it's subjunctive you know."

The same is often true of a cost estimate. Once people hear the dollars, they conveniently forget you said it was "within ±25%." If they heard anything, they only heard the *minus* 25%!

### 17.1.2 It's about the Future

> **If I had asked people what they wanted,
> they would have said faster horses.**
>
> *Henry Ford*

Another issue that makes cost estimation difficult is that it is inherently a prediction about the future. Since projects have not been done before, there is little data to go on, and the more innovative the project, the less reliable the prediction. Some of the most famously innovative projects also have infamously incorrect price tags: Our two top personal favorites are the Sydney Opera House and Boston's "Big Dig."

### 17.1.3 The Dream Factor

We described the Jello® Triangle whereby changing either the scope, the cost, or the schedule leads to changes in the other two. The scope, however, is different, because it represents the customer's dreams, which crash against the hard realities of cost and schedule. Figure 17.1 shows the spirit of this.

---

[1] Remember, in this book, you are the project manager. That tiny change to the scope document that hardly anyone noticed is now estimated to add thousands to the project. Imagine how your customer feels.

Figure 17.1: The scope dreams often crash on the reality rocks of cost and schedule.

### 17.1.4 The Optimism Factor

People want to please, and when it comes to giving a cost estimate to a customer, even more so. We want to give a low number. A mature project manager will distinguish between doing what's right for the project, and the desire to please.

### 17.1.5 Cost Estimation Errors

The accuracy of a project estimate is a function of where you are in the project. Early on, a macro estimate maybe off by 100%! Suppose you estimate the project cost as $10,000. A 100% error means that the project might cost $20,000. Of course, the error cannot be −100%, because then the cost estimate would be zero. We see immediately, that over-runs are much more likely than under-runs. In fact, this is a well-known property of projects, which we describe as follows:

*A project that starts to overrun will stay overrun!*

### 17.1.6 Marketing vs. Technical Estimates

There is an inherent tension between the marketing and technical departments over the budget. Often, marketing has a good estimate what the customer is willing to spend. This may be completely different from the cost estimate derived from the scope by the technical team. Both organizations will appeal to the project manager:

Marketing: The technical bid is too high. We can't win with their number.
Technical: We can't deliver if we use the marketing number.

### 17.1.7 Will it get canceled?

Large public sector projects often experience enormous cost growth. One of the contributing factors is that politicians sometimes believe that if they tell the truth about the cost, the public will not support it, and the project will be canceled.

This is a "failure of nerve" combined with a lousy cost justification argument. A good project manager should be able to make a financially compelling case for the project, and to convince a variety of stakeholders.

### 17.1.8 Protect the Valuables!

Customers are understandably curious about how you came up with the cost estimate. It's their money, and they feel entitled to investigate if you are taking advantage of them. It is a reasonable request.

On the other hand, if you hand over your carefully calibrated cost estimation formula, you risk giving away your competitive edge.

We recommend you educate your customer in *general* cost estimation, especially industry standards if they exist. That way, the customer can work from the scope to determine a reasonable cost estimate. This will be an independent estimate, and if it is close to the one you have submitted, then everyone should be happy.

## 17.2 Cost Estimation

> **It's tough to make predictions, especially about the future.**
>
> *Yogi Berra*

## 17.2. Cost Estimation

There are two types of cost estimates: high level and low level. High level estimates are created early on in the planning cycle, while low level estimates require more detail and so are generated later. Any of the techniques of cost estimation described below can be used at any stage, the real difference is their purpose.

The first estimate for a project is not likely to be very accurate (often referred to as a rough order of magnitude, or ROM. The goal of the ROM estimate is often to decide on the feasibility of the project. If the estimate and the budget are out of line, then adjustments can be made, either to the budget, or more likely, to the project content. The project manager can also begin lining up the cash-flow needs: Will it be necessary to borrow funds?

The early estimates establish the *budget* (the cost baseline) for the project, which is defined as the Budget at Completion (BAC). As soon as the project gets underway, costs will be reported, and progress is measured against the budget. If the budget is not well thought out, the project manager will have to continually ask for more money from the customer, which is not a good situation to be in.

A high level estimate is also referred to as a macro cost estimate, or a top-down estimate. Such estimates are made from the *scope* document, usually before there is a WBS.

*Estimation is the process of forecasting the time and cost of completing project deliverables.*[2]

The question of how long it will take, and how much will it cost are intimately related. Usually, one estimates in person hours, not dollars. Estimates in person hours are independent of hourly rates (and inflation), and so are more reliable. For example, if it takes 8 hours to paint my office today, then it will most likely take 8 hours to paint it next year. Next year, however, the painter's rates may have gone up, so the same job will cost more.

We wish to estimate in terms of some sort of constant productivity rate that is predictable. In the case of painting my office, the painter's estimate should be in hours, because he should have a good idea of how much he can paint in a day. The he multiplies by the cost per day to get the cost estimate. That is why almost all our estimates, are in terms of person hours and not dollars. Dollars change, hours don't.[3]

**Go get some pizza!**

[2] The PMBOK also adds "while balancing stakeholder expectations and the need for control." This is typical of junk added to definitions in the PMBOK. Balancing stakeholder expectations is a good idea, but technically irrelevant to the development of the cost estimate. The cost estimate is defined in terms of project parameters, and the stakeholder needs come later in the negotiation about the cost.

[3] One of the more interesting estimates I learned many years ago (sorry, I don't remember where) is that the cost of a man's tailored suit is approximately equal to the price of an ounce of gold, and has been for over 700 years! That is a great example of a time-independent cost estimate!

## 17. Cost

One of our favorite cost estimation formulae is the one that tells me how many pizza to order:

$$N = 1 + \frac{3G}{8}, \qquad (17.1)$$

where $G$ is number of guests. With 10 guests, I need 4.75 pizza, so rounding up, I order 5! I just have to multiply by the cost per pizza, and I have the cost.[4]

This is a quick and simple formula that does the job. It contains a parameter from the scope (number of guests) and is calibrated, i.e. it works in practice.[5]

Every industry has a standardized set of estimation parameters. You can't do business without them. Here's another example, which despite its simplicity, also has all the features we need.[1]

**The Cost of a Super-Yacht:**

A super-yacht is defined as a yacht whose length is greater than 40 meters (>130 feet) long. The cost estimate is:

Sail:   $1 million per meter
Power:  £1 million per meter[6]

How is this used? Someone saunters into the boat yard, and casually remarks that they just saw a yacht they rather liked. It was about 150 feet long, and they'd like to know how much it would cost to build one. You listen, rub your chin thoughtfully, and ask, *Power or sail?*

Listen carefully to the accent, because the cost depends on the currency. *Sail*, they say in an American accent. You quickly dividing the 150 feet by 3 to get 50 meters, and say,

*"In which case, it's about $50 million."*

Obviously, the eventual cost of the yacht will depend on a lot of factors, but for now you have established the ball park. Assuming your client did not faint at the price, it is now probably a good idea to hedge that number, *"But, of course, the actual cost will depend on the quality of the outfitting."*

This simple cost estimate formula actually has all the necessary features:

- *Parameters.* In this case there are two parameters: the length of the yacht, and whether it is power or sail. These two parameters are the major determinants of the eventual cost.

- *Accurate.* Accuracy depends on the situation, obviously, and there will be a lot of variation in super yacht costs. But this estimate is good enough to begin negotiations.[7]

---

[4] I am indebted to one of my students, Grant MacElhiney for telling me about this formula.

[5] Grant also says that it has worked for him for years, so it is calibrated. What more can you ask of a cost estimation formula?

[7] And, not incidentally, it will immediately sort out the serious buyers.

## 17.2. Cost Estimation

- *Easy to use.* A good cost estimate is practical. You need to be able to be able to immediately give the client a decent answer.

- *Calibrated.* Somebody plotted a chart of super yacht costs vs. length. Then they noticed that the line representing *$1 million per meter* was a decent fit to the data for sail.[8] This rule must be derived by an expert in the field; someone with credibility and access to a decent sized data sample.

- *Uncertain.* An "exact estimate" is an oxymoron. Estimates have uncertainties, which are important to understand.

While few of us will get to purchase such a yacht, the same process is repeated for every project. If someone gives you an estimate for a project, you are entitled to ask, "On what basis did you estimate that?"

There are two types of cost estimates:

1. Top-down (macro) estimate:

   The top-down estimate is made early on in the project, typically from the specification.[9] The estimate may be refined by analogy with other projects. Sometimes, a group of experts confer to reach a consensus. The estimate should be derived through a mathematical relationship, as the super-yacht estimate was.

2. Bottom-up (micro) Estimate:

   The bottom-up estimate is typically derived by estimating the cost of the individual activities in the WBS. Each element of the WBS (at some appropriate level) is independently estimated, and the layers summed to derive a total cost for the project. The estimates may be derived through a mathematical relationship, even at the lowest levels of the WBS.

Figure17.2 shows the accuracy of the cost estimation process as the project proceeds. During the concept phase, the macro estimate is typically within +75% → −25%.

During planning, the micro estimate from the WBS is +25% → −10%. By the time the project is 30%-40% complete, the cost estimate is an excellent representation of the actual, final cost.[10]

Notice the asymmetry in the error. The project is more likely to overrun than underrun.

---

[8] A good analyst would also list the standard deviation and the major factors that increase or decrease the estimate.

[9] Note that the estimate is made from the *spec*, not the *scope*. It is the *spec* that defines the project's content.

[10] There are many projects for which the estimate is consistently incorrect. For example, the estimate for Boston's Big Dig was initially $2.6B in 1984, then $6.4B in 1992. The actual cost of $14.6B was not owned up to until 2002. However, the politicians were not telling the public the truth. The engineers always knew it was a $12-$14B program.

235

## 17. COST

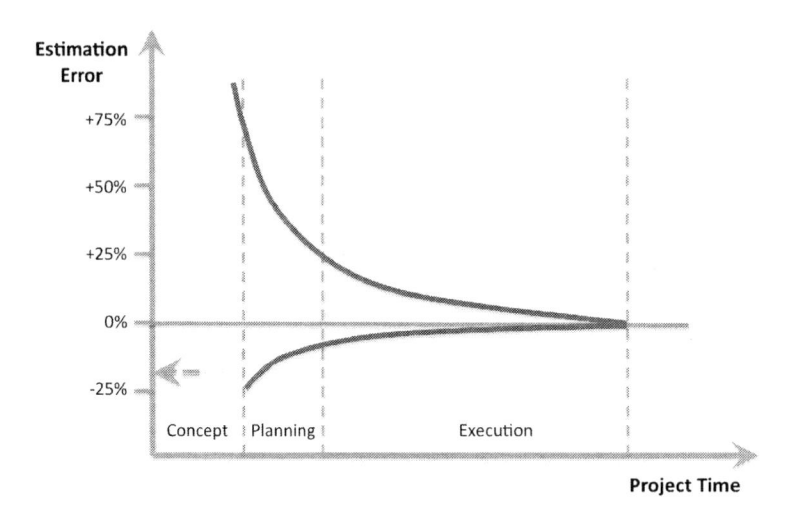

Figure 17.2: The Accuracy of cost estimation during the project life cycle.

Table 17.1 summarizes the situations when you might use the top-down approach, and when the bottom-up. If you need speed, and you only have a preliminary scope, use top-down. If you need accuracy, have the time, and there is a detailed WBS, then use bottom-up.

Table 17.1: When to use Top-Down vs. Bottom-up Cost Estimates.

| Situation | Top Down | Bottom Up |
|---|---|---|
| Strategic planning | X | |
| Speed important | X | |
| Accuracy important | | X |
| Customer needs options | X | |
| Poor scope | | X |

An important rule about cost estimates is that they are always made for the "average" situation, the most likely case. You should never add contingencies into a cost estimate, because that is handled in the risk analysis. It is tempting to add some rainy day funds into the cost estimate, but if you do, you will be adding unnecessary cost.[11]

[11] Besides, when your boss reviews your bid, she will invariably uncover your rainy-day funds, and immediately delete them.

Target costs should be distinguished from cost estimates. Typically, a target cost is proposed by the Marketing department, and is often based on information about the customer's desires, or goals. If marketing knows that the customer has allocated $10,000 for the project, they will press for the estimate to come in at $10,000 (or maybe less). The cost estimate made from the specification may not bear any relation to the customer's needs and wants, as the specification may include a long list of customer wishes, which force the cost well over $10,000.

One way to deal with this situation is for the technical team to estimate the cost of a minimum system, and then propose a series of optional add-ons. The customers can then select which options they can afford, according to their priorities.

Cost estimates that are created during the planning phase are used in strategic planning and feasibility studies. As the scope evolves (progressive elaboration), the cost estimate is refined (rolling wave planning), becoming more accurate. The basic process has three steps:

1. Estimate the size of the product, e.g., the *length* of the super yacht.

2. Estimate the effort (person-months) and convert to a cost, e.g., a 50m yacht will cost $50 million.

3. Estimate the schedule, e.g., a 50m yacht takes 3 years to build.

### 17.2.1 Parametric Techniques

**A dollar per horse per mile.**

*Paul Parnegoli*

The above quotation by Paul Parnegoli was his cost estimation rule for transporting horses in his special truck, from Kentucky Downs to places as far as California and Boston. As we shall learn, it is a parametric estimate.

Parametric techniques are mathematical models that use project characteristics to compute a total project estimate. This is a fast and reliable way to obtain a cost estimate in the early stages. Typically, the project parameters are determined from the specification.

When facing an estimation task the estimator always has to have a particular a model in mind. Most, if not all, cost models use predictors. According to De Marco,

"A predictor is an early-noted metric that has a strong correlation to some later results." [12] Most cost estimating tools have a parametric model inside.

Parametric models consist of equations, constants, and parameters. The values of the constants are determined by calibration using historical data. The parameters are system characteristics.

In an excellent, and quite sophisticated example, the author (Vijay Kanabar) designed and implemented a parametric model called a 4GT Model. But what is 4GT? According to Pressman, the term fourth generation technique (4GT) encompasses a broad array of tools that have one thing in common: each enables the software developer to specify some characteristic of software at a high level. [13] The tool then automatically generates source code based on the developer's specification. There is little debate that the higher the level at which the software can be specified, the faster a program can be built.

Here is Kanabar's formula to estimate the cost of a 4GT software project. The programming effort, $PE$, in person-hours, is.

$$PE = 10.2 \times \#Forms \\ + 7.9 \times \#Reports \\ + 4.9 \times \#Entities, \quad (17.2)$$

This is the programming effort only. The total effort, $TE$, for the project is:

$$TE = 3.1 \times PE. \quad (17.3)$$

The formula consists of several pieces. The parameters are the *number of forms*, the *number of reports*, and the *number of entities* (the data items). These can be estimated by examining the *spec*. The formula also contains several constants: 10.2, 7.9, and 4.9. These are determined by calibration using historical data.

The 4GT model only estimates the Programming effort, which is estimated as 32% of the total effort. This data leads us to recommend a multiplier of 3.1 in the 4GT Model to obtain the total effort for a project.

There were three steps in the development of this parametric cost estimate formula:

1. The parametric formula itself. The formula must conceived in terms of useful *spec* entities that can be counted (e.g., the number of screens).

2. The formula must be calibrated to determine the constants. This requires company data from similar projects.

## 17.2. Cost Estimation

3. Finally, the assumptions that apply to the model's use must be listed, e.g., it applies to 4GT software developments only.

**PMA Cost Estimate**

Suppose we want to add capabilities to the PMA web site to allow referees to register and examine the conference papers they have been assigned to review. The scope would contain information about logging in; presenting screens for referees to enter their data; listing the titles of papers; and allowing the referees to select and reject papers. (The scope would have more specific detail, but this is enough for now.)

We analyze the scope and decide we need 2 login forms for name and addresses; 2 forms for the referee's background and expertise; and 2 forms to select the papers. (A total of 6 forms.) We have one form to print out the paper titles when the referee has completed her assignment. As to data entities, we estimate 50 are associated with the referee's name and address, 20 with their qualifications, and 20 with each paper (title, author data, subject area, accepted/rejected, etc.), for a total of 90 data entities.[12]

The cost estimate for the programming effort, $PE$, is:

$$\begin{aligned} PE &= 10.2 \times 6 + 7.9 \times 1 + 4.9 \times 90 \\ &= 61.2 + 7.9 + 441 = 510 \\ TE &= 3.1 \times PE = 1{,}581 \; person \; hours = 39.5 \; person \; weeks. \end{aligned} \quad (17.4)$$

We immediately see the largest item in the cost is the data, and say that the *cost driver* for the project is the data. At this point we should go back and carefully re-estimate the number of data entities, because the accuracy of our cost estimate is very sensitive to the number of data entities. Do we really need 50 entities for the referee's name and address? After drawing some rough pictures of the screens, we may decide that we could cut that to 20 entities, and re-estimate the cost of the project.

This is an example of a sensitivity analysis.[13]

At this point we have the cost estimate in person hours, but we have said nothing about either the dollar amount, or the schedule. Usually, the customer has a schedule in mind, and here we'll assume it is six weeks. If we put 4 people on the job, it will take 38.25/4 = 9.7 weeks, while if we use 6 people, it will take 38.25/6 = 6.4 weeks.[14]

We now convert to dollars by multiplying by the rates for the proposed mix of people to be employed on the job. Many organizations have a standard job mix of

---

[12] Notice that there may be hundreds of papers, but that is not what is being counted. We are only to estimate the number of different data types.

[13] Since you almost always have to cut the bid, it is also a useful, practical skill.

[14] Of course that assumes that adding more people actually shortens the job. At some point, when you add people they just get in each other's way.

17. COST

people they use to bid on jobs—see Table 17.2. Small organizations may simply bid the rate of the people who will be actually assigned to the project.[15]

Table 17.2: Sample job mix cost rates.

| Job Title | Percent | Rate | Cost |
|---|---|---|---|
| Principal Engineer | 10% | $100,000 | $10,000 |
| Senior Engineer | 20% | $80,000 | $16,000 |
| Engineer | 40% | $50,000 | $20,000 |
| Junior Engineer | 10% | $30,000 | $3,000 |
| Clerical Support | 10% | $20,000 | $2,000 |
| **Total Person Year Cost** | | | **$51,000** |

**Detailed Parametric Estimating**

Parametric estimation techniques can be used at all levels of the estimation process. Here is an example in which the method is used at a very detailed level of the WBS.

In this example, a form in the PMA web site has been assigned to a programmer. During the detail design stage, the total number of data elements on the form, and their properties are completely specified. The *Adjusted Specification Effort*, ASE, is the development effort for the whole form. It consists of the number of data element *specifications* multiplied by the complexity of the elements. The specification of each data element is classified as follows:

- *Simple Element (SE)*. These are simple screen elements that do not have any specification complexity beyond just data entry, e.g., a field that represents a zip code, but with no implied retrieving of the town and state when the zip code is entered.

- *Basic Elements (BE)*. These are data elements that require some validation, and/or some simple additional processing. For example: checking the ZIP code for numeric values, and looking up and automatically populating the city and state fields.

- *Detailed Elements (DE)*. Such screen fields require implementation of a trigger or a stored procedure. For example: when the zip code is entered, the

[15] Of course, all these parameters can be manipulated to get the bid to the desired number.

system accesses a shipping company's web site, and sends some data to calculate the cost of shipping.

The cost estimation formula for the form is:

$$ASEV = \text{No. of SE elements} \times 10 \\ + \text{No. BE elements} \times 24 \\ + \text{No. DE elements} \times 250. \tag{17.5}$$

For example: You are implementing a form in the PMA web site with the following data elements: 20 simple (SE), 5 basic (BE), and one form-function (DE). The application development effort is:

$$ASEV = 20 \times 10 + 5 \times 24 + 1 \times 250 = 570 \, person\text{-}hours. \tag{17.6}$$

This particular form will take about 570/40 ~ 14 weeks of work.

When the programming department is called upon to write the form, the project manager will send over the specification of the form and request a quotation for the work. The programming department manager will carry out the above calculation, and explain to the project manager that the job will take about 14 weeks of work. This is a simple form, and so perhaps a junior programmer will be assigned. The project manager thus knows the estimated cost of the form.

These examples show how the parametric technique is used at all levels of the project WBS—it is not confined to the higher levels.[16]

## 17.2.2 The Delphi Technique

Wideband Delphi is an expertise-based process that a team can use to generate any kind of estimate. Delphi is an anonymous, group approach to estimation, based on the theory that:

- Group opinions are fairly reliable.

- Extreme views get annulled.

- Informal one-on-one conversations are susceptible to bias and intimidation.

- An individual might not estimate frankly in the presence of managers, customers or other stakeholders.

[16] By the way, the *Practice standard for Project Estimating* says that parametric techniques are useful at "level one and level two" of the WBS. Actually, as you can see from this example, parametric models can be used at *all levels* of the WBS.

To begin the Delphi technique, the project manager chooses an estimation team, and asks each person (or small sub-team) to estimate a series of quantities (costs or schedules). The teams are then informed about the other teams' estimates, and the process is repeated. The Delphi technique can be used when no historical data exists, and is useful when implementing unique product or project with no history.

Somewhat amazingly, the Delphi technique seems to converge to the right answer!

### 17.2.3 Bottom-Up Estimation

This is sometimes referred to as a Micro Cost Estimate. Bottom-up estimation is typically carried out at some level of the WBS. The more detailed the WBS level that is used for the estimate, the more accurate will be the cost estimate. When performed on work packages, which is the lowest level of the WBS, the estimate is about as accurate as possible.

In bottom-up WBS estimation you focus on individual project activities, which requires a detailed breakdown, and requires the project manager and team members to precisely estimate individual activities and work packages. Once they are estimated, you roll up the costs of the lower level activities to come up with an estimate for the entire project.

The bottom-up estimation approach is generally considered to be more accurate than top-down estimation methods because it is based on the WBS, which is a refined version of the scope, and so generates an accurate compilation of effort and costs. The major risk is that the project manager is so focused on the project details that he or she might overlook the fact that the WBS is missing some key features.

In Fig. 17.3 we show a summary level snap shot of an estimate for the PMA Project. (All details of the WBS view will not fit in the figure.) The total estimated effort for the PMA Conference Management System project is 522 work-hours.

The final step of the bottom up estimation stage is to compare the results with the top-down (macro) analysis. While the bottom-up estimate is more precise, it is possible to make systematic errors, such as leaving out pieces of the project. Resolution of any discrepancies between the two estimates provides confidence that the final estimate is not only precise, but correct.[17]

---

[17] The precision of the estimate is the number of figures, e.g., $10,271.25 is a very *precise* estimate. However, if a major piece of the project is left out, then it may not be *accurate*.

## 17.2. Cost Estimation

| Task Name | Work |
|---|---|
| **PMA PROJECT** | **522 hrs** |
| − Initiation Processes | 24 hrs |
| − Review Inputs to Initiation | 12 hrs |
| Create Project Statement of Work | 12 hrs |
| − Produce Outputs from Initiation | 12 hrs |
| Develop Project Charter (3.2.1.1) | 6 hrs |
| Develop Stakeholder Register | 6 hrs |
| Initiation Processes COMPLETE | 0 hrs |
| − Planning Processes (3.2.2.1) | 143 hrs |
| − Scope Management Processes | 50 hrs |
| Complete Scope Definition (3.2.2.3) | 30 hrs |
| Create WBS to level of Work Packages (3.2.2.4) | 20 hrs |
| + Activity Planning | 20 hrs |

Figure 17.3: A portion of the micro (or, bottom-up) estimate for the PMA project derived using Microsoft Project.

### 17.2.4 Cost Drivers

What drives the cost? This is a critical question to understand. Here is an enlightening quote from Sarah Susanka. [29]

> Have you ever wondered why there are so many Colonial style houses built around the country? What is it about this form that is so appealing? The shape is very simple, and in terms of getting the most "bang for yout buck," it encloses most space for the least amount of money. In addition, the floors are typically 9 ft. from floor to floor, meaning that the house can be framed easily using standard 8 ft. studs and 10 in. to 12 in. floor joists. Typically, there is a center bearing wall, which makes framing the floor simple, and there are no odd angles or vaulted ceilings. Every square foot of potential space is used for living area. When someone is looking for a way to make their dollars stretch the farthest, it's impossible to ignore the benefits of keeping the form simple. In general, the fewer corners you have in the exterior perimeter, the less expensive the house will be.[2]

Note again that the cost is driven by the design, which is defined in the specification, e.g., the 8' studs.

### 17.2.5 The Budget

The budget requires the cost estimate as the starting point, and adds the times of the cash flow events: When will outgoing costs be paid? When will incoming payments be received?

*A cost estimate is a budget when it is time-phased.*

Time-phased budgets show the project's cash needs (costs) over time. The budget details the expected cash flows, both in and out. Budget variances occur when actual and forecast events do not coincide.

### 17.2.6 Cost Estimation Summary

We summarize the cost estimation process as follows:

- People familiar with the project make the estimate.
- Use several people to make independent estimates.
- Estimate normal conditions, efficient methods, and standard resources.
- Don't make allowances for contingencies.
- Use consistent time units.
- Treat each task as independent.

## 17.3 PERT

How do we estimate things when there is uncertainty? Usually, we use the concept of the standard deviation, which measures the likely spread in a sample of numbers. For example, if we toss a coin 100 times, we expect *on average* that we will get 50 heads. Of course in reality, we also know that we may get 46 heads, but we would be surprised to get 100 heads.

Unfortunately, the Normal distribution doesn't work for project management because once projects start to be late, they stay late. So project management costs and schedules are *not* symmetric. Since the normal distribution is symmetric, we cannot use it. Instead we use something called the $\beta$ distribution.

## 17.3. PERT

To estimate an effort, a cost, or a schedule, a project manager can use the three-point technique, also called the PERT Weighted Average (or simply, PERT).[18]

We begin by assuming that each activity duration has a range of values, and that these durations statistically follow a beta distribution—see Figure 17.4

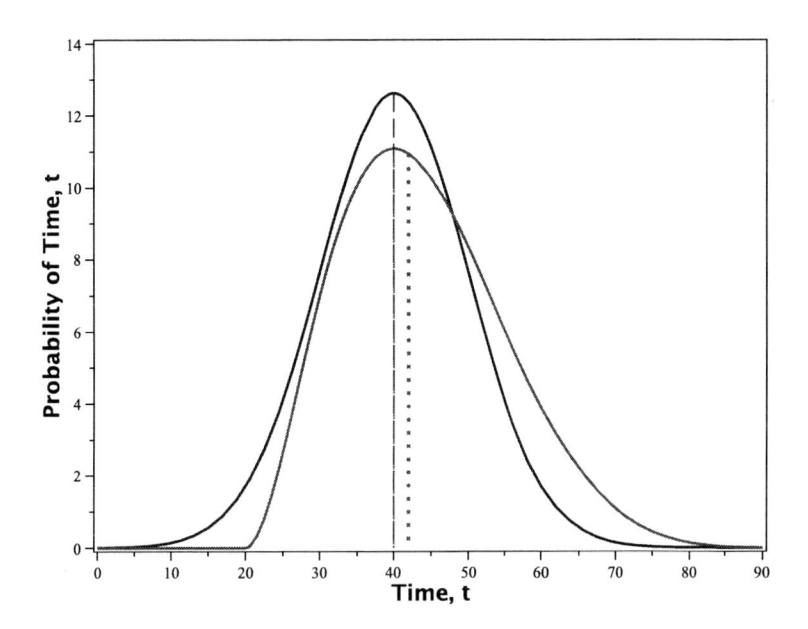

Figure 17.4: A comparison of the $\beta$ and normal distributions for projects with the same total cost. $\beta$ is asymmetric, with less likelihood of being early, and more likely to take longer.

In the PERT technique we use three data points. For example, if we are estimating an activity duration, then:

- *Pessimistic estimate, p.* The pessimistic estimate is used to come up with a worst-case scenario–if all the risks materialize and everything that could go wrong did go wrong. If the project were repeated, 1% of the time this pessimistic estimate of the activity duration would be realized.[19]

- *Most likely estimate, m.* If the project were repeated, this would be the activity duration that occurred the most often. (In statistics, we call this the mode.)

[18] PERT is an acronym for Program Evaluation and Review Technique, and was developed as a quick estimating strategy in the 1950s for the Polaris Missile System. One of its main advantages is that it uses very simple mathematics—this was long before electronic calculators.

[19] This is the Murphy's Law estimate.

# 17. COST

- *Optimistic estimate, o.* The optimistic estimate is defined as the shortest activity duration one has had, or might expect to experience. If the project were repeated, this would occur 1% of the time.[20]

The formula to calculate the Pert Mean is:

$$\mu = \frac{o + 4m + p}{6}. \tag{17.7}$$

The variability in the activity duration estimates is represented by the standard deviation, $\sigma$:

$$\mu = \frac{p - o}{6}. \tag{17.8}$$

The standard deviation, $\sigma$ is used with the PERT Mean to determine how diverse the range in the estimate is likely to be, and allows the assignment of a degree of confidence to the estimate of the mean.[21]

The confidence intervals for the $\sigma$ are as follows:

| | | | |
|---|---|---|---|
| $1\sigma$ | → | 68%. | The actual schedule has a 68% chance to be within $8 \pm 3$ months, i.e. from 5 to 11 months. |
| $2\sigma$ | → | 95%. | The actual schedule has a 95% chance to be within $8 \pm 6$ months, i.e. from 2 to 14 months. |
| $3\sigma$ | → | 99.7%. | The actual schedule has a 99.7% chance to be within $8 \pm 9$ months, i.e. from -1 to 17 months. |

### PERT Example 1

Suppose we are going for an interview. We estimate the drive is most likely to take 60 minutes. Then we consider the worst case, and decide that if there is rain or sleet, it might take 120 minutes. On the other hand, if there is no traffic, we could possibly do it in 45 minutes. These values are shown in table 17.3.

The PERT Mean is:

$$\mu = \frac{o + 4m + p}{6} = \frac{45 + 4 \times 60 + 120}{6} = 67.5 \tag{17.9}$$

---

[20] This is the wishful thinking estimate.

[21] Both the PERT mean and standard deviation formulae are approximations to a *Beta Distribution*, which is more appropriate for projects, in that once a project starts to be late, it stays late. The two PERT formulae are accurate enough for practical work, and their simplicity makes them useful.

Table 17.3: Driving to the interview: The PERT optimistic, pessimistic, and most likely estimates.

| Optimistic | $o$ | 1% chance | 45 min |
|---|---|---|---|
| Pessimistic | $p$ | 1% chance | 120 min |
| Most Likely | $m$ | | 60 min |

The variability in the driving times is represented by the standard deviation, $\sigma$:

$$\mu = \frac{p-o}{6} = \frac{120-45}{6} = 12.5 \qquad (17.10)$$

Our best guess for the time to drive to the job interview is $68 \pm 13$ minutes. But that only gives us a 66% chance of arriving on time. If we wanted to reduce the chance that we arrive late, then we might chose a 95% confidence level, and so we would use $2\sigma$: $68 \pm 26$ minutes, i.e., we should allow 94 minutes.[22]

Table 17.4: PERT interview chances of being on time.

| $1\sigma$ | $68 + 13 = 81$ min. | 66% chance of being on time. |
|---|---|---|
| $2\sigma$ | $68 + 2 \times 13 = 94$ min. | 95% chance of being on time. |
| $3\sigma$ | $68 + 3 \times 13 = 107$ min. | 99.5% chance of being on time. |

Personally, if it were me, and I really was going to a job interview, I'd leave 1 hour and 47 minutes or the trip ($3\sigma$, 99.5%); show up early; and walk around outside if need be.[23]

PERT can be applied to many different types of estimates, not just activity durations. It can be used to estimate costs, schedules, delays, or personnel requirements.[24]

**PERT Example for the PMA Case Study**

The team estimates the time to develop a new system as follows: Most likely, the prototype will take 2 months. Pessimistically, if things go wrong, we estimate that development will take 5 months. Optimistically, the prototype can be completed in one month. Substituting the above numbers in the PERT Mean equation gives:

$$\mu = \frac{o + 4m + p}{6} = \frac{1 + 4 \times 2 + 5}{6} = 2.3 \; months. \qquad (17.11)$$

[22] One of the characteristics of PERT estimation is that schedule accelerations are much more unlikely than delays. This is shown in the above example, which shows how the schedule a acceleration tends to become unreliable for more than 1 or 2 $\sigma$. This is one of the limitations of the beta distribution.

[23] My best friend's father gave me some useful advice when I was a teenager going to meet girls: "If you can't be there on time, be there a few minutes early. Never arrive after the girl!"

[24] We teach PERT in the classroom by having students work in teams to estimate the weight of an Indian elephant. Amazingly, it works, even though the students do not know much about elephants. The key is to spread out the $o$ and $p$ values.

The variability in the activity duration estimates is $\sigma$:

$$\mu = \frac{p-o}{6} = \frac{5-1}{6} = 0.66 \ months. \tag{17.12}$$

Therefore, we would quote our estimate for the schedule as:

$$Project\ Schedule\ Estimate = 2.3 \pm 0.7 \ months. \tag{17.13}$$

For the PMA project, we would like to have a 95% confidence estimate for the project schedule, i.e., $2\sigma$. We therefore quote the following schedule estimate: The project schedule estimate is $2.3 \pm 1.4$ months, with 95% confidence.

**PMA Project Function Point Analysis**

Table 17.5 is an example of a function point analysis.

Table 17.5: PMA Function Point Analysis.

| Measurement Parameter | Number | Weighting Factor |
|---|---|---|
| Number of User Input | 3 | Simple |
| Number of User Outputs | 1 | Simple |
| Number of User Inquiries | 1 | Simple |
| Number of Files | 5 | Average |
| Number of External Interfaces | 6 | Average |
| **Total** | **90** | Function Points |
| **Estimated Effort** | **180** | person-hours |

In the Table 17.5, the function points score of 90 considered Complexity Adjustment Factors for attributes like the operational environment, performance constraints, and distributed processing. Assuming that each Function Point may take 20 Person Hours to implement, the worksheet estimates that for the PMA project we have an estimate of 180 person-hours.

Depending upon the industry, worksheets and templates may be available to help the project team estimate the costs of specific activities. For example, the City of Boston has comprehensive worksheets for construction projects.[3]

## 17.4 Overhead Costs

> **Beware of the little expenses; a small leak will sink a great ship.**
>
> *Benjamin Franklin*

Overhead costs are the costs of running the business. A project team member needs a desk and a place to work. And of course, the work place needs utilities (heat and light), and computers. But, if a team member works on several projects, the company needs a way to divide up the expenses fairly between projects. If someone works 90% on project A, and 10% on project B, then project B should only pay for 10% of the heating bill.

The process of allocating charges fairly across projects is to calculate the percentage overhead to be applied to direct labor, so that you can allocate the overhead appropriately. To do this, we need to calculate the total overhead expenses, and figure out what percentage they are of the direct labor.

The largest overhead cost is almost always the occupancy (mortgage or rent, utilities, supplies, etc.)[25] Overhead costs are all added up, and then the percentages calculated.

It all begins with the direct labor. When you pay a member of the project staff $1, what does it cost the customer? Somewhat surprisingly, usually between $2 and $3. Payments to staff are called direct labor.

*Direct Labor (DL) is the cost to pay the staff.*

Charges for work directly associated with the project are called direct costs.

*Direct Costs are items that are chargeable to a specific work package.*

Direct costs come in two categories: Labor (i.e, staff work), and materials and equipment. Both categories of charges must be directly attributable to the project. Only labor directly performed actually working on the project can be charged to the project. The same applies to materials and equipment: only equipment used directly on the project can be charged to the project. For example, the cost of renting a backhoe used to dig a hole for a construction project is a legitimate cost and will be paid for by the project.

[25] A mentor once told me that 90% of companies fail, not because of profitability, but because of cash flow, and 90% of cash flow problems are due to occupancy.

## 17. Cost

Not all staff time is chargeable to the project. Sometimes, team members perform non-project related work, such as company assignments, attending professional development courses, and even the dreaded committee work. This is called *indirect labor*. Typically, the customer will not pay for staff time that is not directly attributable to the project.

### 17.4.1 What Does $1 Cost?

The "Overhead Rate" is used as a description of all the non-labor costs: benefits (vacation, sick time, and health insurance), office costs (rent, utilities, and computers), the company bureaucracy (payroll, accounting, legal, and human resources), and profit. In this sense, the overhead is the multiplier from $1 of direct labor to the final amount charged to the customer.

If the overhead rate is 2.2, for every dollar of direct labor applied to the project, the customer is billed $2.20. For example, if you take home $17.00 per hour (before taxes), and you work 40 hours on a project, then the bill to the customer is $40 × 17 × 2.2 = $1,496. In this section, we show you how to calculate that important number: the overhead rate, the 2.2.

The overhead rate (here, the 2.2) is a characteristic of the company. For companies that deal with federal, state and local government, the overhead rate is an official, audited number that applies to everything the company does, and has a dramatic effect on the cost of all projects.

The overhead rate is a public number that all customers and clients get to see, because it is an integral part of both the bidding and billing processes. However, the details of how the number is determined is not made public. While the end result, the 2.2, is often a public number, the detailed costs that go into it are not. The overhead rate is audited, to ensure that only legitimate costs are included, but the audit process is not made public.

Even if you do not work for the government, the company still needs to know its overhead rate, if for no other reason than to know when it is making a profit. Often, charities will not pay overhead costs when distributing funds, so even small non-profits need to clearly understand the details of overhead calculations. The project manager must also know what exactly are legitimate project charges, and understand the difference between direct and indirect costs.

The overhead calculation is made each year before the fiscal year starts. Costs are estimated and the overhead rate established. Usually, the costs for the previous

## 17.4. Overhead Costs

year are audited, and the proposed costs verified. This establishes the official overhead rate for the company for the following year.

**Calculating the Overhead Rate**

The process for calculating the overhead rate is the same in all organizations.[26] Suppose you are thinking of starting the Small Beer Company, and want to determine if you should quit your job. Here's how you would go about it.

The first step is to make a cost budget for the organization for the entire year. The Small Beer Company has estimated they need the following staff:

- 3 senior partners, who will make $40,000 per year.

- 4 semi-skilled workers who will make $20,000 per year.

Everyone is allocated 2 week's vacation, 8 holidays and 5 sick days. All employees have a pension plan that costs the company 6% of the labor cost. Medical benefits are 25% of the labor cost.

The company has estimated they need to borrow $250,000 to purchase and set up the beer making equipment, and the loan is to be paid off in 5 years. They require 20,000 square feet of space, rented at $0.50 per square foot per year. Utilities add another 33% to the space rental. Office supplies, computers, etc., are estimated at $10,000 per year. Payroll, legal, and other corporate expenses are estimated at 5% per year.

To be worth the effort and sacrifice, the partners plan for a profit margin of 25%.

They have performed a preliminary marketing study, and believe their specialty beer will be competitive at $30.00 per case. Each case of beer contains $10 worth of ingredients. Their preliminary marketing study also suggests that they can sell around 20,000 cases of beer per year.

The overhead calculation is shown in Table 17.6.

We begin with the direct labor. The three partners earn $40,000 so the yearly direct labor for the partners is $3 \times \$40,000 = \$120,000$. The direct labor for the beer workers is $4 \times \$20,000 = \$80,000$, so the total direct labor is $200,000.

Next, we add all the fringe benefits, such as vacation time and sick pay. For example, the employees receive 10 days vacation. They work 52 weeks, 5 days per weeks, so the percentage vacation time is $10/(52*5)*100 = 3.8\%$. Similar calculations are performed for the holidays and sick pay.

[26] Note again, that this is a forecast and subject to all the vagaries we discussed previously.

Table 17.6: The overhead calculation for the Small Beer Company.

| | | | | | |
|---|---|---|---|---|---|
| **Direct Labor** | | | | | |
| | Partners | 3 | $40,000 | $120,000 | |
| | Labor | 4 | $20,000 | $80,000 | |
| **Total DL** | | | | | $200,000 |
| **Fringe Benefits** | | | | | |
| | Vacation | 10 days | 3.8% | $7,692 | |
| | Holidays | 8 days | 3.1% | $6,154 | |
| | Sick Pay | 5 days | 1.9% | $3,846 | |
| | Medical | | 25% | $50,0000 | |
| | Pension | | 6% | $12,000 | |
| | DL+Fr = | DL*1.398 | | $79,692 | |
| **Total Fringe** | | | 39.8% | | $279,692 |
| **Overhead** | | | | | |
| | Equipment | | | $50,000 | |
| | Interest | 8% | | $4,000 | |
| | 20K sq ft | $0.5 / sqft | | $10,000 | |
| | Utilities | 33% of Rent | | $3,300 | |
| | Total OH | | | $77,300 | |
| **Total OH** | OH% = | 77.3/279.6 | 27.6% | | $356,922 |
| **G&A** | 1.05*(DL+Fr+OH) Payroll, etc. | | 5.0% | $17,850 | $374,842 |
| **Total Cost** | | | | | $374,842 |
| **Sales** | | | | | |
| | **Plan** | 20,000 cas. | $35.00 | $600,000 | |
| | Cost of Goods | Ingred. | $10/cas. | $200,000 | |
| **Gross Profit** | | | | | $400,000 |
| **Net Profit** | | | 6.3% | $25,158 | |
| **Planned Profit** | | | 25% | $100,000 | |

## 17.4. Overhead Costs

The major occupancy items are the equipment, $50,000, and the rent, $10,000. The total overhead is $77,300. Now we are in a position to calculate the overhead percentage:

$$\textbf{Overhead Percentage} = \frac{Overhead\ Expenses}{Direct\ Labor} = \frac{77,300}{279,692} = 27.6\%. \quad (17.14)$$

Notice that the overhead was calculated as a percentage of the Direct Labor **plus Fringe**. This allows us to allocate overhead costs fairly to multiple projects, as follows. Suppose you charge $1 to a project. We immediately add the fringe benefit (here, 39.8%) for a cost of $1.39. The overhead percentage is 27.6%, so we add this also, to get: $ 1.39 × 1.276 = $1.77.

The final item in the overhead calculation is the General and Administrative Cost (G&A). These are the global corporate organizational costs, such as payroll, accounting, human resources, and legal. Typically, these costs are expressed as a percentage of the Direct Labor plus Fringe plus Overhead, e.g., the Small Beer Company allocated 5% for these costs, which is: 5% of DL+Fr+OH = 5% × $356,922 = $17,850. Notice again, this is a percentage of the total DL+Fr+OH.

We now have the total costs to run the Small Beer Company for a year.[27] To pay for these costs, you need sales. The marketing study suggested that the Small Beer Company could sell 20,000 cases of their beer at $35.00 each, for a gross sales of $600,00. We subtract the cost of making that beer ($200,000), to leave a gross profit of $400,000.

The net profit is gross profit minus the costs:

$$\textbf{Net Profit} = \$400,000 - \$374,482 = \$25,158, \quad (17.15)$$

for a percentage profit of 25, 158/400, 000 = 6.3%. This is the best estimate of the percentage profit from the operations for a year. It is a lot less than the plan of 25%! [28]

Note that if the overhead costs go up (the landlord wants a rent increase), the profit will fall unless there are more sales to make up for the increase in cost. Or, as usually happens, suppose the sales do not meet their target. The costs will remain, and so the profit will be reduced. Thus we see that the overhead calculation is a critical component of the planning for the year.

The end result of this process is that we now have the percentages for the overhead, which we summarize in Table 17.7.

[27]A sharp eyed student will again notice that we have used a non-project example; it's another manufacturing case. That is because this case has all the pieces that go into an overhead calculation. Your project might not have a Cost-of-Goods, but if it does, at least you'll know where to put it.

[28]This is quite typical. In fact, the first pass often indicates a loss, never mind a smaller than desired profit. This is where the work really begins: more sales, less cost.

Table 17.7: The overhead summary for the Small Beer Company.

| | | | |
|---|---|---|---|
| **Direct Labor** | | | $1.00 |
| **Fringe** | 39.8% | DL*1.396 | $1.40 |
| **Overhead** | 27.6% | 1.276*(DL+Fr) | $1.79 |
| **G&A** | 5% | 1.05*(DL+Fr+OH) | $1.88 |
| **Total Cost** | | | $1.88 |
| **Profit** | 25% | 1.25*(DL+Fr+OH+G&A) | $2.35 |

### 17.4.2 Cost vs. Price

> **Price is what you pay. Value is what you get.**
>
> *Warren Buffett*

Suppose a friend calls you up and asks if it is possible to create a special brew for a mutual friend's birthday party.[29] We could determine the cost of the job as follows: First, we estimate the labor costs of the special run as $10,000; the cost of the project immediately follows from the overhead calculation:

Table 17.8: The bid for the special party from the Small Beer Company.

| | | |
|---|---|---|
| **Direct Labor** | | $10,000 |
| **Fringe** | 39.8% | $13,980 |
| **Overhead** | 27.6% | $17,838 |
| **G&A** | 5% | $18,730 |
| **Profit** | 25% ($4,683) | $23,413 |

To make the special beer for our friend's party will cost $23,413. We emphasize that this is the **cost**, which is different from the **price**. What we charge the customer, *the price*, can vary considerably.

For example, this special brew might be a lot of bother and interfere with normal operations. In which case, we might inflate the price to make it worthwhile: We explain to our friend that the price is $30,000.

[29] A sharp eyed student will notice that this is (finally!) a project–a unique brew, never been done before, one time, etc.

On the other hand, if we see this as an opportunity to get into a new area we've wanted to get into for a while, we might reduce the profit margin and price the brew below cost at $15,000. Since the cost is $18,700, we would be planning to lose $3,700.

There is an important distinction between the cost and the price. The cost is fixed.[30] The price can be any number at all; it all depends. The Marketing department often wants to win the job by bidding low. As the project manager, you should be quite willing to do the job for $15,000, and make it clear that on this project, the company stands to lose $3,700.

Unfortunately, what often happens is that upper management says, "We'll do the special brew project, just try to do it for $15,000." This is a nasty trap, because what you heard is not what they said. As the project manager, you think that it is OK to go ahead with an $18,700 project, and that the company is willing to invest $3,700. In actual fact, a more correct reading of upper management's position is *We expect you to complete the project for $15,000.*

Our recommendation at this point is to write a project charter for the project, explaining that it is a new venture, with excellent future potential for new business and documenting all the wonderful aspects of the project. Then sneak in there that the project is estimated to cost $18,700, of which the company will invest $3,700. Circulate the charter and ask everyone to sign it.[31]

Then stand back and wait for the sparks to fly!

## 17.5 PMI and Estimating

The Project Management Institute released its *Practice Standard for Project Estimating* in 2011. [14] This standard is intended to provide guidance for applying sound estimating principles for the life of a project and treats estimating as a living process.[32]

[30] Assuming, of course, the labor estimate is correct.

[31] Remember, it is perfectly standard for everyone to sign the charter; you are not asking anything unusual.

[32] This is the first edition, and like many first attempts, it is a bit weak. In our opinion, the estimation examples are not very insightful. For a detailed analysis of the standard, see [15].

# CHAPTER 18

# EARNED VALUE MANAGEMENT

> The more education a woman has, the wider the gap
> between men's and women's earnings for the same work.
>
> *Sandra Day O'Connor*

Earned value management (EVM) is such an important topic that we dedicate an entire chapter to it. Normally, EVM is covered as part of the *Cost Management* knowledge area.[1]

## 18.1 How ya doin'?

This is the question everyone wants the answer to. Customers, upper management, stakeholders, and the project team all want to know the true status of the project. By which they mean they want to know about the cost and schedule. How do you determine that? Earned Value.

While the details of earned value management can get quite complicated, the basic idea is simple.

Suppose I am asked to write a 50 page document. I look at the requirements, and estimate that I can deliver 5 pages per day for 10 days.

[1] We believe that the two most important technical concepts in project management are the critical path and earned value.

## 18. EARNED VALUE MANAGEMENT

I explain to the customer that I earn $10 per hour, and I agree to work 10 hours per day.[2] However, I am paid for all the hours I work and I report the number of pages I write each day, the cost, and the hours worked.

Here's what happened:

Day #1  I worked 10 hours, and wrote 5 pages. The customer accepted the pages, and paid me the agreed amount for my day's work: $100. I am clearly on budget and on schedule.

Day #2  I again worked 10 hours, and produced the planned 5 pages. The customer paid me $100. I am still on budget and schedule.

Day #3  I ran into a problem, and I only delivered 2 pages. Also, I worked an extra 2 hours trying to fix the problem. (I worked 12 hours.) Since I get paid $10 per hour, I submit a bill to the customer for 12 hours: $120.

*I am over budget! I am behind schedule!*

But is my cost overrun significant? Should I be worried? Can I fix it?

So far, the total cost of the project is $320, but I have only delivered 12 of the planned 15 pages. How can I measure my *true* progress? Can I determine the *value* of the 12 delivered pages?

We go back and carefully analyze the *plan*: I estimated I could deliver 5 pages per day, and get paid $100. Therefore each page has a *planned value* of $20. After 3 days, I planned to deliver 15 pages, so the value of the work I planned to deliver is 15x$20 =$300. We refer to this as the *Planned Value* on day #3, $PV(3) = \$300$.

Now let's look at the *Actual Cost, AC*: I have actually spent $320. There is no arguing with this, it is simply the invoiced amount. $AC(3) = \$320$.

I only produced 12 of the planned 15 pages, so the actual cost applies to the 12 pages delivered, not the planned 15 pages. Therefore, I need to determine the *value* of the delivered work.

We noted above that in the plan, each page was worth $20. I have delivered 12 pages, so the value of the completed work is 12x$20 = $240. We call this the *earned value* on day #3, $EV(3)$. It is the value of the work I have actually delivered.

The value of the work accomplished (the earned value) is $240, but the actual cost for that work is $320. Another way to say this is that I have done $240 worth of work (12 pages), but it has cost $320. Therefore, my cost efficiency is: $240/$320 = 75%.

---

[2] We are keeping the numbers as simple as possible.

From the cost perspective, at the end of Day #3, I am working at a cost efficiency of 75%.

This simple example has all the features of an earned value calculation:

1. A planned value for the work over time. This was the budget estimate over time, which was $100 per day.

2. A time at which we wish to estimate the progress. In this case, we decided to measure the progress on Day #3.

3. On day #3, we used a *cumulative* measure of progress. I reported the total number of pages delivered (12), and the total cost ($320). I did not report that on Day #3, I spent $120 to produce 2 pages.

4. A physical measure of progress. I measured progress in terms of completed deliverables (in this case, pages). This is the important feature of earned value. Every deliverable must be measured in some way to actually determine the real progress. This is discussed in detail in section 18.3.3.

We emphasize that earned value calculations use a *cumulative* measure of cost progress. This makes sense, because I did 2 days of work which was on budget, and it was only on day #3 that I ran into problems. I should get credit for the on-budget work in the first 2 days. Therefore, a reasonable measure of my cost progress is 75% ($240 worth of completed deliverables which cost $320).

Now let's examine the schedule.

At the end of day #3, I was supposed deliver 15 pages, and I have only completed 12, so I am behind schedule.

But how much am I behind schedule? I was supposed to complete 15 pages (my planned deliverables), but I have only completed 12 (my actual (earned) deliverables). So a measure of my schedule progress is that I have completed only 12/15 = 80% of the planned deliverables due on Day #3, i.e., I have actually completed 80% of the work I planned to do.

*My schedule efficiency is 80%.*

This simple schedule example also has all the features we need, and they are the same as for the cost example above.

There are some technical details, such as: What is the quality of my work in the first 2 days? I should not get credit for completing pages if they are rejected by the customer and have to be re-written.

Also, we measured progress in pages, establishing that we measure progress in terms of the physical deliverables. We can also measure the progress in dollars, which can confuse things. In general, it is much easier to understand progress in terms of a physical measure of the deliverables. This is discussed in detail in section 18.3.3.

### 18.1.1 EV and Efficiency

The power of *EV* is that it provides measures of efficiency for the work accomplished:

- *Schedule Efficiency:* At the end of day #3, I have completed 12 of 15 planned pages, which is 80%. I can interpret this as: My schedule efficiency is 80%.

  In dollar terms, I have completed 12x$20 = $240 worth of work, compared to the planned work I was supposed to have completed at the end of day #3, which was 15x$20 = 300. So again, my cumulative schedule efficiency is, $EV(3) = 240/300 = 80\%$.

  On day #3, I completed 2 out of 5 pages, so my instantaneous schedule efficiency is 40%. This is distinct from my *cumulative* schedule efficiency, which is 80%.

- *Cost Efficiency:* At the end of day #3, I have spent $320, and I have completed $240 worth of work (12 of 15 pages). I can interpret this as: My cost efficiency is 240/320 = 75%. My cumulative cost efficiency is, $EV(3) = 240/300 = 80\%$.

  On day #3, I completed 2 out of 5 pages, which was worth $40. I actually spent $120, so my instantaneous cost efficiency is: 40/120 = 40%. This is distinct from my *cumulative* cost efficiency, which is 75%.

The key idea is that *EV* provides a measure of the efficiency with which I am completing the project. We will make this more formal with the concepts of cost and schedule variance, and cost and schedule performance indexes.

To calculate this measure of efficiency, we only needed three quantities, *PV*, *AC*, and *EV*. A little thought shows that these are the minimum data that the project manager reports to the customer. The plan was agreed to upon contract signing, and so the planned value is readily available.

The cost is always reported to the customer, because otherwise the team does not get paid. So the customer also has the actual cost. Finally, the project manager reports progress on deliverables, which is nothing more than the earned value.

## 18.2 Formal Definitions

Therefore, the customer has all the data needed to calculate all of the earned value quantities.[3]

### 18.2.1 Planned Value, $PV$

*The Planned Value, $PV$, is the cumulative time-phased budget.*[4]

In the above example, the planned value of the work is $20 per page, or $100 per day for 5 days.

The $PV$ at the end of the project is called the Budget at Completion ($BAC$).

In the above example, the budget at completion is the total planned budget for the project, $500.

### 18.2.2 Earned Value, $EV$

*The Earned Value, $EV$, is the cumulative value of work performed.*

We emphasize that in the standard definition, $EV$ is the *cumulative* value of the work completed to date.

$EV$ can be measured both instantaneously and cumulatively.[5] An instantaneous $EV$ measurement would be: On day #3, I completed 2 planned pages. In dollar terms, I actually completed $40 worth of work on day #3.

### 18.2.3 Actual Cost, $AC$

*The Actual Cost, $AC$, is the total cost incurred to date.*

$AC$ includes all expenditures, including labor costs, overhead costs, equipment rentals, purchases, and subcontractor costs. $AC$ is a also a cumulative measure, but it can be measured instantaneously. An instantaneous measurement of the cost is: On day #3, I spent $120.

---

[3] This is why we say that when customers learn to use *Earned Value*, we will no longer be able to hide the true project status!

[4] The PMBOK definition also includes the idea that the budget is authorized, and allocated over the life of the project. All that just clutters the definition. Somewhat strangely, the word cumulative is left out of the PMBOK definition.

[5] The PMBOK uses the word *incrementally*, rather than *instantaneously*. We believe that an *instantaneous* measurement is a more correct description of what is being performed, since we are measuring the $EV$ at that instant. An *increment* is a change, which is not what we are measuring, unless you regard day #3 as the increment.

18. EARNED VALUE MANAGEMENT

### 18.2.4 Cost Variance

*The cost variance is the earned value minus the actual cost.*

$$CV = EV - AC. \tag{18.1}$$

The cost variance is a measure of the cost performance of the project. When the value of the work actually completed (i.e., work earned, $EV$) is less than the actual cost spent, $AC$, the project is over budget. Simply put, you have spent more than you were supposed to on the work you have actually completed. Therefore, when $EV < AC$, the project is over budget and $CV$ is negative.

In the above example, at the end of day #3, I have spent $320, and I have completed $240 worth of work (12 of 15 pages). Therefore, the $CV$ is negative:

$$CV = EV - AC = 240 - 320 = -80. \tag{18.2}$$

When the project is complete, $CV$ measures the total cost overrun or underrun. At the end of the project,

$$CV_{end} = Budget - AC_{end}. \tag{18.3}$$

Suppose that the budget for the project was $1,000 (the BAC). If at the end of the project you have spent $1,200, the *Cost Variance* is:

$$CV_{end} = BAC - AC_{end} = 1,000 - 1,200 = -200. \tag{18.4}$$

### 18.2.5 Schedule Variance

*The schedule variance is defined as the earned value minus the planned value.*

$$SV = EV - PV. \tag{18.5}$$

The schedule variance is a measure of the schedule performance of the project. When the work actually completed (i.e., the earned work, $EV$) is less than what was planned ($PV$), the project is behind schedule. Simply put, you have not done what you were contracted to have done, so you are behind schedule.

Therefore, when $EV < PV$, the project is behind schedule and $SV$ is negative.[6]

[6] We feel obliged to point out that there are problems with the $SV$ concept. First, it is not actually a variance in the statistical sense. It is really a difference. Also, it is measured in dollars, which is a strange set of units for a schedule delay. You say to your boss, "I am $40 behind schedule." Shouldn't a schedule difference be measured in days or weeks?

262

In the above example, at the end of day #3, I was suppose to have completed $300 worth of work, and I have completed $240 worth of work (12 of 15 pages). Therefore, the $SV$ is negative:

$$SV = EV - PV = \$240 - \$300 = -\$60. \tag{18.6}$$

Notice the weird set of units here. Your boss calls and says, "I hear you are behind schedule. How much are you behind?"

You answer, "I am $60 behind schedule."

Your boss is perfectly entitled to ask, "How can you be $60 behind schedule? How much is that in days?"[7]

When the project is complete, all deliverables will be complete. That is, all of the planned work is finished. Therefore, at the end of the project $EV = PV$, and $SV = 0$. If the project is behind schedule, this may happen after the planned delivery date. While $SV \to 0$ at the end of the project, this may be after the planned end of the project.

### 18.2.6 Cost Performance Index (CPI)

The cost performance index ($CPI$) is a measure of the cost efficiency with which the money is being spent on the project. It is one of the most important concepts is all of project management. The $CPI$ is:

$$CPI = \frac{\text{Earned Value}}{\text{Planned Value}} = \frac{EV}{PV}. \tag{18.7}$$

When $CPI < 1$, the project is over budget, when $CPI > 1$, the project is under budget, and when $CPI = 1$, the project is exactly on budget.

In the above example, on day #3 I have actually spent $320. There is no arguing with this, it is simply the invoiced amount. $AC(3) = \$320$. The value of the work accomplished (the earned value) is $240. Therefore, $CPI$ is:

$$CPI = \frac{EV}{AC} \frac{240}{320} = 0.75. \tag{18.8}$$

From a cost perspective, at the end of Day #3, I am working at an efficiency of 75%.

[7]And you do not know, because $SV$ is measured in dollars, not days!

### 18.2.7 Schedule Performance Index (SPI)

The schedule performance index, ($SPI$), is a measure of the efficiency of schedule progress, indicating the actual schedule progress compared to the planned schedule progress.

$$SPI = \frac{\text{Earned Value}}{\text{Planned Value}} = \frac{EV}{PV}. \tag{18.9}$$

When $SPI < 1$, the project is behind schedule, when $SPI > 1$, the project is ahead of schedule, and when $SPI = 1$, the project is exactly on schedule.[8]

In the above example, on day #3 I planned $300 worth of work. The value of the work accomplished (the earned value) is $240. Therefore, $SPI$ is:

$$SPI = \frac{EV}{PV} \frac{240}{300} = 0.80. \tag{18.10}$$

From a schedule perspective, at the end of Day #3, I am working at an efficiency of 80%.

At the end of the project, the earned value is equal to the planned value. This is most easily seen in a simple example.

Suppose I plan to deliver 4 pages, one per day, and each page costs $1. ($BAC = \$4$) We will refer to this as the "4 page" project. Suppose I deliver 1 page every two days, instead of the planned 1 page per day. It will take me 8 days to complete the 4 pages. The planned and earned values are calculated in Table 18.2.7. The $SPI$ is plotted in Figure 18.1.

Once I have delivered all the pages, my total earned value is $4: I earn the value of the completed deliverables, and when I have delivered them all, I earn the planned value. Therefore, at the end of the project, $EV = PV$, and $SPI = 1$.

Note that this occurs after the planned end of the project, and here not until Day #8. Also note that in some sense, my schedule efficiency was 50% *at all times*, because I was completing 0.5 pages per day. However, the shape of the $SPI$ curve does not reflect a constant page delivery rate of 50%, it rises towards the end of the project.

Figure 18.1 illustrates some of the pitfalls in the use of $SPI$ curves. After about 50% of the project, the $SPI$ rises and is not useful any longer.[1]

The project manager cannot take any credit for the "improving" $SPI$ in Figure 18.1, it is an artefact of the defintion of the $SPI$.

---

[8]At the end of a project, the $SPI \to 1$, always, so the $SPI$ inevitably rises towards the end of the project. This does not actually mean the efficiency is improving, it is just an inherent property of the $SPI$. This makes the use of SPI problematic after about the 50% point.

## 18.2. Formal Definitions

Table 18.1: The SPI for the 4 page project.

| Day | Daily Planned | Daily Earned | Cumulative Planned | Cumulative Earned | SPI |
|-----|---------|--------|---------|--------|------|
| 1 | $1.00 | $0.00 | $1.00 | $0.00 | 0.00 |
| 2 | $1.00 | $1.00 | $2.00 | $1.00 | 0.50 |
| 3 | $1.00 | $0.00 | $3.00 | $1.00 | 0.33 |
| 4 | $0.00 | $1.00 | $4.00 | $2.00 | 0.50 |
| 5 | $0.00 | $0.00 | $4.00 | $2.00 | 0.50 |
| 6 | $0.00 | $1.00 | $4.00 | $3.00 | 0.75 |
| 7 | $0.00 | $0.00 | $4.00 | $3.00 | 0.75 |
| 8 | $0.00 | $1.00 | $4.00 | $4.00 | 1.00 |

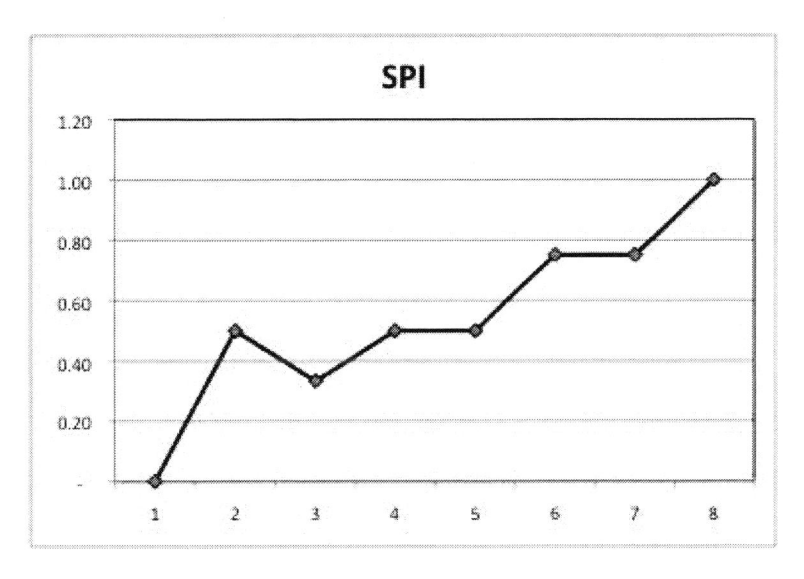

Figure 18.1: $SPI$ for the 4 page project. The $SPI \to 1$ at the end of the project, which here, is on Day #8.

## 18.3 The Estimate at Completion, $EAC$

What every customer wants to know is: *How much is it going to cost?*

When you are in the middle of the project, and have some cost and schedule data, you can estimate the final cost, which is called the estimate at completion ($EAC$). There are several ways to estimate the $EAC$.

### 18.3.1 The Average $CPI$ Method

An quick and easy way to estimate the final cost is to estimate the average $CPI$ for the project, and then,

$$EAC = \frac{BAC}{\langle CPI \rangle}, \tag{18.11}$$

where $\langle CPI \rangle$ denotes the average $CPI$ for the project. If you think you have a decent estimate of this, then equation 18.11 provides a decent estimate for the final cost of the project, the estimate at completion, $EAC$.

Consider another book project. I agree to write 10 chapters, each with an estimated cost of $100. The Budget at Completion, $BAC$ = $1,000. Suppose I immediately run into problems, and deliver the first chapter on time, but at a cost of $133. I also deliver the second chapter on time, but at a cost of $138.

The planned value after month 2 is $PV$ = $200. The actual cost is $AC$ = $135 + $138 = $271. After two months, my $CPI$ = $200/$271 = 0.74. I can now estimate my EAC as:

$$EAC = \frac{BAC}{\langle CPI \rangle} = \frac{1,000}{0.74} = \$1,351. \tag{18.12}$$

I am working at roughly at a $CPI$ = 74%. Therefore, I should increase my original budget by dividing by my $CPI$. If as the project manager, I believe that the team can increase its efficiency, then perhaps I can convince the customer that we will do better than the above estimate.

### 18.3.2 The $EAC$ Formula

A more careful analysis uses the $EAC$ defined as:

$$EAC(t) = AC(t) + \frac{BAC - EV(t)}{CPI(t)}. \tag{18.13}$$

## 18.3. The Estimate at Completion, $EAC$

At any time, $t$, we can estimate the final project cost as follows: First, at the current time, we have spent a specific amount, indicated in equation 18.13 as $AC(t)$. One cannot argue wit this amount, it is the actual amount spent (and presumably invoiced) to date.

Next we have to estimate the cost to complete the project. First, we estimate the remaining work, which is the total work to be done, $BAC$, minus the work completed, which is defined as the earned value to date, $EV(t)$. So the remaining work is: $BAC - EV(t)$. This is the numerator in equation 18.13.

Next we note that our cost efficiency to date is measured by the current $CPI(t)$. If the $CPI = 1$, then we are on budget, and we can expect to complete the work at that rate in the future.

On the other hand, suppose the $CPI = 0.5$, which says we are only performing at a 50% efficiency rate on the cost. For the remaining work, therefore, we should double the estimate of what it is going to take to complete the remaining work. This is accomplished in equation 18.13 by dividing the work remaining by the $CPI$.

Equation 18.13 says that we should use as the current value the $CPI$, which is denoted by $CPI(t)$. This is perfectly fine, as long as the current value of the $CPI$ is a good representation of the efficiency we can expect on the remaining work. If so, then equation 18.13 will give a good value for the $EAC$.

Equation 18.13 says that the estimate of the final project cost is the actual cost to date, plus the remaining work forecast to be completed at the *same efficiency* as the project to date.

### 18.3.3 Measuring Progress

The $CPI$ formula has two terms, $AC$ and $EV$. The actual cost can only be measured in dollars,[9] and so to calculate the $CPI$, the earned must also be measured in dollars—we need all quantities in the same units. Therefore, $EV$ must be converted into dollars.

Sometimes, $EV$ is presented as if the deliverable value is only measured in dollars.[10] It is not! Progress is measured in physical units.

Suppose I hire a painter to paint a room, then the progress is easily measured in square feet actually painted. Suppose the wall is 10' tall by 10' long (area = 100 square feet). The painter discovers that he cannot reach above 8', and needs to borrow a ladder to complete the work. At the end of the day, he has only completed the lower 8' by 10' = 80, which is 80/100 of the area = 80%.

[9] Assuming you get paid in dollars and not euros!

[10] For example, the PMBOK says that $EV$ is the "value of work performed expressed in terms of the approved budget," i.e., it is assumed to be measured in dollars.

Therefore, the value of the work earned is only 80% of the planned work. It is hard to argue with such a simple measure of progress, and here it is the square feet of wall actually painted.

The painter might argue that his efficiency is actually better, and he could have finished the wall if he had a ladder. The painter might ague that it is 'unfair' to say his efficiency only 80%. As a project manager, however, we are only interested in *actual progress*. It really does not matter how fast the painter *might* have finished the work, the *actual* progress was only 80% of planned.

The painter may say that tomorrow, he will 'make it up' because now he has the ladder. But when he starts tomorrow, he is already over budget and behind schedule.

If the painter agreed to a fixed price contract, he may be motivated to catch up and finish on time. Alternatively, he may say that the ladder was not his responsibility, and that he expects to receive more money because the delay was not his fault. If the painter is working on a Time and Materials contract, he has no incentive to work harder to catch up.

The point is that it is pretty easy to see that the painter has only accomplished 80% of the planned work. He is behind schedule and over budget.

Mathematically, the $CPI$ is simply a ratio—there is not much to it. However, even in the simple painting example, we see immediately that the $CPI$ can be interpreted and used in different ways. We refer to this as the 'political' aspect of earned value, and it complicates the discussion.

Some manuals on the use of the earned value are hundreds of pages thick, and propose a process involving dozens of steps. Much of the complication and bureaucracy is intended to define carefully how to collect data, and how to interpret the results, i.e., they attempt to remove the political aspects.[11]

We claim that on any project, if you give it a little thought, the deliverables can be measured in physical units. Some examples of physical units of measure for deliverables are:

- Miles of roadway completed.

- Number of steel girders erected.

- Cubic yards of tunnel dug out. Cubic yards of concrete poured.

- Software modules designed, tested, documented, or delivered. Web pages operational.

---

[11] In our opinion, such unwieldy documents have given *EVM* a bad name.

- Scope pages delivered.
- Book chapters delivered to the publisher.[12]

## 18.4 EV Example: The Re-Paving Project

We now work through an example of using EVM to determine the true status of a project. The state has decide to repave a road, which is 7.7 miles long. The plan is to complete the job in 10 months. The estimated cost of the whole project is $1,470,000.

### 18.4.1 Month Three

The following table represents the status of the project in month three:

Table 18.2: The status of the repaving project after month 3.

| Month | Miles Completed Planned | Miles Completed Actual | Costs Planned | Costs Actual |
|---|---|---|---|---|
| 1 | 0.77 | 0.77 | $147,000 | $147,000 |
| 2 | 0.77 | 0.62 | $147,000 | $161,711 |
| 3 | 0.77 | 0.64 | $147,000 | $158,492 |

We claim that this table is the minimum that any project manager would report to the client on a monthly basis. It consists of the work completed (in miles) and the costs incurred.[13]

From this data we can calculate the earned value as follows: The planned amount to be paved each month is 0.77 miles, and the planned cost for this is $147,000. The planned cost per mile is therefore:

$$\text{Planned Cost per mile} = \frac{\$147,000}{0.77} = \$190,909. \quad (18.14)$$

In month one, we complete all of the the planned 0.77 miles on time and on budget. Our earned value in month one is, therefore, $EV(1) = 0.77$ miles, or in dollars, $EV(1) = \$147,000$.

In month two, we only completed 0.62 miles. So our earned value for month two is $EV(2) = 0.62 \times 190,909 = \$118,364$. The actual cost is $161,711, so we have spent

[12] In our experience, usually with an $SPI \sim 0.4$!

[13] We immediately see that unlike its bad press, EVM actually does not require any extra bookkeeping.

## 18. EARNED VALUE MANAGEMENT

more than was planned to accomplish less than was planned. Let's augment the above table with earned value. Remember: $EV$ requires cumulative data.

Table 18.3: The repaving project after month 3 with cumulative costs.

| | Costs | | | Cumulative Costs | | |
|---|---|---|---|---|---|---|
| Month | Planned | Actual | Earned | PV | AC | EV |
| 1 | $147,000 | $147,000 | $147,000 | $147,000 | $147,000 | $147,000 |
| 2 | $147,000 | $161,259 | $118,364 | $294,000 | $308,711 | $265,364 |
| 3 | $147,000 | $158,492 | $122,182 | $441,000 | $467,203 | $387,546 |

From this we can now compute the $CPI$, $SPI$, and $EAC$. Remember the formula for EAC is equation 18.13.

Table 18.4: $CPI$, $SPI$, and $EAC$ for the repaving project after month 2.

| Month | CPI | SPI | EAC |
|---|---|---|---|
| 1 | 1.00 | 1.00 | $1,470,000 |
| 2 | 0.86 | 0.90 | $1,710,126 |
| 3 | 0.83 | 0.88 | $1,772,149 |

For example, the month two calculation for $EAC(2)$ is:

$$EAC(2) = 308,711 + \frac{1,470,000 - 265,364}{0.86} = 1,710,126. \qquad (18.15)$$

The $EAC(3)$ says that the best estimate for the final cost of the project, based on the expenditures and the efficiency to date is: $1,710,126. The variance at completion is: $VAC = BAC - EAC = 1,470,000 - 1,710,126 = -302,149 = 21\%$. In month three, we are already over a three hundred thousand dollars over budget!

It is interesting at this stage to plot the $CPI$ and $SPI$, which are shown in Figure 18.2. We have selected the current $CPI$ as the one to use in the formula for $EAC$. But an interesting question to ask is: What value of $CPI$ should we really use?

A quick look at 18.2 shows that the $CPI$ is declining. We are entitled to ask, therefore, if the current $CPI(3)$ is in fact a good representation of the overall $CPI$ of the project. One might argue that the $CPI$ is declining and so the current value is in fact an *optimistic* value. In which case, our estimate of the final cost could be higher!

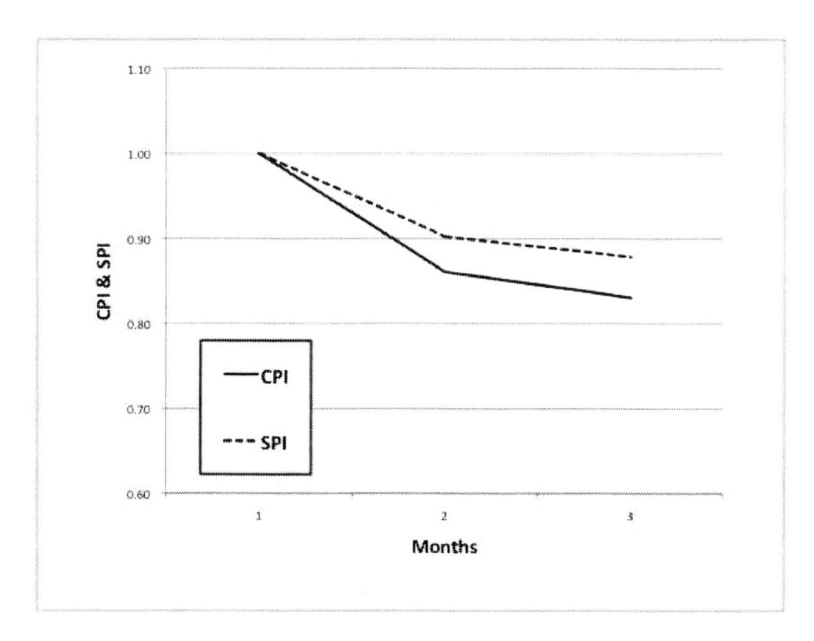

Figure 18.2: $CPI$ and $SPI$ in month 2 for the repaving project.

If the customer plotted this chart, the project manger will have some explaining to do.[14] The customer might well ask how the project manager intends to get back on track.

Here we see the importance of earned value management. Using a few simple concepts, we have in month three, an estimate of the final cost, and it is problematic. The only good news is that it may be early enough for the project manager to take corrective action.

### 18.4.2 Plot Everything

To carefully analyze the project status, we recommend that the project manager plot all quantities because plots explain what is happening far better than do tables. In the next few figures, we show the data for the entire 10 month project.

Figure 18.3 shows the actual miles completed, and it pretty quickly reaches a value of around 0.6 miles per month. We can quickly determine that we are not going to achieve the planned 0.77 miles per month.

Figure 18.4 shows that in the first few months, the $CPI$ and $SPI$ fall and then level off. After a few months, the $CPI$ is pretty well established. This means that the

[14] Remember, this chart is easy to plot. If the project manager reported the miles completed and the costs to date, the customer has everything necessary to plot the chart!

## 18. Earned Value Management

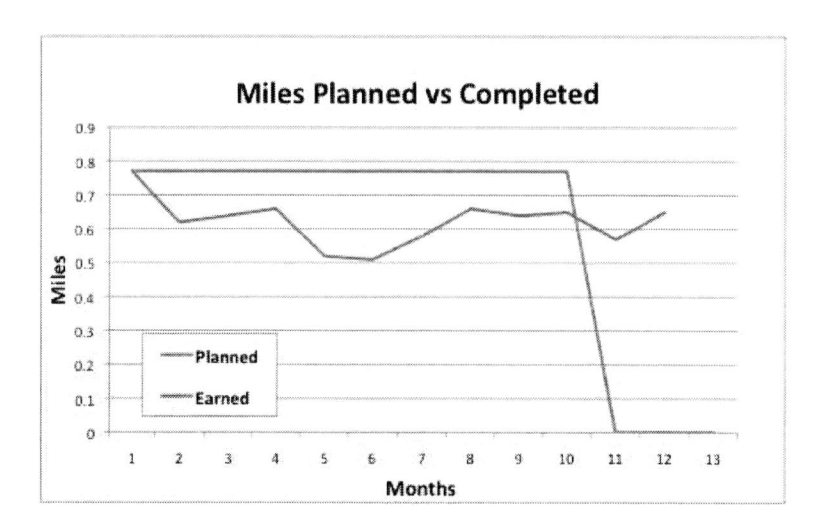

Figure 18.3: Miles (planned and completed) for the repaving project.

final cost estimate, the $EAC$, quickly converged to a reasonable value, which is shown in Figure 18.5.

In fact, data from thousands of projects shows that the $EAC$ is an excellent approximation of the true cost after about 25% of the project. When it is a poor estimate, it is an underestimate! This is because the $CPI$ is often seen to decline over the life of a project, making the $EAC$ a lower bound on the cost.[2]

## 18.4. EV Example: The Re-Paving Project

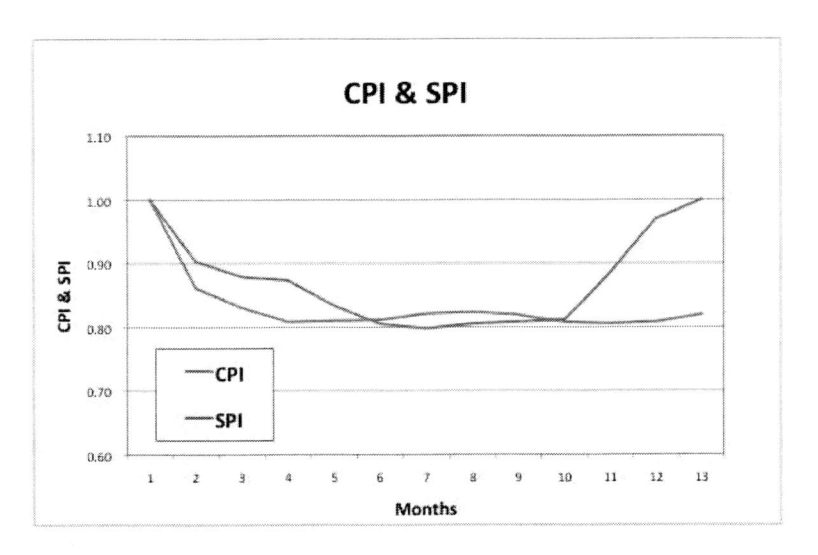

Figure 18.4: CPI and SPI for the repaving project.

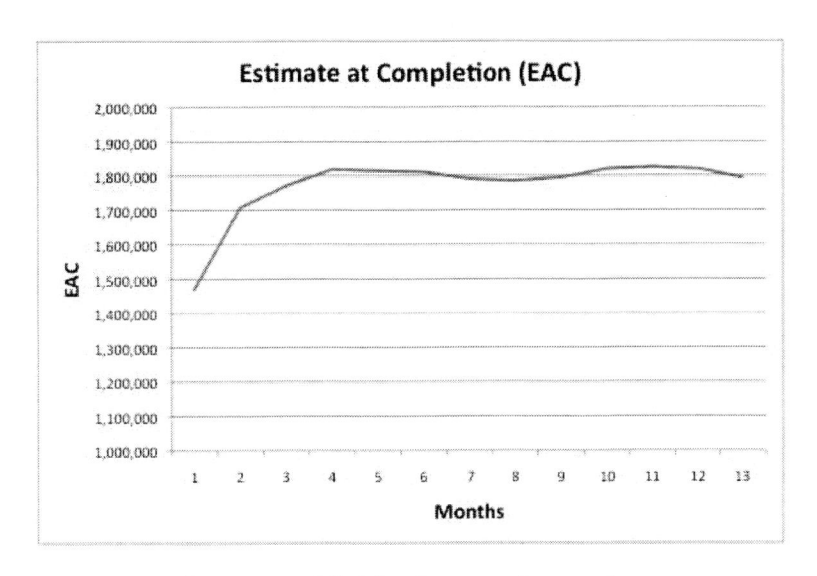

Figure 18.5: EAC for the repaving project.

## 18.5 Using Earned Value

> **The only way to enjoy anything in this life is to earn it first.**
>
> *Ginger Rogers*

Earned value management (EVM) is designed to address an issue that is sometimes known as the *work-in-process measurement problem*. EVM has been established as a valuable, but much neglected tool. It provides early warning signals of project trouble, and its predictions are reliable as early as 15% into the project.[3]

So why doesn't everyone use it? There are many excuses, for example:[16]

- "It is not needed on small projects."

    OK, so let me get this straight. Just because you are working on a small project, you do not want to know if your project is late or over budget. Hmm.

- "It is too hard to use."

    You have to report the cost and completed deliverables to your customer every month. Why not divide the cost of the deliverables by the actual cost to determine the CPI? That doesn't sound too hard.

- "The terminology is complex and the rules are overly restrictive."

    There are two quantities, the *CPI* and the *SPI*, and they are nothing more than percentages. Reporting those every month doesn't seem to be very complex at all. Since you have to report those to the customer anyway, why is this so "restrictive?"

We suspect the real reason that people don't want to report the *CPI* and *SPI* is that their customers will discover the truth about their projects.[15]

### 18.5.1 Using Hours

Many companies and organizations do not track dollars spent, but only "hours worked." This occurs in organizations where the staff are on salary, and assigned to projects.[16] In this case, it is still possible to use Earned Value, one simply calculates everything in hours. A project must be defined in terms of deliverables, and each has a number of *planned hours* over time. As the project proceeds, the hours spent define the *actual cost*. As deliverables are completed, they *earn* the value of the deliverable in *hours*.

---

[15] We have repeatedly suggested, both here and in talks, that the problem with *EVM* is that our customers will find out the truth!

[16] If the organization does not track hours worked on projects, then this is a good time to begin installing real project management, and tracking hours!

18.5. Using Earned Value

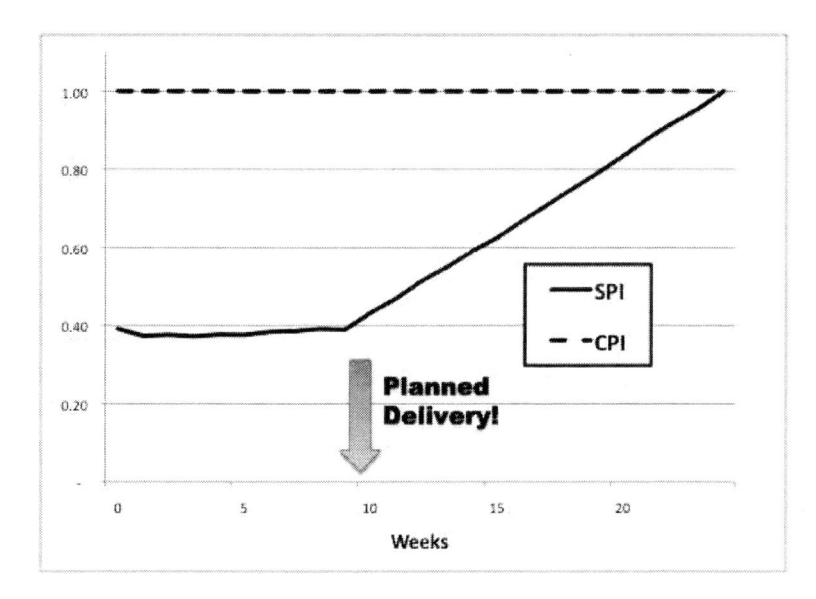

Figure 18.6: CPI and SPI when there is not much progress.

### 18.5.2 No Progress!

Figure 18.6 shows what happens when a project does not start well. The project was supposed to complete many small deliverables at a constant rate. In the early stages, a small fraction of the deliverables were completed, and each one was completed on budget. Therefore, $AC = EV$, and $CPI = 1.0$, as shown in Figure 18.6.

*The project is on budget!*

Where are the trouble signs? The problem is that there is not much progress, and this is indicated in the $SPI$ curve in Figure 18.6, where the $SPI = 0.4$. Only 40% of the deliverables are being completed in the early stages of the project. (The $PV = 100$, but the $EV = 40$.) In fact, this project continued at the 40% completion rate all along, right up until week 24, when the project was completed.

Notice that the $SPI$ eventually begins to increase, which has nothing to do with the actual progress. Actually, the productivity is constant: 40%. of the deliverables are completed each week. Nevertheless, the $SPI$ is useful, particularly early on, when the lack of progress is shown in the $SPI$, not the $CPI$.[17]

[17]One should not allow the project manager on such a project to claim that the rising $SPI$ means progress!

275

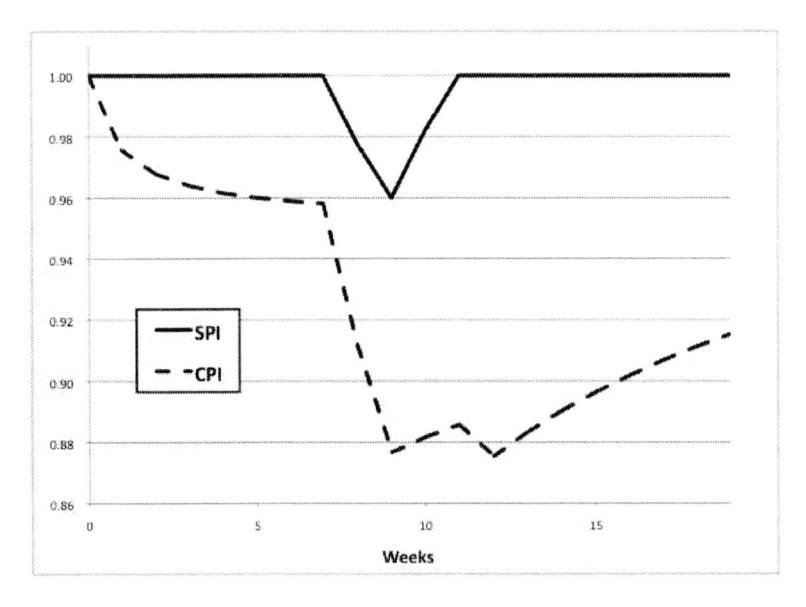

Figure 18.7: CPI and SPI when the project manager throws money at it to get back on schedule.

### 18.5.3 Throw Money At It!

Figure 18.7 shows what happens when a project gets into schedule trouble and the project manager decides to trow money at it to get it back on schedule. This project was *schedule dominated*, meaning that the stakeholders would not tolerate a delay. In the early stages, the project is on schedule, but slightly over budget, which can be seen in Figure 18.7: $SPI \sim 1.0$, and $CPI \sim 0.96$.

*The project is on schedule!*

Around week 8, the project runs into trouble and a few deliverables are late. The $SPI$ falls to around 0.96. The project manager immediately recognizes the trouble, and spends extra money to get the project back on schedule. This is shown in Figure 18.7, where the $SPI$ climbs back to 1.0, and the $CPI$ falls to around 0.88.

This is a combination that is useful to recognize. The $SPI$ falls and then climbs back to where it was. Meanwhile the $CPI$ falls to a new average level. The decline in the $CPI$ shows that money was thrown at the project to get it back on schedule. [18]

[18] Whether the money is well spent, we leave to the reader to decide when they uncover such a combination.

### 18.5.4 Rotten Quality!

Finally, we note that Earned Value will not help with the *quality* of the deliverables. It not unusual for the first few deliverables to be completed on time and on budget, but for a thorough review to uncover errors and missing pieces. The $CPI = 1.0$ (on budget!), and the $SPI = 1.0$ (on schedule!), but the quality stinks.

In this case, one has not actually *earned* the value of the planned deliverable. A good project manager on assigns the value of the deliverable only after a thorough review of the quality of the deliverable!

Earned Value does not tell you what is wrong, or what is causing the problem. Neither does it tell you how to fix it. Think of Earned Value as a Thermometer, it merely *indicates* when there is trouble.

### 18.5.5 At Major Milestones

Earned Value is particularly important at major milestones. Customers will want to see a measure of progress at these important events. At major milestones, the discussion is not going to be about the money spent, but the accomplishment of something useful.[19]

## 18.6 TCPI

> **Once our customers start using earned value, we will no longer be able to fudge the cost!**
>
> *Roger Warburton*

The fourth edition of the PMBOK added a simple formula that could change the world of project management. The new topic carries the unwieldy name of the *To-Complete Performance Index*, or TCPI. It is defined as follows:

> *TCPI is the calculated projection of cost performance that must be achieved on the remaining work to meet a specified management goal, such as the planned budget—the BAC.*

The equation for the $TCPI$, using the BAC, is:

$$TCPI = \frac{\text{Work Remaining}}{\text{Funds Remaining}} = \frac{BAC - EV(t)}{BAC - AC(t)} \quad (18.16)$$

[19] Earned Value doesn't deliver a project, people do!

## 18. EARNED VALUE MANAGEMENT

What is the point of this formula? Why $TCPI$?

We've got $CPI$ and $SPI$, so what else do we need? $TCPI$ is not just yet another formula to measure the status of a project, it is a revolution waiting to happen. But surprisingly, it's a political and ethical revolution.

Here's an illustration of the problem: You're a few months into a project and the first few deliverables have been completed. You diligently calculate the $CPI$ and get the value, $CPI = 0.9$. Your customer asks you about your plans for the cost overrun.

"No problem, we'll make it up," you say.

Once our customers start computing the TCPI, that answer is not going to work anymore. Let us show you why.

### 18.6.1  *TCPI* Example

Suppose we are writing a book, and we estimate that it requires 10 chapters (the scope). We estimate the cost, and negotiate the following deal with our customer: The planned cost of each chapter is $100, and we promise to deliver one chapter per week for 10 weeks. Therefore, the *Budget at Completion*, $BAC$, is the planned (estimated) cost of the book, which is $1,000.

We start the project and dutifully deliver the first 3 chapters on time. While we keep to the schedule, we have to put in some over-time to complete each chapter, and this adds some extra expenses. Table 18.5 shows the status of the project at the end of month three.

Line 1 of Table 18.5 shows the planned costs for the first three months. We delivered the first 3 chapters on time, and so according to the standard earned value approach, we *earn* the value for those (the second line of the table). Line 3 of the table shows the actual costs incurred, which are larger than the planned cost.

We dutifully calculate the $CPI = 0.8$, so we are running a little over in costs, but at this stage we might just shrug it off....no problem, we'll make it up later.

### 18.6.2  Hints of Trouble Ahead: The TCPI Calculation

It is important to note that the work remaining is the *earned value remaining*. The total earned value for the project is $1,000 (the $BAC$) and we have completed three deliverables, so the *earned value*, $EV = \$300$.

Table 18.5: The status of the book project after month 3.

| Month | 1 | 2 | 3 |
|---|---|---|---|
| Planned Value | $100 | $100 | $100 |
| Earned Value | $100 | $100 | $100 |
| Actual Cost | $125 | $125 | $125 |
| Cumulative Earned Value (EV) | $100 | $200 | $300 |
| Cumulative Actual Cost (AC) | $125 | $250 | $375 |
| CPI = EV/AC | 0.80 | 0.80 | 0.80 |

Now let's add the *TCPI* calculation. The work remaining is the total work minus the work accomplished to date:

$$BAC - EV(3) = \$1,000 - \$300 = \$700. \qquad (18.17)$$

The funds remaining are simply the total budget minus the actual costs expended to date:

$$BAC - AC(3) = \$1,000 - \$330. \qquad (18.18)$$

We now calculate the *TCPI* according to equation 18.16:

$$TCPI = \frac{1,000 - 300}{1,000 - 375} = \frac{700}{625} = 1.12. \qquad (18.19)$$

The *TCPI* says that to complete the project within budget, we have to work at a rate of 112%, i.e., 12% greater than we had planned.

We just need a 12% improvement? No big deal, we'll make it up later.[20]

However, we should not be quite so casual. So far, we are working at an 80% rate (remember, our $CPI = 0.80$), and we need to get our production rate up to 1.12. Therefore, to deliver on budget, we need a 32% improvement (from 80% to 112%). Maybe we should worry!

### 18.6.3  2 Months Later

Let's now consider the situation at the end of month 5. We write and deliver 2 more chapters on time, and at the same expenditure rate. Our status is now shown in Table 18.6.

[20] Isn't that what we tell the customer?!

## 18. EARNED VALUE MANAGEMENT

Table 18.6: The status of the book project after month 5.

| Month | 1 | 2 | 3 | 4 | 5 |
|---|---|---|---|---|---|
| Planned Value | $100 | $100 | $100 | $100 | $100 |
| Earned Value | $100 | $100 | $100 | $100 | $100 |
| Actual Cost | $125 | $125 | $125 | $125 | $125 |
| Cumulative Earned Value (EV) | $100 | $200 | $300 | $400 | $500 |
| Cumulative Actual Cost (AC) | $125 | $250 | $375 | $500 | $625 |
| CPI = EV/AC | 0.80 | 0.80 | 0.80 | 0.80 | 0.80 |

We delivered chapters 4 and 5 on time, so we again *earn* the value for those (the second line of the table). We see that our $CPI = 0.8$, which says that our production rate is constant. In reality, this is not an uncommon occurrence, as projects tend to perform at a constant rate.

Let's now perform the *TCPI* calculation at the end of month 5. The work remaining is: $BAC - EV(5) = \$1,000 - \$500 = \$500$. The funds remaining are: $BAC - AC(5) = \$1,000 - \$625 = \$375$. We now calculate the *TCPI* according to equation 18.16:

$$TCPI = \frac{1,000 - 500}{1,000 - 625} = \frac{500}{375} = 1.33. \tag{18.20}$$

To complete the project within budget, we now have to work at a rate of 133% of our plan, i.e., 33% greater than we planned. Since our actual production rate is only 80% of what we planned. We need to raise our production from our current performance rate of 80% to the necessary rate of 133%.

We need a 53% improvement in our production rate!

At this point, it is getting extremely difficult to justify our position: "No big deal, we'll make it up." If our customers compute the *TCPI*, they will have every reason to be concerned.

### 18.6.4 The TCPI does not lie

In month 6, the *TCPI* reaches the value, $TCPI = 1.6$, suggesting we need an 80% improvement to meet the planned budget. The point is that *TCPI* continues to rise, and very rapidly.

18.6. TCPI

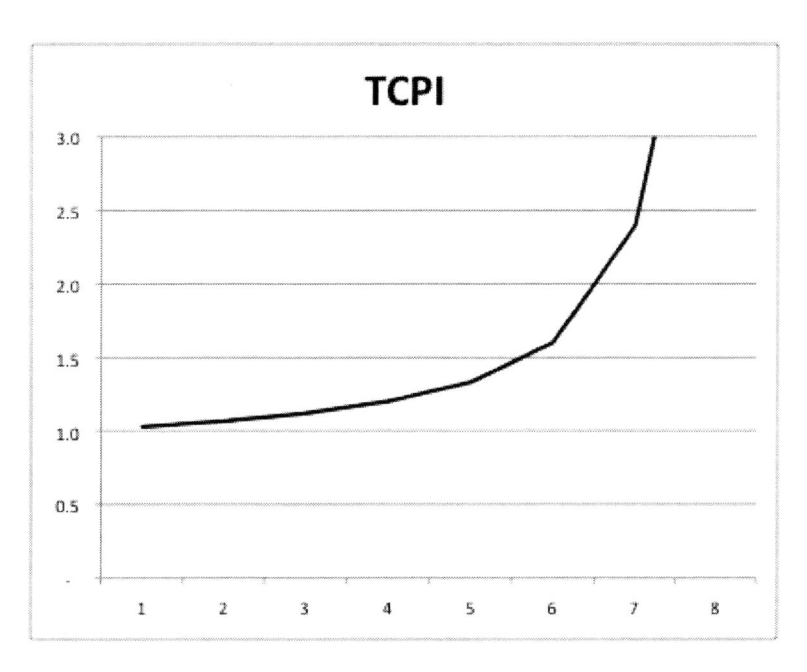

Figure 18.8: The $TCPI$ is the efficiency required to complete the rest of the project on budget. It rises dramatically, clearly demonstrating the project is in trouble. $TCPI \to \infty$ in month 8!

The story does not end here—it gets even more interesting, and very quickly. Figure 18.8 shows a plot of the $TCPI$ for the book project if things continue at the same production rate. The $TCPI$ goes $\to \infty$ in month 8

The fundamental idea is that no matter how great an improvement you think you can induce from your team, the $TCPI$ will eventually overtake that value. You can't fight infinity!

No matter how optimistic you are as a project manager, and no matter what miracle you think you have up your sleeve, the $TCPI$ will show your customers that your project will inevitably reach a point where you just cannot deliver on budget.

### 18.6.5  PMBOK to the Rescue!

At this point, the PMBOK suggests a fix. Buried in the $TCPI$ paragraph is the apparently innocuous comment:

## 18. Earned Value Management

> *If it becomes obvious that the BAC is no longer viable, the project manager develops a forecast estimate at completion (EAC). Once approved, the EAC effectively supersedes the BAC as the cost performance goal.*

This is a fancy way of saying that the *TCPI* formula changes as follows:

$$TCPI = \frac{BAC - EV(t)}{BAC - AC(t)} \rightarrow \frac{BAC - EV(t)}{EAC - AC(t)}. \tag{18.21}$$

The subtle change is that *EAC* replaced *BAC* in the denominator, and this is referred to as the *EAC* version of the *TCPI* formula. Let's see what happens if we use it.

First, we need to determine an estimate for the *EAC*, and using the average *CPI* formula for the *EAC* gives:

$$EAC = \frac{BAC}{\langle CPI \rangle} = \frac{\$1,000}{0.80} = \$1,250. \tag{18.22}$$

This says that since our average *CPI* = 0.80 for five months, then we should probably admit that the final cost will be around $1,250. The PMBOK adds the idea that when the project manager finally owns up to the idea that "the *BAC* is no longer viable," we need to use the *EAC* version of the formula. Since the *BAC* is $1,000 and the new *EAC* is $1,250, we need to own up to the fact that our $1,000 estimate is no longer reasonable.

We can now calculate the new *TCPI* using the right hand version of equation 18.23. At the end of month 5, we get:

$$TCPI = \frac{BAC - EV(t)}{EAC - AC(t)} = \frac{1,000 - 500}{1,250 - 675} = \frac{500}{625} = 0.80. \tag{18.23}$$

The new *TCPI* is equal to the *CPI*!

Remember, the *TCPI* is the "performance that must be achieved on the remaining work to meet a specified management goal." Equation 18.23 simply says that our remaining performance need only be at *TCPI* = 0.80, to meet our goal. However, our new goal is the revised budget of $1,250. In other words, we have been forced to admit to the overrun.

Somewhat ironically, we knew the value of the overrun in month one, but failed to own up to it. Only when forced by the *TCPI* did we admit to the inevitable.

Let's review the process. We calculated the *TCPI*, which eventually told us our original goal was no longer viable. (In fact, the rapid and relentless rise in the

*TCPI*, means that eventually we will have to admit that the cost goal is no longer viable.) We then calculated the new budget using our ongoing, established *CPI*, and this brought our *TCPI* and *CPI* into agreement.

### 18.6.6   *TCPI = CPI*?

When we admitted that the *BAC* was no longer viable, we calculated a new *TCPI* using the *EAC* version of the formula, and our *TCPI* turned out to be equal to our *CPI*. Is this a coincidence? Actually, no, it is a direct consequence of the *TCPI* formula.[4]

This says is that if we own up to the cost overrun and calculate the new *EAC = BAC/CPI* =$1,250, then the efficiency that is required for the rest of the project (the *TCPI*) is simply the current *CPI*. That is, the *TCPI* has the remarkable property that if we own up to the cost overrun and use the *EAC* version of the *TCPI* formula, we can proceed at our current efficiency (defined by our current *CPI*) and hit the new cost target—the *EAC*.

### 18.6.7   Oh-Oh. The customer knows

Fleming & Koppelman suggest that CPI is about the past and TCPI is about the future.[17] While true, this is not as suggestive as the idea that:

1. CPI is what you as a PM, think is happening.

2. TCPI is what your customer is thinking: Can you deliver on time?

One of Albert Einstein's oft-quoted sayings was "insanity is doing the same thing over and over and expecting a different result."[5] As project managers, we are often guilty of this kind of insanity when we measure a few values for *CPI* < 1, and then tell ourselves (and even worse, our customers!) that all will be well.

**PM:**     *We've run into some problems and our CPI = 0.9.*
            *But we believe that we can still deliver on budget.*
**Customer:** *Oh Yeah? I've computed your TCPI = 1.2.*
            *How are you going to get 30% increase in productivity?*

See what we mean? If our customers start computing the *TCPI*, it is going to change the world–no more cheating. *TCPI* will make our customers tougher and smarter.[21]

[21] We keep insisting that your customer can calculate the *TCPI*, and all other EVM quantities from your monthly reports of deliverables and costs. You cannot hide it!

283

## 18.7 Further Reading:

For a gentle introduction to earned value management, see the book by Fleming and Koppleman, who basically invented its modern formulation. [17] Fleming & Koppelman are also a good source of materials on what works in EVM.[18]

Frank Anbari wrote the definitive summary of the state of the art of $EV$. [19]

Christensen & Heise found that EVM provides reliable early warning signals of project trouble as early as 15% into a project. Contracts from the Defense Acquisition Executive Database (DAES) indicate that *without exception, the cumulative CPI does not significantly improve during the period of 15% through 85% of the contract performance; in fact it tends to decline.*[20]

Christensen summarizes this succinctly by saying, "Usually, on a project, things will only get worse!"

For a theory that gives at least one solution to the problem that the $SPI$ is time-dependent, see [21].

# CHAPTER 19

# QUALITY

> **Be a yardstick of quality. Some people aren't used to an environment where excellence is expected.**
>
> *Steve Jobs*

In this chapter we focus on the technical concepts, as well as tools and techniques, associated with the project quality management knowledge area. Project quality management consists of three processes: Plan Quality, Perform Quality Assurance, and Perform Quality Control. The goal of these processes and the activities associated with them, is to assure the stakeholders that the project meets their needs. This is embodied in the definition of quality:

*Quality is the degree to which a set of inherent characteristics fulfill requirements.*

While this is the international standard definition of quality (*ISO 5000*), *meeting requirements* is a complex issue. For example, meeting stakeholder requirements (their wants and needs) is vastly different from meeting performance goals (e.g., speed and throughput).

# 19. QUALITY

Also, quality applies to both the product and the management of the project. For example good quality project management would ensure that the project was delivered within the cost and schedule goals, that changes were all approved jointly with the stakeholder, and that the process for managing deliverables was transparent and efficient. All of this might be accomplished with excellent quality, but is of little value if the product itself has low quality.

*Process quality does not guarantee product quality, and vice versa.*

Mathematically speaking, quality is equal to conformance to requirements plus fitness for use.[1]

*Grade* is also different from quality. ISO defines grade as a category assigned to products or services having the same functional use but different technical characteristics.

For example, international grade specifications for sugar range from very high to low. White refined sugar with a minimum purity of 99.80% is considered to be the highest grade. In comparison crystal sugar which has a minimum purity of 99.60%, or brown sugar which has purity in the range of 94% to 97% is classified as lower grade sugar.[2]

However, from a quality perspective all the above three grades of sugar meet the internationally accepted quality standards for human consumption.[3]

## 19.1 Key Concepts

Before we begin our discussion of tools and techniques, we review some basic approaches to quality management and some terminology.

The International Standards Organization (ISO) is widely known to provide resources pertaining to quality standards. The PMBOK approach is compatible with a variety of approaches, such as Total Quality Management (TQM), Six Sigma, and Continuous Improvement, as well as approaches from quality theorists such as Deming, Juran, Crosby and others. Here is a quick overview of some of the above concepts.

*TQM* is a quality management philosophy from the noted expert Dr. W. Edwards Deming. It is uses statistical analysis to measure whether a process is in control. More importantly, Dr. Deming introduced the concept that quality should be planned in, not inspected in, and that investing in quality saves money.

---

[1] This says nothing about the quality of the development process!

[2] But you might prefer it in your muffins.

[3] Sugar specifications can be found at genesisny.net.

*Six Sigma* is a methodology also rooted in statistics. The focus of the Six Sigma Quality standard is to reduce process output variation, for instance, focusing on processes continuously over time to reduce the defect rate to no more than 3.4 defects per million opportunities. In terms of standard deviation, for instance, Six Sigma translates to being 99.99966% defect free.[4]

*Continuous Improvement*, also known as by its Japanese word Kaizen, is a proactive approach to quality management. It focuses on not being content with things the way they are today, but instead seeking continuous process improvement.

*Zero Defects* is a quality management philosophy from Philip Crosby. As the name suggests, its basic approach is to do something right the very first time. Investing money up front will minimize the need for rework and further expenses down the road to fix defects.

*Fitness for Use* was designed by Joseph Juran, and focuses on identifying and meeting the real needs of stakeholders.

Gold plating is the practice of providing a customer more features than they requested, typically in the scope. From a project management perspective, gold plating can result in a project that is risky and expensive.

An example of gold plating is when a programmer implements a digital clock for the website home page of a North American business, assuming that it adds value to the website. Something like this could create complexity and additional cost down the road when the product is used in multiple time-zones, or the European users want to see the clock in a 24-hour format.

Gold plating might even be unethical if the customer was not informed of the add-ons and is later compelled to pay for them.

## 19.2 Tools and Techniques for Quality Planning

The key inputs and outputs for the Plan Quality process are the quality management plan, quality metrics, the quality checklist, the process improvement plan and the quality baseline. The project team uses tools and techniques to generate these outputs. The following concepts are relevant for the Plan Quality process:

- *Cost-Benefit Analysis* The concept of a quality cost-benefit analysis is similar to a traditional cost-benefit analysis. The team focuses on creating a business scenario for several quality activities and compares the investment in

[4] It is worth pointing out that a project is *unique*, so the idea of defects per million does not apply, as there would need to be a million copies of the project.

# 19. QUALITY

such activities with the perceived benefits, such as higher productivity, less rework, lower-cost and better reputation.

- *Benchmarking.* This refers to comparing a project's internal production process with industry standards with the idea that the comparison will result in establishing a viable quality standard for the project at hand.

- *Cost of Quality.* This refers to determining the total cost of quality over the life of a project, and includes both the cost of conformance and non-conformance.

  A cost of conformance example is prevention costs, such as investing in quality through testing and inspection. Examples of cost of non-conformance include internal failure costs, such as rework, and external failure costs, such as fixing a failed product as required by warranty, or meeting liability expenses. Investing in cost of conformance is money well spent as it reduces costs due to failure.[5]

- *Control Charts* graphically describe performance data. They include upper and lower limits within which a healthy process runs. Such a chart is usually used to reveal if equipment is producing products outside the defined specifications. Control charts can be used both to establish standards and to monitor various types of output variables.[1]

  Figure 19.1 gives an example of a control chart. The target (usually the mean of the process) is the solid line in the middle. We see in the chart that one data point, "x" is outside the upper control limit, and we conclude therefore the entire process is out of control.

  A process can also be out of control if too many data points are all on the same side of the mean. The "rule of seven" declares that an entire process out of control if seven data points lie on the same side of the mean. The process is out of control even if the points are within the limits—see Figure 19.2.[2]

- *Design of Experiments (DOE).* This is a statistical method for identifying the factors influence specific variables of a product or process under development or in production. From a quality planning perspective, it is used to determine the number and type of tests, and their impact on quality. An example given in the PMBOK guide describes automotive designers using DOE to determine which combination of suspension and tires will produce the most comfortable ride at a reasonable cost.[6]

---

[5] We have already explained that defects found by the user are the most expensive to fix.

[6] Another non-project!

## 19.2. Tools and Techniques for Quality Planning

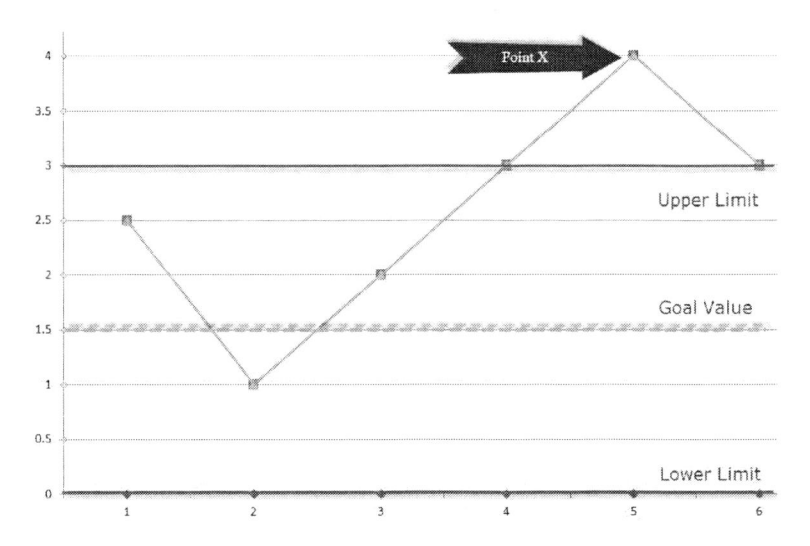

Figure 19.1: A simple control chart with one data point outside the control limits. This point should be investigated.

- *Statistical Sampling* is the study of a population of interest, and it involves gathering information from the sample domain and then analyzing it. As a tool, knowledge about various statistical sampling techniques is very helpful to a project manager. For example, during the project, many choices may be made during the design phase, and selecting the right representative sample choices for consideration is critical if the project outcome is to produce the right results. A type of statistical sampling which is commonly used is random sampling. An example would be to use a random number generator function to select 20 data points from a population of 1000.

- *Flowcharting* is a graphical depiction of a process flow. It consists of rectangles, which represent processes, and a diamond, which represent decision points. A review of a visual flowchart during quality planning can help identify stumbling points.

19. QUALITY

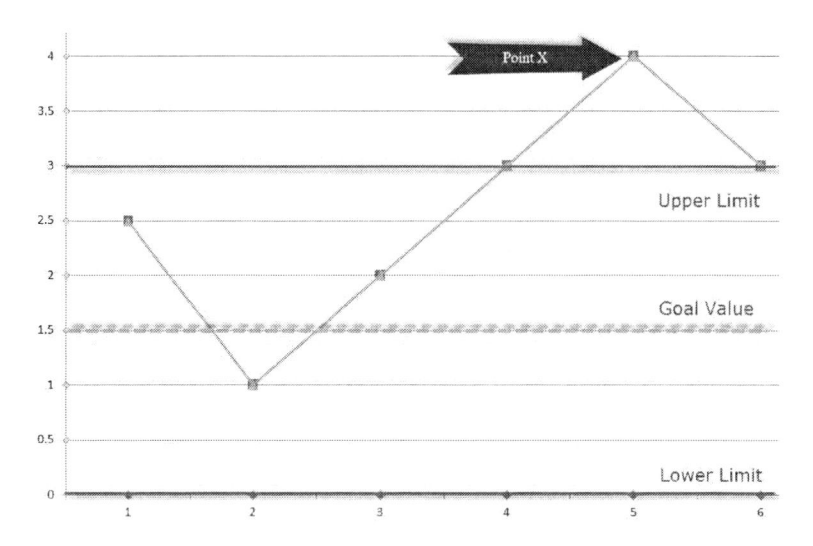

Figure 19.2: A control chart showing an out of control process: There are more than seven data points on the same side of the mean–the rule of seven.

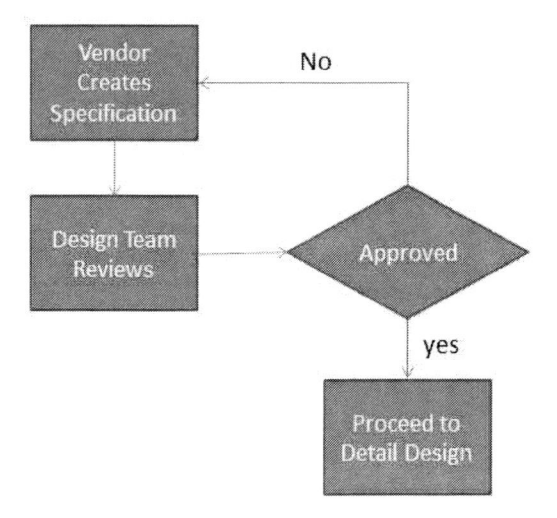

Figure 19.3: A simple flow chart.

## 19.3 Tools and Techniques for Quality Assurance

Once the quality plan is produced, the team proceeds to quality assurance. Here, the team ensures that the project is meeting the quality standards established during the quality planning phase. Quality Assurance is a prevention-driven process. The key outputs are change requests, project management plan updates, and process asset updates. The tools used by the project team to conduct quality assurance are Quality Audits and Process Analysis.

- *Quality Audit.* A quality audit should confirm if the quality processes are functioning correctly and deliverables are meeting the project's objectives. If the benchmark cannot be achieved then a comprehensive review is undertaken to see if the initial goals were not appropriate. Otherwise, steps are taken to get the project to the expected level of quality.

    Quality audits are formal reviews and should be scheduled at key intervals during the project. They can also be conducted randomly as needed. The internal QA department is involved along with experts from outside as required. The lessons learned from a quality audit should be documented so that both shortcomings and strengths are evident to stakeholders.

- *Process Analysis.* The current processes are analyzed to determine if improvements are needed. For example, a process analysis may reveal an opportunity to reduce waste or save time, in which case the project manager might recommend a new process be implemented. Process analysis may include a root cause analysis—a tool we describe in the next section.

## 19.4 Tools and Techniques for Quality Control

In this process the project deliverables are inspected, monitored for overall quality, and corrective action taken if defects are found. Several tools play an important role in evaluating the quality of the outputs.

*Cause and Effect Diagrams.* These are also called Ishikawa Diagrams and are a useful tool for getting to the root of a problem. Ishikawa diagrams are useful in team meetings to investigate a problem, and getting to the *root cause*. Working with the team, the source of a problem is uncovered by asking the 'Why?' question three times.

For example, suppose it is observed that pizza delivery is more likely to be late on weekends. The analysis of this problem begins by asking the following question:

## 19. QUALITY

**Low Quality** — Wrong Addresses Recorded; Wrong Order details resulting in pizza redelivery

**Staffing Issues** — Employees Quit Frequently; No Benefits; Low Wages; Weekend Employees Not Trained

**Resource Issues** — Run out of Heated Delivery Bags; Frequently Out of Pizza Boxes; Insufficient Delivery Vehicles

→ Pizza Delivery is Late on Weekends

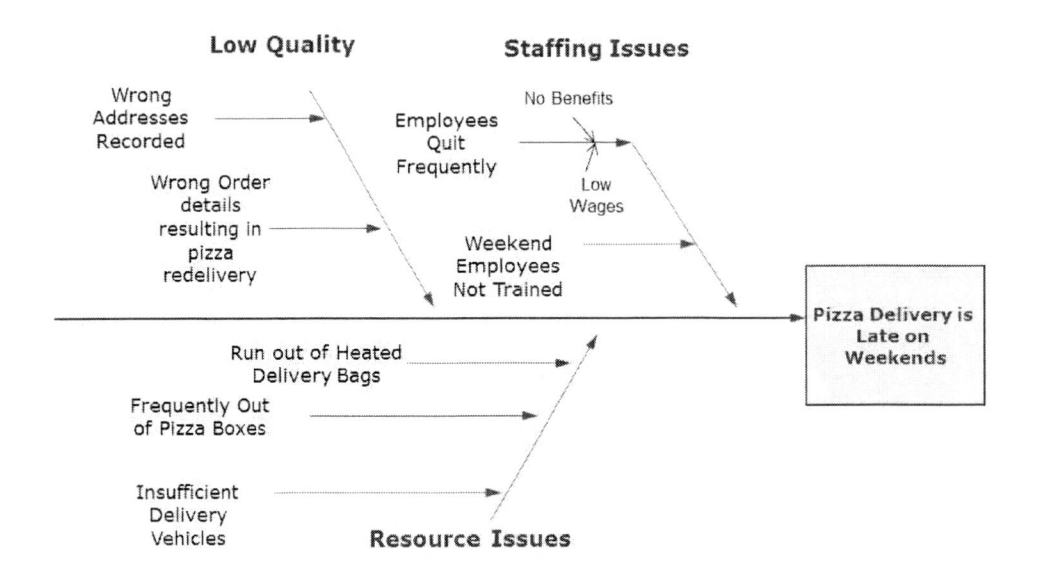

Figure 19.4: An *Ishikawa Diagram* analyzing the causes of late pizza delivery on weekends.

- *Why is pizza delivery late on weekends?*

  Let us assume the response is that there are employee issues, resource issues, and quality issues. Brainstorming continues with a second round of 'Why?'

- *Why are employees inadequate on weekends?*

  The second 'Why?' is trying to uncover possible causes. Suppose the reasons provided are that: Weekend employees are not happy and quit frequently and, therefore, adequately trained staff is not available on weekends.

  Brainstorming continues with a third 'Why?'

- *Why are employees unhappy?*

  Suppose that reasons provided this time include: Wages are low and benefits non-existent. Also, funding is not available for training and instructors are not available to train the weekend crew.

We now have a possible root cause to the employee problem, which is inadequately trained staff due to poor pay. We may even have a possible solution: If it is not possible to raise wages, then at least provide better training. The other issues can be similarly analyzed (quality and resource issues).

## 19.4. Tools and Techniques for Quality Control

*Control Charts* were described in the Plan Quality process, and are a useful tool in quality control as well. A control chart gives a picture of the process output over time.

*A Pareto Chart* is a histogram ordered by frequency of occurrence. It shows data by type and rank ordering is used to focus on the problem. This is commonly known as the "80-20" rule, where we typically conclude that 80% of the defects are due to 20% of the causes.

For example, a car with poor alignment can create all kinds of problems, such as wear and tear on tires, pulling to one side, vibration, loss of control during acceleration, and more. Addressing the poor alignment issue can fix a substantial number of problems.

In projects, poor cost estimation is responsible for many problems, such as schedule pressure, running over budget, and quality issues with deliverables. Addressing cost estimation as a cause might result in fixing many problems associated with cost, schedule and quality!

*Inspection* is a useful technique for examining product quality. It goes by other names such as reviews, audits, and walks-through. Depending upon on the organization, inspection may occurs in several different formats.

# CHAPTER 20

# HUMAN RESOURCES

**Never hire anyone you wouldn't want to run into in the hallway at three in the morning.**

*Tina Fey*

Human Resources (HR) management is one of the areas where project management borrows heavily from general management principals.

The key skills that a project manager must have include leadership, communication, negotiation, influence, and conflict resolution. A project manager must also be a mentor, and be able to motivate the project team after the initial excitement of project kick-off has faded. A project manager also needs strong skills in delegating, follow-up, developing the team and managing them throughout the life of the project.

In this chapter we will cover some of the traditional HR theory and wrap up with the tools and techniques that are associated with HR management as it applies to projects. The PMBOK processes are: Develop Human Resource Plan (a Planning process), Acquire Project team (an Execution process), Develop Project Team (an Execution process), and Manage Project Team (an Execution Process).

## 20. Human Resources

### 20.1 Develop Human Resource (HR) Plan

*Develop HR Plan* deals with organizing, managing, and leading the project team, and there is only one output: The HR Plan. To assemble the HR Plan, the project manager uses company organization charts and position descriptions to define the positions. To acquire the team requires soft skills, such as networking.

A project manager needs an excellent grasp of organizational theory, including organization charts. Organization charts are classified under the following types: Hierarchical; Matrix, RACI; and Text-Oriented formats.[1]

*Hierarchical Charts* are the organizational charts that most organizations publish. They are hierarchical and show titles, positions, and reporting relationships, and are easy to understand—see Figure 20.1.

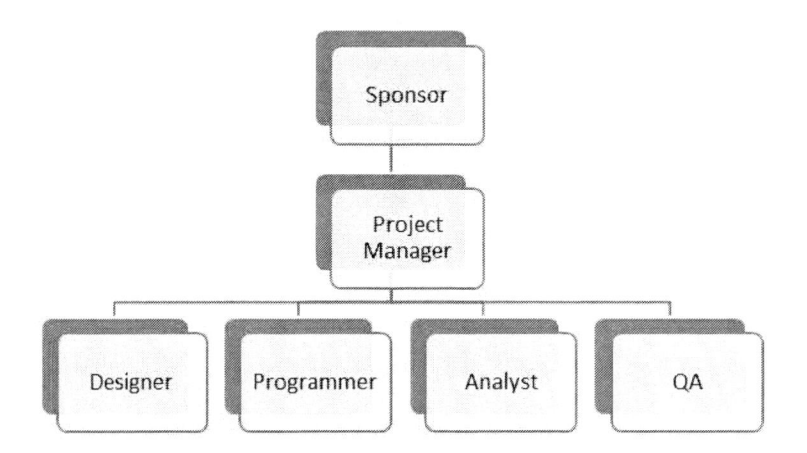

Figure 20.1: A simple organization chart.

*Matrix Charts* are useful tools that associate a resource name with a work package and project responsibility. One such chart frequently used during the planning stages is the Responsibility Assignment Matrix (RAM). There are various formats for depicting a RAM, but the one used most frequently is the Responsible, Accountable, Consult, Inform (RACI) chart.

Typically, only one resource is assigned the Responsibility (R) label. The person accountable for the work is given the (A) label. Of course, there might be sharing or delegation or work involved. Typically, the sponsor is given the Inform (I) label as they need to be kept up-to-date on progress. Staff members who are consulted are designated with the Consult (C) label. An example is shown in Figure 20.2.

[1] Note: Organization charts should not be confused with organizational structures: functional, matrix (weak, balanced, strong), and projectized.

You should try to avoid giving a person more than one label. Someone is either responsible, accountable, consulted, or informed.

| Work Package | Analyst | Designer | Programmer | QA |
|---|---|---|---|---|
| Analysis | R | C | C | A |
| Design | C | R | C | I |
| Build | C | C | R | I |

Figure 20.2: An RACI Matrix.

*Text Oriented Formats* are typically generated from historical templates. The text document provides information such as the name of the person, their role, responsibility, authority, and qualifications.

## 20.2 Acquire Project Team

During the execution phase, the project manager assembles the team. The project manager develops staff assignments and *resource calendars*, which explain who is assigned to what activity and when. In acquiring the team, the project manager makes sure that it is a balanced and effective mix.

When assigning resources, the project manager considers previous experience, matches skills with activity requirements, and assesses leadership and communication styles. The personal desires and interests of a team member should not be overlooked.

The key concepts in acquiring a team are:

*Pre-Assignment:* This refers to the fact that some project team members may be selected in advance.

*Negotiation:* In a matrix structure, resources are controlled by the functional manager. The project manager has to influence the functional manager to obtain the best mix of resources.

*Acquisition:* This is the procurement of resources and services from outside the project.

*Virtual teams:* This refers to teams that are not co-located and have very little opportunity for face-to-face contact. Some of the team members could be in another city or even another country.

Since distributed project development occurs in many large organizations, the project manager must be able to assure an effective pattern of communication, and develop a team where the members trust each other.

## 20.3 Develop Project Team

After the project staff assignments have been completed and calendars created for the resources, the next step is to *Develop Project Team*. The following skills, tools and techniques are used during this process:

*Soft skills*: Project managers that have good soft skills can ensure smooth running of projects. This requires sincere communication with project team members and true empathy. Such skills are vital when it comes to communication, negotiation, and influence of stakeholders.[2]

*Training*: This is essential to ensure that the team members are well prepared to accomplish their tasks, preferably before they start working on them. Scheduling training proactively can mitigate quality risks and reduce costs.

*Team-Building Activities*: Good team building activities help teams to perform synergistically. Depending upon the scope and length of the project, the team building activities may include simple introductions (which help through communicating previous experience and hobbies), clarifying roles and expectations, and describing the management process.

More significant team building may include comprehensive off-site, facilitated, workshops focusing on bonding and integration of diverse personality types.[3]

*Phases of Working Teams*: The project manager must understand the classic stages that teams go through. Dr. Bruce Tuckman published a classic model in 1965, which explains the typical phases that teams go through:

- *Forming:* The team is formed and they look to the project manager for guidance and direction.

- *Storming:* Team members compete for position, as they establish their relation to other team members. The project manager might be challenged at this stage. The project manager must intervene proactively, before conflicts

---

[2] Do not forget that project team members are stakeholders.

[3] All of these activities need a line item in the budget.

get out of hand. If a project manager has defined clear roles and responsibilities, the storming stage will be brief.

- *Norming:* Agreement and consensus occurs in the norming phase and the team works well under the direction of a project manager.

- *Performing:* The team is "strategically aware" and motivated, knows what it is doing, and where it is going.[4]

- *Adjourning:* The team breaks up, which occurs during the closing stage of the project.

### 20.3.1 Recognition and Rewards

Motivation recognizes and promotes desirable behavior and is effective when carried out by the management team and the project manager. This is an important key skill for the project manager: Encouraging the required behavior from the team. To develop teams requires understanding of the following theoretical concepts:

**Maslow's Hierarchy of Needs**

Dr. Abraham Maslow proposed that a person's needs must be satisfied in the following hierarchy: Physiological, Safety, Social, Self-esteem, and Self-actualization. See Figure 20.3. [22]

The primary motivation for an individual is to satisfy their basic physical needs, such as food, drink, shelter and warmth. Only when these needs are satisfied can a person begin to deal with the higher level needs.

The next level deals with safety, and applies to needs such as protection, law and order, and stability. Social needs deal with the desire to belong to a group and involves family, affection and relationships.

The next level in the hierarchy is where individuals are motivated by self-esteem, which includes achievement, status, responsibility, and reputation.

Finally, when all of the needs in the lower end of the hierarchy have been fulfilled, a person can begin to deal with self-actualization. Such an individual is motivated by personal growth and fulfillment.

[4]The plane is on auto-pilot and the project manager can relax.

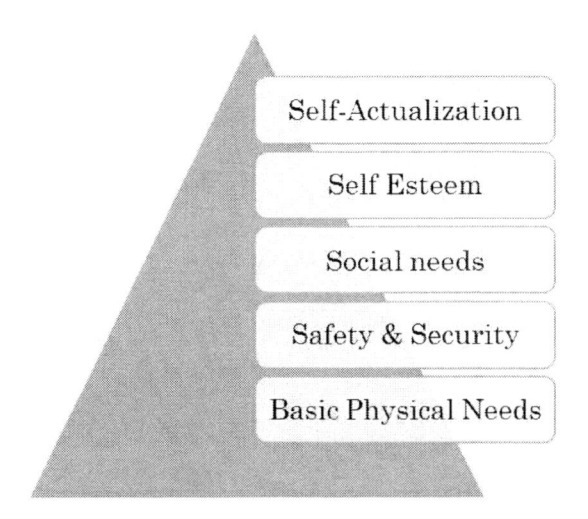

Figure 20.3: Maslow's hierarchy of needs.

A project manager must realize that team members are usually motivated by personal growth and fulfillment and so must take time to identify each member's interests and how to achieve them.

**McGregor: Theory X and Theory Y**

Douglas McGregor defined two models of worker behavior: Theory X and Theory Y. Theory X managers believe that team members will not perform their duties unless threatened or closely supervised.

On the other hand, Theory Y managers believe the team will perform well if given the right motivating environment and appropriate expectations.

Managers that practice *Theory Y* behavior are much more likely to succeed in a project environment because, as we learned from Maslow's Hierarchy, project team members tend to be motivated by personal growth and fulfillment.

**Herzberg's Theory of Motivation**

Herzberg's "motivation-hygiene" theory proposes that certain motivator and hygiene factors affect job satisfaction and dissatisfaction. The *hygiene factors* merely prevent dissatisfaction. Examples are pay, benefits, the conditions of the work environment, and relationships with peers and managers.

The *motivation factors* are those that lead to satisfaction and deal with the substance of the work itself. These include the ability to advance and the opportunity to learn new things.

According to Herzberg, pay (a hygiene factor) will not motivate project teams, but new responsibilities (a motivation factor) might.

**Expectancy Theory**

Expectancy theory deals with how the expectation of a positive outcome can motivate people to perform and drive outcomes. People will behave in certain ways if they think there will be positive rewards for doing so.

If a project manager expects the team to succeed, they will. If the project manager believes they will fail, they will not be motivated and just might fail![5]

## 20.4 Manage Project Team

In this final HR process, the project manager tracks each team member's performance, provides feedback to their manager, manages resources, and resolves conflicts. The following tools and techniques are used when managing project teams:

*Observation and Conversation:* A simple example of communication with team members is inquiring about their work and the issues they face.

*Project Performance Appraisals:* Periodic feedback can help team members, especially if constructively given.

*Use of Issue Logs:* The project manager should keeps a written log of issues with target dates for them to be resolved.

*Interpersonal Skills:* This involves an appreciation of:

- *Leadership:* Varying leadership styles exist, such as, directing, facilitating, coaching, supporting, autocratic, consultative, and consensus.

- *Influencing skills:* This requires good listening skills, the ability to persuade and articulate points and positions, and building trust.

[5]We expect our students to succeed!

## 20. Human Resources

- *Effective Decision making:* This requires clearly understanding the project goals, having a well-defined process to follow, consideration of risks and opportunities, and the ability to come up with creative solutions.

*Conflict Management:* Conflict and frustration occurs in most projects. Conflict is natural in all organizations due to different values. The modern theory is that conflict is good as it can create deeper understanding and respect. Two skills that a project manager must develop are:

- *Encouraging Functional Conflict:* The project manager encourages dissent by asking tough questions, encouraging different points of view, and even asking the team to consider an unthinkable, or even unpopular, alternative.

- *Managing Dysfunctional Conflict:* This involves working through the natural stages of a conflict: mediate, arbitrate, control, accept, and closure.

The following techniques are methods for resolving conflict:

- *Withdraw:* Avoid or retreat from an actual or potential conflict scenario.

- *Smooth:* This is also called "accommodate," and involves emphasizing areas of agreement, rather than the conflict at hand.

- *Compromise:* This involves concession and conciliation. Neither party involved in the conflict gets what they value the most. This is generally considered to be a *lose-lose* strategy!

- *Force:* One of the parties involved in the conflict imposed their view point at the expense of the other. This is a win-lose scenario!

- *Collaborate:* This leads to consensus and commitment and involves consideration of multiple viewpoints.

- *Confront:* This is also known as "problem solving," and involves facing the conflict boldly, and brainstorming to come up with a win-win alternative. This takes more effort than *collaborate* or *compromise*, but is generally considered to be the best approach for resolving conflicts.

If good team building has occurred early on in the project, the project manager can avoid conflicts that are destructive and harmful.

Project managers generally do not have formal, legitimate power. Team members often report to functional managers, so project managers rarely have direct authority over them, and cannot order them around. It is important, therefore, to use soft skills to motivate and lead a project to a successful completion.

A key concern for managers in many organizations, and certainly for project managers, is motivating employees and teams, and this problem is more acute for a project manager as limited financial resources are available at his or her disposal. In such situations, an effective form of power is *expert power*, where the project manager leverages "technical expertise" to drive the project towards success. We also note that good project managers trust their teams, while poor manager tend to exhibit "Theory X" behavior, where they constantly intervene and micro-manage. This can result in frustration and dissatisfaction, and drives down productivity.

### 20.4.1 The Technical Director

The role of the project manager (PM) is to manage the customer, the money, and the schedule. The PM manages the deliverables' cost and schedule, but who manages their content? [6]

For example: Do the deliverables meet customer requirements? Does the project actually work?[7]

In every project there is always a role for a person we call the *Technical Director* (TD) whose job it is to ensure and manage the technical aspects of the project. [8] There is a natural tension between the PM and the TD:

**PM:** Ship it on time on Friday!
**TD:** No! It's not ready!

Another word that describes the role of the TD is *architect*, in its most general sense. For example, on an IT project, there may be an architect, whose job it is to create the design, including the human interface, the database structures, etc.

In the movie industry, we suggest that the TD is the director, who controls the performance factors: directing, casting, camera angles, staging, lighting, etc. The producer controls the money, the schedule, and interfaces to the studio (the customer). The producer is fulfilling the role of the PM. What makes the movie case interesting is that it is one of the few cases where the TD often has more power than the PM.

On most projects, conflicts often arise when major deliverables are due. The situation typically evolves as follows: The project manager is pressing the team to meet

---

[6] This entire topic is neglected in the PMBOK and most books. We happen to think it is really interesting and the subject of much discussion.

[7] We are deliberately staying away from the word *quality* here. Many organizations have a Quality Control group, but they work after the design and construction to check everything. What we are referring to is the responsibility for the creative design aspects and the idea that the project satisfies the mission and objectives.

[8] For small projects the PM and TD may be the same person, which leads to schizophrenia.

## 20. Human Resources

the schedule for a major deliverable. The technical director is resisting, explaining that:

- The performance is not up to the *spec*.
- The delivery is going to be late.
- To meet the required performance, extra time and money is required.

*This is really bad project management!*

It is not the team's fault, it is the fault of the project manager. A bad project manager will continue to insist that the team deliver on time, and more forcefully as the deadline approaches. Meanwhile, the PM assures the customer the project is on schedule and budget.

When the delivery date rolls around, lo and behold, the product is not ready, is over budget, and behind schedule.[9]

Let's roll the clock back and suggest a better approach. First, as soon as the TD is assigned, the project manager sets about getting to know the TD. They discuss the tasks, the budget, and the schedule. They discuss all of the estimates, and where problems might lie.

The PM and TD jointly develop a workable project. The TD designs the approach, and the PM the cost and schedule, but they cooperate. The project manager sells the cost and schedule to the customer. The TD sells the product to the customer who agrees to the *spec*.

When trouble arises, the TD comes to the PM and explains the problem. Together they work out the impacts and discuss options.

In our view, if you are a project manager, it's your problem. Whatever it is.

Late? Your problem.

Over budget? Your problem.

TD whining? Your problem.

As the project manager it is your job to *induce* the team to perform, to *induce* the stakeholders to approve the project, and to *induce* the customer to pay for it. No exceptions. No excuses.

---

[9] Meanwhile, the team are all whispering, "We told you so!"

# CHAPTER 21

## COMMUNICATIONS

**It is better to keep your mouth closed and let people think you are a fool than to open it and remove all doubt.**

*Mark Twain.*

Communications Management is all about keeping upper management, stakeholders, and the project team in the loop throughout the life of a project. In large projects, communications can become a very complex because the number of communication paths rises rapidly as the number of people increases. Projects led by project managers with strong communication skills have a much better chance of success.[1]

Examples of communications skills include listening and understanding people, in all modes of communication, speaking, writing, and presenting. Communication management skills also include communication planning, information distribution, performance reporting, and stakeholder management. We introduce some communications theory as well tools and techniques to assist the project manager in these activities.

[1] It is often said, especially by Vijay Kanabar, that project management is 80% communications.

## 21.1 Identify Stakeholders

Very early on in the project, the project manager must identify stakeholders and categorize them according to their influence, identify their needs, as well as understand their perceived threats. An easy way to identify the stakeholders is to ask "Who will be impacted by this project?"

It is necessary to consider stakeholders who are both internal and external to the project. Examples of external stakeholders include the project sponsor,[2] upper management, government agencies, customers, and users of the product. Internal stakeholders include functional managers, and the project team.

One should also consider people impacted by the process. For example, a construction project might be disruptive to businesses in the neighborhood.

To identify stakeholders, the first activity is the performance of a stakeholder analysis, which first identifies them, and then classifies them as to their influence on the project.

Once the project manager has identified the stakeholders, the next step is to create a *stakeholder register,* which lists the attributes for each stakeholder, such as name, role, expectations, and potential influence.

For the PMA case study, Table 21.1 provides example illustrating stakeholder roles, expectations, and influence.

---

[2] Remember, the sponsor is paying!

Table 21.1: Stakeholder identification for the PMA web site.

| Role | Expectations | Influence (1-5) |
|---|---|---|
| Executive Sponsor | **Key Stakeholder.** Provide direction and ground-rules for the project. Guidance by request. | IL = 4. Defines project success and adjudicates rewards for accomplishments. |
| Project Sponsor | **Key Stakeholder.** Provides guidance for the project in a weekly review of the website and develops recommendations. | IL = 4. Defines project success and adjudicates rewards for accomplishments. |
| Steering & Guidance | **Key Stakeholder.** Provides guidance for the project in a weekly review of the website and develops recommendations. | IL = 4. Provides direction for the team. |
| Project Manager | **Key Stakeholder.** Management oversight of all activities. | IL = 5. Handles all status reporting to upper management. |
| Designer & Architect | **Key Stakeholder.** Implement website design. | IL = 5. Website design experience. |
| Lead Developer | **Key Stakeholder.** Implement website. | IL = 5. Website development experience. |
| Business Analyst | **Key Stakeholder.** Provide direction to maximize the effectiveness of the website. | IL = 3. Knowledge of markets. |
| PMA Members | **Key Stakeholders.** End Users. Consumers expected to be the most active users of the website. | IL = 3. Will dictate the success of the project by frequency of visitation. |
| IT Dept. | **Medium Stakeholders.** Website maintainer upon completion. | IL = 3. The quality and timeliness of website maintenance will influence end users' perception of the quality. |
| Prospective Employers | **Medium Stakeholders.** End Users. Prospective employers will use the website to locate PMs. | IL = 2. Use by employers could contribute to success. |
| Alumni | **Minor Stakeholders.** Alumni may visit website. | IL = 1. |
| Prospective Students | **Minor Stakeholders.** End Users. Masters and certificate students may use site for networking. Students may add content. | IL = 1. |

## 21.2 Communications Planning

Inexperienced project managers often spend too little of their time planning their project communications. This should be a big concern, however, as project managers spend a substantial fraction of their time communicating. It is less glamorous and more challenging to identify communication requirements and to create a communications management plan than to create a risk management plan.

There are four main types of communication and, generally, a combination of all four occurs in all projects. The four types of communication are: formal, informal, written, and verbal. They are used in the following combinations:

| | |
|---|---|
| Formal Written: | Used to communicate specifications, product requirements and change control. |
| Formal Verbal: | Used in the official presentations such as status reviews. |
| Informal Verbal: | This includes project team meetings. |
| Informal Written: | This includes non-legal documents and general notes. |

The Communication Management Plan is the primary output of the communications planning process, and becomes part of the project plan. It informs all stakeholders how and in what form communications will be handled on the project. An example of a portion of a communications plan is given in Figure 21.1.

> **Steering Committee**
> A project steering committee will be created, and will include faculty, the executive sponsor, project management team, a member of the IT Infrastructure and one alumni.
> Project steering committee meetings will be held on a weekly basis. The role of the committee will be to make decisions on any outstanding items, address issues, review change requests, and review resource utilization. Steering committee meetings will be held every Friday at 9:00AM. This will allow for issues to be raised and addressed without spanning the weekend.
> **Issues Tracking**
> Unplanned issues will occur during the duration of the project. These issues will be collected and tracked by the project manager and any issues that cannot be resolved will be presented to the steering committee. All issues reported will have an owner and a resolution date.
> All issues will be captured and tracked in an issues database, managed by the project manager. The issues will be assigned a severity based on potential impact to the project. The Issues Tracking Database will be reviewed during weekly project team meetings.

Figure 21.1: A portion of the *Communications Plan* for the PMA web site

## 21.3 Identify Communication Requirements Techniques

The following resources are helpful in identifying communication requirements: organization charts, project structures, the stakeholder register, and data on the functional departments involved with the project.

Communication complexity and communication channels increase rapidly as the number of people on the project rises. For example, the number of interactions between $n$ people is $n(n-1)/2$. For example if a project has two stakeholders $n = 2$ and the number of communication channels is $2(2-1)/2 = 1$.

If the project has four stakeholders the project has $4(4-1)/2 = 6$ communication channels. If a project has 12 stakeholders there would be 66 communication channels indicating a challenging communication problem if the project manager needs to manage them all.

A theoretical communication model is helpful in understanding the communication process. This model consists of the following components: Encode and decode; message and feedback; and medium and noise. The *message* refers to the verbal (spoken or written) symbols, as well as nonverbal signs, which also represent information that the sender attempts to convey.

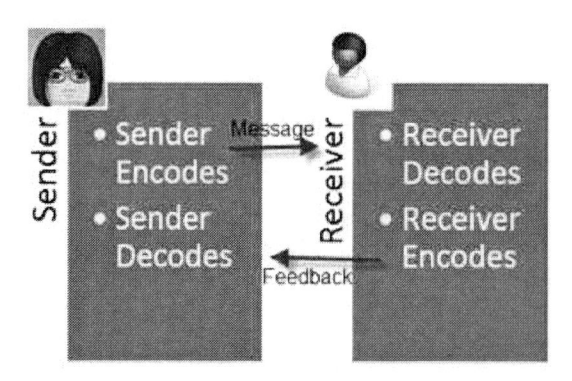

Figure 21.2: Maslow's hierarchy of needs.

The first issue in the above simple model is that unless the sender receives feedback of the message just communicated (e.g., via parroting), the sender cannot be sure that the message was properly received (let alone understood). The model also indicates that both the sender and the receiver have to be good listeners, otherwise the message cannot be decoded properly.

Adding to the complexity of the basic communication model is that many things can interfere with the transmission of the message. We classify such barriers as filters and noise, and list some examples below:

- Distance, unfamiliar technology, lack of background information.

- Different spoken languages or use of unfamiliar technical jargon, physical separation, different cultural, educational, or social backgrounds.

- Sabotage also hinders communication and could include hidden agendas, and power plays.

- Having a pre-determined mind-set or a self-fulfilling philosophy, can result in miscommunication.

- Historical considerations, such as the manner in which a task was "always done in the past," can also jeopardize communication.

A project manager facing the challenges described above must create a communication plan which clearly specifies the appropriate format, duration and frequency of communications to mitigate the risk of communication failure.

## 21.4 Distribute Information Tools & Techniques

The goal of *Distribute Information* is to share information with the team, project sponsors, and stakeholders. The PMBOK guide classifies this under communication *methods*. Examples used to distribute information include individual and group meetings, video and audio conferences, and computer chats.

Examples of information distribution *tools* include electronic communication and conferencing tools, such as e-mail, telephone and web conferencing, as well as web portals and project management software.

## 21.5 Manage Stakeholder Expectations Tools and Techniques

The PMBOK guide lists interpersonal skills and management skills under this category. Examples of interpersonal skills include building trust, resolving conflict, active listening, and overcoming resistance to change. Examples of management skills include presentation, negotiation, writing, and public speaking.

Project managers can learn from Steven Covey's *Seven Habits of Highly Effective People* to communicate more effectively and manage stakeholder expectations. [23] The steps are pretty self-explanatory and are listed below:

1. Being proactive
2. Beginning with the end in mind
3. Putting first things first
4. Thinking win/win
5. Seeking first to understand, then to be understood
6. Achieving synergy
7. Sharpening the saw

### 21.5.1 Report Performance Tools & Techniques

Four tools and techniques are introduced in the PMBOK guide: Variance analysis, forecasting methods, communication methods, and reporting systems.

## 21. Communications

*Variance analysis* refers to tools and techniques to analyze the difference between what was planned and the actual performance. Earned value management techniques can help you calculate cost and schedule variance. According to the PMBOK, the following steps can be performed during a variance analysis:

- Verify the quality of the information collected to ensure that it is complete and credible.

- Determine variances and document if they are favorable or unfavorable to the project's outcome.

- Determine the impact on project cost and schedule, as well as the impact on quality and scope.

- Analyze the trends of the variances and note the sources of variation.

*Forecasting method:* On the basis of the actual performance, a project manager may have to predict the future project performance. For example, earned value analysis is used to predict the estimated cost at completion.

*Communication methods:* The project manager conducts periodic status review meetings to gather and exchange information about the project progress and performance. The project manager can use electronic methods to distribute status updates and reports.

*Reporting systems:* A project management information system helps the project manager to capture, store, and distribute information to stakeholders. An example of such a reporting system could be Microsoft Project or Primavera.

Table 21.2: Issues tracking for the PMA web site.

| **Project Issue** | **Severity** (H, M, L) | **Owner** | **Resolution Due Date** |
|---|---|---|---|
| Need to sign a release form from PMI to get certain content to be utilized by the site. | H | PM | 07/01/2011 |

# CHAPTER 22

# RISK MANAGEMENT

> **Risk?! Risk is our business!**
>
> *Captain James T. Kirk*

*Risk Management* is the art and science of dealing with risks. During planning this involves defining the approach to risk management, identifying risks, quantifying them, and creating a risk response plan. During the execution of the project the project manager monitors and controls risks.

Historically, risk management was considered an optional, add-on process, as distinct from activities such as project scheduling or cost estimating, which were always considered to be an essential part of project management.[1] However, the reality is that every project faces risks and, inevitably, some will materialize.

Starting in the mid-1980s project management standards, such as early versions of the PMBOK, formally began to recognize that comprehensive and integrated risk management is fundamental to project success. Today, managing risk is considered an indispensable and integral part of every stage of project management, and that it must be practiced diligently throughout the life of the project.

Risk management is a proactive attempt to recognize what can go wrong and to plan ahead. Just as in medicine, prevention is better than cure. Here are some questions the project manager should ask: What can go wrong? How can we minimize the impact? What can be done in advance? What will our response be?

## 22.1 Risks

We begin with the definition of a risk:

> A *risk* is an uncertain event or condition that, if it occurs, has a positive or negative effect on the project.

Risks have *causes*: People get sick; the scope changes; a construction permit takes longer than anticipated.

Risks also have *consequences*, and some consequences associated with the above risks are:

| **Risk** | **Consequences** |
| People get sick | Inexperienced, replacement personnel make mistakes. |
| The scope changes | The change in scope increases the cost. |
| Permit delayed | The completion date is delayed. |

Notice that the cost increase is a *consequence*, not a risk. Technically, it is incorrect to say there is a *cost risk*. It is also incorrect to speak about a *schedule risk*, one should explain that there are risks that may impact the schedule.

There are many sources of risks:

- Scope Creep.[1]

- Insufficient or poor resources. An expert may be needed simultaneously in two places.

- Pressure to compress the schedule from customers or management.

- Pressure to reduce the cost from customers or management.

- Lack of a formal project management process. Uncontrolled changes are a major source of confusion and delay.

- Stakeholder friction. Stakeholders can hold up approvals if they feel their particular interests are not being satisfactorily addressed.

---

[1] Can you make this small change for me?

- Poor communications. Team members will not know what to work on, or how to prioritize their time. Customers will not understand the status of the project. Stakeholders will not know what is going on.

Examples of risks on the kitchen project are shown in Table 22.1. The consequences were that the occurrence of each one contributed to an increase in the cost.

Table 22.1: Sources of risk on the Kitchen project.

| Risks in Cost Estimate | Source of Risk |
| --- | --- |
| Unforeseen circumstances. | When the plumber opened the cabinet to replace the faucets, he found rusted pipes that had to be replaced. |
| Use of wrong estimation parameter. | The estimator used the parameter for a new house, instead of a renovation. |
| Formula inaccuracy. | The estimation formula is only good to $\pm 20\%$. |
| Optimistic estimate. | The PM Knew the customer's budget, and agreed to do the project for that amount. |
| Junior plumber assigned. | The estimate assumed an experienced plumber. |
| The estimate was made by "analogy." | The project turned out not to be "analogous," it was completely different. |
| It took longer. | Sometimes, this just happens. |

### 22.1.1 Good Risks and Bad Risks

It often comes as a surprise that the definition of a risk includes the idea that it can be positive. People usually assume that a risk has only negative consequences, and that risk management consists of mitigating the impact of the things that can go wrong. The following example includes both positive and negative risks. During *Human Resource* planning, the project manager identified the following risks:

1. *The staff do not have the required technical skills.*

   This is a negative risk, and the job of the project manager is to develop a strategy either to prevent the risk from occurring (e.g., by changing staff assignments), or mitigating the risk (e.g., by implementing a training plan).

2. *The subcontractor can provide the deliverable earlier than planned.* This is a positive risk. If the deliverable is on the critical path, this may result in accelerating the schedule. The project manager should work to maximize the

positive impact of the subcontractor's early delivery, perhaps by providing extra staff to help with delivery documentation.

Project managers should diligently investigate all risks and apply the correct tactic: Preventing and mitigating negative risks, and enhancing positive risks.

### 22.1.2 Known Unknowns and Unknown Unknowns

When trying to identify risks, one is always looking into the future, so it is an uncertain business. When describing risks, their degree of uncertainty can be classified as follows:

- *Known knowns:* These are the things that we know.[2]

- *Known unknowns:* These are risks that can be fairly well anticipated. They may be identified by reviewing similar projects. A good example from the New Kitchen project is:

    *We have to install a gas line in the kitchen and on the last project the permitting process was delayed by 6 weeks.*

    Known unknowns are risks that we can "kind-of-anticipate." According to David Logan, "much of the scientific research .... (about risks) .... is based on investigating known unknowns." [24] That is, we tend to allow for the things we expect![2]

- *Unknown unknowns:* These are the events we did not expect, things we had no idea about, as in:

    *What?! You can't quit, you're our best programmer!*

    NASA space exploration missions provide fascinating examples of things that went wrong that no one could possibly have anticipated. On a more mundane level, it is just not humanly possible to anticipate all risks.[3]

The lesson for project managers is serious: Risks will materialize, so plan ahead.[4]

## 22.2 Risk Strategies

The approach to dealing with risks is to formulate a strategy for both negative and positive risks.

---

[2] One should not be too smug about these.

[3] And if experience is anything to go by, we are not very good at this. Unknown unknowns constantly catch us by surprise.

[4] You can't anticipate all eventualities. Plan to bury some funds and schedule some slack. You never know when you will need them.

### 22.2.1 Strategies for negative risks

The negative risk strategies are: avoid, transfer, mitigate and accept.

- *Avoid:* If possible, this risk *prevention* strategy should be the first choice.

    A technique of risk avoidance is to change the scope, which changes the project's functionality so that the risk cannot occur. For example, if the kitchen does not have gas, and its installation introduces an unacceptable delay, then propose an electric stove. Another avoidance strategy is to defer risky parts of the specification to a future delivery.

- *Mitigate:* In this approach, one attempts to reduce either the likelihood of the event occurring or the impact, or both. This can result in lowering the ranking of risk from high to medium, or even low. In practice, it is unlikely that a risk can be entirely prevented from occurring.

    An example of *mitigation* is as follows: Assume that an information technology project plans to use a sophisticated development system, and the organization does not have any previous experience with it. One *mitigation* strategy is to send the inexperienced staff members for training.

    Notice that *mitigation* almost always involves extra cost. In the above case, training funds were required to mitigate the risk of inexperienced staff.

- *Transfer:* In this strategy, we outsource the risk to a third-party. Often, risk *transfer* involves investing in insurance, performance bonds, or warranties.

    An example of risk *transfer* is the hiring an expert consultant to build a difficult piece of the project.

- *Accept:* In this strategy, we accept the reality that the risk can neither be avoided, mitigated, nor transferred. The project team then decides to take a chance and *accept* the risk. The team recognizes that they will have to deal with this risk if, and when, it occurs. To allow for the risk, the project manager should set aside contingency reserves of time, money and staff.

    An example of *accepting* a risk is: A deliverable is to be supplied by an unreliable subcontractor who holds a monopoly on the technology and there are no alternatives. The only option is to accept the risk.[5]

[5] Note that all risk strategies involve adding costs. You did put that in your budget, didn't you?

### 22.2.2 Strategies for positive risks

There are also four strategies for dealing with positive risks: Exploit, enhance, share, and accept. The strategies for positive risks parallel to those for negative risks.

- *Exploit:* Here we leverage our strengths and attempt to take advantage of the risk. For example, the company might have talented programmers and assigning them to critical deliverables may result in early completion at a lower cost.

- *Enhance:* In this strategy, we attempt to increase either the likelihood or the impact of the risk occurring. An example of risk enhancement is as follows: If an activity is finished early freeing up staff, then they can be assigned to activities on the critical path to shorten the schedule.

- *Share:* Here, we enhance the opportunity for project success by teaming with a third party and delegate to them pieces they are better equipped to perform. Large projects usually share risks among several companies, each with their own expertise. For example, Boeing, subcontracts the design and development of jet engines to third-parties.

- *Accept*: Here we acknowledge that we cannot construct a viable strategy for maximizing the benefits of the positive risk, so we accept the status quo.

Despite the best efforts of the team to mitigate them, some risks will actually occur, and often in unexpected ways. Therefore, the final piece of the strategy is to *respond.* The project manager creates a *Contingency Plan*, which defines how the team will react to the risks in a timely manner to reduce their impact.

The following processes are part of the *Risk Planning* process group: *Plan Risk Management, Identify Risks, Perform Qualitative Risk Analysis, Perform Quantitative Risk Analysis,* and *Plan Risk Responses.* The process *Monitor and Control Risks* is part of the *Monitoring and Controlling* process group. We now discuss the tools and techniques that apply to each process.

## 22.3 Tools for Plan Risk Management

The purpose of the *Plan Risk Management* process is to create the overall management approach to risks. Since this is a plan, the most appropriate tool is a template. The key components in the plan are:

- Risk management scope and objectives.

- The methodology to be used for risk identification, quantification, and response, as well as for monitoring and control.

- The participants in the risk analysis process.

- The risk analysis tools to be used, and identification of helpful templates and other organizational process assets.

- Risk prioritization, e.g., risks impacting cost take priority over schedule. Risk weights, labels, and selection guidelines.

- Communications approach to including risks when distributing status reports, and protocols to elevate risks to sponsors and senior management.

## 22.4 Tools for Identify Risks

The goal of the *Identify Risks* process is to create the *Risk Register*, which contains a list of risks, and evolves to include their assessment, ranking in importance.

According to PMI's *Practice Standard for Risk Management* [25], a useful method of identifying risks is to continually repeat the following mantra:

> Because of **<one or more causes>**, **<risk>** might occur, which would lead to **<one or more effects>**.

The standard also contains a comprehensive description risk analysis tools and techniques, their strengths and weaknesses, as well as critical success factors for effective application of each technique. We present some risk identification techniques below:

- *Assumptions and Constraints Analysis:* Each assumption and constraint in the project scope statemen represents a risk. This can be used as a starting point to identify risks during the planning stage.[6]

- *Brainstorming:* The project team, and other stakeholders, should be encouraged to generate a list of risks in a facilitated process.

- *Cause-and-effect (Ishikawa) diagrams:* This visual diagram promotes brainstorming, clarifies root causes, and helps develop mitigation strategies.

[6]Assumption: The permit will be available in 30 days ... Risk: Permit schedule delay.

- *Checklists:* By examining historical data from similar projects, a list of relevant issues can be developed. Project lessons are sometimes available in industry databases, and are a great source for risk identification.

- *Delphi Technique:* This is similar to brainstorming, but is a structured and formal process that requires formal facilitation and anonymity.

- *Influence Diagrams:* Risks can be inferred from this diagram, which shows the main project entities and decision points, uncertainties and outcomes, and the relationships among them.

- *Interviewing:* This is similar to brainstorming in that expert consultants are interviewed to help identify and understand risks.

- *Historical information:* Organizations with good project management assets have a repository of lessons learned—an invaluable resource for identifying risks.

- *Questionnaires and Software:* Software that prompts the project team or stimulates creativity can help with risk identification.

- *Risk Breakdown Structure (RBS):* The RBS is a valuable tool for identifying and classifying risks.

- *SWOT analysis:* A SWOT analysis might be available, since it is often part of the business case. If not, the team can perform a SWOT analysis, focusing on threats and weaknesses.

- *WBS:* The work breakdown structure provides a comprehensive overview of all activities and can act as a starting point for brainstorming to provide another source of risks.

The *Risk Identification* process results in a *risk register*, in which each has the following attributes: ID, Name, Description, Impact (area and at what stage), Type (positive or negative), Likelihood, and Estimated Severity.

## 22.5 Tools for Risk Assessment

Given a list of risks in the *risk register*, the next step is to assess them, and there are two steps: qualitative and quantitative. The qualitative assessment considers all risks and calibrates them in terms of their likelihood of occurring and potential impact. As part of the qualitative analysis, the risk data are updated in the risk register by adding their ranking (High, Medium, Low). Unlikely risks and those with little impact may be placed on a "watch list."

The goal of the qualitative assessment is to develop a list of risks with the potential to significantly affect project outcomes, either negatively or positively. These significant risks are further investigated in a quantitative analysis. Tools to accomplish this include a sensitivity analysis, an Expected Monetary Value analysis, and a Monte Carlo analysis.

## 22.6 Techniques for Qualitative Risk Assessment

In a qualitative risk analysis, each risk is analyzed to determine its likelihood of occurring and its impact. Tables 22.2 and 22.3 provide examples of how the likelihood and impact might be defined on a project.

Table 22.2: Definition of risk *Likelihood* values.

| Rating | Likelihood | Definition |
| --- | --- | --- |
| 1 | Rare | Occurs in exceptional circumstances |
| 2 | Unlikely | Could occur at some time |
| 3 | Possible | Might occur at some time |
| 4 | Likely | Will probably occur in the project |
| 5 | Very Likely | Expected to occur in most situations |

Table 22.3: Definition of risk *Impact* values.

| Rating | Likelihood | Definition |
| --- | --- | --- |
| 1 | Insignificant | No Damage or Loss |
|   |               | No cost or schedule impact |
| 2 | Minor | Minor damage or loss |
|   |       | Minor cost or schedule impact |
| 3 | Moderate | Some damage and/or loss |
|   |          | Significant cost or schedule impact |
| 4 | Major | Extensive loss and damage |
|   |       | Extensive cost and/or schedule impact |
| 5 | Catastrophic | Damage to reputation |
|   |              | Huge financial loss |
|   |              | Unrecoverable cost and/or schedule impact |

## 22. RISK MANAGEMENT

Risks are scored on a scale from 1 to 5 in both likelihood and impact, with 5 being 'high.' These scores are used as coordinates on the *Risk Assessment Matrix*—see Figure 22.1.

In the *Risk Assessment Matrix*, bands of color are used to help visualize the overall risks in the project. The top right hand corner is red, and risks in this area have **high likelihood** of occurring and **high impact** if they occur. Many risks in this area is a sign of trouble. The middle band represents medium risks, while the bottom left corner represents **low likelihood** and **low impact**.

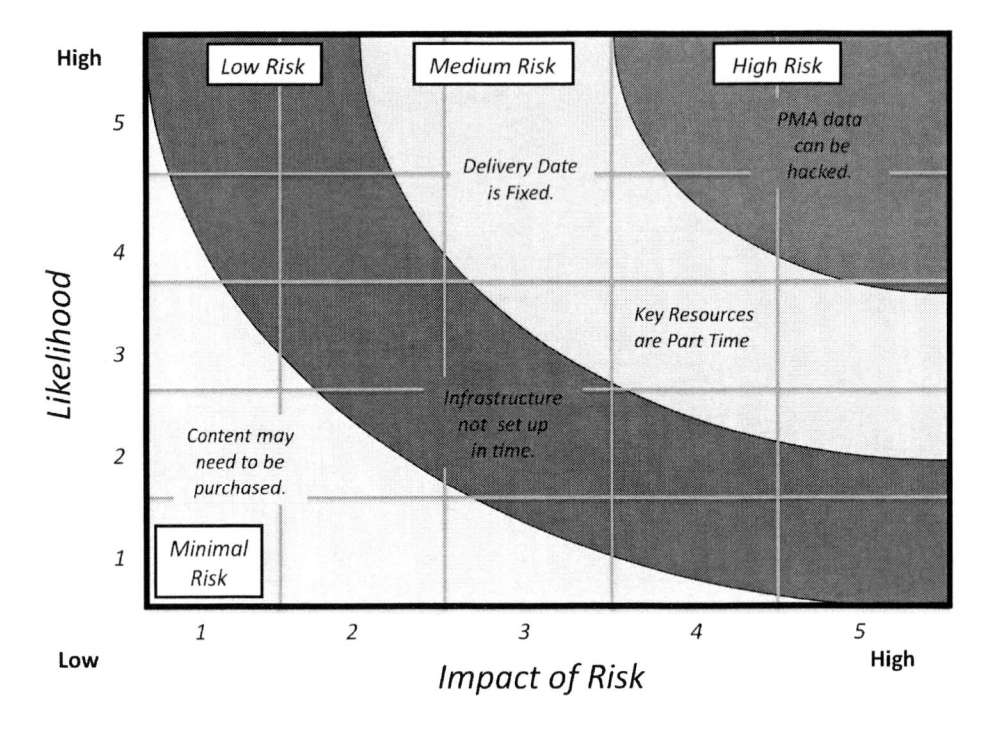

Figure 22.1: The *Risk Assessment Matrix* tool for *Qualitative* assessment.

## 22.6. Techniques for Qualitative Risk Assessment

Table 22.4: The *Risk Assessment* for the PMA web site.

| Risk ID | Category | Risk | Impact | Likeli-hood | Mitigation Action |
|---|---|---|---|---|---|
| 1 | Infrastructure | May not be able to get server infrastructure operational before planned launch. | 3 | 1 | Select and work with a highly recommended VAR to deliver servers. |
| 2 | Architecture | Wordpress may not be robust enough to support the designed solution | 4 | 2 | Work with developer skilled in other development tools. If cannot meet requirements, shift environments. |
| 3 | Time | Project delivery date is fixed and aggressive. Schedule relief will not be provided regardless of delays or issues. | 5 | 4 | Accept the risk. Progress will be closely monitored. Re-assess risk if schedule slip occurs occurs. |
| 4 | Skills | Development team is not familiar with Wordpress. | 3 | 2 | Tool is rudimentary and should be easy to learn. If needed, conduct training sessions. |
| 5 | Resources | Available resources may be assigned to other projects. | 3 | 3 | Establish relationship with contractors to provide resources with skills needed. |
| 6 | Budget | Fixed price contract. Some content may need to be purchased from PMI, which could increase the cost | 1 | 2 | Include a contingency fund of $2,500 to allow for unforeseen PMI expenses. |

323

## 22.7 Tools for Quantitative Risk Analysis

Significant risks identified in the qualitative assessment are investigated further using a quantitative analysis, which goes beyond the qualitative analysis by attempting to provide numerical estimates of their impact. When risks occur, they usually impact the cost and schedule, so at this stage it is necessary to have a detailed project plan.

The goal of the quantitative assessment is to *numerically* estimate the impact of the risks on the cost and schedule. These are called contingencies, and there should be a contingency for cost and a contingency for schedule, often called a time buffer.

### 22.7.1 Expected Monetary Value (EMV)

EMV is a technique used to calculate a weighted average, or expected cost, when the outcomes are uncertain. We illustrate the EMV technique with three examples:

1. *Rank Ordering Risks:*

    EMV is a good tool to prioritize and rank order risks. Suppose that all the risks in the risk register are negative. First, we express the risks in monetary form, e.g., *The cost of a one-week delay is $10,000.*

    Next we assign a probability to each risk, e.g., *The probability of the risk is 50%*. Finally, we multiply the monetary impact by the probability to determine the expected value of this event:

    $$Expected\ Value\ of\ Risk = \$10,000 x 0.50 = \$5,000. \qquad (22.1)$$

    One can then rank order all of the risks by their expected value to reveal which ones are most important and require more attention.

2. *Calculating Contingency Amounts:* The contingency budget is the amount allocated to cover the cost of the risks. (There should be a similar allowance for the schedule.) The contingency budget can allow for the fact that some risks are positive and some negative, as shown in Table 22.5.

    Table 22.5 suggests the project manager should set aside around $35,000 to cover the identified risks.[7] The probabilities, gains, and losses are all **estimates**. A wise project manager will conduct a sensitivity analysis in which

[7] This does not guarantee that this is the right amount, it is simply the best guess. Both (or neither!) of the risks might occur.

Table 22.5: Calculation of the contingency budget.

| Risk Event | Amount at Stake | Probability | Contingency (EMV) |
|---|---|---|---|
| Project will incur cost overrun resulting in financial penalty | $50,000 | 0.8 | -$40, 000 |
| Vendor supplies component early. Early completion of project | $10,000 | 0.50 | +$5,000 |
| **Potential Project Impact** | | | **-$35,000** |

the amounts and probabilities are varied, and a range of values determined for the contingency.

3. *Alternative Outcomes:* When calculating the contingency budget, several alternate outcomes for risk events might have to be considered. To show how this is accomplished, we expand the EMV calculation to include several possible events. We then weight the possible outcomes by their probabilities of occurrence—see Table 22.6.

Table 22.6: Calculation of the contingency budget using multiple outcomes.

| Outcome | Amount at Stake | Probability | Contingency (EMV) |
|---|---|---|---|
| When reward is high demand for new software in financial penalty | $40,000 | 0.6 | -$24,000 |
| If reward is Low | $10,000 | 0.4 | -$4,000 |
| **Potential Project Impact** | | | **$20,000** |

### 22.7.2 Decision Tree Analysis

A decision implies there are several alternative approaches, each with different potential outcomes. The *decision tree* is a tool for evaluating decisions, and showing which alternative provides the highest payoff.

We illustrate a decision tree with an example from the PMA case. The PMA board proposed a campaign to increase membership, and the team thinks the quality of the web site will be a significant factor in the success of the campaign. Therefore,

## 22. RISK MANAGEMENT

the team proposed investing in a development environment, which would cost around $50,000.

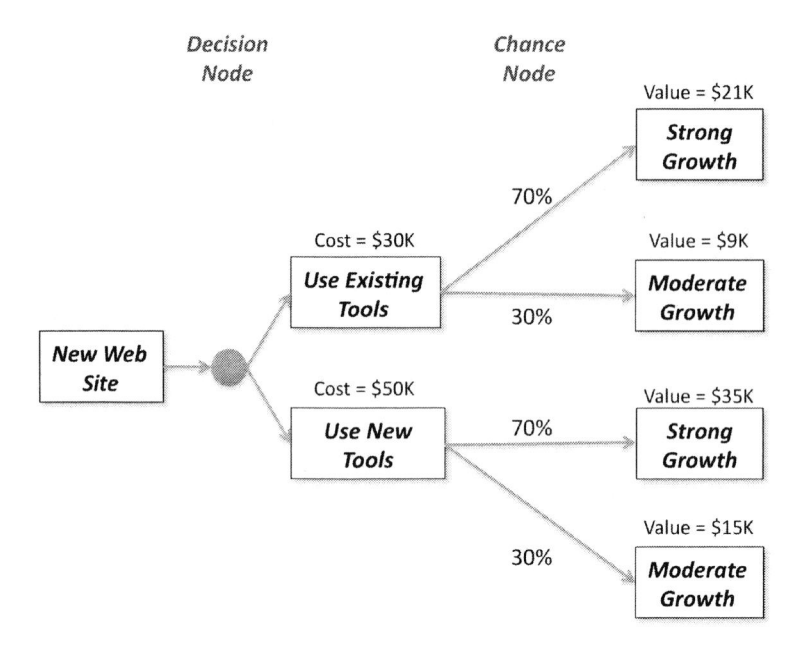

Figure 22.2: A *Decision Tree* analyzing the investment in new web site tools.

Figure 22.2 shows the way in which a decision tree is structured. The decision node, which is represented on the diagram by a small circle, has two options:.

1. *Use Existing Tools:* In this option, the investment is $30,000, which is the estimated cost of upgrading the existing tools. This should include staff costs to implement the upgrades, training, and any new hardware.

2. *Use New Tools:* In this option, the investment is $50,000, which is the investment amount for new tools, including staff, training, and hardware.

Next we allow for multiple outcomes, which is accomplished by assessing and evaluating the potential of the campaign to increase membership. After some analysis, the team proposes that there are two likely outcomes:

1. *Strong Growth. Likelihood: 70%:* The team believes that the campaign is very likely to succeed, and they propose that there is a 70% chance that the membership growth campaign will be successful.

2. *Moderate Growth. Likelihood: 30%:* Since nothing is certain, the team admits that there is a 30% chance that the membership campaign will be only moderately successful.

We now calculate the payoff for each outcome. The PMA team estimated that each new member is worth around $1,000 to the organization. Therefore, to determine the payoff, we must estimate the increase in membership for each branch in the decision tree.

When the team uses the existing tools and the growth is strong, they estimate an increase of 21,000 members. However, when new tools are used, that number should increase to 35,000, as the new tools will allow the team to reach a wider audience and process potential new members more efficiently. For moderate growth, the corresponding numbers are 9,000 for existing tools, and 15,000 for new tools.

The final analysis step is to determine which is the most effective option. To do this, we calculate the *Expected Monetary Value* of each branch of the tree:

$$\text{Existing Tools} = -\$30,000 + \$21,000 \times 0.7 + \$9,000 \times 0.3 \quad = -\$12,600. \quad (22.2)$$
$$\text{New Tools} = -\$50,000 + \$35,000 \times 0.7 + \$15,000 \times 0.3 \quad = -\$21,000. \quad (22.3)$$

The decision with the highest payoff is *"Existing Tools"*.[8]

Because both options have negative payoff, one may reasonably ask what happens if the team decides to do nothing. That is, conduct the campaign with no upgrade of web tools at all.

In that case, we can add a third decision, *Do Nothing*, with an investment of zero. Further, suppose we estimate that the growth in membership for the two scenarios are *Strong = 2,000* and *Moderate = 1,000*. If we add the *Do Nothing* decision node to the diagram, we will get the following expected monetary value for that branch of the tree:

$$\text{Do Nothing} = -\$0 + \$2,000 \times 0.7 + \$1,000 \times 0.3 = +\$1,700. \quad (22.4)$$

This option produces a positive payoff, and is the best option.

This is an example of a sensitivity analysis. After constructing the decision tree, we evaluated which parameters drive the decision. In this case it was the investment amounts, which are large. Therefore, a natural question to ask is, "What happens if we eliminate the investment?" This led to a third decision option, *Do Nothing*, which turned out to be the best option.[9]

[8] It has the smaller negative number.

[9] Only by conducting the sensitivity analysis did we uncover the best option. If we had blindly followed the "best" decision tree outcome, we would have lost a lot of money.

## Using Decision Trees

A major problem with decision trees is the so-called, "Myth of Analysis."[3] This covers a wide variety of issues:

- *All options are included.* Not all of the decisions may be included, or even analyzable. In the first version of the decision tree, we omitted the *Do Nothing* option, and that turned out to be the best approach.

- *All consequences are included.* We can easily add a third outcome: *Weak Growth*. If the economy declines, such an option may be important.

- *The data are valid.* The costs and probabilities are fundamental in assessing the usefulness of the decision. Questions that might be asked in a sensitivity analysis, include: Do small changes in either probabilities or payoff change the decision? If so, all outcomes should be considered to be equally valid.

- *The tree rapidly gets complicated.* It is confusing to analyze multiple decisions with multiple outcomes. A useful approach here is to prune obviously bad branches.

- Belief of impartiality. A fallacy is that the data, because they are probabilities, are somehow impartially developed. They are not. Analysts bring their biases and preconceptions to the assignment of probabilities and costs.

- *It is not about the cost.* As we have stated several times already, making a decision based on the estimated future costs is a poor approach. We pointed out in Chapter 2 that the most important critical success factor for new products is a "unique differentiated product."

- *Intermediate decisions.* Sometimes, a branch of the tree may have a decision point built in. For example, when pursuing the option of a new development environment, there may be an initial investment followed by optional add-ons. If the membership growth is going well, the team may decide to purchase the options.

    Such conditional decisions make the decision tree very complex. The best approach is often to wait until the decision is imminent, at which time one will have better data on the costs and income.

On the other hand, there are definite benefits in the use of decision trees:

- *There is a decision.* The first and most important aspect is that it informs everyone that there is indeed a decision to be made. The tool formalizes the process and allows stakeholders a chance to give input.

- *Open analysis.* The assumptions, data, and resulting decision are all open to everyone.

- *Team discussion.* The process generates an informative discussion. In particular, a sensitivity analysis will strengthen the confidence of the stakeholders that the decision is correct.

## 22.8 Risk Monitoring and Control

This is where risks are tracked and responded to. Different risk categories warrant different approaches.

- *High Risk:* These must be continuously monitored. Throughout the project, high risks should be analyzed to determine if there are actions that might reduce the likelihood of occurrence and the impact if it occurs. If possible, risks should be *prevented* from occurring, e.g., change the scope.

- *Medium Risks:* These should be monitored closely and continuous mitigation should attempt to contain their effects, and to ensure that they do not escalate to high impact risks.

- *Low Risks:* These should be routinely monitored at regular meetings to ensure their status remains as 'low.'

### 22.8.1 Tools for Risk Response

This is where the project manager *responds* to the risks when they arise. If significant planning has occurred, and a response strategy is in place, then this is where the contingency plan is implemented.[10]

There are several tools and techniques to help the project manager to respond to risks, including brainstorming and scenario analysis. In both, participants suggest solutions and analyze their effects.

[10] If there is no contingency plan, then the strategy becomes: *Dig Out!*

## 22. Risk Management

### 22.9 Tools to Monitor and Control Project Risk

During the execution of the project, we monitor and control risks. This occurs throughout the life-cycle of the project by regularly reassessing and updating the *risk register*. Status meetings and periodic team meetings are an excellent opportunity to review the risks, which should be an agenda item.

Other tools and techniques that can be used during execution include risk audits, variance and trend analysis, technical performance measurement, and reserve analysis. Table 22.7 lists some potential responses to risks when they occur.

Table 22.7: Risk events and some potential responses.

| Risk Event | Risk Response |
|---|---|
| Personnel shortfall | Hire subcontractors. Enhance productivity through training. |
| Scope unclear | Develop prototype with user input. |
| Subcontractor not performing adequately | Conduct frequent site visits. Co-locate with team. Invoke performance clauses in contract. |

### 22.10 Risk Occurrence Over Time

The PMBOK suggests the probability of risks occurring is high initially and then declines throughout the project's life. We claim that this only applies to the known risks, probably because the project manager is looking at them and containing them.

We are not at all convinced that the likelihood of occurrence of "unknown unknowns" declines over time. The following examples from the kitchen project illustrate the issue:

- When the refrigerator arrived, it did not fit in the cabinet opening. The contractor, Mark, immediately measured the opening size, which was correct according to the specification.

    Mark then measured the refrigerator and found that it was 1.2 inches higher than the specification. Mark was furious and called the refrigerator manufacturer. There was a lot of yelling and screaming, which came to a head when the refrigerator manufacturer said, "Standard practice is to allow an extra inch."

"I allowed two inches!" Mark yelled back.

Fortunately, the refrigerator had leveling screws on the bottom, and some careful adjustments allowed the refrigerator to *just* fit in the opening. This is an example of a specification error that could have been expensive to fix.[11]

- Hurricane Irene barreled through town and ripped the roof off the finish carpenter's house. Only less skilled carpenters were available, and the finish work was delayed. This is an example of a personnel risk.

- The ceiling was scheduled to be insulated with foam. The insulation contractor told us that we could not sleep in the house the night the foam was installed. We planned to stay with friends.

  However, when the insulation contractor showed up, he said that nobody could stay in the house while the foam was being blown in.[12] That happened to be a day when the plumber, painter, and carpenters were all scheduled to work! This is an example of a communication risk.

- Peter the electrician, suffered an accident in which his hand was cut rather badly. Fortunately, there was no tendon damage, but he was out of commission for a week. His assistant filled in, but could only do low level electrical work and the project was delayed. This is another example of a personnel risk.

Hurricanes, injuries, and specification errors were all "unknown unknowns," and completely unanticipated. They are all examples of high-impact, low-probability events, and most risk analytical models fail miserably in predicting and allowing for such situations.

[11] This is also a good example of Mark's planning ahead. When everyone had calmed down, Mark drolly observed, "This is why we add tolerances."

[12] He actually said this at 8:30 am when Eileen not had a chance even to dry her hair. The insulation contractor was less than popular! The project manager was not happy.

# CHAPTER 23

# PROCUREMENT MANAGEMENT

> **I wish to be cremated. One tenth of my ashes shall be given to my agent, as written in our contract.**
>
> *Groucho Marx*

*Procurement management* defines how the project manager purchases products or services from sellers outside the project. This is accomplished by developing and awarding a contract. There are many types of contracts, and the project manager selects the type that assigns to the seller both a reasonable risk and the greatest incentive for efficient and cost-effective performance.

We begin with the definition of a contract:

*A contract is a mutually binding agreement that binds the seller to provide specified products and services, and also obligates the buyer to provide monetary or other valuable consideration.*

For a project, the contract will usually reference the scope document as the definition of what is to be provided. We note here that the scope not only includes the specification (the definition of the project), but also major milestones, schedule

## 23. Procurement Management

constraints, etc. Thus the scope becomes the fundamental basis of the contract, and every statement carries legal implications.

The above definition is a simplified version of that found in legal books.[1] The project manager is considered to be the *buyer* of the services and the contractor providing the goods or services is called the *seller*.

There are two contracts that the project manager must be aware of. The first is the contract for the project itself. That is, the project manager is probably working on a contract to deliver the project to the buyer. This contract defines what it is that the project manager must do. In this case, the project manager is the seller.

The second type of contract occurs during the execution of the project, when the project manager decides it is necessary to employ a third party to perform some of the work. This is called a subcontract, and the project manager is the buyer.

The fact that the project manager is both a seller and a buyer means the project manager has to understand all aspects of contracting, its terminology, and the different types of contracts.

In order to pursue a subcontract, the project manager must have a clear description of the physical product or service to be delivered. Therefore, the project manager begins the subcontracting process by separating out a well-defined piece of the scope. Next, the project manager creates a Statement of Work (SOW), which is the most important contracting document.

When developing a subcontract, the project manager must answer the following questions:

1. What should we procure and how?
2. When should we procure it?
3. What type of contract will we use?
4. What metrics will we use to measure completion and success?
5. How will we administer the contract?

[1] Legal definitions add phrases such as "often in writing." We believe a PM needs practical guidance on contracts and we leave the legal technicalities to the lawyers.

The work to be completed may not be well specified. This occurs when someone is asked to perform some research on a problem where the answer is not known. In that case, the SOW should define the problem to be solved, along with goals and objectives and success criteria. The document that defines the goals is called a Statement of Objectives (SOO).

## 23.1 Contract Types

There are three broad categories of contracts:

1. *Fixed Price:* The contractor is awarded a total sum as payment for performing the project, no matter how much time, effort, and money it took to deliver the project.[2]

2. *Cost Reimbursable:* All legitimate project costs for performing the work of the project are reimbursed to the contractor. A fee (or profit) is also added. This is also known as cost-plus contract.[3]

3. *Time and Materials:* The buyer pays a fixed hourly rate for the labor spent working on the project and also reimburses the contractor for all the materials and expenses associated with the project work.

A major theme of modern contracting involves the movement to *performance-based* contracting (PBC), where the project manager defines the desired results or outcomes. This is in contrast to *cost-plus* contracts, where one looks for best effort. When a contract is performance-based, the project manger must carefully define both the desired outcomes and the criteria for assessing the performance. Contract incentives (positive or negative, or both) are also included.

There are two major advantages of performance-based contracts. The first is that the seller can determine the best technical alternatives and the most cost effective approach. The second is that the buyer is relieved of detailed contract administration and can focus on helping the seller to achieve the specified goals. Incentive and award contracts are a good compromise for risky projects, which has accelerated the trend towards performance-based contracts.

Contractors may be awarded extra fees, i.e., incentives, for completing the project early, or for controlling costs. If the contractor finishes a project at a cost less than specified in the contract, the buyer and seller may split the savings. The opposite of incentives is *penalties*, which are imposed on the seller for poor performance.

Many variations and combinations of the basic three types are possible. The most frequent types of contracts a project manager will encounter are:

- *Firm Fixed Price (FFP) Contract:* The amount to be paid for the project is determined at the time the contract is signed. In this type of contract, the contractor bears all the risk. It is a very common contract type, because both the buyer and the seller want relative certainty as far as costs are concerned.

[2] While the total amount is fixed, it may be paid out over time.

[3] The key word here is *legitimate*. There are strict accounting and government rules and regulations for what is *legitimate*.

The buyer must be willing to put significant effort into providing a clear, well defined specification. The seller must be willing to deliver the entire project for a firm fixed price.

FFP contracts work well when the project is well defined, and the specification is clear.

- *Fixed Price Plus Incentive Fee (FPIF) Contract:* This is similar to the FFP contract in that the conditions are determined at the time of signing the contract. However, the buyer is willing to give a bonus to the seller based on some clearly identified superior project performance. Performance criteria may include delivering ahead of the defined schedule or under the defined budget. Penalty clauses may be imposed for late delivery or cost overruns.

- *Costs Plus Fixed Fee (CPFF) Contract:* This provides for the reimbursement of all *allowable costs* plus the award of a fixed fee upon completion. This type of contract is common with projects in which the scope is uncertain such as research and development contracts and many Department of Defense contracts.

- *Costs Plus Award Fee (CPAF) Contract:* This is also a cost-plus contract, except that instead of paying a fee, the buyer pays an award based on the buyer's evaluation of the seller's performance. The award amount is earned based on defined criteria, such as completion time, cost effectiveness, quality of work, or technical ingenuity.

    An important issue in CPAF contract is: Who decides the amount of the award? If the criteria are subjective, the award fee may be determined by an independent external board. The award amount may also be based upon objective performance metrics, e.g., the range of a battery powered car or a web site response time with 1,000 users accessing it simultaneously.

- *Costs Plus Incentive Fee (CPIF) Contract:* This also provides for the reimbursement of contract costs, but the buyer is willing to award a fee if well defined performance goals are met. For example, if the final cost of the project is less than the budgeted cost, the buyer and seller may share the savings based on a predetermined, legally documented incentive arrangement.

- *Cost Plus Percentage of Cost (CPPC) Contract:* This provides for the full reimbursement of allowable costs. The seller is also given a fee which is an agreed percentage of the allowed project cost. In this arrangement, the buyer bears all the risk. It is used only when there is major uncertainty associated with the project.

This type of contract is banned in U.S. Federal Contracting and you can understand why.[1] There is no incentive for the contractor to hold down costs, because the more they spend, the more profit they earn.

CPPC is used only occasionally in the commercial sector. For example, in the pharmaceutical industry, there is so much uncertainty and risk when searching for a new drug that only the CPPC contract type provides the appropriate motivation for contractors to take on the work.

## 23.2 Selecting a Contract

### 23.2.1 Fixed Price Contracts

In a *Fixed Price* contract, the seller agrees to pay a fixed amount to the seller. The period over which the fixed sum is paid out depends on the contract. Usually the seller requests a certain percentage at the start (or award) of the contract. The buyer will usually hold back a certain percentage of the amount until the job is successfully completed.

For large contracts, a third party may be employed to define when the seller's work is satisfactorily complete. This is called a Validation and Verification contractor. The remaining amount due to the seller is divided up into installments, the schedule for which is included in the contract.

The installment payments are often driven by the seller's cash flow. For example, in the New Kitchen contract, Mark requested major payments at times when he was facing expensive purchases. One such contract payment condition was: *$3,000 at delivery of blue-board.* Since the purchase of blue-board was a major expense, Mark inserted into the contract a provision for a payment at that time. Notice Mark did not specify a date, but tied the payment to a deliverable. If Mark accelerated the schedule, he would still receive a payment when he needed to pay for the blue-board.

Table 23.1 shows the positive and negative incentives of a fixed price contract from both the buyer's and seller's perspectives.

### 23.2.2 Cost-Plus Contracts

In a *cost-plus* contract, the seller is reimbursed for all allowable costs, which include labor, materials, and travel. The seller must have an audited overhead rate,

## 23. PROCUREMENT MANAGEMENT

Table 23.1: The positive and negative aspects of a fixed price contract.

| Buyer's Perspective | |
|---|---|
| **Advantages** | **Disadvantages** |
| Known price | More costly to prepare |
| Incentives for lower cost | Requires a good spec & knowledge of needs |
| | Mistakes in the spec are costly |
| | Incentive for fast completion at lowest cost |
| | May require contingency costs |
| **Seller's Perspective** | |
| **Advantages** | **Disadvantages** |
| Potentially larger fee | Underestimated costs mean a loss |

which determines the rate at which overhead costs are reimbursed by the buyer. The seller also receives an additional prior-negotiated fee, which is often set as a percentage of the initially specified contract cost.

For example, suppose you negotiate a CPFF contract for $100,000 with a 6% fee. Your fee is $6,000. You successfully perform the project and your costs are $90,000. The buyer audits your project, and your overhead rate, and agrees that these are all legitimate costs. You receive $90,000 for the costs, plus your fee of $6,000.

On the other hand, suppose you successfully perform the project but your costs are $200,000. The buyer audits your project, and your overhead rate, and agrees that these are all legitimate costs. You receive $200,000 for the costs, plus your fee of $6,000. In this case, you do not lose money, but your boss will probably be unhappy that your fee rate is down to 3% ($6,000/200,000 = 3\%$).

The major disadvantage with cost plus contracts is that the buyer must rely on the seller's best efforts to contain costs. Table 23.2 shows the positive and negative incentives of a cost plus contract from both the buyer's and seller's perspectives.

Table 23.2: The positive and negative aspects of a cost plus contract.

| Buyer's Perspective | |
|---|---|
| **Advantages** | **Disadvantages** |
| Maximum Flexibility | Relies on seller's best efforts to contain costs |
| Minimizes early negotiation costs | No assurances of actual cost |
| Eases selection of best-qualified rather than lowest bid | |
| Allows use of same contractor for design and implementation | |
| **Seller's Perspective** | |
| **Advantages** | **Disadvantages** |
| Can undertake risky efforts | High costs reduce fee rate |
| Can undertake long projects | |

## 23.3 Incentive Fee Contract Example

The best way to understand an incentive fee contract is through an example.

The project manager of the PMA website decides to subcontract out the work of building the web site. The project manager prepares a detailed specification, and a scope document, including a Statement of Work. The project manager uses a macro estimation formula to determine an estimated cost of $10,000. The project manager then does a PERT analysis of the major components and assesses all the risks. As a result, the project manager decides that a creative subcontractor might get the job done for less. But the project manager also needs to be able to establish a firm budget, which will not exceed $13,000.

The project manager therefore selects a CPIF contract with a 70%/30% sharing of the savings. The budgeted cost is $10,000 and the project manager proposes that a profit of 10% will be a sufficient incentive for sellers to take on this small job. The contract summary is shown below.

> Target Price: $11,000
> Target Cost: $10,000
> Target Fee (or Profit): $1,000
> Contract Ceiling: $13,000
> Profit / Loss Sharing: Seller Share: 30%
> Buyer Share: 70%

We now explore what happens in three scenarios:

### Case 1: Under Run

The subcontractor (the seller) completes the contract at a cost of $8,000, i.e., less than the originally budgeted cost of $10,000. The fee, or profit, calculation is as follows:

| | |
|---|---|
| Seller Cost: | $8,000 |
| Cost Savings: | $2,000 |
| Profit / Loss Sharing: | Seller Share: 30% of $2,000 = $600 |
| | Buyer Share: 70% of $2,000 = $1,400 |
| Seller Profit: | $1,000 + $600 = $1,600 |
| Contract Price: | $8,000 + $1,600 = $9,600 |

We note that incentive fee contract calculations are based on the costs, since these are always auditable and verifiable. In this case, the seller made an additional profit of $600, while the buyer's total cost is $9,600.

### Case 2: Over Run

The subcontractor completes the contract at a cost of $11,000, i.e., more than the originally budgeted cost of $10,000. The fee, or profit, calculation is as follows:

| | |
|---|---|
| Seller Cost: | $11,000 |
| Cost Savings: | -$1,000 |
| Profit / Loss Sharing: | |
| | Seller Share: 30% of -$1,000 = -$300 |
| | Buyer Share: 70% of -$1,000 = -$700 |
| Seller Profit: | $1,000 - $300 = $700 |
| Contract Price: | $11,000 + $700 = $11,700 |

In this case, the seller made a slightly smaller profit of $700, while the buyer's total cost is $11,700.

### Case 3: Exceeding the Ceiling!

The seller's cost is $15,000. The buyer informs the seller that the contract ceiling is $13,000 and so the buyer receives only $13,000. The seller has lost $2,000 on the contract, and these costs will have to be paid by the seller's company.

If the project were not very risky, then the percentage share of the profit might be adjusted. For a low risk project, the buyer might adjust the share to a 30%/70% ratio, so that the contractor gets less in the case of an overrun. Using a 30%/70%, Case 2 becomes:

Seller Cost: $11,000
Cost Savings: -$1,000
Profit / Loss Sharing:
Seller Share: 70% of -$1,000 = -$700
Buyer Share: 30% of -$1,000 = -$300
Seller Profit: $1,000 - $700 = $300
Contract Price: $11,000 + $300 = $11,300

The seller's profit is reduced significantly.

## 23.4 The Scope and Contract Types

There is direct relationship between the quality of the project scope (and particularly the specification) and the type of contract that should be employed. The specification defines what is to be produced, so when the specification is well defined and complete, the buyer is in a position to request a fixed price contract. If the specification is incomplete, has unknowns, or is or risky, the buyer should move towards cost-plus contracts.

The buyer risk versus contract type is shown in Figure 23.1. Buyer risk is lowest for fixed price contracts, because the cost is known in advance. The buyer risk increases for cost plus contracts because the seller's costs are not known, and may increase as the specification is refined.

The seller's risks are shown in Figure 23.2. Sellers have more risk on a fixed price contract because they must specify the bid in advance, with only the scope document to go on. Seller risk is lower for a cost-plus contract, because they will be reimbursed for all contract costs.

## 23. PROCUREMENT MANAGEMENT

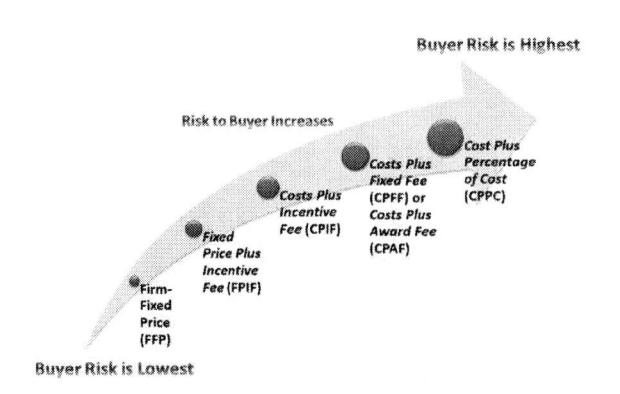

Figure 23.1: Buyer risk versus contract type.

Figure 23.2: Seller risk versus contract type.

## 23.5 Statement of Work

Figure 23.3 shows an example of a Statement of Work for the PMA contract.

> Project Start Date:     March 10th, 2010
> Projected Finish Date:  April 25th, 2010
> **Budget Information:** Hosting investment has already been made for this site to the tune of $200 per year. The majority of costs for this project will be internal labor. An initial estimate provides a total of 40 hours per week per team. Other proposed budget items will be considered.
> **Project Manager:** Dr. Vijay Kanabar
> **Project Objectives:**
> The PMA web site is a social network site dedicated to all BU students interested in project management, including alumni. The primary stakeholders are students interested in becoming certified as PMPs, as well as those wishing to maintaining their certification status. The website provides a channel for PMPs to earn PDU's to maintain their certification. Other stakeholders include any students interested in PM who will benefit from the website.
> It is conceivable that a non-BU audience interested in the field of project management will access the site. Therefore, the website will have resources that anyone can use, such as templates, links to project management websites, and links to interesting research.
> Only the following personal information will be captured and maintained: First name, last name, email address. The email address will act as proof of a current or past BU association. MailChimp will be used to store all student names and email addresses, because it comes with a built-in database. Students with data in the system will be considered to be *registered*.
> The web site will have a designated *Director*, who will email to registered students: the the newsletter and special information such as job postings and internships. Students will be requested to link to resources such as facebook, wordpress, and linkedin. Jobs and internships will also be posted.
> While we are not dictating functionality, Social Networking site features that will be useful to members are: A News and Announcements Section; User Blogs and Forums; a Reading Room (document repository); an Event Calendar; BU TV PM related videos; Resource Links – split into two PM and IT PM categories; a link to the Project Management in Practice Conference website; Job tips and opportunities; PMP Certification links and resources; PM templates and papers; and an "Ask the Expert" feature, for users to post questions about their projects and receive advice from other PMA members.

Figure 23.3: Statement of Work for the PMA contract.

## 23.6 DoD Contracts and Costs

> **Thoroughly read all your contracts. I really mean thoroughly.**
>
> *Bret Michaels*

In the early 1980s, Norman Augustine produced Figure 23.4, which exploded into the consciousness of the defense establishment in the first edition of *Augustine's Laws.* [26] [4]

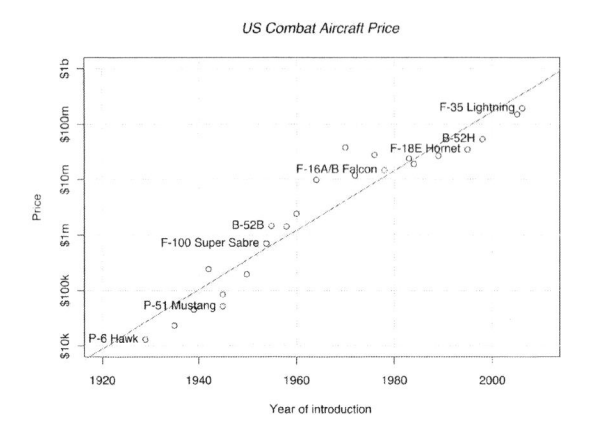

Figure 23.4: Norman Augustine's data on combat aircraft price.

[4] The data has since been updated, and is available at the Augustine's Laws page at Wikipedia.

The thing to note about this chart is that the vertical scale is logarithmic, i.e., aircraft prices are rising *exponentially*![5] Aircraft prices go up by a factor of ten, every ten years. It is actually more impressive to plot the data on a linear scale, see Figure 23.5.

[5] People often use the word "exponentially" to mean large. Here we really do mean exponentially!

Augustine also noticed that the Department of Defense (DoD) budgets are rising linearly. In Figure 23.6, we have projected the DoD budget out to 2050,[6] and also projected the exponential growth of combat aircraft prices.[7] The chart is not half so impressive when plotted logarithmically, as in 23.7.[8]

[6] Based on the DoD budget from 2000 to 2010 and a linear fit.

[7] For the technically minded, I obtained a decent fit with $ln(P) = m * yr + c$, where $m = 0.15$ and $c = -280$.

Somewhere around 2050, the entire DoD budget will purchase exactly one combat aircraft! This is Augustine's most cited Law, Number XVI:

[8] which is the way it usually shows up in print and on the web.

> *In the year 2054, the entire defense budget will purchase just one aircraft. This aircraft will have to be shared by the Air Force and the*

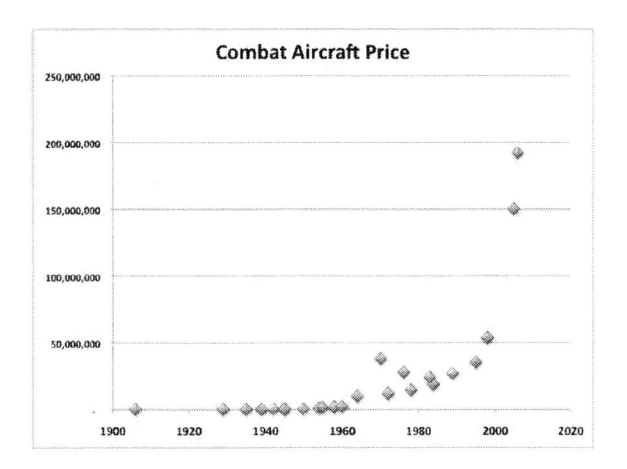

Figure 23.5: A linear plot of Norman Augustine's data on combat aircraft prices.

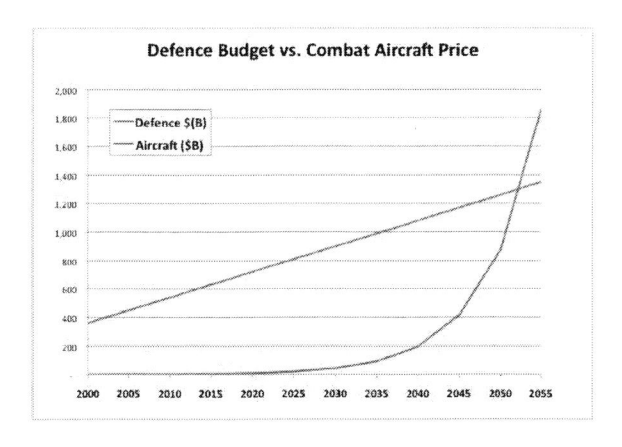

Figure 23.6: Norman Augustine's Law: The DoD budget vs. combat aircraft prices.

*Navy 3½ days each per week except for leap year, when it will be made available to the Marines for the extra day.*

[26]

## 23. PROCUREMENT MANAGEMENT

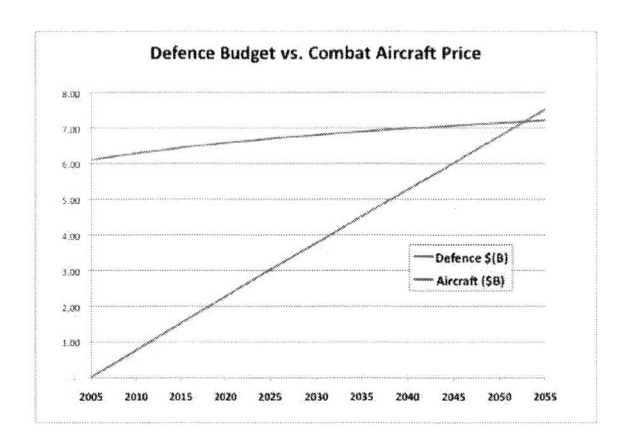

Figure 23.7: The same graph as Fig. 23.6, which is just not as impressive in this log form.

# CHAPTER 24

# ETHICS

**Relativity applies to physics, not ethics**

*Albert Einstein*

Ethics plays an important role in project management. The Project Management Institute (PMI) continually stresses that ethics is an integral part of the project management profession and has defined a rigorous *Code of Ethics and Professional Conduct*, which we will refer to as the *code*. [27]

PMI has emphasized their position by including questions about ethics in the PMP exam. In addition, PMPs are continually held accountable to the the *code*.

The *code* defines the rules for the professional practice of project management. More important from a practical perspective is that it communicates to stakeholders the values and standards that project management professionals will bring to their work. Values that the PMI community defined as most important were responsibility, respect, fairness, and honesty. [28]

Some of the more interesting aspects of the *code*, at least to us, are:

- We do what we say we will do.[1]

[1] Since we are both PMPs, the word "we" applies to us, too!

- When we make errors, we own up promptly, accept responsibility, and make amends.

- We listen to others' points of view.

- We negotiate in good faith.

- We provide accurate information in a timely manner.

- We disclose conflicts of interest of stakeholders.

- We report unethical or illegal conduct.[2]

In a 2010 PMI Member survey, awareness of the *code* rose to 83%, and virtually everyone found it useful in helping to resolve ethical issues. Ethics is not just a theoretical concept. The practical implications are illustrated by the fact that 'loss of trust' was cited as a major reason motivating workers to seek new jobs.

## 24.1 An Example of an Ethical Issue

You are the project manager holding a team staff meeting. In last week's meeting, the Technical Director (TD) reported that his design group had run into technical difficulties, which had resulted in a delay in the delivery of a deliverable. You assigned the Assistant Project Manager (APM) the task of determining the impact on the cost and schedule.

In this week's staff meeting, the TD said that the design issues were now resolved. The APM reported that the because of the delays, the new $CPI = 0.93$. The APM projected a small, but significant, overrun in both the budget and the schedule. The following conversation took place between the TD and the APM:

TD: The technical issues are resolved and we will be able to get back on track. I don't foresee this as a problem.

APM: The issue was an error in the spec. The $CPI = 0.93$, which reflects the true productivity. We should not assume that was the only spec error. We should inform the customer.

TD: It is way too early to go to the customer. We have fixed the only error.

APM: We owe it to the customer to explain the situation.

TD: We don't want to bother the customer yet. It will work out.

As the project manager, what do you do?[3]

---

[2] The real challenge is not just to behave ethically yourself, but to report unethical conduct. What do you do if your good friend is behaving unethically?

[3] *Beware! This is not an easy question.*

## 24.1. An Example of an Ethical Issue

First, let's discuss some of the surrounding issues:

- *Legal vs. Ethical:* We should immediately remove any legal issues. Nobody in this meeting is suggesting that the team should deliberately hide data, pad estimates, or engage in dubious behavior. If that were to happen, the approach of the project manager is clear: Call the police!

- *Difficult vs. Ethical:* Not all difficult decisions involve ethical issues. For example, a really difficult decision that project managers often face is to lay someone off (perhaps their task is complete, and there is no more work). This would indeed be difficult for anyone, but if there is no money to hire someone, it is inevitable. Although difficult, we would not consider this an ethical dilemma.[4]

- *Competence:* We assume that all of the actors are well qualified and that their conclusions are based on reasonable data and informed opinion.

- *Integrity:* All actors are behaving well and genuinely believe in their respective positions.

Project management is complicated and invariably involves many gray areas of judgment and interpretation. For example, let's examine the claim of the TD that he can make up the cost and schedule. Consider the following alternatives:

1. The TD is deliberately falsifying his estimate.

2. The TD has made an error in his estimate.

3. The TD is exaggerating his estimate due to optimism.

4. The TD believes that he can complete the project within his estimate.

We suggest the first three interpretations of the TD's behavior are: illegal (#1), incompetent (#2), and dumb (#3). The fourth is legitimate, but creates an ethical dilemma. How does the project manager proceed? At this point, some terminology is required. First, we define an ethical dilemma as:

> *An ethical dilemma is one in which it is difficult to decide on the right outcome.*

[4]We often say that laying off good people is the hardest thing we've ever had to do.

## 24. ETHICS

An ethical dilemma usually a complex situation that involves a choice. Often however, the issue is not resolved by the selection of *any* of the alternatives. Part of the complication is that your ethics are your own *personal* standards of right and wrong.

It's not just about opinions and personal differences, and here's at least one reason why: There are two approaches to ethical decisions that philosophers use in handling ethical dilemmas:[5]

1. *Deontology:*

    Deontology is from the Greek "deon" meaning duty, and "logos" meaning logic. Deontology is therefore the study of ethics based on *duty*. You do it because you think it is "right." The basic duties are usually considered to be:

    | | |
    |---|---|
    | Fidelity | Keeping promises |
    | Reparation | Righting the wrongs you've done |
    | Justice | Distributing goods equitably |
    | Beneficence | Improving the lot of others |
    | Self-Improvement | Improving one's own intelligence and virtue |
    | Gratitude | Exhibiting when appropriate |
    | Non-injury | Avoiding injury to others |

2. *Teleology:*

    Teleology is from the Greek "telos" meaning end, and "logos" meaning logic. Teleology is therefore the study of ethics based on *the end result*. This is often summarized as "The end justifies the means." You evaluate whether the decision is a good one by examining the consequences or outcomes. Correct actions produce the most good, while wrong actions do not contribute to the general good. Outcomes are usually classified as:

    | | |
    |---|---|
    | Egoism | Focusing on self-interest goals, and asking if the action benefits oneself. |
    | Utilitarianism | Operating in the public interest rather than for personal benefit. |
    | Altruism | Maximizing the benefits of some, even at the expense of oneself. |

Altruism is generally regarded as the highest moral virtue. Notice that Deontology and Teleology are alternative views, and that neither is right nor wrong. They are different approaches to an issue.

---

[5] Our intent is not to debate philosophy, but to provide practical guidance.

350

A project manager must be able to recognize and understand these different world views in order to understand conflicts within the team. If two people are arguing from two different sets of ideals, then it is difficult for them to compromise—they both think they are right.[6]

## 24.2 More Ethical Examples

A student was explaining to the class that his company had not reported their earnings correctly. He was carefully explaining the rationale for dealing with the failure by updating the latest reports, and explaining the legal and political issues.

Suddenly, another student yelled, "That's just wrong!"

Everyone immediately took sides and chaos ensued. This is a classic example of an ethical issue!

The students were approaching the problem from two different ethical points of view. The first student was going through the *teleological* argument: Justifying company actions by the idea that it would be OK in the end. Meanwhile, the second student reacted from the *deontological* viewpoint: It's just not right!

This is a also good example of the dilemma faced by a project manager. The project manager (in this case the teacher) needs to understand that the two students have completely different world views and it is unlikely they will agree. Proposing a compromise is unlikely to work in this situation!

In our experience, progress can be made when everyone understands the difference between Deontology and Teleology, and that there are two legitimate, but different points of view.[7] Notice that we are not presenting an easy fix. All we can say is that when people understand the different ethical approaches, they can begin to work on the practical issue: Shall we tell the customer?

Here's an approach that produces interesting discussions and helps to resolve the issue: The deontological camp tends to take a righteous stand, and refuse to compromise. Therefore, pick a member of the other—the teleological—camp, and try to modify the issue gradually until they reach the point of saying, 'That would be wrong!' At that point they have reached a deontolological truth, and begin to understand the other point of view.

Or, take the opposite approach: Move the teleologists until they are in the deontology camp. Once the camps begin understand each other, the project manager can get back to discussing the cost and schedule!

[6] And they both will be right!

[7] The next time someone asks you what you learned in your project management class, you can say 'I learned the difference between deontology and teleology!'

Here's another example from a classroom discussion. Students were asked to list things they thought were of personal importance. Ned said:

*I always call my mother on Sundays.*

How do we classify this? Deontology or Teleology? I asked Ned why he did that. Ned quietly said, "It's the right thing to do." He clearly regarded it s his *duty* to call his Mom on Sundays. Ned was practicing Deontology.

Suppose you tried to convince Ned to go out and get some Pizza, and that he really doesn't need to call his Mom this week. You might suggest that his Mom won't mind if he misses a week, and that his Mom will understand that he's busy.

In fact, when I tried this in class, Ned just sighed, looked down, and politely shook his head. 'I have to,' he said. When someone is motivated by duty, they will resist attempts (strongly!) to make them change their behavior, especially if you are using an *end-justifies-the-means* argument.

Here's another example: Julie said:

*I always do my homework.*

I asked Julie why? She said, "I want to get a good grade." Julie was not doing her homework because she thought it was her duty to do so, she was was doing it because of the end result—a good grade. Julie was practicing Teleology.

It is important to realize that the same action can result from different ethical perspectives. Two different students said:

*I am always good to my classmates.*

When asked, 'Why?' one student said "It is the right thing to do." (Deonotology) The other student said "Because they will be good to me in return." (Teleology).

Here we have two students with the same action, but motivated by completely different ethical perspectives.

## 24.3 TD vs. PM Revisited

We now return to the project management discussion above. Table 24.1 provides a summary of the ethical positions.

Table 24.1: An *Ethical Analysis* of the TD vs. APM positions.

| Role | Argument | Ethical Position |
|------|----------|------------------|
| TD | I don't expect any more issues. We will get back on track | The outcome justifies the position —Teleology |
| APM | We owe it to the customer to explain the situation. | It is our duty —Deontology |

Both actors are approaching the issue from a sound ethical position. The project manager must recognize when team members believe that they are operating ethically, because an attempt at compromise might be viewed as an attack on their integrity.

It might be impossible for the project manager to resolve this issue.

## 24.4 PMI Sample Ethical Problem

Here is the classic PMP test problem on ethics. Try to decide for yourself the correct approach. Hint: Read the words carefully, it is very tricky.

Your project is being performed overseas. On a visit to the project site, you need to take some valuable equipment with you that is essential for the project. You rent a car at the airport and drive into the countryside where you are stopped by the police at a check point. The policeman says that there are bandits in the hills and the police offer to escort you through the danger for a fee.

*Do you pay the police?*

Look again at the definition of an ethical dilemma. Do you pay?

**Hint**: You are probably thinking that this is a bribe. Do you pay bribes? Even in a foreign land where bribes are a normal way of doing business?

**Answer:** First of all, bribes are illegal. If you follow the PMI rules, you never pay bribes. Never!

So that suggests that you do not pay the policeman, right?

Not quite. The key issue is: **Fee for service.** If the person asking for money provides a legitimate service, for which you can reasonably be expected to pay, then it is acceptable to pay the fee. So now, do you pay the policeman?

Well, we still cannot quite decide yet. We have to distinguish if it is a reasonable fee for service. To do this we have to look very carefully at the words of the problem.

## 24. ETHICS

If the fee is standard in some sense, and reasonable, then you can pay it. If it is extortion, then you do not pay it.

Since it is a policeman, who can reasonably be expected to provide escort services, then you are allowed to pay the fee. That is the standard PMI answer.[8] You may not agree. That's OK, the process is as important as the answer.[9]

## 24.5 Ethical Situations Test

Look at Table 24.2. Decide on whether the issue in the left hand column is an "ethical dilemma" or not.

*Hint: When analyzing you need to pay very careful attention to the words and think about them. Don't rush in.*

We emphasize that in Table 24.2, we are giving our *opinion*. It is guidance. There may be situations where you disagree with us.[10]

Answering questions on ethics, more than any other topic, involves a very careful inspection of the precise words used and an understanding of terminology. Complicating the situation is the fact that the audience may come from different cultural perspectives.[11]

Ethical issues require a subtle and patient approach on the part of the project manager, as emotions can run high on questions of integrity. One must be careful. A calm, unemotional presentation usually works best.

### 24.5.1 Sleeping at Night

As a final comment, we summarize by saying that making the right ethical decision is a personal issue and the image of an 'internal compass' is frequently used as a metaphor for guiding oneself to the right decision. At some point in your career, you will be confronted with a very difficult choice. Beware! Fate has a way of constructing the exact situation guaranteed to give you the most discomfort:

- Should you quit a good job and risk your family's well-being because you are uncomfortable with management?
- Should you tell what you know and risk censure?

The only advice we can offer is that you are the one who has to sleep at night. Only you can make this decision. Only you will know whether you sleep peacefully.

---

[8] And an immediate lesson in how tricky the ethical questions on the PMP test are!

[9] Our late colleague, Jim Cormier, used to say that the correct answer to all ethical questions on the PMP exam is the one you would never do in the real world!

[10] As always, you can disagree, but you have to back up your claim.

[11] PMI is often accused of imposing U.S. ethics on the world, a criticism with which we sympathize.

Table 24.2: Ethical Issues Test.

| Issue | Ethical Dilemma? |
|---|---|
| Padding a cost estimate because you know the customer can afford it. | Not really–this is basically lying. You have a responsibility to make money. The key word here is "padding," implying a deliberate act, hence lying. |
| Report an environmental violation by your own company. | Yes. A classic ethical dilemma. You have a conflict: 1) Company loyalty, which may even be protected by legal non-disclosure agreements. 2) A desire to do the right and honorable thing. |
| You discover confidential information in the copier. Do you report it? | This is not an ethical dilemma. The right thing to do is to report it. It may be your own salary review (tricky!), but using the information is wrong. |
| Approving sub-standard work to shorten the schedule. | No. This is a difficult decision, but not an ethical dilemma. Do not approve the work. Take the cost and schedule hit. |
| Changing the schedule due to pressure from your boss. | This is an ethical dilemma that depends on circumstances. You and your boss disagreed, but she insisted you report her version to the client—a genuine ethical dilemma. If your boss pressures you, then the path is clear: Tell the truth! |
| Assuring customers the project is on track when you suspect it's not | Trick Question! We deliberately added the word "suspect." The answer depends on why you *suspect* the project is late. A "gut feeling" you do not have to report. If it is based on earned value, you should report it. |
| Falsifying the schedule data. | No! This is not an ethical dilemma. It is just plain unethical, and maybe even illegal. |
| You listen to your team about the schedule and report the optimistic case to your boss. | Yes. This is an ethical dilemma. If you lie, then it's not an ethical dilemma. If there is genuine disagreement among the team, and you believe you can accelerate the schedule (for valid reasons!), it might be OK to report the optimistic version. |
| Firing a problem employee. | This may be an ethical dilemma, depending on the "problem." If he is simply annoying, it is wrong to fire him, and the right path is to work with him. If he disrupts the team, it might be best to remove him. |
| An employee tests positive for an illegal drug. Do you fire them? | Not an ethical dilemma. Nasty perhaps, but not ethical. The company policy should be clear on this. Unless you discover the test results accidentally, then you have ethical issues. |
| Accelerating progress by ignoring standards. | Not an ethical dilemma. Probably illegal. |

# Part IV

# The "New Kitchen" Project

# CHAPTER 25

# A NEW KITCHEN

**You're not using that project management stuff on me, are you?**

*Eileen Warburton*

In this chapter we follow a project through all its phases, and give examples of the essential project management tools and techniques.

## 25.1 Conceptual Development

Like many projects in our house, it all started with a book: *The Not So Big House*, by Sarah Susanka.[1] [29] Sarah is a brilliant architect, who suggests that most people do not need a bigger house, they need to examine the way they live, and how they use their existing space. The key idea is that many houses have "dead spaces," and rethinking their use can lead to innovative redesign. That proved true of our kitchen space.

In the summer of 2009, we began reading Sarah's books and discussing the kitchen project. Except that at this stage, it was not yet a project. It would take a year to get to preliminary planning.[1]

[1] Projects do not spring fully formed from nothing. They begin with an idea, which is explored and worked on until it begins to look like a project.

## 25. A New kitchen

Figure 25.1 shows a plan of the house before construction. The kitchen had old units and appliances and Eileen had been campaigning for a while to redo it. *The Not So Big House* inspired her. We never used the 'fireplace room,' it looked over the street and was dark. The living room looked over the garden and was a much nicer room in all respects. Eileen's key realization was that the fireplace room was dead space and could go![2]

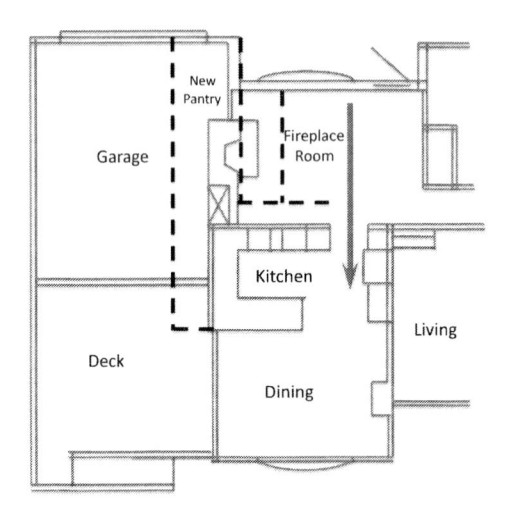

Figure 25.1: Conceptual plan. The dotted lines show the proposed new position of the kitchen and closet walls. The arrow indicates the goal of creating a sight line from the front door through to the garden.

The second key idea of the project emerged when we admitted that the garage was really a *1.8 car garage*. It was never going to hold two cars! The chimney was awkwardly placed and the garage door was too small, so Eileen proposed to expand the kitchen in two directions: Into the garage to create a pantry; and, into the fireplace room to generate more space.

We needed an architect!

---

[2] Of course, this plan did not exist back then. It is used here to explain the problem.

## 25.2 The Requirements Analysis Phase

We knew that we did not yet have a project. We did not know enough to define the project—we needed to develop the requirements: What did we want?[3]

We needed to answer the following questions: Is a new kitchen design possible? Can the chimney be eliminated? Will the the new garage space reasonably hold one car? Also, we needed a rough cost estimate.[4]

Therefore, in late September 2010 we selected an architect, Scott, who had redesigned several rooms in a friend's house, and we liked what we saw. Thus began the pre-kitchen project, which we refer to here as *Pre-K*.

The goal of *pre-K* was to specify the kitchen project.[5] We invited Scott to look around and discuss the project. We liked him immediately. Scott did not freak out at the over-stuffed bookcases everywhere. He also indicated that he "liked the challenge" of our particular problem. Scott sent us a contract and we signed it.

We then had a requirements session. We discussed everything we thought we might want, the idea being that Scott should design everything. We could eliminate things later if the cost was too high (which of course, it was!). However, it would be much harder to add to the design later. We also discussed planning issues, such as breaking the work into phases, the cost, and the schedule.

We ran into our first problem: Scott explained that he did not do cost estimates or schedules, and neither was he good at detailed kitchen layout. We would need a kitchen designer to do that. This required a new plan for the *pre-K* project. Scott would produce a preliminary design, which we would discuss and evaluate. Then we would put the kitchen project out to bid to three contractors. After we had selected the contractor, all of us together would modify the plans and produce a complete specification for the job.[6]

The immediate impact was that the *pre-K* project had just become much longer. Scott's design would take 4-6 weeks, and the bidding process would take another month. That put us into December, 2010. Nothing much happens in December, so a realistic date for contractor selection was January, 2011. The next step was that we would all meet and revise the plans; probably have to go through a bid modification; develop new plans; and get the loan.

In October 2010, we realized that the kitchen project would not start before March, 2011.

Scott went ahead and produced the preliminary design, Figure 25.2. While we made some major changes, we were thrilled.[7] Scott had several new ideas, which

---

[3] One of the first mistakes that people often make, is that they assume they have one project, when they really have two or more. In this case, there are at least two projects. The first project is to answer the question, 'What is the kitchen project?'

[4] Requirements analysis requires preliminary design work because the purpose of the requirements phase is to produce a *feasible* project.

The project must be both technically and financially feasible: the design must resolve all (or most) of the issues; and the cost must be affordable. You cannot simply list a series of wants and desires, the resulting project will almost certainly be unaffordable.

[5] You have to iterate. In fancy project management language, the project is progressively elaborated. You produce a rough design and estimate the cost and schedule. You modify the design (usually to reduce the cost!), and try again.

[6] I would get to referee a bidding cycle. Cool!

[7] Our fantasy of a new upper-floor bedroom was quickly eliminated by the cost!

## 25. A New Kitchen

we thought were excellent, but the "lav" in the middle of the kitchen had to go. However, Scott's proposal to move the front door to get a clear line of sight all the way to the rear windows was an excellent idea.

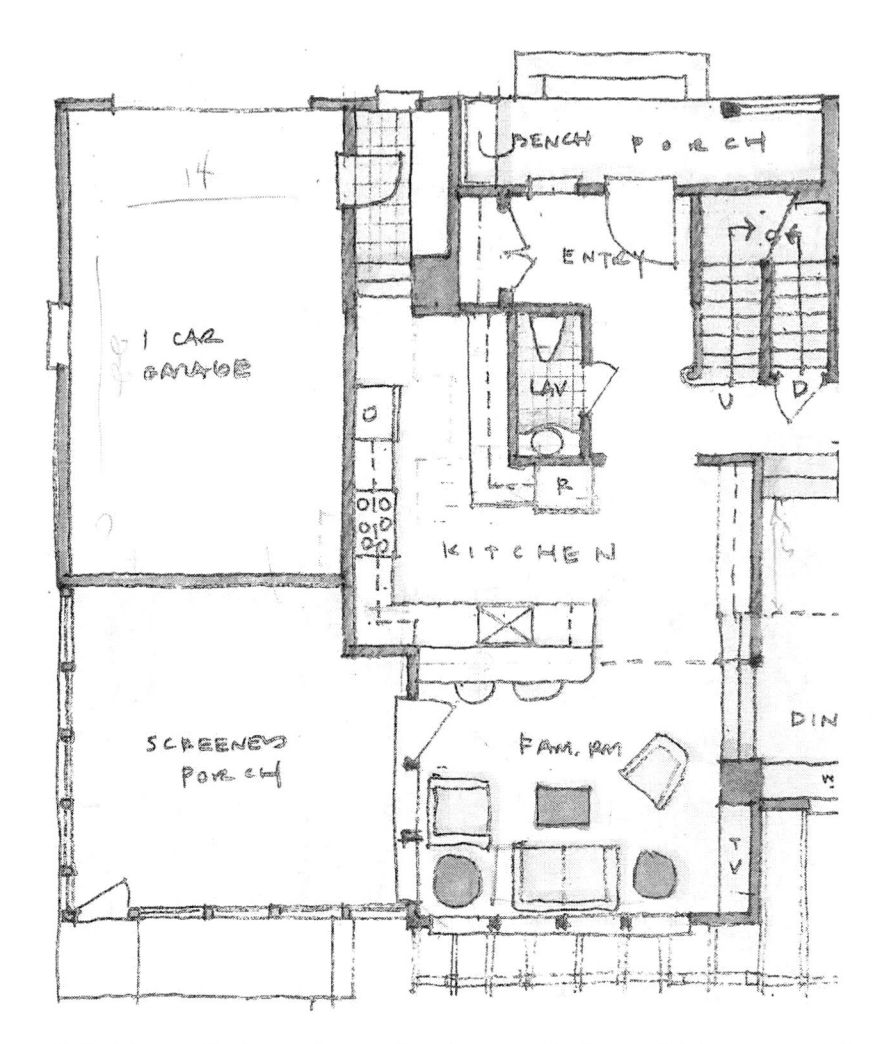

Figure 25.2: The preliminary design for the new kitchen, which was used for the bidding cycle. The lav in the middle of the kitchen had to go!

## 25.3 The Bidding Cycle

We invited three contractors to bid. Scott recommended someone from up-state and we contacted two locals that we knew.

The up-state guy was the first to visit and a week later delivered an outrageously expensive bid. We eliminated him.[8] His bid was simply a one page statement of the cost. While not very useful for our purposes, it was interesting from a project management perspective, it was a classic macro estimate: He simply measured the square footage of the job and multiplied by $200 per square foot.

The two local contractors walked through the house, discussed the project, and examined the plans. Both were pleasant, eager for the work, and had creative suggestions. Joe had done a large addition for a friend of ours and was well thought of around town. Mark had done some work for us before and his finish work is excellent. He is smart, courteous and a great planner. We thought it was going to be a tough decision and felt bad that we would have to chose.

Two weeks after the walk through, Mark produced a 10 page bid, carefully laid out with multiple options. Each piece was clearly explained and estimated. Mark also suggested several cost saving measures, and proposed a kitchen designer he had used in the past for the detailed kitchen layout. It was a well thought out bid.

Joe did not get back to us, so we called him again. He said he was working on it. A week later, we had still not heard from Joe, and with the holidays approaching, we decided to go with Mark. We called Mark, he came over and we congratulated him. We also felt good about the whole process.[9]

The next step was the production of a detailed design, which would involve the architect, the contractor, and us. Scott estimated that it would take a couple of months. From Scott's design, Mark would produce a detailed cost estimate, to be followed by the the bank financing activity, which would take 4-6 weeks.

We now had a project!

## 25.4 The Charter

We now had all the elements of a project: The detail design provided the scope; Mark had produced a rough cost estimate, which was within our budget; and the schedule was realistic.

The charter is the next step, it grants authority to the project manager to spend money and assign resources. Therefore, before a project can formally begin, a

---

[8] The bidding process is not just about cost, it is also about evaluating potential bidders. Can you work with them? In the case of the up-state guy, the answer was a comfortable, 'No'.

[9] One of the key ideas of the bidding cycle is that you end up comfortable with the contractor you have selected. It is not just about the cost.

*Charter* must be created and a project manager assigned.[10] The Charter for the new kitchen project is shown below in Figure 25.3.

---

1. Increase the kitchen size by moving the garage wall and the fireplace room wall.
2. Create a walk-in pantry.
3. Create a one-car garage.
4. Re-purpose little used spaces.
5. Create lines of sight from the front door through the kitchen.
6. New doors and windows to let in more light as appropriate.
7. Investigate more efficient utilities.
8. Cost: Budget $60,000 plus appliances.[11]
9. Schedule: Begin indoor work around March 1st. Outdoor work as weather permits. Work essentially complete within 6 months to comply with city permit restrictions.

---

Figure 25.3: *Charter* for the new kitchen project.

## 25.5 The Scope

> **Few things are harder to put up with than the annoyance of a good example.**
>
> *Mark Twain*

Fig. 25.2 shows a part of the detailed design of the kitchen. The diagram also shows a new screened in porch. This was eliminated as too expensive during cost estimation.[12]

Here we see an example of the scope being refined—progressive elaboration. The scope evolved from concept design, through preliminary design and finally detailed design. Note that there is little scope creep (the project did not grow in scale), it was merely refined.

### 25.5.1 Deliverables

Deliverables include:

- The Scope. This actually consisted of three separate deliverables: The Concept Design, the Preliminary Design, and the Detailed Design.

---

[10] This is the preferred order, but few projects follow it!

[12] This is a good example of a *Technical Requirement:* The existing deck was sound, but not within the new code, which required that any small change would require an entirely new deck.

25.5. The Scope

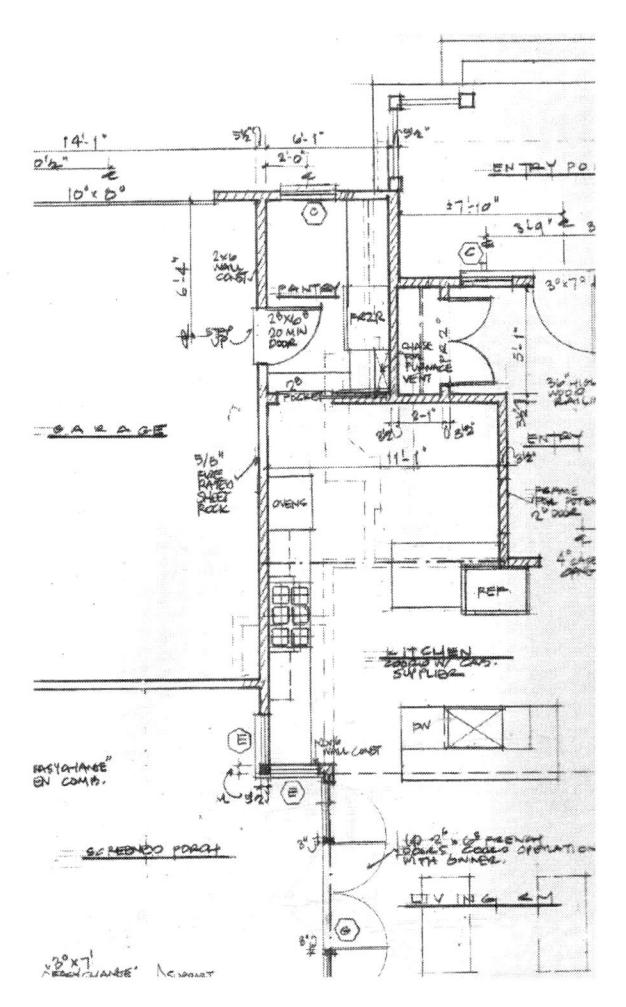

Figure 25.4: The detailed specification: The detailed design, showing the new entry closet, pantry and kitchen island.

- Cost Estimate. A multi-page spreadsheet of the estimated costs.
- Cabinets.[13] The cabinets turned out to have the longest delivery time, so determined the critical path, i.e., the schedule.

### 25.5.2 Milestones

Milestones included:

[13] These turned out to be a big deal.

25. A NEW KITCHEN

- Demolition Complete. Estimated March 31st.
- Gas line installed. Estimated April 15th.
- Cabinet Delivery. Estimated July 1st.

## 25.6 WBS

The high level WBS is given in graphical form in Fig. 25.5. This is suitable for managing the project and estimating the costs.

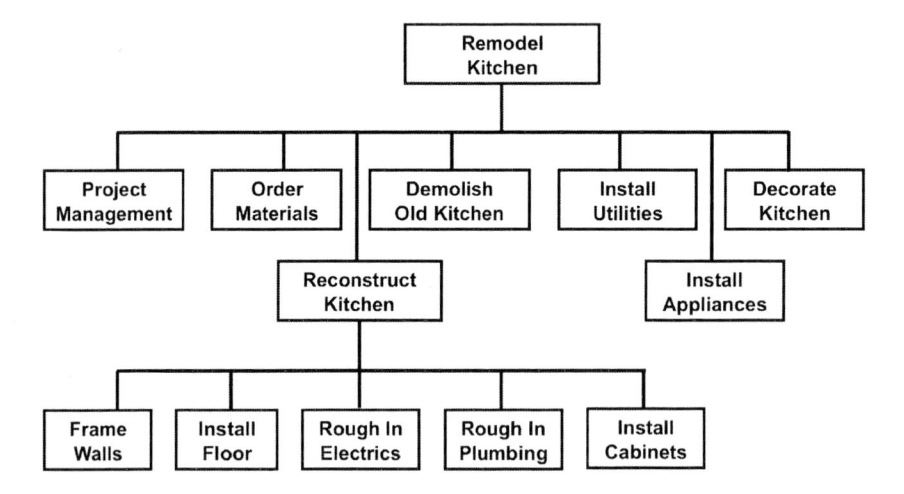

Figure 25.5: The graphical form of the WBS.

The Low level WBS is given in outline form in Figure 25.6. This is suitable for managing the project and estimating the costs.

```
0   Kitchen
  1.  Plan Project
      1.1   Obtain Loan
      1.2   Obtain Permit
      1.3   Detailed Architectural Plan
      1.4   Detailed Cost Estimate
  2.  Order Everything
      2.1   Select & Order Cabinets
      2.2   Select & Appliances
  3.  Demolish Old Kitchen
  4.  Manage Utilities
      4.1   Install Rough Plumbing
      4.2   Install Rough Electrics
      4.3   Install Appliances
          4.3.1   Install Gas Range
          4.3.1   Install Refrigerator
          4.3.1   Install Appliances
              4.3.1.1   Install Dishwasher
              4.3.1.2   Install Garbage Disposal
      4.4   Finalize Utilities
          4.4.1   Install Lights
          4.4.1   Install Refrigerator
          4.4.1   Install Electric Appliances
  5.  Do Carpentry
      5.1   Install Floor
      5.2   Install Frame Walls
      5.3   Install Blueboard
      5.4   Install Under Floor Heating
  6.  Decorate Kitchen
      6.1   Plaster Walls
      6.2   Paint Walls
      6.3   Install Floor
      6.4   Install Counter Tops
```

Figure 25.6: Outline WBS Format for the new kitchen.

## 25.7  Cost Estimate

The cost estimate is shown in Table 25.1.

We were already over budget.

## 25. A New Kitchen

Table 25.1: The cost estimate for the new kitchen

| Code | Item | Cost |
|---|---|---|
| 1.0 | Plan Project | |
| 1.1 | Obtain Loan | |
| 1.2 | Obtain Permit | $3,000 |
| 1.3 | Architectural Plan | $5,000 |
| 1.4 | Cost Estimate | $35,000 |
| 2.0 | Order Everything | |
| 2.1 | Select & Order Cabinets | $10,000 |
| 2.2 | Select & Order Appliances | $7,500 |
| 3. | Demolish Old Kitchen | |
| 4. | Manage Utilities | |
| 4.1 | Install Rough Plumbing | |
| 4.2 | Install Rough Electrics | |
| 4.3 | Install Appliances | |
| 4.4 | Finalize Utilities | |
| 5. | Carpentry | |
| 6. | Decorate Kitchen | |
| 6.3 | Install Floor | $1,500 |
| 6.4 | Install Counter Tops | $1,000 |
| | **Total Cost** | **$63,000** |

## 25.8 The Network Diagram

The first step in the creation of the network diagram is the development of the Table of Activity Times and Predecessors—Table 25.2. The most important aspect of the table is the estimated activity times. The predecessors are the first pass in the design of the schedule and will change as the schedule evolves.

From Table 25.2, we developed the network diagram using Microsoft Project®. The overall look of the GANTT chart is shown in Figure 25.7.

In Figure 25.8, the GANTT chart for the end of the project is blown up to show the interaction of the activities. Microsoft Project can also output a network diagram, and examples of this are shown in Figures 25.9 and 25.10.

### 25.8.1 Designing the Schedule

A careful look at the network diagram in Figure 25.11 will reveal that the list of tasks and their predecessors is different from the activities in Table 25.2. This is because

## 25.8. The Network Diagram

Table 25.2: The time estimates for the activities in the new kitchen

| Code | Item | Predecessors | Time (days) |
|---|---|---|---|
| 1.0 | Plan Project | None | |
| 1.1 | Obtain Loan | None | 30 |
| 1.2 | Obtain Permit | 1.3 | 30 |
| 1.3 | Architectural Plan | None | 30 |
| 1.4 | Cost Estimate | 1.3 | 14 |
| 1.5 | Project Approval | 1.1, 1.2, 1.3, 1.4 | 0 |
| 2.0 | Order Everything | | |
| 2.1 | Select & Order Cabinets | 5.2 | 60 |
| 2.2 | Select & Order Appliances | 1.5 | 10 |
| 2.3 | Select & Order Counter | 1.5 | 60 |
| 3. | Demolish Old Kitchen | 1.5 | 10 |
| 4. | Manage Utilities | | |
| 4.1 | Install Rough Plumbing | 3.0 | 5 |
| 4.2 | Install Rough Electrics | 3.0 | 3 |
| 4.3 | Install Cabinets | 4.1, 4.2 | 4 |
| 4.4 | Install Appliances | 5.1, 6.1 | 2 |
| 4.4.1 | Install Gas Range | 5.1, 6.1 | 1 |
| 4.4.2 | Install Refrigerator | 5.1, 6.1 | 1 |
| 4.4.3 | Install Appliances | | |
| 4.4.3.1 | Install Dishwasher | 5.1, 6.1 | 1 |
| 4.4.3.2 | Install Garbage Disposal | 5.1, 6.1 | 1 |
| 4.4.4 | Appliances Complete | 4.3, 4.4 | 0 |
| 5.0 | Do Carpentry | | |
| 5.1 | Install Floor | | 3 |
| 5.2 | Install Frame Walls | 3.0 | 10 |
| 5.3 | Install Blueboard | 5.2, 4.1, 4.2 | 5 |
| 5.4 | Install Under Floor Heating | 5.2, 4.1, 4.2 | 2 |
| 6.0 | Decorate Kitchen | | |
| 6.1 | Plaster Walls | 4.1, 4.2 | 2 |
| 6.2 | Paint Walls | 6.1, 4.4.4 | 4 |
| 6.3 | Install Floor | 5.3 | 2 |
| 6.4 | Install Counter Tops | 4.3 | 2 |

the predecessors in the table are used to create the first pass at the network diagram. Once you get into it, you will quickly find yourself moving tasks around to clarify the schedule. This is perfectly normal and acceptable.

A good example is the movement of the install tasks.[14] When creating Table 25.2, we placed them in the same order as they occurred in the WBS. Once we started working on the schedule, it became clear that installation of the appliances came

[14] We are using the word *task* here because *Project* uses it. Normally, we prefer to stick to the PMBOK terminology and use *activity*.

## 25. A NEW KITCHEN

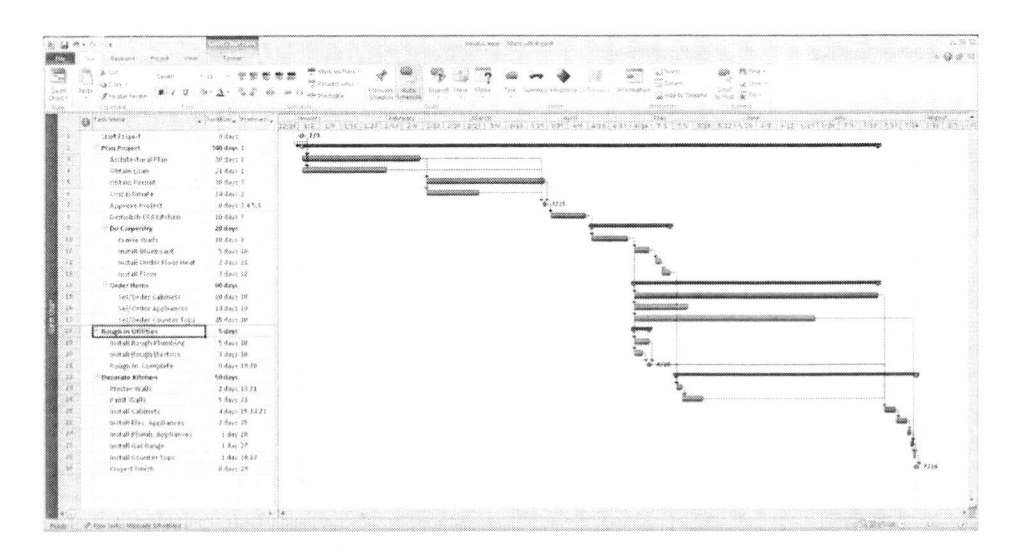

Figure 25.7: The Microsoft Project look in GANTT chart format.

at the end of the project, after most of the *Decorate* tasks. Therefore, we made the install tasks into sub-tasks of *Decorate Kitchen*.

Moving the install tasks produced a GANTT chart that flowed from top left to bottom right, which is easier to read and to manage.[15] This is an example of the analysis that occurs as the project planning proceeds.

Microsoft Project can produce a WBS automatically and this is shown in Figure 25.11.[16] However, because we moved the tasks around, this WBS is different from the previous version. We have two different WBS!

After all the design effort to create the WBS, the structure was ruined when the tasks were moved around to get a better network diagram. Our opinion at this point is that the original WBS is still the right one to use. Why? The original WBS was *designed* to help manage the project. Remember, we kept insisting that the construction of the WBS is a *creative* process, and that well-designed WBS was essential to a well-managed project.

We grouped activities so they could be managed coherently. For example, we collected all of the plumbing activities (and their deliverables) together so we could manage them effectively. Loosely speaking, everything to do with plumbing went into one box.

From the WBS, we estimated the costs for the all plumbing activities, which made

[15] If you don't move tasks around, the arrows begin to look like spaghetti, and you can't figure out what is going on.

[16] Right click on the column header, select *Add Column*, go to the bottom of the list that pops up, and select *WBS*.

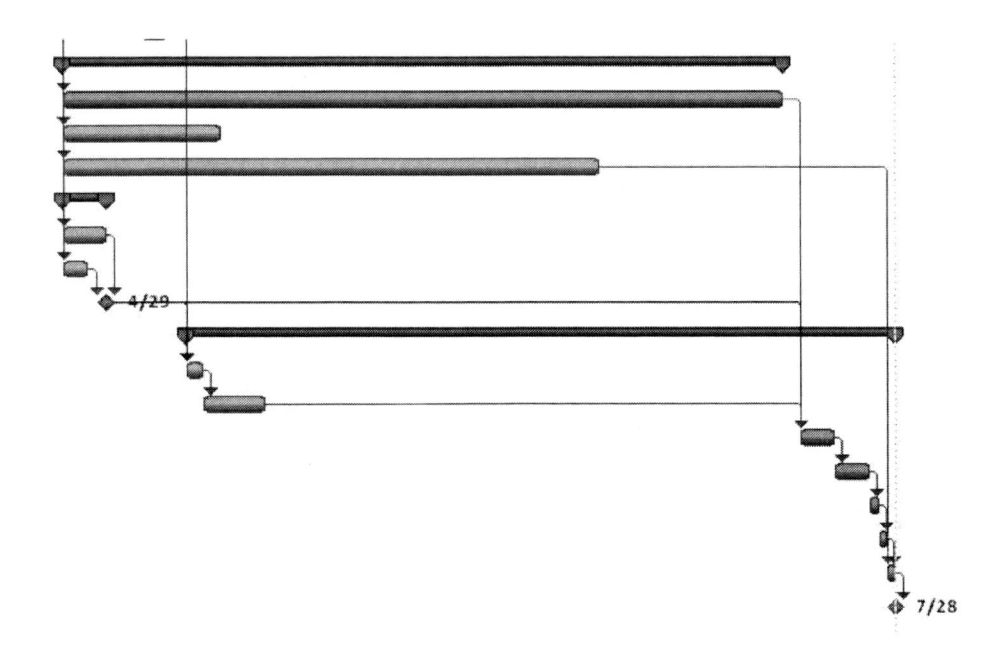

Figure 25.8: The GANTT chart for the end of the project.

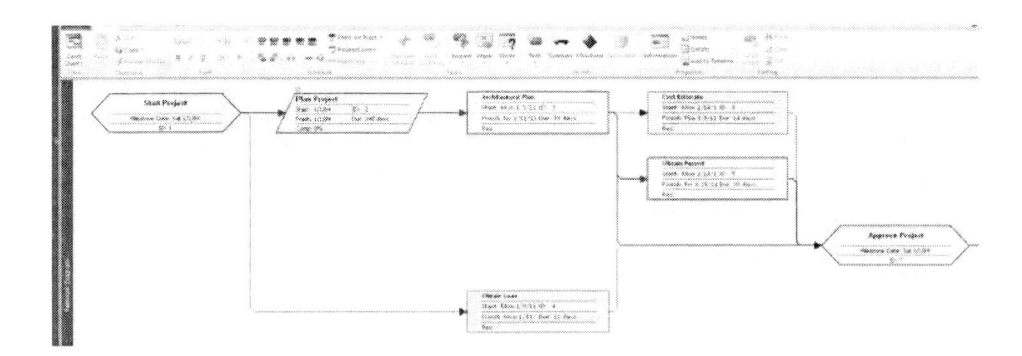

Figure 25.9: The network diagram for the start of the project.

things easier for the plumber, who had a list of all plumbing-related things in one place. Also, when the plumbing work begins, the actual costs can be monitored against planned costs of the deliverables. If we had scattered the plumbing tasks throughout the WBS, it would be easy to miss something.

When we moved the tasks in the network diagram, *Project* re-numbered them.

## 25. A NEW KITCHEN

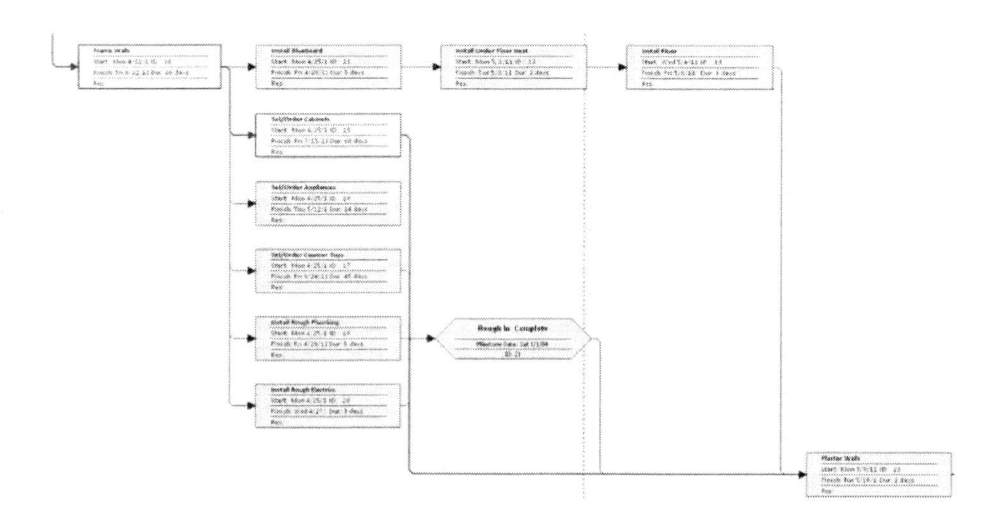

Figure 25.10: The portion of the network diagram that follows on from Figure 25.9.

From a scheduling perspective, this was acceptable, as it made the *network diagram* clearer and easier to manage. However, the resulting WBS produced automatically from *Project* destroyed our carefully designed WBS![17]

So which WBS do we use? The well-designed version, of course! *In our opinion, the WBS produced from Project is not a real WBS, it is a merely a task numbering scheme that has some use in managing the schedule during the actual work of the project.*

The WBS that was designed previously should be used to manage the project.[2]

---

[17]Which is why we refer to the *Project WBS* as the "lazy person's WBS."

| | Task Name | Duration | Prede | WBS |
|---|---|---|---|---|
| 1 | Start Project | 0 days | | 1 |
| 2 | ⊟ Plan Project | 140 days | 1 | 2 |
| 3 | Architectural Plan | 30 days | 1 | 2.1 |
| 4 | Obtain Loan | 21 days | 1 | 2.2 |
| 5 | Obtain Permit | 30 days | 3 | 2.3 |
| 6 | Cost Estimate | 14 days | 3 | 2.4 |
| 7 | Approve Project | 0 days | 3,4,5,6 | 2.5 |
| 8 | Demolish Old Kitchen | 10 days | 7 | 2.6 |
| 9 | ⊟ Do Carpentry | 20 days | | 2.7 |
| 10 | Frame Walls | 10 days | 8 | 2.7.1 |
| 11 | Install Blueboard | 5 days | 10 | 2.7.2 |
| 12 | Install Under Floor Heat | 2 days | 11 | 2.7.3 |
| 13 | Install Floor | 3 days | 12 | 2.7.4 |
| 14 | ⊟ Order Items | 60 days | | 2.8 |
| 15 | Sel/Order Cabinets | 60 days | 10 | 2.8.1 |
| 16 | Sel/Order Appliances | 14 days | 10 | 2.8.2 |
| 17 | Sel/Order Counter Tops | 45 days | 10 | 2.8.3 |
| 18 | ⊟ Rough in Utilities | 5 days | | 3 |
| 19 | Install Rough Plumbing | 5 days | 10 | 3.1 |
| 20 | Install Rough Electrics | 3 days | 10 | 3.2 |
| 21 | Rough In Complete | 0 days | 19,20 | 3.3 |
| 22 | ⊟ Decorate Kitchen | 59 days | | 4 |
| 23 | Plaster Walls | 2 days | 13,21 | 4.1 |
| 24 | Paint Walls | 5 days | 23 | 4.2 |
| 25 | Install Cabinets | 4 days | 15,24,21 | 4.3 |
| 26 | Install Elec. Appliances | 2 days | 25 | 4.4 |
| 27 | Install Plumb. Appliances | 1 day | 26 | 4.5 |
| 28 | Install Gas Range | 1 day | 27 | 4.6 |
| 29 | Install Counter Tops | 1 day | 28,17 | 4.7 |
| 30 | Project Finish | 0 days | 29 | 4.8 |

Figure 25.11: The WBS output from *Microsoft Project*.

## 25.9 Risks

### 25.9.1 Known Unknowns

Known unknowns are the risks identified during the planning stage. These included:

- *Cabinet Schedule Risk:*

    The longest activities on the critical path were the purchase, delivery and installation of the cabinets.[18] The cabinets could not be ordered until the

[18] The longest critical path items should always be analyzed carefully.

kitchen studs were in place, becasue only then were the exact measurements available. Once ordered, the delivery time was 12 weeks.

The mitigation strategy was for the contractor to work to get the kitchen studs up as soon as possible so the kitchen designer could finalize the measurements and order the cabinets. After the studs were up, the contractor worked on other tasks while waiting for the cabinets.

- *Counter Top Schedule Risk:*

We selected counter tops that were not in production–only pictures were available in brochures. They were scheduled to be delivered June 1st, but the company had not even delivered prototypes to the store for display.

The mitigation strategy was to pick an alternate counter top design that was readily available.[19]

### 25.9.2 Unknown Unknowns

*Unknown unknowns* are the risks that actually occur that you had no idea about during planning. These included:

- We realized that during construction there was nowhere to store the good china.[20] We hired a moving company to pack the china and put it in storage, which added storage costs of $100 per month for the length of the project.

- Mark applied for a gas permit from the city, but it took four weeks. Only after the city gas permit was granted would the gas company schedule the installation of the gas line, which took another three weeks. As a result, the installation of the new gas boiler was delayed three weeks.

**The week things really went awry ....**

Every project reaches a point where frustrations boil over. In one week, the following happened:

1. On Monday morning the electrician called to say he had badly cut his hand and sent over his assistant. Eileen had planned to select sconces, and the junior assistant was not up to the task.

---

[19] This risk would occur as the company did not make samples available, and rather than wait two months, we selected the other design.

[20] Breakage would be catastrophic!

2. Over the weekend, the finish carpenter's roof was damaged in a storm, so he was at home fixing his roof. The substitute was not a finish carpenter and could not handle the week's activities.

3. The kitchen appliances were delivered on time on Tuesday morning. The refrigerator did not fit in the opening. The contractor called the the appliance store, who condescendingly said "You should have left an extra inch." The contractor yelled back "I left two inches!"

   Investigation determined that the refrigerator specification was incorrect.[21] Fortunately, the refrigerator was carefully nudged into place using the leveling screws.

4. The insulation contractor showed up in a chemical protection suit. He said that everyone had to leave the house, which at the time included the contractor, plumbers, and electricians. Eileen was less than thrilled about having to leave the house when working on a writing deadline.[22,23]

### 25.9.3 Enhance Risks

Risks can be positive or negative. A good example of a positive risk was the new gas boiler. During planning, the plumber examined the heating system and discovered an old and inefficient boiler. He proposed that we could save on heating bills by installing a new, efficient gas boiler.

After analyzing the efficiencies, we decided to purchase a new gas boiler.[24] This was a positive risk, that we attempted to enhance.

## 25.10 Acceptance

The last few weeks of the construction involved a lot of negotiation about the remaining activities to be completed. Mark's original contract included a final payment upon completion of $8,000. We held back part of that payment until he had completed the "punch list."

This was not confrontational. Mark had his own punch list that he was working on. He also understood that when he finished our list, we would be happy, and he would get paid. We also understood that complaining at this stage would only annoy Mark and delay things even further.

---

[21] Remember, spec errors are the most expensive if they are not caught until implementation. A good example.

[22] For the first time in 20 years, Eileen wrote a theater essay on a yellow pad with a pen, sitting in her car.

[23] When I explained it all to Vijay, he said, "Oh Cool. Communication risk. Be sure to put it in the book!

[24] Project management in action: Examine the proposed change for cost and schedule impacts before deciding!

## 25. A New Kitchen

Some of the items on our list were clearly *add-ons* and would increase the cost. But the entire process went smoothly, because we were in constant communication about what was to be done. The process dragged out several weeks because Mark had started another job and showed up intermittently, but he always told us what was happening. We had to accept that as the reality and concentrate on keeping the punch list up to date.

# Chapter 26

# Acknowledgments and Copyrights

Quotes are slippery things and, like any currency, they get passed around. We've made every attempt here to give credit where credit is due and to respect the rights of everyone quoted, but for some quoted remarks it hasn't been possible to identify the original use, or even to confirm the author with certainty.

In an interview with Tasha Robinson, Steven Wright[1] described the widespread mis-attribution of quotes, commenting "Someone showed me a site, and half of it that said I wrote it, I didn't write. Recently, I saw one, and I didn't write any of it." Wright also expressed the distress this can cause for an author: "I wish it was just my material, and people could like it or not like it. Just as long as it was really mine."

Our goal in presenting this information is to honor the contributions and rights of all the authors quoted, so if you have concerns about the accuracy of an attribution or the appropriateness of use, please contact the authors.

## Preface

*I like prefaces. I read them. Sometimes I do not read any further.*

Malcolm Lowry (1909-1957). British poet and novelist. Original publication unknown, but the line is referenced by Lowry in a 1947 letter to Jonathan Cape.[2]

Lowry paraphrases this quote himself in a letter to his editor, pleading for more time to write a preface. He writes "I like prefaces. I read them. Especially if they come at the end of the book." The authors of this text appreciate the advances in publishing technology that have made this pleading unnecessary, but are still grateful for the patience of their editors.

---

[1] Wright, S. (2003, Jan 29) Interview by T. Robinson. Retrieved from http://www.avclub.com/articles/steven-wright,13796/.

[2] Grace, S. (1997). Sursum Corda: The Collected Letters of Malcolm Lowry. Toronto: University of Toronto, p. 5.

# 26. Acknowledgments and Copyrights

## Introduction

*The important thing is not to stop questioning. Curiosity has its own reason for existence.*

Albert Einstein (1879-1955). German theoretical physicist who derived the most famous equation, ever: $E = mc^2$.[3] From Miller, W. (1955, May 2). "Death of a genius: His fourth dimension, time, overtakes Einstein." *Life*, **38(19)**, p.64.

## Chapter 1

*Don't undertake a project unless it is manifestly important, and nearly impossible.*

Edwin Herbert Land (1909-1991). American scientist who invented inexpensive filters for polarizing light and the Polaroid instant camera, which first went on sale in 1948.

*I think it's wrong that only one company makes the game Monopoly.*

Stephen Wright (born 1955). American comedian, actor, writer, and famous Red Sox fan.

*You want to study project management? Read more, sleep less!*

Mr. John Cable is the Director of the Project Management Program at the A. James Clark School of Engineering at the University of Maryland. John is a superb speaker who brings astute and pithy observations to the teaching of project management.

*Managing is essentially a loser's job, and managers are about the most expendable pieces of furniture on the earth.*

Ted Williams (1918-2002). The Splendid Splinter, American baseball player and manager. From Williams, T. & Underwood, J. (1969, revised edition 1988). *My turn at bat: The story of my life*. New York: Simon & Schuster, p. 241-242.[4]

## Chapter 2

*There are two ways of being creative. One can sing and dance. Or one can create an environment in which singers and dancers flourish.*

Warren G. Bennis (born 1925). American scholar, widely regarded as a pioneer in field of Leadership. In 2005, James O'Toole claimed that Bennis developed the "then-nonexistent field that he would ultimately make his own–leadership." He further observed that Bennis "challenged the prevailing wisdom by showing that humanistic, democratic-style leaders are better suited to dealing with the complexity and change that characterize the leadership environment."

*I don't know the key to success, but the key to failure is trying to please everybody.*

Bill Cosby (born 1937). American comedian, actor, author, television producer, educator, musician and activist.

*If it doesn't matter who wins or loses, then why do they keep score?*

Vincent Thomas "Vince" Lombardi (1913-1970) is best known as the head coach of the Green Bay Packers during the 1960's. He led the team to three straight league championships and five in seven

---

[3] Except the first time he actually wrote $L = mc^2$, and then crossed out the $L$ and wrote $E$.

[4] Williams actually made this statement in a description of his years as the manager of the Washington Senators. But it seems likely he was still thinking of newly appointed Red Sox manager Lou Boudreau's 1950 remark that all players, including Williams, were expendable (ibid, p.172).

years. Under Lombardi the Packers won the first two Super Bowls and the Super Bowl trophy is named in his honor. He was enshrined in the NFL's Pro Football Hall of Fame in 1971.

## Chapter 3

*Life isn't a matter of milestones but of moments.*

Rose Fitzgerald Kennedy (1890-1995). American philanthropist and matriarch of the Kennedy family.

*It's a funny kind of month, October. For the really keen cricket fan it's when you discover that your wife left you in May.*

Denis Norden (born 1922). British comedy writer and television presenter.[5]

## Chapter 4

*There's no crying in baseball!*

Tom Hanks. From Marshall, P. (Director); Wilson, K., Candaele, K., Ganz, L., & Mandel, B. (Writers). (1992). A League of Their Own. USA: Columbia Pictures.

*A nation's culture resides in the hearts and in the soul of its people.*

Mohandas Karamchand Gandhi (1869-1948), known as Mahatma Gandhi, was the leader of Indian nationalism in British-ruled India. Employing non-violent civil disobedience, he inspired movements for non-violence, civil rights and freedom across the world.

As leader of the Indian National Congress in 1921, Gandhi campaigned to ease poverty, expand women's rights, build religious and ethnic amity, and end untouchability. Gandhi protested the salt tax by marching 250 miles, theDandi Salt March, in 1930 for which he was imprisoned.[6] He was assassinated on 30 January 1948. 30 January is observed as Martyrs' Day in India and his birthday, 2 October, is commemorated world-wide as the International Day of Non-Violence.

*Peace is a daily, a weekly, a monthly process, gradually changing opinions, slowly eroding old barriers, quietly building new structures.*

John Fitzgerald "Jack" Kennedy (1917-1963). The 35th President of the United States, serving from 1961 until his assassination in 1963.

After military service as commander of the Motor Torpedo Boats PT-109 and PT-59 during World War II in the South Pacific, Kennedy represented Massachusetts's 11th congressional district in the U.S. House of Representatives from 1947 to 1953 as a Democrat. Thereafter, he served in the U.S. Senate from 1953 until 1960. Kennedy defeated then Vice President Richard Nixon in the 1960 presidential election. Kennedy is the only president to have won a Pulitzer Prize.

## Chapter 5

*Life is what happens to you while you're busy making other plans.*

[5] Like the baseball season, the cricket season also runs April through September.

[6] Winston Churchill ridiculed him as a "half-naked fakir."

## 26. Acknowledgments and Copyrights

John Lennon (1940-1980). British musician, artist and writer. From *Beautiful Boy (Darling Boy)*, Double Fantasy (1980).

### Chapter 6

*When one has finished building one's house, one suddenly realizes that in the process one has learned something that one really needed to know in the worst way—before one began!*

Friedrich Nietzsche (1844-1900). German philosopher.

*If you want to build a ship, don't drum up people together to collect wood, but rather teach them to long for the endless immensity of the sea.*

Antoine de Saint-Exupery (1900-1944). French pilot and writer

*To live means to finesse the processes to which one is subjugated.*

Bertolt Brecht (1898-1956). German poet, playwright, and theater director.

*If a man empties his purse into his head no one can take it away from him. An investment in knowledge always pays the best interest.*

Benjamin Franklin (1706-1790). One of the Founding Fathers of the United States. A major scientist for his theories on electricity, he invented the lightning rod, bifocals, the Franklin stove, and a carriage odometer. He formed the first public lending library in America and earned the title of "The First American" for his early campaigning for colonial unity.

Always proud of his working class roots, he became a successful newspaper editor and printer in Philadelphia, played a major role in establishing the University of Pennsylvania, and was elected the first president of the American Philosophical Society. Later in life, he freed his slaves and became a prominent abolitionist.

### Chapter 7

*He who has begun has half done. Dare to be wise. Begin!*

Horace (65 BCE-8 BCE). Roman lyric poet, satirist, and critic. In Latin, "Dimidium facti qui coepit habet: sapere aude, incipe." Horace. (20 BCE). *Epistles* **1.2.40** (Letter to Lollius).

*We must, indeed, all hang together, or most assuredly we shall all hang separately.*

Benjamin Franklin (1706-1790). Comment made in the Continental Congress just before signing the Declaration of Independence, 1776.

### Chapter 8

*Give me six hours to chop down a tree and I will spend the first four sharpening the axe.*

Abraham Lincoln (1809-1865). 16th president of the United States. Though the original source of this quote has not been found, Lincoln's expertise in building rail fences with raw timber was well known and frequently referenced in his political life. In 1860 he ran for president as "The Rail Candidate," playing on his frontier background, and later in his presidency was frequently referred to as "The Rail Splitter," so presumably he knew something about chopping down trees!

*By looking at the questions the kids are asking, we learn the scope of what needs to be done.*

Buffy Sainte-Marie (born 1941). Canadian musician and activist. From Silber, S. (1998, June 1). Sharing the fire online. *Wired*, accessed 6/1/2012 at http://www.wired.com/culture/ lifestyle/ news/ 1998/ 06/ 12630.

*Lost time is never found again.*

Benjamin Franklin (1706-1790). From Franklin's 1758 essay, "The Way to Wealth."

*The sooner you fall behind, the more time you'll have to catch up.*

Steven Wright (born 1955). American comedian, actor and writer

*The cost of living has gone up another dollar a quart.*

W. C. Fields (1880-1946). American comedian, film star, and vaudeville performer.

*Large increases in cost with questionable increase in performance can be tolerated only for racehorses and fancy women.*

William Thomson, Lord Kelvin (1824-1907). British mathematical physicist. Unsourced, though widely quoted. Still, this seems a strange remark for a life-long bachelor and scholar who was devoted to his research and teaching at the University of Glasgow. [7]

*Risk comes from not knowing what you're doing.*

Warren Buffett (born 1930). CEO of Berkshire Hathaway, investor, and philanthropist.

*The quality, not the longevity, of one's life is what is important.*

Martin Luther King, Jr. (1929-1968). American clergyman, activist, and prominent leader of the Civil Rights Movement.[8] From America's Gandhi: Rev. Martin Luther King, Jr. (Man of the Year cover story, unsigned.) (1964, Jan 3). *Time*, **83(1)**.

*The human mind is our fundamental resource.*

John F. Kennedy (1917-1963). 35th president of the United States. From Kennedy's Special Message to the Congress on Education, February 20, 1961.

*The single biggest problem in communication is the illusion that it has taken place.*

George Bernard Shaw (1856-1950). British literary critic, playwright and essayist.

*The universe never did make sense; I suspect it was built on government contract.*

Robert A. Heinlein (1907-1988). American author and winner of the first Grand Master Award from the Science Fiction Writers of America From Heinlein, R. (1980). *The Number of the Beast*. New York: Fawcett Publications (p. 6).

## Chapter 9

*Everything should be made as simple as possible, but not simpler.*

[7] Far from being born into aristocratic circles, Kelvin was raised to the peerage only when he was 68 years old.

[8] Boston University's most famous alumnus.

## 26. ACKNOWLEDGMENTS AND COPYRIGHTS

Albert Einstein (1879-1955). German theoretical physicist.

*We cannot direct the wind, but we can adjust the sails.*

Unknown. The comment is attributed a number of people. However, all online sites that have investigated this in detail conclude that the source is unknown.

*Excellence, then, is not an act but a habit.*

Will Durant (1885-1981), American writer, historian, and philosopher. Commenting on a quote from Aristotle (384 BCE-322 BCE), Greek philosopher, student of Plato, and teacher of Alexander the Great. From Durant, W. (1926) *The Story of Philosophy: the Lives and Opinions of the Greater Philosophers*. New York: Simon & Schuster, revised edition 1933 (p. 98).

In commenting on Aristotle's philosophy, Durant added this interpretation of his own, which is now widely quoted as coming directly from the Greek philosopher. Durant actually wrote, "[W]e do not act rightly because we have virtue or excellence, but we rather have these because we have acted rightly; 'these virtues are formed in man by his doing the actions'; we are what we repeatedly do. Excellence, then, is not an act but a habit." The internal quote from Aristotle ("these virtues are formed...") comes from *Nicomachean Ethics*, **ii**, 4.

*Talent wins games, but teamwork and intelligence wins championships.*

Michael Jordan (born 1963). American NBA Basketball Player. From Jordan, M., Vancil, M. & Miller, S. (1994). *I can't accept not trying: Michael Jordan on the pursuit of excellence.* San Francisco: Harper San Francisco (p. 24).

*A person will sometimes devote all his life to the development of one part of his body—the wishbone.*

Robert Frost (1874-1963). Pulitzer Prize-winning American poet, teacher and lecturer.

*As a coach, I play not my eleven best, but my best eleven.*

Knute Rockne (1888-1931). American football player and coach who played and coached exclusively for the University of Notre Dame.

*The speed of communications is wondrous to behold. It is also true that speed can multiply the distribution of information that we know to be untrue.*

Edward R. Murrow (1908-1965). American broadcast journalist and producer. On receiving "Family of Man" Award (1964).

*Oft expectation fails, and most oft there*
*where most it promises; and oft it hits,*
*where hope is coldest; and despair most sits.*

Helena in *All's Well That Ends Well*. William Shakespeare (1564-1616). English poet and playwright. The "Bard of Avon" is widely regarded as the greatest writer in the English language.

*I'm not going to buy my kids an encyclopedia. Let them walk to school like I did.*

Yogi Berra (born Lawrence Peter Berra, 1925). American baseball player and manager.

## Chapter 10

Kirk: *You're not exactly catching us at our best.*
Spock: *That much is certain.*

Captain Kirk and Mister Spock are the captain and science officer respectively of the starship Enterprise in the Star Trek series of television shows and movies (though Spock holds other titles as the series matures). From Nimoy, L. (Director). Meerson, S., Krikes, P., Bennett, H., & Meyer, N. (Screenplay writers). (1986). *Star Trek IV: The Voyage Home*. USA: Paramount Pictures.

*If everything seems under control, you're just not going fast enough.*

Mario Andretti (born 1940). Italian American racecar driver, the only person ever to win the Indy 500, the Daytona 500, and the Formula One World Championship.

*Change is inevitable....except from vending machines.*

Steven Wright (born 1955). American comedian, actor and writer

## Chapter 11

*Acceptance of what has happened is the first step to overcoming the consequences of any misfortune.*

William James (1842-1910). American psychologist and philosopher.

## Chapter 12

*I'm not for integration and I'm not against it.*

Richard Pryor, American comedian and actor. From a 1977 interview with New York Times writer Guy Flatley, accessed 6/1/2012 at http://www.moviecrazed.com/outpast/pryor.html. The full quote is "I'm not for integration and I'm not against it. What I am for is justice for everyone, just like it says in the Constitution."

## Chapter 13

*If you can't explain it simply, you don't understand it well enough.*

Albert Einstein (1879-1955). German theoretical physicist.

*Sometimes I can't figure designers out. It's as if they flunked human anatomy.*

Erma Louise Bombeck (1927-1996). American humorist and newspaper columnist. From 1965 to 1996, Bombeck wrote over 4,000 humorous newspaper columns chronicling the ordinary life of a midwestern suburban housewife. Bombeck also published 15 books, many of which became best-sellers.

*The most essential gift for a good writer is a built-in, shock-proof sh\*\*t-detector.*

Ernest Hemingway (1899-1961). American novelist and author. From an interview with Hemingway in *The Paris Review* (**18**), Spring 1958.

# 26. Acknowledgments and Copyrights

## Chapter 14

*The secret of getting ahead is getting started. The secret of getting started is breaking your complex overwhelming tasks into small manageable tasks, and then starting on the first one.*

Unknown. The origin of this comment has not been found. Several online sites attribute the first sentence to Agatha Christie but more cite Mark Twain; the quote as a whole is always attributed to Twain. In rebuttal, a number of sites devoted to Twain specifically identify this as a mis-attribution. Since the second sentence sounds surprisingly unskeptical for Twain, we are going with "Unknown."

## Chapter 15

*Time is nature's way of keeping everything from happening at once. Space is what prevents everything from happening to me.*

John Wheeler (1911-2008). American theoretical physicist who coined the term "black hole." The first sentence is often attributed to Einstein, Pauli, and others. The second sentence, however, is pure Wheeler, so Wheeler gets the credit.

## Chapter 16

*Even if you are on the right track, you'll get run over if you just sit there.*

Will Rogers (1879-1935). American humorist of the vaudeville stage and of silent and sound films.

*Life can only be understood backward, but it must be lived forward.*

Søren Kierkegaard (1813-1855). Danish philosopher and author.

*The show doesn't go on because it's ready. It goes on at 11:30.*

Lorne Michaels (b. 1944), Canadian-American television producer, writer, and comedian. Quoted by Tina Fey (born 1970), American comedian, writer, actress, and television producer. From the section headed "Things I Learned from Lorne Michaels" in Fey, T. (2012). *Bossypants* (paperback edition). New York: Reagan Arthur / Back Bay Books (p. 23).

## Chapter 17

*The first 90% of the job took the first 90% of the money. The remaining 10% of the job took the other 90% of the money!*

Anonymous.

*If I had asked people what they wanted, they would have said faster horses.*

Henry Ford (1863-1947). The founder of the Ford Motor Company and innovator in mass production. His Model T automobile revolutionized transportation and American industry.

*It's tough to make predictions, especially about the future.*

Yogi Berra (born Lawrence Peter Berra, 1925). American baseball player and manager. This comment has the distinction of being attributed to both Yogi Berra and Niels Bohr. A debate on the authorship in the Letters section of *The Economist* (July 15, 2007) offers some evidence in favor of Bohr, but it sure sounds like something Berra would say. Of course, as Yogi himself noted "I really didn't say everything I said!"

*A dollar per horse per mile.*

Paul Parnegoli is a carpenter who works in Rhode Island. On his lunch break, he once regaled the crew about how he used to haul horses for a living. Always on the look out for unusual cost estimation metrics, RW asked him how he bid the cost of hauling a horse from Kentucky to Boston.

*Beware of the little expenses; a small leak will sink a great ship.*

Benjamin Franklin (1706-1790). From Franklin's 1758 essay, *The Way to Wealth*.

*Price is what you pay. Value is what you get.*

Warren Buffett (born 1930). From the 2008 Berkshire Hathaway Letter to Shareholders (p. 5), where Buffett attributed the origin of the idea to Benjamin Graham, author of the classic text, *The Intelligent Investor*. Accessed 6/1/2012 at http://www.berkshirehathaway.com/ letters/ 2008ltr.pdf.

## Chapter 18

*The more education a woman has, the wider the gap between men's and women's earnings for the same work.*

Sandra Day O'Connor (born 1930). The first woman to be appointed to the United States Supreme Court. She served as an Associate Justice from 1981 until her retirement from the Court in 2006.

*The only way to enjoy anything in this life is to earn it first.*

Ginger Rogers (1911-1995). American stage and film actor and dancer, noted primarily as the partner of Fred Astaire in motion-picture musicals.[9]

*Once our customers start using earned value, we will no longer be able to fudge the cost!*

Roger Warburton in a lecture to the Project Management Institute's Massachusetts Bay Chapter entitled *Miss the Memo? How TCPI makes customers tougher and smarter*, February 18, 2010.

## Chapter 19

*Be a yardstick of quality. Some people aren't used to an environment where excellence is expected.*

Steve Jobs (1955-2011). American businessman, designer and inventor. Co-founder of Apple.

## Chapter 20

*Never hire anyone you wouldn't want to run into in the hallway at three in the morning.*

Lorne Michaels (b. 1944), Canadian-American television producer. Quoted by Tina Fey in *Bossypants*.

[9] In a 1982 Frank and Ernest comic strip, award winning cartoonist Bob Thaves wrote about Fred Astaire: "Sure he was great, but don't forget that Ginger Rogers did everything he did, backwards ... and in high heels."

## 26. ACKNOWLEDGMENTS AND COPYRIGHTS

### Chapter 21

*It is better to keep your mouth closed and let people think you are a fool than to open it and remove all doubt.*

Mark Twain (born Samuel Langhorne Clemens, 1835-1910). American author and humorist. This quotation is widely attributed to both Mark Twain and Abraham Lincoln, among others. Whoever said it was probably paraphrasing Proverbs 17:28, "Even a fool, when he holdeth his peace, is counted wise: and he that shutteth his lips is esteemed a man of understanding."

### Chapter 22

*Risk! Risk is our business!*

Captain Kirk. From Roddenberry, G. & Kingsley, J. (1968, Feb 3). *Star Trek: Return to Tomorrow* (Television program). Los Angeles: Paramount Television.

### Chapter 23

*I wish to be cremated. One tenth of my ashes shall be given to my agent, as written in our contract.*

Groucho Marx (Julius Henry Marx, 1890-1977). American comedian and film and television star.

*Thoroughly read all your contracts. I really mean thoroughly.*

Bret Michaels (born Bret Michael Sychak, 1963). American musician and television personality.

### Chapter 24

*Relativity applies to physics, not ethics.*

Albert Einstein (1879-1955). German theoretical physicist.

### Chapter 25

*You're not using that project management stuff on me are you?*

Eileen Warburton, writer and independent scholar.

*Few things are harder to put up with than the annoyance of a good example.*

Mark Twain (born Samuel Langhorne Clemens, 1835-1910). American author and humorist. From Twain, M. (1894). *Pudd'nhead Wilson.* Hartford, CT: American Publishing Company (p. 246).

# NOTES

## Chapter 0 Introduction

1. This is a chapter note for Chapter 0, the Introduction. The extra information being provided here is that this is how a chapter note looks.

## Chapter 2 The Project Environment

1. For an excellent practical book on new product development, see the book by Cooper.[30]

2. We are actually quoting research on what makes successful new *products*, not projects. There is little research to report on what makes successful projects, but there is a significant, growing body of evidence for what makes a successful product. Since each new product development is a project, we feel comfortable presenting this as "project selection."

## Chapter 3 Deliverables and Milestones

1. This definition is a technical convenience, which makes milestones equivalent to activities. This allows the linking of a milestones to activities, which is useful. If the completion of an activity has a linked milestone, and the activity is delayed, then the milestone is also delayed.

## Chapter 5 Project Life Cycles

1. More information on the pharmaceutical life cycle can be found in [31].

2. This is based on a template for Microsoft Project [32].

3. The approach was pioneered by Barry Boehm in his *Spiral Model* [33].

4. *The Agile Manifesto* consists of 12 philosophical statements, which were first described in the *Manifesto for Agile Software Development* by Beck, Kent; et al. in 2001. [34]

NOTES

5. The name *scrum* is borrowed from the game of rugby, and was first described by Peter DeGrace, Leslie Stahl, and Leslie Hulet in *Wicked problems, righteous solutions*, Peter DeGrace and Leslie Hulet Stahl. [35]

6. We have adapted the attributes from earlier research conducted by Mo Mahmood. [36] Table 5.2 was adapted from Richard Fairley's *Managing and Leading Software Projects*. [37] Note that Fairley has a more liberal interpretation of the waterfall as he includes incremental builds.

## Chapter 7 Initiating Process Group

1. Quintus Horatius Flaccus, known as Horace, was the leading lyric poet during the time of Augustus. In Horace's first book of Epistles the epigraph to this chapter is the moral of a story where a fool waits for the stream to stop before crossing it. Horace values human endeavor, persistence in reaching a goal, and the need for effort in overcoming obstacles.[38]

*Sapere aude* is Latin for "Dare to be wise." It challenges us to experience discovery and to be passionate about it. But thinking is not enough, one must also, "Begin!"

Kant suggested that *Sapere Aude* was the motto of enlightenment: "Have courage to use your own understanding!" Kant charged his readers to follow a program of intellectual self-liberation, the tool of which is *reason*. Kant suggested the mass of "domestic cattle" have been bred by unfaithful stewards not to question what they've been told. It is the courage of individuals to follow *Sapere aude* that will break the shackles of despotism and, for the benefit both of the population and the state, reveal through public discourse better methods of governance or legitimate complaints.

In other words, we start as we intend to continue, *Challenge Everything!*

2. For an excellent book on the softer skills of project management, see Meredith and Mantel [39].

## Chapter 8 Planning Process Group

1. There is considerable debate as to whether the activity resources are estimated before or after the activity durations. In the text, we have presented the standard PMBOK approach, which says that resources are estimated first, then durations. The argument to support this is that you can't realistically estimate how long it takes to do a job unless you know what type of person is working on it. Is the assigned person an expert or a novice? The duration obviously depends on the skill.

However, many organizations have an estimating procedure that estimates activity costs directly from the parameters in the scope. For example, a painter may estimate the time to paint a room based on the number of square feet. The cost is then determined by assigning a person (the resource) to it, and by multiplying by their hourly cost, the activity cost is determined.

Software cost estimation does not follow the PMBOK either. Typically, one first determines the program parameters (e.g., number of function points, or forms and screens) and then derives the estimated number of hours to complete the job. After that, an allowance is made for the type of staff assigned.

2. See the NSP Preliminary Cost Estimate form at cityofboston.gov in the dnd/ PDFs/ section.

3. Dr. Gawande is a surgeon at the Brigham and Women's Hospital in Boston, a staff writer for The New Yorker, and an assistant professor at Harvard Medical School.

## Chapter 12 Integration

1. This Charter was developed as a homework assignment by Vicky Morrissey in Fall 2011 in the undergraduate PM class. We are grateful to Vicky for allowing us to use this excellent example of a charter.

## Chapter 13 Scope

1. I'd like to find the person who said this, but can't. Sorry.

2. As described by our colleague *Steve Leybourne* in [40]. People unfamiliar with the complexity and magnitude of superyacht projects may learn more by visiting www.feadship.nl and www.lurssen-.com.

## Chapter 14 The WBS

1. We are burying the answer to this claim in this note to give you a chance to think about it. The answer is: The *Project Management* is missing from the WBS!

## Chapter 17 Cost

1. This example comes from our colleague Steve Leybourne, a professor at BU, who studied the nature innovation in super yachts. See [40].

2. On page 135 of *The Not So Big House* Sarah Susanka gives a construction primer. If you are at all interested in the topic, this is a great book. It is also a magnificent explanation of cost drivers.

3. The city of Boston has a comprehensive worksheet at their web site: www.cityofboston.gov, in the section dnd/PDFs. See NSP_Preliminary_ Cost_ Estimate_ form.pdf.

## Chapter 18 Earned Value Management

1. One of the techniques for addressing the issue of the time-dependence in the SPI is called *Earned Schedule*, and was pioneered by Walter Lipke.[41]

NOTES

2. Christensen has conducted several landmark studies on the accuracy of the *CPI*. Using Department of Defense data he found that, "without exception, the CPI does not improve during the period 15% to 85% of the contract."[20, 42]

3. For a theoretical justification of this statement, see [21].

4. If we substitute the *EAC* from equation 18.13 into the *TCPI* formula, we get:

$$TCPI = \frac{BAC - EV(t)}{EAC - AC(t)} = \frac{BAC - EV(t)}{AC(t) + \frac{BAC - EV(t)}{CPI(t)} - AC(t)} = CPI! \qquad (26.1)$$

The *EAC* version of the *TCPI* formula is an identity: $TCPI = CPI$. Presumably, this is what the PMBOK means by: "If it becomes obvious that the *BAC* is no longer viable .... the *EAC* effectively supersedes the *BAC* as the cost performance goal."

5. The expression probably dates from much earlier, but Einstein quoted it a lot and so is credited with it.

## Chapter 19 Quality

1. We think it is hard to find an example from project management. For example, cost and schedule variances can be tracked against their goals and flags raised if they depart from acceptable upper and lower limits. However, control charts are based on the idea that things are independent, and the *CPI* is a cumulative measure and so correlates the variables. Personally, we don't see how they apply to PM at all!

2. We have al;ready established that all *CPI* charts values are less than 1.0, which says that the "process is out of control!"

## Chapter 22 Risk Management

1. For example, Metzger's *Managing a Programming Project* [43] does not even make reference to the practice of risk management!

2. Even worse, scientists develop a hypothesis to be tested, and then in an ideal situation perform experiments that are at-best designed to test the null hypothesis. At the outset the researcher does not know whether or not the results will support the null hypothesis. However, it is common for the researcher to believe that their result will be within a range of known possibilities. Occasionally, however, the result is completely unexpected—it was an unknown unknown!

3. For an interesting discussion of the use of decision trees in medicine, see Farrokh Alemi's web page, *http:// gunston.gmu.edu/ 730/ DecisionTrees.asp*. The page is based on a chapter with the same name in the book *Systems to Support Health Policy Analysis: Theory, Model and Uses*. [44]

Decision trees can be very useful in the analysis of medical issues. There is often good data on the cost of a treatment or drug, along with actual probabilities for patient outcomes, e.g., cure rates, death rates, etc.

## Chapter 23 Procurement Management

1. For example, see an interesting discussion of contracts in the Iraq war at http://www.dodig.mil/audit/reports/fy06/06-007.pdf

## Chapter 25 A New kitchen

1. This is a simplified account of the design and construction of Roger's new kitchen. The conceptual and design work was done by his wife, Eileen. We took the opportunity to record what was happening as an example of a project. Fortunately for the book, but not so for the real implementation, the new kitchen project seemed to go through all the typical project management issues.

2. The perfect tool would help you to create the graphical WBS diagram and then add outline format for the lower levels of the hierarchy, and with automatic numbering. These activities (along with their WBS numbers) would then automatically populate a network diagram in which tasks can be moved around without destroying the WBS numbering. I can dream!

# BIBLIOGRAPHY

[1] Paul McDonald. It's time for management version 2.0: Six forces redefining the future of modern management. *Futures*, 43:797–808, 2011.

[2] V. Kanabar and R. D. H. Warburton. *MBA Fundamentals: Project Management*. Kaplan Publishing, New York, NY., 1st edition, 2008.

[3] David B. Guralink, editor. *Websters New World Dictionary*. William Collins Publishers, Inc., Cleveland, OH., Second College edition, 1979.

[4] *A Guide to the Project Management Body of Knowledge*. Project Management Institute, 4th edition, 2009.

[5] K. Jugdev and R. Muller. A retrospective look at our evolving understanding of project success. *Project Management Journal*, 36(4):19–31, 2005.

[6] The Standish Group Report. The chaos report, 1995.

[7] L. Eveleens and C. Verhoef. The rise and fall of the chaos report figures. *IEEE Software*, 27(1):30–36, January/February 2010.

[8] Erik Larson and Clifford Gray. *Project Management: The managerial process*. McGraw-Hill Irwin, NY, NY, 5th edition, 2011.

[9] James Wilson and Michelle Harrison. The necessity of driving to Abilene. *Organization Development Journal*, 19(2):99–109, 2001.

[10] Andrew Crowe. *Alpha Project Managers*. Velociteach Press, GA., 2006.

[11] A. Gawande. *The Checklist Manifesto: How to Get Things Right*. Metropolitan Books, 1st edition, 2009.

[12] T. DeMarco. *Software State-of-the-Art: Selected Papers*. Dorset House Publishing, New York, NY, 1990.

[13] R.S. Pressman. *Software engineering: a practitioner's approach*. Mcgraw Hill: Higher Education. McGraw-Hill, 2005.

[14] PMI. *Practice standard for project estimating*. Project Management Institute, Newtown Square, PA, 2011.

# BIBLIOGRAPHY

[15] V. Kanabar and R.D.H. Warburton. Leveraging the new practice standard for project estimating. In *PMI World Congress, Dallas*, October, 2011. PMI.

[16] EunHong Kim. *A Study on the Effective Implementation of Earned Value Management Methodology*. PhD thesis, The George Washington University, 2000.

[17] Quentin W Fleming and Joel M Koppleman. *Earned Value Project Management*. Project Management Institute, Newtown Square, PA, 3rd edition, 2005.

[18] Q. W. Fleming and J. M. Koppelman. The two most useful earned value metrics: the CPI and the TCPI. *PM World Today*, XI(VI), June 2009.

[19] F. T. Anbari. Earned value project management method and extension. *Project Management Journal*, 34(4):12, 2003.

[20] David S. Christensen and Scott Heise. Cost Performance Index Stability. *National Contract Management Journal*, 25(Spring):7–15, 1993.

[21] Roger D. H. Warburton. A time-dependent earned value model for software projects. *International Journal of Project Management*, 20:1082–1090, 2011.

[22] A. Maslow. A theory of human motivation. *Psychological Review*, 50(4):370–396, 1943.

[23] S. R. Covey. *The 7 Habits of Highly Effective People*. Free Press, 1st edition edition, 1990.

[24] David Logan. Known knowns, known unknowns, unknown unknowns and the propagation of scientific enquiry. *Journal of Experimental Botany*, 60(3):712–714, 2009.

[25] PMI. *Practice standard for Risk Management*. Project Management Institute, Newtown Square, PA, 2011.

[26] Norman R. Augustine. *Augustine's Laws*. Viking Penguin, NY, NY, 1983.

[27] Project Management Institute. Code of ethics and professional responsibility. Technical report, 2006.

[28] Louis Mercken. Ethics has proven a useful tool for the project management profession. *PMI Today*, page 3, December 2011.

[29] S. Susanka and K. Oblensky. *The not so big house: A blueprint for the way we live*. The Taunton Press, Newtown, CT, 2nd edition, 2008.

[30] Robert G. Cooper. *Winning at New Products: Accelerating the process from idea to launch*. Perseus Publishing, Cambridge, MA, 3rd edition, 2001.

[31] Oracle. Oracle agile product lifecycle management pharmaceuticals, Oct 2011.

[32] Microsoft. Home construction project plan.

[33] Barry Boehm. A spiral model of software development and enhancement. *ACM SIGSOFT Software Engineering Notes*, 11(4):14–24, August 1986.

[34] Kent Beck. Manifesto for agile software development, 2001.

# Bibliography

[35] P. DeGrace and L. H. Stahl. *Wicked problems, Righteous solutions: A Catalog of Modern Engineering Paradigms.* Prentice Hall, 1990.

[36] Mo A. Mahmood. A comparative investigation of system development methods. *MIS QUARTERLY*, 11(3), 1987.

[37] R. E. Fairley. *Managing and Leading Software Projects.* Wiley, IEEE Computer Society, 1st edition, 2009.

[38] Wikipedia page for "sapere aude", 2011.

[39] Jack Meredith and Samuel Mantel Jr. *Project Management: A Managerial Approach.* John Wiley & Sons, Hoboken, NJ, 8th edition, 2012.

[40] Stephen Leybourne. Project Management and high-value superyacht projects: An improvisational and temporal perspective. *Project Management Journal*, 41(1):17–27, 2010.

[41] H. Lipke, Walter. *Earned Schedule.* Lulu Publishing, Lexington, KY, 1st edition, 2009.

[42] David S. Christensen, Richard C. Antolini, and John W. McKinney. A review of estimate at completion research. *Journal of Cost Analysis*, 25(Spring):41–62, 1995.

[43] P. W. Metzger and J. Boddie. *Managing A Programming Project: Processes and People.* Prentice Hall, 3rd edition, 1996.

[44] D. H. Gustafson, W. L. Cats-Baril, and F. Alemi. *Systems to Support Health Policy Analysis: Theory, Model and Uses.* Health Administration Press, Ann Arbor, Michigan, 1992.

[45] Lars Madsen. *Various chapter styles for the memoir class.* MemoirChapStyles.pdf, 2009.

[46] Peter Wilson. *The Memoir Class for Configurable Typesetting: User Guide.* The Herries Press, Normandy Park, WA, 8th, maintained by lars madsen edition, August 2009.

# INDEX

Abilene paradox, 46
AC, *see* actual cost
acquire project team
    process, 131
acquisition, 297
activities, 96
activity, 100, 209
    attributes, 100
    burst, 223
    concurrent, 223
    dependencies, 223
    duration, 211
    earliest finish, 213
    earliest start, 212
    identification, 210
    latest finish, 216, 220
    latest start, 216
    merge, 223
    predecessor, 212, 223
    successor, 223
activity attributes, 100
activity list, 100
activity on arrow, 227, 228
activity on node, 227
activity sequencing, 210
actual cost, 258, 263
    definition, 261
administer procurements
    process, 152
agile, 59
ajourning, 299
AOA, *see* activity on arrow
AON, *see* activity on node
arrow
    definition, 212
assumptions, *see* scope
Augustine's Law, 344

BAC, *see* budget at completion
backward pass, 215–217
basis of estimates, 109
budget
    definition, 244
budget at completion, 233, 261
budget estimate, 108
burst activity, 217
    definition, 223
business case, 168, 170
buyer, 334

cause and effect diagram, 291
CCS, *see* change control cystem
change control board, 143, 146
change control system, 142, 143
change request, 143, 145, 166
charter, 166, 167
    Vicky's party, 167
close procurement
    process, 160
close procurements
    process, 157
close project or phase
    process, 157
close project or phase process, 174
closeout report, 158
closing
    process group, 71
closing process
    group, 155
CMS, *see* configuration management system
Code of Ethics and Professional Conduct, 347
collect requirements
    process, 92
communication channels, 309
communication complexity, 309

# INDEX

communication model, 309
communications management plan, 123, 308
compliance projects, 23
concurrent activity
    definition, 223
conditional branch, 227
conduct procurements
    process, 136
configuration management system, 145
conflict resolution, 302
constraint, 181
contingency, 108, 324
contingency budget, 324
contingency funds, 118
contract
    buyer, 334
    cost plus, 335
    cost plus award fee, 336
    cost plus fixed fee, 336
    cost plus incentive fee, 336
    cost plus percentage of cost, 336
    cost reimbursable, 335
    cost-plus example, 338
    definition, 333
    firm fixed price, 336
    fixed price, 335, 337
    fixed price plus incentive fee, 336
    incentive fee example, 339
    incentives, 335
    penalties, 335
    performance based, 335
    seller, 334
    SOW, 334
    time and materials, 335
control chart, 288
control costs
    process, 147
control schedule
    process, 146
control scope
    process, 145
corrective action, 172
cost driver, 239, 243
cost estimate, 233
    accuracy, 236
    bottom-up, 235, 242
    macro, 233
    parameters, 234
    parametric, 237
    rough order of magnitude, 233
    top-down, 235
cost estimation, 233
cost performance baseline, 109
cost performance index
    definition, 263
cost reimbursable contract, 335
cost variance
    definition, 262
cost vs. price, 254
CPAF, *see* cost plus award fee contract
CPFF, *see* cost plus fixed fee contract
CPI, *see* cost performance index
CPIF, *see* cost plus incentive fee contract
CPPC, *see* cost plus percentage of cost contract
create WBS
    process, 96
critical path, 104, 206, 209, 218, 221, 222, 225
    definition, 219
    longest path, 219
    multiple, 219
    shortest time, 219
critical success factors, 23, 24
    scoring, 27
    scoring matrix, 27
CSF, *see* critical success factors
cultural clash, 47
cultural clashes, 48
cultural norms, 43
culture, 43
CV, *see* cost variance

decision gate, 56
decision node, 326
Decision Tree, 325
defect repair, 172
define scope
    process, 73, 95
definitive estimate, 108
deliverable
    definition, 36
    examples, 36
    one-to-two rule, 38
    small, 38
deliverables, 129, 180
Delphi technique, 74, 241
deontology, 350

# Index

dependencies, 223
design of experiments, 288
determine budget
    definition, 109
    process, 109
develop charter
    inputs, 80
    outputs, 81
    process, 79
    tools and techniques, 81
develop HR plan
    process, 121
develop project management plan
    process, 92
develop project team
    process, 131
develop schedule
    process, 103
direct and manage project execution
    process, 129
direct costs, 249
direct labor, 249
discretionary dependency, 224
distribute information
    process, 134
duration, 209
dysfunctional conflict, 302

EAC, *see* estimate at completion
earliest finish, 214, 216
earned value, 257, 258
    definition, 261
earned value management, 147, 257, 274
EMV, *see* expected monetary value
enterprise environmental factors, 80
    definition, 169
estimate activity durations
    process, 103
estimate activity resources
    process, 101
estimate at completion, 149, 266
    formula, 266
estimate costs
    process, 108
ethical dilemma
    definition, 349
ethical issue
    example, 348
ethics, 347

EV, *see* earned value
EVM, *see* earned value management
evolutionary life cycle, 60
executing
    process group, 70
executing process group, 127
expectancy theory, 301
expected monetary value, 324, 327
external dependency, 224

FFP, *see* firm fixed price contract
finish-to-start constraint, 212
fixed price contract, 335
float, 218
flowcharting, 289
forecast report, 149
formal acceptance, 157
forming, 298
forward pass, 213, 214
FPIF, *see* fixed price plus incentive fee contract
fringe, 251
fringe benefits, 251
functional conflict, 302
functional manager, 48, 158
functional organization, 48, 50

G&A, *see* general and administrative costs
GANTT chart, 104
GANTTER, 100
general and administrative costs, 253
GERT, *see* Graphical Evaluation and Review Technique
goals, 21
gold plating, 142, 188, 287
grade
    definition, 286
Graphical Evaluation and Review Technique, 227

Herzberg's theory, 300
HR, *see* human resources
human resources, 121, 295
human resources plan, 121, 296
hygiene factors, 300

identify risks
    process, 73, 115
identify risks process, 319

identify stakeholders
    process, 83
indirect labor, 250
initiating
    process group, 70
initiating process group, 77
    processes, 77
inspection, 293
integrated change control
    process, 142
integration knowledge area, 165
Ishikawa diagram, 291, 319

knowledge area
    integration, 165
knowledge areas, 67, 74
known knowns, 316
known unknowns, 111, 316

lag, 224, 225
    definition, 225
latest finish, 215, 217
latest start, 217
lead, 225
lessons learned, 158
life cycle, 53
    construction, 59
    pharmaceutical, 58
    product vs. project, 54
    software, 57
loops, 226

macro cost estimate, 233
manage project team
    process, 133
manage stakeholder expectations
    process, 135
mandatory dependencies, 223
Maslow's hierarchy, 299
matrix chart, 296
matrix organization, 49, 51, 158
McGregor Theory X and Y, 300
merge activity
    definition, 214, 223
micro cost estimate, 242
Microsoft Project, 100
milestone, 221
    definition, 39, 221
    zero duration, 39

milestone list, 101
milestones, 180
mission, 21
    company, 21
monitor and control project work
    process, 141
monitor and control risks
    process, 151
monitoring and controlling
    process group, 71, 139

negotiation, 297
net present value, 32
    example, 33
network
    if, 227
    loops, 226
network diagram, 101, 104
new kitchen project, 359
    introduction, xxxviii
node, 211
norming, 299
NPV, *see* net present value

objectives, 22
    SMARTO, 22
order of magnitude estimate, 108
organizational asset updates, 158
organizational chart, 122, 296
organizational process assets
    definition, 170
overhead
    fringe, 251
    profit, 251
overhead costs, 249
overhead rate, 250

parallel activity, 223
parametric cost estimate, 237
Pareto chart, 293
payback, 32
PDM, *see* precedence diagramming method
perform integrated change control
    definition, 143
perform qualitative risk analysis
    process, 117
perform quality assurance
    process, 129
perform quality control

# Index

    process, 148
perform quantitative risk analysis
    process, 117
performance based contract, 335
performance report, 149
performing, 299
PERT, 245, *see* program evaluation and review technique
    mean, 246
    mode, 245
    optimistic, 246
    pessimistic, 245
    sigma, 246
plan communications
    process, 123
plan procurements
    process, 125
plan quality
    definition, 119
    process, 118
plan risk management
    process, 112
plan risk responses
    process, 118
planned value, 258
    definition, 261
planning
    process group, 70
planning process group, 89
PMA
    activity list, 100
    business case, 171
    change management, 143
    charter, 81, 168
    closeout, 161
    closeout report, 159
    communications plan, 124
    cost estimate, 239
    critical success factors, 26
    decision tree, 326
    earned value status report, 149
    estimate activity durations, 103
    estimate activity resources, 102
    estimate at completion, 149
    function point analysis, 248
    GANTT Chart, 104
    milestone list, 101
    operating agreement, 132
    organizational chart, 122

    performance assessment, 132
    PERT, 247
    project ranks, 28
    project selection, 26
    project strategies, 28
    QA audit, 130
    quality control measurements, 149
    quality management plan, 119
    requirements document, 94
    resource breakdown structure, 102
    risk audit, 152
    risk management plan, 113
    risk register, 151
    risk register updates, 115
    scope verification, 145
    scoring matrix, 27
    stakeholder identification, 306
    statement of work example, 343
    team directory, 132
    time phased budget, 110
    variance analysis, 146, 148
    WBS, 97
PMA case
    description, xxxviii
    introduction, xxxviii
PMBOK, *see* Project Management Body Of Knowledge
    definition, 5
PMBOK Guide, 9
PMI, *see* project management institute
PMO, *see* project management office, *see* program management office
portfolio, 20, 23
    definition, 20
portfolio management, 23
pre-assignment, 297
precedence diagramming method, 227
predecessor
    definition, 212
predecessor activity, 210, 212
    definition, 223
preventive action, 172
price vs. cost, 254
Primavera, 100
priority matrix, 186
process, 67, 72
    acquire project team, 131
    administer procurements, 152
    close procurement, 160

401

close procurements, 157
close project or phase, 157, 174
collect requirements, 92
conduct procurements, 136
control costs, 147
control schedule, 146
control scope, 145
create WBS, 96
define scope, 73, 95
determine budget, 109
develop charter, 79
develop HR plan, 121
develop project management plan, 92
develop project team, 131
develop schedule, 103
direct and manage project execution, 129, 172
distribute information, 134
estimate activity durations, 103
estimate activity resources, 101
estimate costs, 108
identify risks, 73, 115, 319
identify stakeholders, 83, 306
integrated change control, 142
manage project team, 133
manage stakeholder expectations, 135
monitor and control project work, 141, 173
monitor and control risks, 151
perform integrated change control, 174
perform qualitative risk analysis, 117
perform quality assurance, 129
perform quality control, 148
perform quantitative risk analysis, 117
plan communications, 123
plan procurements, 125
plan quality, 118, 287
plan risk management, 112, 318
plan risk responses, 118
procurement management, 333
report performance, 149
verify scope, 144
process analysis, 291
process assets, 157
process group
closing, 71, 155
executing, 70, 127
initiating, 70, 77
monitoring and controlling, 71
monitoring and controlling, 139
planning, 70, 89
process groups, 67, 69, 74
processes, 71
42, 69
product, 73
project management, 73
procurement management
process, 333
procurement management plan, 125
product
processes, 73
program, 19
definition, 19
program management office, 19
progressive elaboration, 38, 84, 143, 194, 237, 364
project, 3
companies' role, 42
definition, 6
environment, 17
external environment, 18
financial evaluation, 31
internal environment, 17
life cycle, 53
life span, 7
multi-disciplinary, 7
non-profits, 34
objective, 7
phase, 68
PMBOK definition, 5
schedule, 7
sponsor, 8
stakeholders, 8
unique, 6
project document updates, 96
project management
benefits, 12
definition, 9
processes, 73
success, 13
project management institute, 5
project management office, 14, 51
project management plan, 91, 92, 166, 171
project manager
authority, 11
constituencies, 12
definition, 11
induce, 11

# Index

role, 11
project phase, 68
project selection, 30
projectized organization, 50, 51
projects
    cultural norms, 43
    cultures, 43
PV, *see* planned value

QA, *see* quality assurance
quality
    audit, 291
    benchmarking, 288
    cost-benefit analysis, 288
    definition, 285
quality assurance, 129
quality checklists, 121
quality control, 129
quality management plan, 119
quality metrics, 119

RACI chart, 296
RAD, *see* rapid application development
RAM, *see* responsibility assignment matrix
rapid application development, 60
RBS, *see* resource breakdown structure
report performance
    process, 149
requirements
    enhancements, 94
    refinements, 94
requirements document, 93
requirements management plan, 94
requirements traceability matrix, 95, 145
resource breakdown structure, 102
resource calendar, 131, 297
responsibility assignment matrix, 296
return on investment, 25, 31
rewards, 47
risk
    accept, 317, 318
    avoid, 317
    causes, 314
    consequences, 314
    contingency, 324
    definition, 314
    enhance, 318
    exploit, 318
    identification techniques, 319

    mitigate, 317
    qualitative, 321
    quantitative, 324
    share, 318
    transfer, 317
risk assessment matrix, 322
risk audit, 152
risk breakdown structure, 320
risk impact, 321
risk likelihood, 321
risk management, 313
risk management plan, 112, 151
risk prevention, 116
risk register, 74, 111, 114, 116, 319, 320
risk register updates, 115
ROI, *see* return on investment
rolling wave planning, 91, 194, 237
    definition, 70
ROM, *see* rough order of magnitude
rough order of magnitude cost estimate, 233
routine activities, 5

schedule baseline
    definition, 105
schedule performance index
    definition, 264
schedule variance
    definition, 262
scope, 175
    acceptance criteria, 180
    assumptions, 182
    baseline, 97
    budget, 180
    business goals, 179
    complete, 178
    constraint, 181
    constraints, 181
    contents, 179
    definition, 175
    exclusions, 182
    limits, 182
    PMBOK definition, 176
    precise, 178
    priority matrix, 186
    risks, 181
    specification, 178
    statement of work, 184
    technical requirements, 184
    theme, 177

# INDEX

triple constraints, 185
scope baseline, 97, 145
scope creep, 142, 188
scope statement, 95, 96
scoring matrix, 25, 27, 29
scrum model, 62
seller, 334
sensitivity analysis, 239
slack, 217–219
    definition, 217
SMARTO, *see* objectives, 34
sociocultural skills, 10
SOO, *see* statement of objectives
SOW, *see* statement of work, 334
spec, *see* specification, *see* specification
specification, 96, 176, 178
    definition, 178
SPI, *see* schedule performance index
stakeholder, 7
    definition, 83
    influence, 85
stakeholder analysis, 306
stakeholder management strategy, 87
stakeholder register, 85
stakeholders issues log, 135
start node, 211
statement of objectives, 334
statement of work, 125, 176, 177, 184, 193
    customer interface, 184
    definition, 184
    example, 343
statistical sampling, 289
stop node, 211
storming, 298
strategy, 22
successor activity
    definition, 223
SV, *see* schedule variance

target cost, 237

task, 219
TCPI, *see* to-complete performance index
technical skills, 10
teleology, 350
time and materials contract, 335
to-complete performance index, 277
    BAC formula, 278
    EAC formula, 282
transition plan, 158
triple constraints, 185

unknown unknowns, 111, 316

validation
    definition, 95
variance analysis, 145
verification
    definition, 95
verify scope
    process, 144
virtual teams, 298

waterfall cycle, 60
WBS, *see* work breakdown structure
WBS dictionary, 96
work breakdown structure, 36, 95–97, 191, 235, 240, 242, 320
    active verbs, 193
    activity, 100
    definition, 192
    deliverable oriented, 194
    design, 194
    dictionary, 97, 203
    graphical format, 196
    node, 192
    outline format, 198
    work package, 192, 201
work package, 192
    definition, 201

**Colophon**

This book is set in Computer Modern Roman, 11 point size using the LaTeX typesetting system created by Leslie Lamport. The layout follows the *memoir* class with Lars Madsen's chapter styles. [45] Acknowledgments go to Peter Wilson for creating the memoir class and to Lars Madsen for maintaining it. [46] And of course, none of this would be possible without Donald Knuth who wrote the original TeX. The bibliography was produced in Bibtex. LaTeX produced the final POSTSCRIPT file that was sent to the printer.